THE ARTS
IN SOCIETY

edited by

Robert N. Wilson

University of North Carolina

Prentice-Hall, Inc.

Englewood Cliffs, New Jersey

PRENTICE-HALL INTERNATIONAL, INC., *London*
PRENTICE-HALL OF AUSTRALIA, PTY., LTD., *Sydney*
PRENTICE-HALL OF CANADA, LTD., *Toronto*
PRENTICE-HALL OF INDIA (PRIVATE) LTD., *New Delhi*
PRENTICE-HALL OF JAPAN, INC., *Tokyo*
PRENTICE-HALL DE MEXICO, S.A., *Mexico City*

PRINTED IN THE UNITED STATES OF AMERICA
04935-C

For Lynda and Debbie

PREFACE

This symposium was first considered during 1957 when I was a Fellow at the Center for Advanced Study in the Behavioral Sciences and an interested participant in a seminar on art and human behavior. At that time such a collection began to seem feasible; indeed, four other members of that seminar are now represented in this volume: Leo Lowenthal, Harrison and Cynthia White, and Hans Speier. In a more general sense, I have been deeply concerned about the relations between the humanities and the social sciences since my student days when I was dismayed to find that there seemed to be such a slight connection between my college studies in literature and my graduate studies in sociology and psychology. I determined to explore this connection further, the first effort being an investigation of modern poets, later published under the title, *Man Made Plain*.

The present book grows out of my conviction that it is exceedingly important for the student of society to attend to the arts achieved by various social groups.

Behavioral scientists can learn a great deal from artists and art, primarily because writers and painters are sensitive perceivers who often see what is going on in the society or the psyche a good bit earlier than other men do. Moreover the arts are symbolic representations of *something* (no one is quite sure what) in the societies that give them birth. It is commonplace to say that people who study human behavior can gain heightened understanding through art; part of the task in this book is to enunciate more clearly what sorts of understanding may be thus derived.

Complementing the idea that literature, painting, music, and the dance have something vital to say to the social scientist is the belief that social scientists have themselves a contribution to make. One may propose, audaciously enough, that a sociologist or psychologist brings to the arts a trained intelligence and a point of view, and that he is therefore potentially equipped to enhance our comprehension of the arts themselves—for their own sakes. Further, those who believe with Edward Shils that the high culture of any age is of immense value and must be cultivated may take heart from the attempt of the social scientist to define and ultimately help to conserve the arts as a realm of social life.

The authors gathered here are concerned with both the major themes in the reciprocal pairing of art and society: what can art and artist teach us about society? what can the perspectives of the social sciences teach us about artistic careers and created works? It would be difficult to say that one theme or the other was clearly dominant, since most of the selections illuminate both ranges of questions. However, there has been throughout an emphasis on close study of the creator and the art product in the conviction that at this early stage in the development of a sociology of art we need to know much more about the precise character of the objects of our attention. That is, literature and other expressive media are not taken merely as illustrations of already-framed social psychological issues, but are seen as phenomena of intrinsic interest. It is very unlikely that any scholar can do excellent work in this field unless he has such an abiding interest and resists the temptation to use the arts as mere adjuncts to social research or convenient repositories of data.

The editorial comments attempt to place the various contribu-

tions in perspective and relate them to one another. There is, however, no intention of trying to impose a single, rigid conceptual
scheme on these diverse essays; art is long and social science is short,
and our correct posture should be one of humility toward the fact
of art rather than an arrogant and premature disposition to sort and
count. Whatever the long-run possibilities, we are surely in no position at this date to erect an accepted, conventional taxonomy or to
compose textbooks on the sociology of the arts. The theoretical view
which informs my discussion is catholic in nature and modest in
claim. It argues only that the analysis of art cannot proceed on the
sole basis of internal criticism, psychological explanation, or sociological association. The art object is complex and the artist is complex; a single-factor or unidimensional analysis is almost certain to
be inadequate. To "understand" a work of art in the fullest sense
requires intimate acquaintance with the created work itself, with
the personality of its creator, with the social milieu which is an
environing frame for artist, art, and audience. One can never know
enough or see with sufficient clarity. Art is at once profoundly individual—the sacred private vision of its creator—and resolutely social—a pervasive transaction among a symbolic tradition, an artist,
a medium, a company of perceivers, and a species of social organization.

I have not sought to impose form upon this volume by culling
appropriate selections from extant work or suggesting topics to contributors. With few exceptions, the essays are written expressly for
the symposium and printed here for the first time. From the authors
I have asked only excellence, leaving them quite free to pursue any
topic or point of view within the general field. This orientation is
in keeping with the contention that the sociology of art is not ripe
for formalization. There is no effort to "cover" all the subjects that
might be suggested by the title; for the present, a collection of lively
individual voices seems more fitting than an arid comprehensiveness.

As is always the case with a book carried over several years and
involving many associates, there is no accurate way to express thanks
for the varieties of help received. I should nevertheless wish to mention a few of the persons whose encouragement and labor were
important: Ralph Tyler, Charles Morris, Henry A. Murray, Neil
Leonard, Ronald D. Scibilia, Lowell Hagan, Alys Venable, and Gay

Preface

Goss. In addition, my students in Social Relations 90 at Harvard and Sociology 70a and 26a at Yale were a constant stimulus to thought.

Robert N. Wilson

Chapel Hill, North Carolina

THE CONTRIBUTORS

Sanford M. Dornbusch is Professor of Sociology at Stanford University.

César Graña is Associate Professor in the Social Sciences at the University of Chicago.

Mason Griff is Professor of Sociology, Anthropology, and Social Work at Montana State University.

Leo Lowenthal is Professor of Sociology at the University of California at Berkeley.

Dennison Nash is Associate Professor of Sociology at the University of Connecticut.

Carol Pierson Ryser is a candidate for a Ph.D. in sociology at Harvard University.

Edward A. Shils is Professor of Sociology and Social Thought, University of Chicago, and Fellow of King's College, Cambridge.

Hans Speier is a member of the Research Council of The RAND Corporation.

Cynthia White is a painter and a graduate of Radcliffe College *magna cum laude* in Fine Arts.

Harrison White is Associate Professor of Sociology at Harvard University.

Robert N. Wilson is Professor, School of Public Health, and Professor of Sociology at the University of North Carolina.

CONTENTS

One

THE POET
IN AMERICAN SOCIETY

This essay analyzes poets as defined by poets, but pays remarkably scant attention to the other parties involved in the artistic transaction; we learn little about the critics, publishers, readers, and others whose roles presumably join the poet's and whose actions and attitudes circumscribe the poet's universe of operations. In part, these omissions are deliberate. Small-scale individual research must have a limited scope of empirical attention, and it seemed better to probe as deeply as possible into the subjective aspects of the artistic role than to cover superficially what a great many people thought about poets. In part, too, the neglect of associated roles, of those sets of actions and expectations which complement the artistic task, may be traced to intrinsic difficulties in the analysis of creative behavior: how firm is the image of the poet others *do* carry in their minds? How can the expectations of the audience be teased forth? How can the researcher observe the interactions between poets and significant related figures?

1

We ordinarily define a social role in terms of mutuality and reciprocity; we ask what are the rights and obligations of the parties to a transaction, what each owes to and claims from the other. But it may be questioned whether very many persons apprehend any set of rights and obligations where poets are concerned. Perhaps in contemporary America the chance of meeting a poet in his role as artist is even more slight than that of reading his poems. Further, the writer himself may have no clear conception of a possible audience to whom he owes the products of his craft and from whom he may expect reward. The artist as artist does not seem to be entangled in a social fabric which would provide a defining context for his activities.

Roles of physician or businessman, father or friend, appear to be more susceptible to analysis than roles of artist or saint. We can observe the interpersonal relations which form the core of the role, can fasten on the patterned anticipations held by the members of the relationship. The artist, however (with the exception of the performing arts), does not typically express himself in face-to-face intercourse with his audience. Thus the sociologist has an obligation and a challenge, as this essay contends, to develop ways of thinking about unusual social roles. In particular, he must be aware of the symbolic "interaction once-removed" (the reader and the page, the viewer and the painting) in which the fruits of artistic and intellectual creativity are so often embedded. In the present analysis, for example, virtually nothing is said—and perhaps at this stage of social science development little *could* be said—about the experience of reading a poem or about the social-psychological import of poetic content itself.

Another area omitted from this account is what might be termed the antechamber to the artistic role. We do not learn much about the process of being an apprentice or novice poet. Because the individuals studied here had already attained a certain stature, we lack information about earlier impelling motives and about the hazards of recruitment into the role. Fortunately, although the cases are not precisely comparable, several other essays in this book do focus intensively on the younger artist.

THE POET
IN AMERICAN SOCIETY

Robert N. Wilson

Introduction

The poet's role is a special case of unregulated and unplanned vocation. It is an exceptional, personally chosen position which has deep roots in the artistic tradition of Western society but is virtually excluded from the major patterns of contemporary occupational or recreational life. In David Riesman's terms[1] the poet is acutely inner-directed, devoting his best energies to the elucidation of idiosyncratic visions of experience. Although the medium in which he works is thoroughly social, and the words with which he grasps reality are supposed to communicate intensively and extensively, his central activity is basically solitary. Of those who work alone in an American society dedicated to the abolition of solitude, the poet is perhaps most nearly comparable to the scientist. But he differs strikingly in that the scientist enjoys a fabric of external support and prestige, as well as a well-defined realm of objective data; the scientist is linked to research money, nuclear charisma, and circumscribed phenomena of interest. The number of scientists who actually work alone is also steadily diminishing. Poets, in their roles as verbal innovators, are adventurers in the minds and hearts of men. As such, they have no appreciable economic leverage, their names are unknown, and the potential field of attention is as wide as the universe. The fundamentally lonely nature of the task has been well described by Stephen Spender:

. . . above all, the writing of a poem brings one face to face with his own personality with all its familiar and clumsy limitations. In every other

3

phase of existence, one can exercise the orthodoxy of a conventional routine: one can be polite to one's friends, one can get through the day at the office, one can pose, one can draw attention to one's position in society, one is—in a word—dealing with men. In poetry, one is wrestling with a god.[2]

It is impossible to understand the poet's relation to the social milieu without taking into account his relation to himself and to the expressive medium—language—in which he is absorbed. Unless this private world is recognized as the locus of the artistic role, we shall seriously misjudge his intentions and importance. For the poet does not set out to tell the public a beautiful tale, nor is his impact to be gauged by the total readership of the tale he does tell. He sets out to capture for himself the essence of experience. In his attempted elucidation of the ineffable, he works in and through the distinctively human medium of words. The obsession with language means that experience recaptured in privacy is in a fundamental sense more "real" to the poet than are everyday face-to-face encounters. Since one cannot look to overt, observable social interaction as the source of basic understanding about the role, he is thus to some extent disabled as a sociological investigator. In effect, since the investigator can hardly watch poets at work or devise a controlled experiment to assess their propensities for various sorts of artistic behavior, the study of this distinctive social role is largely confined to an intensive probing of the subjective dimensions of the task as they appear to the poet himself. There are certain types of tangential information which offer some clues, such as literary criticism, psychological analyses of literary work, publishing and sales figures, and popular reactions to the artist as expressed in magazines and newspapers. Yet in the end one is compelled to look at the poet's personality, style of life, methods and goals, and above all the created product itself, through the poet's own lens. Only then is it justifiable, and indeed possible, to analyze his role from a social psychological perspective. In John Ciardi's words, "Modern poets, in one sense, are the poets we know least about, and until time has made clear to us (and to them) their whole intent, until time has completed the circle whose arc they are now projecting, the poets themselves are likely to be their own best guides to themselves." [3]

4

The Poet in American Society

The present research was initiated as an effort to explore the reactions of creative writers to a projective test. During the testing, we grew increasingly interested in the poet's behavior and writing habits and in his place in American society. It was decided therefore to enlarge the investigation, visiting the sample of writers a second time for a lengthy semistructured interview. The two visits, often occurring at summer homes far from public accommodations, afforded an exceptional opportunity for informal discussion and casual observation extending well beyond the limits of a normal interview. Fortunately, most of the respondents rejected Auden's dictum:

> Thou shalt not answer questionnaires
> Or quizzes upon World Affairs,
>   Nor with compliance
> Take any test. Thou shalt not sit
> With statisticians nor commit
>   A social science.[4]

This study is based primarily on a group of twenty-four poets who were the focus of intensive research, although relevant data were secured from many other sources. The group interviewed and tested was thus small in numbers. It was, however, large in artistic excellence, so that it constituted an elite sample. The poets, all published writers of some stature, included several Pulitzer Prize winners and holders of the consultantship in poetry at the Library of Congress. They were for the most part residents of the northeastern United States, recipients of critical acclaim, and members of the more "advanced," experimental artistic sector often loosely termed *avant-garde*. There were no newspaper versifiers and no strictly regional writers, only one author of light verse, and only three women poets. It may be seen that the sample was sufficiently homogeneous to be internally comparable, but that it necessarily can afford only a partial picture of the very ill-defined entity, "the American poet." For an exploratory venture, it was felt that a limited range of cases studied in depth was preferable to a survey of any substantial number of persons who might be designated as poets. Because of the limitations of the sample and the fact that writing is a highly individual operation, generalization is exceed-

5

ingly hazardous. We shall nevertheless speak of "the poet" for convenience of exposition, without qualifying each statement in the several ways required for absolute precision.*

A Psychological Note

The psychology of creativity cannot be developed in a brief treatment of the artist's social role. In another paper, the creative process in poets and the personality characteristics that seem to accompany the process were analyzed in some detail.[5] Yet the writing job itself has such important implications for the general behavior of the writer that we should mention a few prominent psychological concomitants of poetry making.

Creative writing is a process that involves the whole individual at his most alert level of activity. It demands great energy coupled with a capacity for probing and using the materials of one's own personality. The subjective immersion of the poet at work exposes him to psychic strain, as the deliberate use of the self tends to reveal and accentuate the deficiencies and conflicts, as well as the rich integrations, of that self. Creative involvement is critical to the social role in that much of the behavior often labeled eccentric or deviant in the artist's life, such as difficult family relationships, failure to keep social engagements, refusal to get caught up in community activities, should really be seen as a part of the writer's job rather than as evidence of perverse Bohemianism or inherent marginality.

In addition to the vitality and flexibility required for intensive creative effort, the poet cultivates a particular gift for experiencing the world fully. He can write only out of that experience, that combination of stored impression and current sensation which forms his creative fund. The poet is sensitive, then, but not in a mode of mere flabby impressionability; rather, he is selectively sensitive to his environment. Though it may be true that he actually experiences a larger quantity of physical stimuli and ideas than do most people, it is perhaps more true that he experiences with a heightened keen-

---

* Since the poets were quite candid in interviews, their privacy has been respected by quoting them anonymously to illustrate many of the themes discussed later in this essay.

ness and selectivity. For this is, after all, his job. The task is only begun by sharp perceiving, however; there remains the crucial element of ordering experience, of molding and trapping it in the web of language. The poet has a remarkably developed capacity for the use of language. One informant has emphasized that the predominance of the verbal is in him so acute that sense impressions must usually be immediately transformed into words if they are to be fully meaningful. W. H. Auden has remarked that the love of words is the distinguishing mark of the aspiring poet. Linguistic virtuosity, backed by a strong desire to make experience as meaningful as possible, is the poet's chief weapon in the creative endeavor.

Supplementing these required qualities of personality are technical skills of a high order. A knowledge of the forms and techniques of verse is essential. Technique alone is not enough, yet the most sensitive and gifted perceiver does not become a poet without mastering the formal properties of poetry. These skills should be emphasized, for the poet is sometimes wrongly seen as an untutored person engaged in a purely emotional response to the world about him. On the contrary, his technical equipment is quite as important and hard won as are the conceptual tools of any other professional. If the poet is more than a fine technician, he is also more than a primitive celebrant of sensuous joy. He is in the strict sense a maker, a craftsman, an artisan of language who transmutes the flux of perception into a fulfilled order for his own (and others') pleasure.

The labor of writing is long. It moves through stages from first conception to finished poem, and each stage exacts from the poet a substantial measure of alert effort. If the artist then demands some privacy, some extra degree of disassociation from worldly concerns, his social solitude should be related as much to the intrinsic nature of his craft as to any conscious alienation from the social context. His main connection with nature and human nature is through language, as he makes experience meaningful to himself and thereby provides the tongue and the knowledge for increasingly sensitive perception in society at large. The poet's primary function is not to lecture or serve on committees or lead political movements, but to write poems. The psychological satisfactions of art and the intensity of self-definition in the poet's role will be prominent in the following discussion. Satisfaction and self-definition must be

7

recurrent themes, for they are too easily lost in the rather clumsy and abstract framework of sociological consideration.

The Poet's Historical Role

It has been hypothesized by aesthetic and literary scholars that in some era of prehistory all men were artists, or perhaps better that each member of society had skills which permitted him to assume the creative role at some time. The seemingly spontaneous elaboration of the primitive dance would lend credence to this view. Otto Rank[6] has maintained that the selection of an individual to voice the sentiments of the group occurred only in conjunction with certain religious forms. At any rate, the role of the artist in the West has typically been specialized and distinct, although in a few places and times it has been expected that educated men would occasionally indulge in art making apart from their "full time" occupations. If the role has been specialized, it has also been traditionally arduous and unrewarded by the society in which it takes place. As Sir Arthur Quiller-Couch reminds us, "The inequity of it is accepted, proverbial, and goes back even to legend, to Homer—Seven wealthy towns contend for Homer dead/Through which the living Homer begged his bread." [7]

The paucity of recognition enjoyed by most poets during their lifetimes may of course be related to the fact that the validation of artistic worth is a matter for posterity, that the poet as prophet may seem much more congenial and valuable to a later age than to his own. Yet it is true that the writer is an exceptional man among nonwriters, and that a private excellence may be deprecated as a public excellence is exalted. The poet, after all, has seldom been able to offer anything of immediate public utility. At many times in the past, however, he has appeared to be more nearly woven into his society's major patterns of interest and behavior than he is today. Pindar wrote odes to military victory, and Elizabethan playwrights and musicians created for the monarch's pleasure; it is rather difficult to imagine T. S. Eliot celebrating the Battle of Okinawa or Tennessee Williams being commissioned to write a new drama for a presidential inauguration. (And yet the appearance of Robert

Frost at the late President Kennedy's inauguration may prefigure a somewhat closer alliance of artistic and civic spheres.)

The poet has been an object of suspicion, to be sure. Plato excluded the "honeyed muse" from his ideal republic, and one of the first moves of modern dictatorships has been an attempt to force artistic conformity with the dogmas of the state. Perhaps only in the contemporary Western democracies has the poet been so sedulously disregarded. Critics have sometimes assumed that the writer, as producer of a cultural luxury, was dependent on the favor of aristocratic patronage, so that the decline of aristocracy left him without a social anchor. Without the patronage of a ruling elite, he was exposed to the winds of the commercial marketplace. In the nineteenth and twentieth centuries it became a European fashion to speak of the artist *versus* society, as if there were some unalterable opposition between the creator and the social order. We are heirs of this romantic stereotype of the alienated writer. It is significant that the writer enunciated the enmity, and that there are very few instances of attack on the artistic role by government officials, businessmen, or whomever. It might be more appropriate for the contemporary poet to sue his society for nonsupport than for alienation of affection. A classic statement of the poet's feeling that he is hounded by an unsympathetic social environment is Baudelaire's:

. . . if a poet asked the state for permission to keep a few bourgeois in his stable everyone would be greatly astonished; but if a bourgeois asked for some roast poet, it would be considered perfectly natural.[8]

The case of the poet in America is especially interesting because the very trends toward mechanization and bureaucratization of life which repelled European artists have here reached most acute form. It is generally accepted that the colonial and post-Revolutionary periods in the United States failed to produce artists of the first rank. One assumes that citizens of that age were much too busy staking out a new republic and dominating the physical environment to devote much attention to the arts. Most of the productions of that and later periods were either too clumsy to merit critical consideration or too derivative of English models to stand as truly American literature. We note then (de Tocqueville) as in the latter part of the nineteenth century (Henry Adams) the primary antithesis between a pragmatic penchant for getting things done fast and efficiently and a much less common resolve to get things done beautifully if slowly.

Most critics point to the mid nineteenth century as the golden years of artistic intensity in America. The Concord group and other figures in F. O. Mathiesson's "American Renaissance" stand for the plenitude of literary fruition. The names of Melville, Poe, Emily Dickinson, Walt Whitman, Emerson, Thoreau, are taken as climactic. Of the poets, it is Poe, Whitman, and Dickinson who are singled out for special praise as the progenitors of a native verse.

Matthew Josephson[9] develops the thesis that after this literary high noon the serious writer became progressively alienated in spirit from the main facets of American life. Of course he can point to anonymity and marginal status of the artist even before the late 1800's. But it is in the booty stage of American capitalism, the post-Civil War expansion of railroads and industry, that he finds the locus of disenchantment. The mercantile emphasis, the stress on unaesthetic utility, the lack of public response, all contrived to produce in the artist a feeling of separation from society. Josephson assumes that this society rejected the artist; if the public indeed did so implicitly, it is certain that many writers proclaimed an explicit rejection of their country. The exiles went the length to physical rejection, as in the expatriation of Henry James, of Whistler, of Eliot and Pound in the early twentieth century. The stay-at-homes were in many cases unhappy with their lot. Recall Melville's "I feel I am an exile here." The individual who stayed in America seemed doomed to eccentricity: "The fatalistic, the silenced Melville, the outcast Whitman, the mysteriously secluded Emily Dickinson. . . ." What reasons are adduced for this situation, which may err on the gloomy side but is nevertheless a largely correct summary of what writers felt their lot to be? Leveling and standardization of values and mechanization of life, which may be expressed sociologically as the dominance of a rational-legal, bureaucratic industrial system, are most often put forth as antecedents of artistic discontent:

The artist, then, appears most vulnerable. In a society increasingly collective and uniform in its interests, no place has been left for his lonely and personal labors. With such a world art in the older sense can no longer co-exist.

Under mechanism, the eternal drama for the artist becomes resistance to the milieu, as if the highest prerogative were the preservation of the individual type, the defense of the human self from dissolution in the horde.[10]

In this dilemma the poet represents one of the critical issues of contemporary Western civilization. Simmel stated the problem in general terms:

The deepest problems of modern life derive from the claim of the individual to preserve the autonomy and individuality of his existence in the face of overwhelming social forces, of historical heritage, of external culture, and of the technique of life.[11]

To balance the picture of the artist as a social isolate of ignoble status, we may think of the "Indian Summer" of New England, of Chautauqua with its idolatry of "culture," of the general (and genteel) fashionableness of literary activity. Yet the critics affirm that those artists of sterner vein, who were to be recognized as giants by a later generation, were for the most part badly treated. So Dahlberg weeps for Melville buried in a poor grave:

Is it not fitting, so American, that the most astonishing genius that ever came out of the Western hemisphere, should be so uncleanly slabbed down in mean cheap dirt not among the pitiable poor but with the common drab bulk of rightly unremembered dead. Look upon his homely sparse tombstone and read the frugal inscription written thereon, "Occupation, Writer," and then utter aloud the pity for the artist, in America, alive or deceased, it matters not, that Hamlet so dolorously sighs forth before his father's apparition, "Alas! Poor Ghost." [12]

In 1913 we find Ezra Pound advancing a somewhat brighter view, although it is still weighted toward the dark strains of isolation and rejection. For Pound, while stating in definite terms the obstacles to poetry in this country, had hope of a development toward better days: "I have declared my belief in the imminence of

11

an American Risorgimento. I have no desire to flatter the country by pretending that we are at present enduring anything except the Dark Ages." [13] He sets up American vigor and "clumsy energy" against the flowering of the arts, noting that politics and business drain talented individuals away from the arts. Of the Americans he said:

> One knows that they are the dominant people and that they are against all delicate things. They will never imagine beautiful plaisaunces. They will never "sit on a midden and dream stars," as the Irish peasant said to Joseph Campbell.[14]

The status of the American poet today is difficult to describe, for it is an ambiguous and various complex of attitudes and values. While certain observers profess to see a general raising of artist and intellectual in the public eye, stimulated by increased literacy and leisure, it is apparent that the poet's craft is far from the concerns of most members of American society. In one sense the poet's position is bettered by the wide influence of poets and critics in academic circles and by a resultant increase in intelligent interest. Public readings of poetry have drawn large audiences, recordings by poets are stocked in libraries, and one poet a year has been formally recognized by the Library of Congress as Consultant in Poetry. Yet it would be false to suppose that the appellation "poet" evokes an unusually affirmative response from the mass of Americans, or that it implies any great respect. He is no culture hero but is probably more nearly disregarded than disvalued in any explicit sense. A *lack* of attribution of high status is not the same as the attribution of low status, for broadly speaking the poet is not scorned but neglected. His role is simply not in the public ken, and this despite a healthy, important production of poetry in modern American. Many leading observers, in fact, emphasize that the writing of contemporary and recent native poets is of extremely fine quality, a true growth of poetic tradition matching other high points in aesthetic history.

Auden sums up the mixed, uncomfortable status of most poets today:

Everyone in his heart of hearts agrees with Baudelaire: "To be a useful person has always seemed to me something particularly horrible," for, subjectively, to be useful means to be doing not what one wants to do but what someone else insists on one's doing. But at the same time, everyone is ashamed to admit in public that he is useless. Thus if a poet gets into conversation with a stranger in a railway coach and the latter asks him: "What is your job?," he will think quickly and say: "A schoolteacher, a beekeeper, a bootlegger," because to tell the truth would cause an incredulous and embarrassing silence.[15]

Why should the artist, the specialist in symbolic creativity, hold a tenuous position in American society? He originates form and content which afford pleasure and more than pleasure, the rich insights and stark perceptions to make experience meaningful. Yet he can seldom earn a living in his vocation, seldom count on any broadly based support in his chosen role; he must be as ready for depreciation as for appreciation, and this according to criteria seemingly remote from consideration of artistic excellence. If we analyze the poet's work and life in the context of American values, it may be possible to see the frail roots of his insecure role in our cultural soil. It should be stressed, however, that American society only accentuates the traditionally precarious role of the artistic innovator. In nearly every place and time the truly creative individual has represented a threat to the norms men live by, since he promises to shatter or transcend or at least drastically amend those norms. The creative individual in art is the more dangerous because he challenges our ways of perceiving and our habits of expressing what we see. Unlike the political revolutionary or social reformer, who would change the forms of social intercourse, the artist would change our total response to the universe of man and nature. In this he is like the scientist revising our perceptions of physical reality or the charismatic religious leader enhancing our moral perceptions.

The Poet and American Values

The texture of American culture is so rich and complicated that generalizations about specific themes of value and behavior are

13

always hazardous. For every statement that this or that pattern is dominant or recessive, one can easily adduce contrary evidence. Although an analyst must arbitrarily break through the almost oppressive heterogeneity of social forms, it is well to begin by recognizing that pluralism is itself perhaps the most prominent theme. Pluralism of values is in fact a chief support of the artist, in that it lets him work out a unique destiny of vocational fulfillment. Although it is true that cultural diversity complicates his effort to communicate, reducing the scope of any single shared tradition or contemporary frame of reference, diversity also provides the poet with a range of alternative life styles, with economically rewarding pursuits other than poetry, and with several potential kinds of audience. Again, the habit of tolerance in religious and political matters tends to insure the tolerance of artistic heresy. If we let artists die of neglect it can scarcely be said that we hound them with demands for conformity to any particular doctrine of state or ideology. Underlying pluralism of tradition, however, there are a few generally recognized clusters of dominant themes against which the artist may be viewed.

THE PROTESTANT ETHIC AND THE SPIRIT OF POETRY

The Protestant Ethic as adduced, for example, by Max Weber, is in a very fundamental sense antipathetic to poetry. This is true despite the high rank of the greatest Puritan poet—Milton—and despite certain superficial congruities between the Calvinist ethical ideal and that of the artist-as-ascetic. While the concept of the "calling," of devotion to a disciplined activity, is very relevant to poetic dedication, the context of the poet's calling is singular. For his work by its very nature demands a breadth of enjoyment, an appetite for the pleasure of this world, which is foreign to the religiously derived work ethic. The Protestant Ethic, like the utilitarian doctrine, emphasizes the extrinsic goals of striving; salvation and profits are alike in their displacement from the work activity itself. Weber has shown how the goal of election into a celestial state of grace became subordinated, in the later development of Calvinist-inspired work ethics, to the idea that work is good for its own sake.

Yet this Calvinist work is not the poet's work, since it is not to be enjoyed but grimly endured. Obviously an entrepreneur could not legitimately derive pleasure from a calling which had been imposed as dutiful striving.

The poet is too apparently a man who derives pleasure from his task, and that pleasure is a sensuous one. The immediacy of symbolic creation implies acceptance and deep enjoyment of affective nuances. The poet plays with words and loves them for their own sweet verbal sakes; he is stimulated by his own productions. The Protestant Ethic, rightly internalized, involves a positive distaste for pleasure, and especially for sensuous pleasure. We might recast Macaulay's famous remark about the Puritans and bear baiting by noting that American society rejects the poet not because of the pain (or ease) he gives his readers, but because of the pleasure he obviously gets from writing. It is furthermore a peculiar feature of the artist's work that he rarely appears, to a casual observer, to be working at all. Actual writing is known to consume a rather small portion of the writer's day, even when he is in high gear. And there are periods, well described by E. D. Hutchinson as "Periods of Renunciation" in creative endeavor, when nothing happens to be going just right, no new idea has jelled, and the artist must stick it out. This "sticking it out" may take the form of loafing; although everyone agrees that a certain kind of loafing is crucial to any intellectually creative activity, it still seems to the public not quite right or wholly just. The public, as Bergler notes, envies the writer while scorning him for his (seeming) ease. In a country where occupational life is characterized by intensity, especially "busy work" and routine, the person of no fixed outer demands is looked upon somewhat askance. This occurs despite the fact that there may be inner personal demands, in poet or scientist, more strict than anything the time clock or straw boss imposes.

ROUTINE AND ORIGINALITY

In the rational-legal society of the West, occupations are very generally routinized. The complexity of huge bureaucratic-industrial organizations demands that the specific task assigned through

15

division of labor be amenable to definite planning. The characteristic job should be ordered to standards of performance, technique,
and interrelation with other closely allied functions. Not only is the
job itself routinized, but the training that fits an individual for the
position is specified and clearly established with an end in view of
competent task fulfillment. All of this ordering and accountability
means further that the vast majority of occupations are institutionalized; that is, the activities involved cluster into a set of definable
expectations on the parts of mutually interactive role players. Performance of certain roles is an accepted feature of the social system,
and both role players and significant others know what is legitimately to be expected. The "public" or mass of social actors has, too,
a disposition to regard as justified an activity for which formal
social provision is made, which can be objectively "certified." None
of these strictures applies to poetry as a profession. It is true that
strict standards of competence are applied by literary critics, but
even here the criteria are amorphous. Writing is a sedentary activity; the poet grows no calluses, goes to no offices, punches no time
clock, gains no diploma, earns no certificate of competence. There
is no current, universal measure of his success or fitness; his credentials are intangible, a passport without date, country, or occupation.
Poetry is an undefined profession. It lacks either the institutional
support or the popular appeal of science, with which alone it is
comparable in terms of originality of contribution.

THE POETIC ROLE AND THE "REVOLT OF THE MASSES"

Ortega y Gassett has given a profound analysis of the tremen-
dous power of the "mass man." He posits the rise to dominance of
the great bulk of average individuals, through the democratic fran-
chise and the weakening of older hierarchical social organizations,
as the primary fact of our times. Nowhere is the phenomenon more
fully exemplified than in the United States. That this should result
in a vast pressure toward conformity and mediocrity is not surprising. De Tocqueville made careful note of "leveling" tendencies in
America over a century ago. Perhaps genius and talent are always
suspect; one doubts that physicists or chemists are wholly under-

stood or accepted in this country, despite the practical efficacy of their sciences. Mass dominance implies a standardization of values and a distrust of the unique. These tendencies are accentuated enormously by the media of mass communication, which insure that the value standard becomes a common denominator. The common denominator is not necessarily low for being common; it may be quite high, as exemplified in a very real intensifying of the interest in classical music, but it *is* weighted toward uniformity.

The poet is by definition the teller of a personal truth. He is unique and abides by an uncommon denominator. His vision is necessarily too exacting for a generation schooled in the comforting prose of the *Reader's Digest* or the artificial excitement of quiz shows. As a minority of one, he falls under many of the strains imposed on other, more obtrusive minorities.

PRAGMATISM AND POETRY

Americans do things and go places. The poet does things and goes places too, only he does unusual things and goes to uncharted places. This in itself may make him an object of suspicion. But he is guilty of a worse crime, and one that sets his role more incontrovertibly against the American temper: his efforts have no obvious utility. In this aspect he is more deviant than the gangster, whose role at least has an objective utility for himself in that it may make him rich before it makes him dead. The molder of aesthetic symbols may reform the language, transmute and communicate experience, delight the reader with originality of form. But, the popular pragmatist might ask, to what end are these things done? We accept the notion of "pure research" in the sciences because we have learned by experience that such efforts generally result in efficacious and profitable by-products. The poet does pure research in the human heart, but few Americans could be convinced that his work compares in importance with that of a specialist on coronary thrombosis.

THE ARTIST AND THE FEMININE ROLE

In American culture, women have most often been the carriers of the arts. They have not usually been of the first rank artistically

17

or critically, but overall they have been the sustaining and encouraging audience. In a very real sense American males have delegated to their wives, and even more definitely to women of the "old maid schoolteacher" stereotype, the responsibility for what is popularly known as "culture." A superficial explanation of this phenomenon might point to the frontier imperatives, which later became the business imperatives, of energetic effort, devotion to externals, and resolute "toughness" on the part of the male. As Erikson has so beautifully shown, one of the duties of the mother in this country has been to push the son firmly in the direction of untrammeled maleness and striving, meanwhile sedulously smothering his impulse to things sensual and immediate. This emphasis of course leaves the pursuit of poetry to women or to males whose socialization somehow did not "take."

Yet this is not the whole story. When Carol Kennicott, protagonist in Sinclair Lewis' *Main Street,* tried to bring the arts to Gopher Prairie (a typically womanish project), she was met not by a plain refusal to be concerned but by positive male hostility. Why should American men avoid the artist's calling and tend to deprecate those who follow it?

We may suggest that, going deeper than the fact of the female as the functional art bearer in the American tradition, there are elements intrinsic to the roles of male and female which militate against men-as-artists. What has been called the American man's "panic fear of homosexuality" may be relevant to the ambiguous position of the male poet. As the Kluckhohns and others have stressed, it is comparatively easy for men to be "scared" out of being artists. A major basis for this fear may be found in the observation that the themes of diffuseness and affectivity which characterize the feminine role, for example as outlined by Parsons, are also quite typical of the artist role. In this connection, Parsons has remarked upon the revealing use of the term "longhair," to describe artists and their works. We note that the term is ordinarily employed in a derogatory vein. May it not be a dramatic symbol of the hostility often directed against the artist who oversteps role boundaries? This correspondence of themes suggests that the fear and hostility the poet often meets are contingent on his not "acting like a man" in role terms. The poet incorporates too much, refuses to be bound by conventions of role differentiation, and exhibits an "unmasculine" concern with senses and sensitivity. He is not well socialized, for he breaks the mold by overincorporation. Related to his greater *capacity* for experience is the possibility that his actual intake is too large for an easy distinction between masculine and feminine elements. Thus he takes in elements of both male and female roles, as do all men, but then refuses to be disabused of "feminine" affectivity and diffuse responsibilities at a later stage. Perhaps he never succeeds in unlearning the infant's play impulses or warmly sensuous responses to the world. An hypothesis might be, then, that the artist role and the feminine role are intimately related—often to the social detriment of the artist—not because artists are constitutionally "queer" but because our culture demands a role differentiation on the thematic, learned level which the artist is unable or unwilling to make. Unable to suppress his affective resonance and diffusely generalized response to life in favor of the more strict male occupational model, the poet finds himself too versatile in a specialized world. As "the apple tree, the singing and the gold" do not promote the world's work, so they do not provide a wholly acceptable costuming of social role for the male poet.

THE IDEAL OF SELF-FULFILLMENT

The American belief in an individual, self-determined destiny that will express the essential talents of each person is one of the strongest props for marginal roles. The idea that one's social role, far from being predetermined by accidents of birth or environment, represents the choice made by a relatively free agent implies the right to choose odd life styles and seemingly incomprehensible goals. Thus, despite the very real pressures toward conformity, and especially toward a materially validated success, there is a range of tolerance for the artist who is doing the kind of thing that appeals to him. The shocked disbelief that greets the announcement that one's son has turned to poetry or painting is not unmixed with a respectful envy, an admiration however grudging for the individual who hews to his own path. The spate of popular volumes which preach self-fulfillment and unique personal development bespeaks the resonance Americans have for such concepts as well as the need for reinforcement of the ideal in a society which seems to force people into roles they might not choose again as free agents. It is true that the notion of an individual's "doing what he wants to do" is usually implicitly qualified by criteria of financial gain, but one must attach great importance to the fact that parents in this society feel guilty about pushing their children into uncongenial vocations. So a way is left open for the artist, who corresponds to an ideal type of self-fulfillment. There can be little doubt that of all men the poet is most concerned with the burgeoning of his own personality, his sensitivity, and his perceptivity. It is, after all, his only stock in trade, the only instrument he will ever have to perform miracles of words. The dramatic moment when Sherwood Anderson walked out of his paint factory, family life, and routine set of social roles to become a professional writer is perhaps a symbol for the right of self-expression. Today it is debatable whether an aspiring novelist would even have to walk out of the factory or out of his settled life style; he might be encouraged in his native circumstances to the point where flight was meaningless.

EDUCATION AND LEISURE

Americans now have the highest general level of education and the most leisure time ever enjoyed by a society as a whole. The effect of this situation on the arts and the artist is not yet clear, but it will undoubtedly change the artist's role by transforming the nature of the audience. More people now have the humanistic acquaintance which is necessary to make the arts individually meaningful, and they have free time to read, or visit museums, or listen to concerts. Respect for the professional artist may increase as more amateurs try to master the techniques of painting and writing. The tiny leisure class which has traditionally provided aristocratic patrons is being expanded in this country toward a kind of classless leisure, a potential source of broad support for artistic activities. It is certainly conceivable that creation and recreation may tend to merge if the mass media do not succeed in consuming all of everyone's spare hours. The great world of events piped to our livingrooms may come to be too much with us, so that the private world of one poet and one reader becomes an attractive sanctuary.

Innovation and Deviance:
The Paradox of the Creative Role

Although we have seen that American values in their variety both harbor and reject the poet, it is obvious that his role diverges rather sharply from the vocational paths which men in this society are expected to follow. In part the divergence is negative, consisting of his not embracing certain common goals such as economic gain or social position and not employing certain common means such as professional training or climbing the rungs of an organizational hierarchy. These negative elements are the core of the concept of the artist as deviant, but they do not lead us very far, because in these terms the poet is indistinguishable from the hobo or the psychotic. The really important questions arise when one asks what the artist puts in place of the behaviors he has rejected.

The poet as maker rejects the conventional perceptions of the world of men and nature. His implicit goal is to make his reader more aware of the complexity and ambiguity of existence, not by preaching but by vigorous example of fresh ways of seeing. The artist forces us to give up, at least momentarily, those routine, comfortable perceptual stereotypes on which we depend to keep the world under safe control. This is why full participation in aesthetic communication may be nearly as psychologically threatening for the appreciator as for the creator. The threat, like almost all challenges to an established behavioral system (for example, neurosis) has as much potential for growth and refreshment as for confusion or debilitation. Yet we naturally resist the challenge to follow the poet into novel modes of reacting to experience and novel words for expressing that reaction. It not only bestirs us, since art may in one sense be seen as the opposite of a state of rest, but it also confronts us with the imperative to grow, to enlarge our own perceptions enough to assimilate some part of the artist's perceptions.

Because the heightening of awareness is an endless occupation, halting only with death or complete unawareness, the poet cannot be said to have a "goal" in the usual sense. His essential goal is more of the same, that is, renewed involvement in the process of living and writing. It is true that he wants to achieve the perfect line, the absolute phrase; but this is an intangible end, really the prelude to the next perfect line, and it is so elusive that many writers would agree with the aphorism that, "a poem is never finished, it is abandoned in despair." If the artist's goal is difficult to define and tends to be a process rather than a static accomplishment, what may one say about his means? They are so extraordinary, when compared with the instrumental maneuvers of most individuals in society, that the question of "how he does it," may put the poet further from the dominant patterns of behavior than the question of "why he does it." In large part, his means are simply to live as fully and sensitively as possible, to be a mobile perceptual antenna at the boundary of human consciousness. Because he spends so much of his time doing and being these things, he may be and often is accused of being a noncontributing member of society. When he comes to the job of writing itself, he performs in a private world. Only when some reader happens to receive his gift and enter to a certain degree the universe of cognition and emotion he has elaborated, does the poet come to have an obvious function.

As the creator of expressive symbols, the artist eventually has an effect. It is likely to be a slow and subtle one, like that of the religious leader, the philosopher, or the scientist, for it consists in changing the basic views of men and reforming the tongue they use to express those views. We then face an interesting conceptual problem: the very innovators whose transcendence of common values has in the long run the most highly valued effect are treated as marginal men in the contemporary social scheme. Many reasons may be adduced for this treatment, including the uncomfortable wrench the artist gives to conventional ways of seeing, and the time lag between what the artist does and what his potential publics may grow to accept. Fewer good reasons may be found, however, for the failure of social scientists to devote adequate attention to the exceptional person, the creative individual in whatever sphere. The theorists of social control and general societal maintenance have tended to accept their own cultural framework to the extent of dividing people into those who follow social prescriptions closely and those whose refusal to follow them results in deleterious (criminal or ill) behavior. They have neglected to consider the talented person who transcends social prescriptions in search of something better or fuller. Psychologists too, as Allport has recently maintained,[16] have been bound to a model of man as reactive organism, who could be seen as responding to external stimuli (therefore capable of accepting or rejecting sensations, including social norms) but not as initiating creative activity (therefore capable of devising new structures and refining old ones).

Since the creative individual is demonstrably important to society, we need a sophisticated theory of innovative behavior. Such a theory is required both for what might be termed *institutionalized* innovation, as in science, and for the singular creativity that occurs in noninstitutionalized spheres, as in art and religion. Some clues exist, in such diverse contexts as Max Weber's concept of charisma, psychoanalytic studies of the genesis of artistic behavior, and current investigations of personality characteristics of talented individuals. But a true social psychology of creativity needs to be grounded in a series of detailed researches, embracing everything from childhood development to the style of life of the mature innovator. As Henry A. Murray has expressed it, the sociologist must turn from an exclusive preoccupation with "associational" roles which are characterized by observable patterns of social interaction toward some cognizance of "monadic" or individually creative roles. The problem of analyzing the role of the artist or scientist is not an exotic or peripheral one merely because their behaviors are complicated and they are a numerically tiny segment of the population. The poet and the physicist are not only highly significant in their society, but in their vocational paths they raise the major issues for the student of man: conformity and social control, the relation of the individual to his various social groupings, the learning of cultural norms, the creation of percepts and values by which the social fabric is torn or mended or graven with bold new designs.

Aspects of the Poetic Vocation

CHOICE OF THE CAREER

The absence of the trappings of institutionalization means that in one sense there is no career for the aspiring individual to choose. That is, the job of poet is a unique system of literary and experiential patterns without many of the familiar guideposts we normally associate with an occupation: there are no training schools, no diplomas, no starting salary, no series of position to which the able beginner might order his progress. This paucity of external criteria is quite fitting, since in other professions such criteria guide rational choice whereas in poetry the decision to follow the muse is seldom a matter for mature deliberation. It is, rather, a decision which generally occurs fairly early in life. Paradoxically, by the time one could accept or reject poetry as a way of life, he would have already to be a considerable poet. It might even be said that the role of poet overtakes the persistent and talented writer of poetry.

Literature as experience is the major force attracting recruits to the poetic role: they read, are astonished, and determine to create for themselves. Symbolic experience, the environment of the printed page, is often neglected in our quest for causal chains in human development, but it may be an important agent of growth, especially for personalities whose career fulfillment lies in literate sectors of the arts, professions, or government. One poet who made an early, explicit choice of the vocation recounted this event:

I have never wanted to be anything else. At the age of nine, I read *Tom Brown's Schooldays,* which had an introduction containing two lines of verse:

"I'm the poet of White Horse vale, sir,
With liberal notions under my cap."

I asked my parents what a poet was, and when they told me I was fascinated. I went to school and saw several words listed on the board; I

24

made a rhyme scheme, and this was my first poem. I always *knew* I would be a poet.

Even those who came to poetry somewhat later in life tend to stress the importance of literary stimuli:

It was not deliberate, and was based on the pleasure principle. I read modern poems in high school, not dreaming that I could write one. Then one day I wrote one, loved the experience and wanted to repeat it.

The exposure to literature is important; poetic activity must spring from somewhere. I wrote some poetry in college, but was not very involved with it. I wrote much prose, and becoming dissatisfied with it, turned to poetry.

The power of the poetic tradition is of course reinforced by the presence of some few mentors and colleagues, themselves sharers of the verbal heritage and partners in the creative enterprise. It is often an older colleague who will call one's work to the attention of editor or publisher. Ezra Pound's reputation in literary circles is actually based quite as much on his letters and encouraging overtures to young poets as on his own artistic contribution; many older writers feel that the nurture of young talent is a duty imposed on the established person, although it is to be sure a duty of enthusiasm rather than compulsion. Contemporary poets are vividly aware of influential exemplars:

I had to quit athletics because of my health. After trying all the arts, I fixed on poetry. I met _____ at the university. He was a major influence on me, giving me good freshman literary criticism, not vague but in clear declarative sentences.

I firmly settled on poetry while at Cambridge, largely under the influence of I. A. Richards and William Empson.

What I need most is someone to fight like hell with. Women are to go to bed with, men are to fight with. My association with Ezra Pound helped inspire me to continue writing poetry. For years we waged a battle over the proper goal of the poet; I would say, "bread" and Pound would say, "caviar."

25

Finally, the inner drive toward poetic innovation appears to many artists as a "given," an historical personal fact which must somehow be accommodated and woven into one's style of life:

> It was an accidental, not a conscious, decision. But I felt a lack when I was doing something else, as if I were not using myself.

> You're generally a poet because you have to be, not because you decide you want to be.

> In this art, in distinction from painting, one must begin early. There is the necessity of much practice, so that one achieves technical mastery before the finding of his individual voice. Poetry is always there. If it is with you, you will make a place for it.

Modern poets are under no illusion that the vocation they have embraced is likely to bring them any of the usual rewards of a profession. Twenty years ago the most famed contemporary, T. S. Eliot, put the matter bluntly:

> As things are, and as fundamentally they must always be, poetry is not a career but a mug's game. No honest poet can ever feel quite sure of the permanent value of what he has written: he may have wasted his time and messed up his life for nothing.[17]

ECONOMIC AND SPIRITUAL SUPPORT

The poet requires at least two kinds of support from his environment: a "living" that makes his existence economically feasible, and a variety of social response or reward that can bolster his own belief in the value of his writing. Economic maintenance cannot be based wholly on the sale of verse; among modern poets, perhaps T. S. Eliot and Ogden Nash could now survive on royalties, but even they were not in a position to do so until their careers were well advanced. Book sales bring in a few hundred dollars a year at best, so they will not support a writer despite a steady production. The average sale of a volume of poems is fewer than 1000 copies. Publication is, moreover, quite difficult, since the publisher must anticipate a loss and usually prints poetry only as a prestige item, an unprofitable but good book published as an aesthetic service. The magazine market for verse is not a great deal better. Serious poets are rarely published in mass-circulation magazines. *Harper's Magazine* and the *Atlantic* cannot afford to pay high prices; *The New Yorker* does pay well for serious work, but it stands almost alone. The "little magazines" often maintain high standards of quality, but they can pay little or nothing to their contributors.

In addition to sales of published work, there is a variety of more or less fortuitous chances for income or its equivalent in subsidized free time. These include prizes, gifts, appointments to summer art colonies, and occasional odd strokes of luck. Some few patrons still may help the artist with gifts of money or nonrepayable "loans"; colonies such as Yaddo or McDowell afford several months of quiet, secure living for a few painters, composers, and poets at work. Sheer windfalls sometimes occur: Conrad Aiken once began to throw an "advertisement" in the wastebasket when the figure of $750.00 caught his eye; it was a letter from a pharmaceutical house offering him this sum for a one-page poem to be written for the annual publication.

When all the possibilities are exhausted, it is obvious that most poets must earn a living through some other activity than writing poems. Thus the follower of a pervasive vocation, one which demands a more nearly total investment of the personality than most, has to fit this vocation into spare-time or part-time occasions. Poets feel the money-making job should be far enough removed from creative work that it does not drain their energy or capture their time to an intolerable extent. They try to avoid the kind of high-pressure involvement demanded by news magazines or films or many sorts of organizations. Yet they do hold a wide range of jobs in business, the professions, and the writing-editing-publishing complex, and these jobs do not appear to interfere greatly with serious artistic production. William Carlos Williams and Merrill Moore were physicians, Wallace Stevens was a business executive, and a great many poets hold academic posts. There is an idealistic conceit that the artist should remove himself to pastoral pursuits or manual labor, but this is not a common happening. Most poets are forced to double up on their outstanding talent, that is, a high skill with

27

language. Academic jobs are a matter of controversy. Those who teach maintain that it is a decent complement to writing; those who do not tend to view the university as a carefully designed trap in which the artists are hamstrung if not prostituted. Poets affirm that it makes no great difference what one does for an income. If a person is a creative artist he will manage in some way to continue his work. Few contemporaries would approve of a system of outright subsidy for the artist; the objections are that subsidy is not only an unfair advantage in a democracy and a potential restriction to artistic freedom, but that the struggle for economic support is a necessary challenge to the writer's initiative. An unostentatious self-confidence generates the theme that the poet as interior man is superior to external conditions.

What of the poet's nonfinancial support from persons? However dedicated and self-propelled, he needs a measure of human response to his efforts. The general public is not an important source of support, because the general public does not read poetry. Poets note that members of the "public" usually like their work for the wrong reasons—or are the wrong persons. Liking for the wrong reasons is decried because the artist is not eager to be misunderstood; his pride is not enhanced by having someone admire the lovely sentiment of a poem whose intent is ironic or satirical. The unintended consequences of poetic action need not be, but often are, harrowing to the conscientious professional. Liking by the wrong persons indicates that the artist is not having the kind of effect he desires, that his efforts may be at least temporarily wasted because ignored by those he respects. Auden gives a succinct analysis of this situation:

> The ideal audience the poet imagines consists of the beautiful who go to bed with him, the powerful who invite him to dinner and tell him secrets of state, and his fellow-poets. The actual audience he gets consists of myopic schoolteachers, pimply young men who eat in cafeterias, and his fellow-poets. This means that, in fact, he writes for his fellow-poets.[18]

If the general public is not prominent in shoring up the poet's morale (and one must note that the public's disregard is often matched by a defensive rejection of popular taste by the poet), he must gain his rewards from more selected, specialized publics. This he does, and the primary characteristic of the specialized audience is, of course, literary sophistication. Family and friends are important, in this context, only as they fill the role of literary expert; otherwise, wife or boon companion is not to be trusted in matters of art. It is the in-group of critics and fellow professionals whose opinion weighs most in the scales of self-assessment. Again and again, poets speak of the vital place held by a few true perceivers, a handful of persons who judge the artist's intent by strict but sympathetic criteria and rightly gauge the inevitable discrepancy between a vision conceived and a poem executed.

In many other fields we think it only sensible that specialists should receive their primary response from other specialists. Especially in scholarship and science, no one expects that the expert will speak to an extended popular audience. Perhaps modern technology and role differentiation have grown together, so that one anticipates specialization of function as a natural thing in science. The poet, however, is expected to create something widely enjoyable, or at least understandable. The image of the artist spans Western society in its prespecialized and postspecialized aspects; thus artists whose work does not emit the familiar ring of common evaluative and stylistic coin are thought of as deviants or cultists. Actually, the poet who has traditionally been the "whole man" seems now to be in one sense a technical specialist whose prospective audience has also become split and specialized. The width of his potential appeal is an unsolved question and probably rests as much on the extensity of common symbolic meanings in the total culture as on the poet's own attempt to elaborate the universal in the unique.

GROUP MEMBERSHIP

The American poet, in contrast to poets of many other countries, does not today associate himself with particular small groups or artistic coteries. While there may be an occasional banding together for launching a new journal or taking a specific public action (for example, awarding a prize or collecting funds for a distressed artist), contemporary poets tend to resist the attractions of the

tightly knit artistic in-group. They feel that the comfort and intimacy afforded by such groups may be bought at too high a price
of artistic conformity. They try to avoid labels and are fairly consistently truant from "schools" of thematic or stylistic dicta. It
might be noted, too, that the poet's preference for catholicity rather
than parochialism is abetted by geographical dispersion and the
absence of congenial informal centers like the cafés of Paris.

If he seeks to avoid the limiting and labeling of coterie membership, however, it is not necessarily true that each artist is an isolated
worker. There are various informal groups, loosely bound together
by spatial or ideological propinquity. The Fugitive poets, a Southern group which flourished at Vanderbilt University in the 1920's,
is an example of a small group sharing many characteristics yet
generating very diverse types of writing and artistic careers. In Cambridge, Massachusetts, five or six established poets meet fairly regularly to read and discuss their work. Geographical proximity, which
is seldom entirely accidental, tends to throw artists together, particularly in the case of summer homes.

In another sense the modern poet is a working member of an
ill-defined group: contemporary professional poets. This craft membership is exceedingly important, although by ordinary sociological
criteria one might hesitate to term poets a "group." That is, they
may exhibit a paucity of overt interaction, a refusal to agree on the
identity of a leader, and a heterogeneity of sentiments. Yet they are
bound together by some few group norms, such as the primacy of
poetic activity and the integrity of critical judgment. Like an extended family, modern poets carry on an internecine war of attrition
but rally to one another's defense if poetry itself seems threatened
by outside forces. Interaction is actually vigorous, quite apart from
interpersonal contact at parties, visits, or art colonies; the symbolic
interplay of the printed word knits writers together through personal correspondence and, more importantly, through mutual cognizance of the created products. Possibly the poet has more profound
knowledge of his fellow professionals from reading their work than
the member of an organized group gains from daily superficial
contacts with his coworkers. We usually overlook this type of interpersonal network because the impulses which travel its channels
cannot be measured, and the channels themselves are seldom visible.

Yet the influences of second-level interaction, employing means other than face-to-face confrontation, are sociologically pervasive and are likely to become more so as modern society enhances its communicative virtuosity.

An artistic fellowship extending forward and back in time, sometimes grandly called "the republic of letters," constitutes the major reference group for the poet's behavior. The paradox of the role, the fact that it is a passionate devotion yet socially marginal, is partially resolved in the realization that the poet does not take business or professional elites as his referential anchors. He does not, then, suffer from invidious comparison with individuals whose vocations entail unusual rewards of income and prestige. Growing as it does from the use of "relative deprivation" as an explanatory concept in *The American Soldier*,[19] the idea of the reference group leads one to ask, "Deprived relative to whom?" The modern poet is not deprived of reward or isolated from the dominant streams of action if he is seen (as he sees himself) in the context of an historically validated artistic community. Indeed, his essential behavioral genealogy is most distinguished and durable. When a poet defines his role as important he is no isolated figure, brashly affirming a transitory place in the sun; rather, he envisions himself as a link, however great or small, in a chain reaching back to Homer and the ancient Chinese lyricists. Since art as symbolic vehicle is a time-defying element of culture, poets can conceive their role as almost infinitely extensible. The vocational faith has been kept, and the writer can find support for his current behavior and exalted role ideal in the achievements of the past. He looks also to the future, to the artists and audiences yet unborn. If the investment in posterity is intangible and hazardous, it is by the same token irrefutable; the poet leaves something behind, and considering the history of aesthetic taste few would scorn him for banking on "a paper eternity."

The relation of poet to poet in the contemporary scene is ambiguous and complex. Fellow poets of today do comprise the primary reference group for each of their number; in a sense, they are "all in it together," and one's peers must be assumed to have the most precise basis for judging one's efforts. As in other groups of specialists, notably the scientific and scholarly fraternities, reputation and hence subjective prestige rest on the good opinion of peers. Again, the jealousy and bitterness which often characterize competitors in specialized fields, particularly those vocations demanding great personal devotion, are apparent in poets. The most skilled artist is of course not necessarily the most attractive personality; as one writer expressed it, "Most of the people one knows aren't poets, and most of the poets one knows aren't people." Yet the very zeal and discrimination which tend to make for unstable interpersonal ties among poets may also enrich those ties with a rare tenderness and significance. By reason of their common sensitivity, poets, of all men, can go "proudly friended."

THE SELF-DEFINED ROLE

It is evident that a faith in their vocation,
mystical in intensity, sustains poets.
——Stephen Spender

. . . Does Madame recall our responsibilities? We are
Whores Fraulein: poets Fraulein are persons of
Known vocation following troops: they must sleep with
Stragglers from either prince and of both views:
The rules permit them to further the business of neither.
. . . The things of the poet are done to a man alone
As the things of love are done—or of death when he hears the
Step withdraw on the stair and the clock tick only
Neither his class nor his kind nor his trade may come near him
There where he lies on his left arm and will die:
Nor his class nor his kind nor his trade when the blood is jeering
And his knee's in the soft of the bed where his love lies:
I remind you Barinya the life of a poet is hard—
A hardy life with a boot as quick as a fiver:
Is it just to demand of us also to bear arms?
——Archibald MacLeish[20]

To paraphrase Thomas and Znaniecki's trenchant aphorism, if poets define poetry as real, it is real in its consequences. It is significant that they do define poetry as real and that they view their role in terms of the intrinsic attributes of art rather than in terms of the writer's individual behavior. The social function of poetry as an art form merges with the function of the poet as person. There is in fact an ascetic tendency to think of the poet as important only in and through his poem; a writer remarked, "Let the language lead the dance—put the self behind."

Poetry is seen as a valuable thing in itself, primarily because it affects the hearts and minds of men by means of the distinctively human pattern of language. The poet sees his role as a strenuous, concentrated effort to refine his own perceptions and trap them so exactly in words that others' perceptions may be sharpened. Conrad Aiken probably speaks for most modern poets in his philosophy that the artist's job is to increase awareness, to promote an ever more acute consciousness of the subtle ties and riches, the "invariant doublets" of experience. The poet thinks of himself as part of a vast company, the companionship of all who have tried to assess experience through art. His creative activity draws meaning and definition from this context, but in daily behavior it is the battle with language, the endless struggle to wring from words an experiential exactitude, that gives him the keenest sense of role fulfillment. The faith of which Spender speaks previously is informed with love and challenged by the hazards of the creative process.

Modern poets do not seem concerned that they fall short of being "the unacknowledged legislators of mankind": they view their role as primarily judicial rather than legislative and are content if their judgments have an implicit relevance for society. They think of themselves as responsible citizens doing a responsible job, not as culture heroes or Commissars of Aesthetic Enlightenment. Their responsibility is essentially to themselves, to write the best verse of which they are capable.

The poet is tough and self-confident. Although he would welcome large sales of his poems and increased stature in the total society, his belief in the intrinsic value of his work is strong enough to sustain him. Today he is not generally tempted to flee to some supposedly more congenial climate or to ally himself with popular political or economic ideologies. Rather, the poet intends to pursue his vocation and maintain his special integrity, relying on the pluralistic vigor of American society to accommodate him if it does not reward him.

The Poet in American Society

[1] David Riesman, *The Lonely Crowd* (New Haven: Yale University Press, 1961), pp. 14ff.

[2] Stephen Spender, "The Making of a Poem," in *The Creative Process,* ed. Brewster Ghiselin (New York: Mentor Books, 1955), p. 124. © 1946 by Stephen Spender. Reprinted by permission of Harold Matson Co., Inc.

[3] John Ciardi, *Mid-Century American Poets* (New York: Twayne Publishers, 1950), p. xxvi.

[4] W. H. Auden, "Under Which Lyre," in *Nones* (New York: Random House, 1951), p. 69. Copyright 1951 by Random House, Inc.

[5] Robert N. Wilson, "Poetic Creativity: Process and Personality," *Psychiatry,* Vol. XVII (May 1954), No. 2.

[6] Otto Rank, *Art and Artist* (New York: Alfred A. Knopf, Inc., 1932), pp. 235ff.

[7] Sir Arthur Quiller-Couch, *The Poet as Citizen* (New York: The Macmillan Company, 1935), p. 2.

[8] Quoted in Martin Turnell, "The Writer and Social Strategy," *Partisan Review,* Vol. XVIII (March-April 1951).

[9] Matthew Josephson, *Portrait of the Artist as American* (New York: Harcourt, Brace and World, Inc., 1930).

[10] *Ibid.,* pp. xii-xiii.

[11] Georg Simmel, "The Metropolis and Mental Life," in *The Sociology of Georg Simmel,* ed. K. Wolff (New York: Free Press of Glencoe, Inc., 1950), p. 409.

[12] Edward Dahlberg, *Do These Bones Live?* (New York: Harcourt, Brace & World, Inc., 1941).

[13] Ezra Pound, *Patria Mia* (Chicago: Ralph Fletcher Seymour, 1950), p. 41.

[14] *Ibid.*

[15] W. H. Auden in *Poets at Work,* by Charles D. Abbott (New York: Harcourt, Brace & World, Inc., 1948), p. 175.

[16] Gordon W. Allport, *Becoming* (New Haven: Yale University Press, 1955).

[17] T. S. Eliot, *The Use of Poetry and the Use of Criticism* (Cambridge: Harvard University Press, 1933), pp. 147-148.

[18] W. H. Auden, *op. cit.,* p. 176.

[19] Samuel A. Stouffer, *et al., The American Soldier* (Princeton, N.J.: Princeton University Press, 1949), p. 125.

[20] Archibald MacLeish, "Invocation to the Social Muse," *Collected Poems 1917-1952* (Boston: Houghton Mifflin Company, 1952), p. 94.

Two

THE ALIENATED COMPOSER

To call the modern composer of serious music "alienated" is to label him with a term which has become
increasingly fashionable in intellectual criticism of
contemporary society. Marx saw the worker alienated
from his job; twentieth century psychiatrists see patients alienated from their inmost selves. A sense of
pervasive estrangement of man from man, man from
the physical world, man from vocation has come to be
commonplace as observation and as experience. Nash,
however, does more than voice a vague unease. He
analyzes with some precision the sources of the composer's disengagement and the modes of coping with
an isolated and unrewarding vocational identity.

In singling out the market situation—the artist
as producer of a product subject to economic competition for the attention of a mass audience—as chief
villain in shaping the composer's present estate, Nash
agrees with most analysts of the modern artist's condition. His general argument that the rise of the
market loosened the artist's ties to the elite patron

audience and thrust him into a struggle for popular favor where he was certain to be defeated by the purveyors of mediocre popular art has been expressed most tellingly in terms of literature by Leo Lowenthal (in *Literature, Popular Culture, and Society,* particularly for eighteenth century England). The cultivation of fresh markets or peculiarly elite markets would seem to be an imperative for the artist as long as he creates in a complex industrial economy; the great trick is to invent an audience which is at once aesthetically responsive and economically able.

Nash's use of the Balinese musical contrast is instructive. Although in practical terms it is unlikely that the Balinese sense of aesthetic community can be reproduced in any large-scale literate society, it is important for us to recognize that the prevailing Western European model of artist-audience relationships is not ordained by nature. We are heirs to the Romantic stereotype of the lonely artist at odds with society. If a valid sociology and psychology of artistic roles is to be achieved, we obviously need far more searching comparative analyses. A less extreme comparison than that of the Balinese and American composers might be focused on artists who are within the European tradition but differ in their relations to the government as a patron. How do modern American composers compare with their counterparts in France, Britain, or the Soviet Union? A really sophisticated and detailed analysis of the varieties of institutional (including governmental) support for the arts in several societies would be immensely valuable.

The "role versatility" exhibited by some of the composers Nash studied seems to be crucial in sustaining most careers in the arts today. It was exemplified in the double, or multiple, job held by poets as an economic necessity. But the cases of poets and composers both point to several issues raised by this versatility: can the creative individual nurture a personality flexible enough to encompass disparate roles? Does the forced choice of complementary remunerative roles adulterate or dissipate creative energy?

Finally, Nash poses the important but vexing question of what functions artistic creativity may serve for the creator's psyche. The composers in his sample appear, on the basis of his analysis of projective test responses, to be dependent on their art work for the maintenance of a stable personality system. And indeed many artists have seen art as their ultimate salvation, without which life would be meaningless. It would be unfortunate, however, if the patterned satisfactions composers evidently find in composing, the outlets this activity provides for their personal needs, were to be taken as strong confirmation of the idea that the artist is typically a mentally disturbed individual. We do not know how commonly a man's vocation may be central to the organization of an otherwise precarious psychological structure; as Lionel Trilling has observed, the notion that the artist is uniquely disturbed is quite untested, since there is no demonstration that the ratio of ill to healthy artists differs from the ratio of ill to healthy doctors or merchants or Indian chiefs.

Exploration of the creative personality is nevertheless a valuable enterprise, and psychological research is beginning to penetrate the ancient mysteries of innovation if not of genius. These investigations are integral to a social psychology of the arts, because we want to know what goes on inside the artist's head as well as what happens in his interactions with the audience. We urgently require what Nash suggests: analysis of the connections between the creator's personality, his art, and the matrix of social life in which he moves.

THE ALIENATED COMPOSER

Dennison Nash

> . . . I am become as sounding brass or
> a tinkling cymbal. (I Corinthians 13)

The social scientist is committed to seeking out (by the method of science) the social and psychological elements underlying human activity. Art is one kind of human activity. In this essay I would like to take the social condition of one art, music, in one society,

ours in America today, and explore its connections with the composer and his music. To subject art to scientific scrutiny is to cause
for the moment the scientist's approach to the world to prevail over
that of the artist; but I do not mean that science should dominate
more than temporarily, nor do I contend that its approach is "truer"
than the artist's. It is only one man's way of looking at things.

I. The Musical Process

In an earlier work I suggested that the immediate social condition of serious music in modern American society could be viewed
as a social process leading from composer to audience.[1] The roles
which are crucial—and universal—in this process are those of
creator (composer, with or without collaboration by another artist),
performer (singer or instrumentalist), and listener (audience).
Music is a performed art (so are the dance and drama) as opposed
to those arts in which a performer is not essential (literature, the
graphic and plastic arts). The number and kind of participants in
the musical process vary from society to society, but it is the com-
poser-performer-listener triumvirate which is basic to the art.

The primary social function of music (and all other extrinsic
symbol systems) is communication. It is not necessary to settle here
an argument about the essential nature of the musical "message"
in contrast to that of other arts and symbol systems such as language
and religion.[2] We have only to assume some kind of "message"
which is communicated well or poorly. The amount and kind of
communication which takes place in the musical process depends
on the shared immersion of the participants in the process in the
same community of musical experience. If the orchestra plays Bach,
and the audience wants—and understands—Offenbach, communication will be poor, and malfunction of the musical process will be
a result. If, on the other hand, Mozart is played and all participants
are sophisticated devotees of that composer, the process will function
well.

The communication of the musical "message" not only pre-
supposes a community of musical experience, but also it reinforces
the solidarity of its participants by performing those secondary func-

tions which further a shared intellectual and emotional orientation.[3] Viewed this way, the musical process becomes a social system
of a temporary or permanent nature which may or may not be
identical with a society. There is no attempt here to maintain that
the furtherance of such a system is good or desirable, but only that
its use as a concept has heuristic value in charting the condition of
the composer and his music. In modern American society, for example, the system is fragmented, which implies a malfunction of the
musical process and a minimal community of musical experience.
In this brief essay I want to explore the consequences of such conditions for the American-born composer and for contemporary
American serious music.

II. Where Community of Musical Experience is High: Bali

In order to crack our culture-boundedness, we should try to
conceive of a situation where the community of musical experience
is high (the opposite of our own society). Bali provides us with
such an example.

In Bali, Covarrubias points out, music and the dance are highly
valued and widely appreciated. Communities seek to outdo one
another in the quality and quantity of their orchestras and dancers.
Despite this, the artist is no prima donna. Rather, he is a kind of
amateur craftsman whose "only aim is to serve his community."
A work of art may even be the work of two or more men. The composer, who usually is an orchestra leader also, often develops a new
composition gradually "through criticism and suggestions from
other orchestra members." [4]

The composer is, strictly speaking, an amateur, since he also
is engaged in occupations outside of music, but even so, musical
standards are extraordinarily high and composition a major effort.
For instance, Covarrubias says of the two composers in Belahin that
"one was a chauffeur and the other . . . worked occasionally carrying loads to ships. . . . I Letring, leader of an orchestra with a
great reputation, spoke and thought of nothing but gamelans and
music, and it was said that he dreamed his compositions." [5]

It is customary for the Balinese composer to have his work

regularly performed before an enormously responsive audience which is fully aware of the conventions of his musical style. He usually plays a part in the performance as leader of the orchestra. Considering such involvement in the musical process, one would expect to find the audience entering into the musical creation of the composer, if not in the very work that is being performed, then perhaps the next one. If this is so, then the audience would tend to become a part of the composer's musical self.

Leonard Meyer, using Mead's psychology, suggests that self-awareness and objectivity in the creative process result from the composer's constantly taking the attitude of some listener.[6] If Meyer is right we should expect that since the Balinese audience is a definite entity which is fully aware of the conventions, the Balinese composer would tend to become a "definite" musical personality who communicates meaningfully to his audience because he is an intensive participant in their community of experience.

Bruno Nettl's *Music in Primitive Culture* suggests that the Balinese situation is rather typical of the "primitive condition." He mentions the general absence of specialization and professionalization in primitive music, comparatively slight differentiation between composer, performer, and listener, and broad participation by members of the society in music.[7] Helen Roberts reached similar conclusions in an earlier work.[8]

III. Music in the West: The Decline in the Community of Musical Experience

In Western society the most recent historical parallels to the "primitive" state of affairs in general, and Bali in particular, were established under the patronage of the church and nobility. Though folk and popular music provide obvious parallels as well, they will not be considered here where the focus is on serious or art music.[9]

The term patronage may be an ill-chosen word for cross-cultural application, since it usually connotes support of some cause (in this case, musical) by specially interested and usually well-heeled persons. In some primitive societies it would be extremely difficult to locate a patron because support is provided by the entire society. Such was the case in the early Christian church. In that institution members of the clergy—many of them of the highest ranks—participated in the musical process as composers, performers, or both. In the Byzantine church, for example, there existed an essentially amateur state of affairs, musically speaking, in which such notable figures as Justinian the Great (483-565 A.D.) and St. Germanos (645-745 A.D.), famous for nonmusical achievements, were important composers as well.[10] In the Occidental church Gregory the Great, Venantius Fortunatus, and Thomas Aquinas were among those who made contributions to the liturgy of the church.[11] Usually the composer created both poetry and the melody for canons, although sometimes new poetry was adapted to older music. There was comparatively slight importance attached to individual composership. The great repertory of Gregorian chants, for example, is almost entirely anonymous work.

As late as the thirteenth century we find church music to be a fairly cooperative undertaking in which "the performers" (clergy) had to improvise on the bare outline left by the composer.[12] Leonin, the choirmaster and composer at Notre Dame, was the first to control time by indicating the time value of notes. Thus we can see that, in the early church, musical socialization and professionalization were not very far advanced. The composer, *qua* composer, tended to be submerged in the entire institution, as were other participants in the musical process. The requirements of a powerful belief and ritual system tended to set up strong conventions upon which there was a large measure of agreement. The early (and later) Christian church composers worked within the framework of these conventions, and they composed for performance in a congregation of which they frequently were a part. Even with specialization farther advanced in the fourteenth century, the eminent Palestrina and Victoria accepted "the considerations of the church as taking precedence over everything else."[13] The developing picture of the church composer during this period shows an individual who is gaining an increasing identity as a composer, but who always is subordinate to the aims of the institution and who fits into the community of experience which it provides.

Particularly humiliating to generations which have been nourished on romantic notions is the fact that those pre-eminent classicists, Haydn and Mozart, had the status of servant-craftsmen. We may deplore the fact that Haydn had to wear livery in his post as court musician for the family Esterhazy; and we may be surprised to learn that Mozart needed to beg noble patrons to allow him to move from one place to another. Yet these facts serve to remind us that as late as the eighteenth century the composer existed by virtue of the patronage of the court, the church, and in some cases, the town. Mueller says that in such a position:

> It would not have occurred to Bach, Mozart, Haydn, and the other Kapellmeister of the day to ignore the interest of the current generation by writing Zukunftmusik, nor could they have had the temerity to expect their socially superior patrons to sit through repeated hearings of a suite or symphony on the chance that they or their descendants might possibly enjoy it at some future time.[14]

The music production of such composers was dictated primarily by order or contract, and it was composed in a style which generally was well understood by a comparatively small, but sophisticated, audience. This does not mean that these composers could not, and did not, solve aesthetic problems of their own magnificently. They did, of course. But it does mean that the solution to these problems took place within a framework of conventions upon which there was considerable agreement by the essential participants in the musical process. The audience to which the composer directed his musical "message" was a definite, to-be-counted-upon entity. There was community of musical experience, and the major social function of music was well performed.

Then of a sudden, as far as historical trends go, the student of music history finds the composer alone in the marketplace and presenting his wares to the masses who come there. The public concert hall, which was rarely found in the baroque era, now comes to the fore.[15] Hauser is of the opinion that this historical condition dates from about the middle of the eighteenth century when town concert societies were founded. These organizations hired large halls in which music was presented to ever increasing, if less sophisticated, audiences.[16] Einstein thinks that the Handel oratorio marks the entrance of the masses.[17] Whatever was the exact turning point, and whatever were the specific causes at work, the musical scene from the late eighteenth century onward was to be dominated by the bourgeois audience. This situation poses increased difficulties for the composer. There comes to be no audience as such, but many potential audiences, and the composer's work must compete with that of other composers for their favor. The transient public introduces an uncertain and shifting element into the musical process.

At the same time, at the other end of the process, there is a trend toward more specialization, professionalization, and subjectivism in the composer's role. No longer is musical composition considered a craft only. It is an extraordinary calling. It is Art. The romantic composers are preoccupied with making very serious and highly personal musical statements. Though the composer may not be sure where he belongs in society, he sometimes appears to be striving toward making his position secure in eternity. Along with this development there occurs a decline in the number of composers who are "compleat" musicians. This trend, which Hindemith laments in our time, tends to remove the composer from the other essential role in the musical process—the performer. Thus, the composer becomes increasingly preoccupied with the development of his art, while significant others in the musical process are further removed from him. Einstein summarizes the composer's resulting condition. He says:

More and more the creative musician freed himself from society; he placed himself more and more in opposition to it, and he became increasingly isolated when he did not succeed in conquering it.

The Romantic era created the opposition between the "artist" and the "Philistin" . . .[18]

If some artists accepted their isolation and independence reluctantly, others positively asserted it. In the life of Mozart there are some not very successful struggles against authority. But Beethoven strikes out independently from the very first—and wins. In him the composer becomes a great man before whom the audience sits in awe and wonder. But some composers during his time and after were not all-conquering. The fiery career of Berlioz illustrates the ups and downs of the genius *vis-à-vis* the bourgeois audience. These examples certainly illustrate a very different situation from the essentially cooperative atmosphere of Bali.

The separation of the roles of composer and performer has in the West generally meant lower status to the former as compared with the latter. The performing virtuoso is one of the salient facts of music in our time, but he is not confined to the modern era. The Heifetz' and Rubensteins of our age were preceded by the Liszts and Paganninis of the nineteenth century and the *castrati* of still earlier times. Indeed, the virtuoso performer generally overshadows the composer at least as far back as the sixteenth century. The key to the relative status of composer and performer probably lies in the cultural distance between composer and audience. Where it is great, as in modern times, the large, comparatively uninformed audience probably finds its idols in the performer rather than in the creator behind the scenes.

Considering all of these developments, upon what kind of foundation is the musical process in modern America erected? First, the community of musical experience has departed with the rise of mass society. The musical situation with *Gemeinschaft*, or *folk*-like, characteristics has become *Gesellschaft*, or *urban*-like. In such a situation the normal mode of communication is via the mass media, the natural style for which is popular music and not serious art. Only a comparative few of the audience to which the serious composer addresses himself are apt to listen to his work in terms of the same conventions in which his musical message is couched. Therefore, communication is poor, and the composer finds it difficult to attract and hold a sufficient audience to support him financially. His comparatively poor financial condition is a direct result of the malfunction of the musical process.

A second feature of the modern musical condition concerns the nature of music. It is a commodity which is bought and sold in the marketplace. In selling his wares the composer must compete with an ever increasing list of other composers, living and dead, for a place in the performed repertoire. Moreover, the composer no longer does much of his "selling" directly to performer and audience. The musical businessman enters the scene as a middleman in the musical process. The fact that music is a commodity with a market increases the importance of the businessman in the overall transaction. He tends to become an "expert" on matters relating to audience taste, much as any businessman becomes acquainted with the attributes of his market. His assessment of taste is liable to be conservative as a means of maximizing his profit in the long run.[19]

Music is composed according to certain aesthetic norms, of course, and the flux in musical styles is a characteristic of the modern musical scene. Such a situation tends to block communication with any extensive audience in the musical process and further the isolation of the composer. Modern composers (still following at least one aspect of the Romantic tradition) tend to be oriented toward the unique and the new in musical compositions, and their musical styles have changed rapidly since the beginning of the twentieth century. The period of the 1920's was a time of extensive experimentation in musical styles in which the work of Schoenberg and Stravinsky is noteworthy. A long period of consolidation or integration of musical styles in which a truly modern—or even American—idiom would develop was to have set in, but composers are even now making bold leaps forward in the realm of electronic music and in music composed to an aesthetic of chance. How does this strike the listener who has just managed to accept Debussy and feel at home with him? This listener has had a leisure interest only, whereas composers, totally involved in their work and constantly oriented toward the new, have been moving along their individual ways. Whether modern works all sound the same or very different from each other, they do not come across very meaningfully to him. The listener's angry or indifferent response is a product of the disappearance of the community of musical experience which once saw the essential participants in the musical process similarly immersed in the same musical sea.[20]

An increase in the specialization or division of labor may very well be the basic condition from which all of the aforementioned conditions of music in modern society are derived. The composer has become more and more a specialist-professional. He has tended to jettison other skills (for example, instrumentalist) for the sake of his creative art. At the same time, increasing numbers of specialists stand between him and the audience. Not only the performer and businessman, but the critic and teacher have some effect on the destiny of his work. Conventions are necessary for communication and interaction in his complex musical process, but fewer significant others share the composer's musical assumptions. Nor do most modern composers have the power and prestige to force others to share these assumptions, or at least take them on faith. If any assumptions are shared throughout the musical process, those of the businessman or manager probably are pre-eminent. His assumptions are generally based on "what the audience will like"; and unfortunately for the immediate destiny of modern works, most of the public for serious music still has not entered the twentieth century, musically speaking.

IV. The Role of the Modern American Composer

Before getting down to the empirical meat of this essay, I want to provide a brief transition from what has been a fairly general discussion of modern music (particularly in nineteenth century Europe) to the specific condition of contemporary American composers. American serious music springs from this modern heritage. Until recently, almost all of our eminent composers were trained in Europe or with Europeans. Moreover, we have had in our midst for extended periods the giants of the Western musical scene: Schoenberg, Stravinsky, and Hindemith. People have been talking for some time about the development of an American musical idiom, but none of the magnitude of the splash recently made by American abstract expressionism in painting has occurred. What we have had is a series of international styles to which both Europeans and Americans have made contributions. Jazz, which is not by definition in the domain of serious music, seems to be the most significant American contribution to these styles.

How does the social condition of the American composer compare with that of his European counterpart? Probably the European lives in a more artistic milieu, which may account for American composers' enthusiasm about their sojourns there. Perhaps more modern music is heard by European audiences. But European composers (exclude the Russians) are not provided with anything like the same opportunity to gain a living which is offered by the many teaching positions in our colleges and universities.[21] Probably the Europeans are less well off financially because of the lack of large-scale organizational support, but in balance I would suggest that the Europeans are less alienated from their milieu on the grounds that aesthetic support and response, rather than financial, is more "necessary" to the artist.[22]

Social alienation is, perhaps, the outstanding social characteristic of the American composer's role as viewed through the condition of twenty-three eminent composers which I studied recently.[23] These individuals, who look to be a fairly good sample of eminent American-born composers, are heavily represented in the National Institute of Arts and Letters—an organization of artistic elite, membership in which is based primarily on artistic esteem—and ASCAP and ACA—the American performance-right societies, membership in which is limited to more frequently performed composers. Despite these signs of their prowess, their comparatively high gross income (mean: $10,000 for 1951), and the long period of specialized education which they negotiated to achieve competence, they are comparatively neglected by the bulk of society. A look at the evidence obtained from an analysis of repertoire content of symphony orchestras, the musical taste of a symphony orchestra audience, and statements by various people in the musical process shows that most of the long-hair audience (to say nothing of the vast majority of Americans who do not "dig" serious music) can get along quite happily without hearing any contemporary American serious music; and, in general, the attitudes of those specialists who must cooperate with the composers to bring their music to performance reflect the feelings of the audience in this regard.

The typical composer has much to say musically, but there are not many who want to hear him, which, translated into crude terms of money, means that *as a composer* he does not have much earning power. The mean income of this sample of "most successful" composers was $2640 for the year 1951.

To put this into sociological terms, these composers occupy a peripheral role in modern American society, which puts them in a dependent and subordinate position in their contacts with others in the musical process. Their status as composer is one of weakness and low esteem in relation to others in the musical process. Despite this, the institutional structure appears to provide sufficient channels and inducements for composer recruitment. All of the talented people in the sample were taught privately by European-born teachers of composition. Such instruction appears to be on the wane with the rise of large and competent music schools in America. At Juilliard, for example, the student has personal contact with a noted composer-teacher, but this contact is limited by the large number of students in his class. By such institutionalization of the training process, the way toward the composer's role has become fairly clear; but what happens to one when he reaches that role is not at all certain. The composer finds himself in what must be, at best, a difficult position from the social standpoint. How does he make the best of it?

Of course he makes the best of it, first of all, by his preoccupation with his art. But there are various kinds of preoccupation. Within the overall composer's role he must make adjustments in two crucial behavioral dimensions. On one, the ivory tower-commercial continuum, we can locate him by the proportion of the music he writes in the media that sell readily. His position on the second, the role versatility continuum of behavior, is plotted in terms of the number of noncompositional roles he has played. As a fictitious example, we might take the composer who shows considerable versatility by functioning as a conductor, instrumentalist, and teacher. At the same time, his musical output contains a very small proportion of music written in the commercial media of expression, for example, chorus, radio, television, and movies. Though the composers are fairly well spread over the ivory tower-commercial dimension, nearly all of them show considerable role versatility. Considering the professional level only, we find that the twenty-three composers have played a total of fifty-nine other roles in the musical process (and more outside of it).[24] The presence of sometime teacher-lecturers, instrumentalists, critic-writers, conductors, and businessman-managers among these composers indicates that specialization has not yet gone so far as the historical trend may have suggested. Such role versatility obviously provides a counter-pull back into the musical process against the alienating forces which were discussed earlier. At the same time, as compared with the commercial "solution," it represents the lesser evil in terms of capitulation to popular taste. Various combinations of positions on the two dimensions may enable the composer to make a go of it financially.

The crucial factor in a composer's location on the two dimensions of behavior would appear to be his kind of personality. How much he needs the praise and support of the world about him, for example, should have much to do with whether or not he can erect an ivory tower in which to write grand operas with horses in them.[25] If there are a variety of adjustments, therefore, to what is in general a nonsupporting role situation, there must be a variety of personalities who make them.

V. Personality and Role Behavior

A rough and ready way to set up an hypothesis about the relationship between personality and role behavior is to compare composers who fall at the extremes of the *ivory tower-commercial* and *role versatility* dimensions of behavior. An element of control may be introduced by selecting for each dimension extreme cases of similar age. Since there is only one female in the sample, it was not difficult to control for sex by selecting men only.

Composer VV represents the extreme of commercial musical expression.[26] He composes for motion pictures and (with considerable popular content) for the concert hall. He is a New Yorker of early middle age who believes that the movie composer is the true musical pioneer and that you cannot make a distinction of quality between serious and popular music. His credo is to get along with others in the musical process. He wants to compose music that can be performed readily. He seeks to communicate with the audience. He will accommodate musically to suit the film makers. He does not show much role versatility, but he can compose music in almost any style to suit the demand.

Composer AA represents the extreme of ivory tower composition. He is five years younger than VV and is a provincial. (He lives outside the New York metropolitan area, which is the musical center of the United States.) Both he and VV are married and have children. AA is indifferent about communicating to the audience. He says that money and prestige are unimportant to him. He believes that musical businessmen and conductors are against contemporary music. He does not accommodate to people in the musical process who suggest changes in his music. He is not markedly versatile in role playing, and he thinks that he is middle-of-the-road in his musical style.

The Rorschach test was used to take a deeper look at the personalities of these composers. This widely used clinical instrument is one of the so-called projective techniques. There is considerable evidence that it taps the basic personality structure, that is, the more stable functions of the personality, though many problems of its validity and reliability still remain to be solved. O. W. Lacy did the semiblind analysis according to a middle-of-the-road typology which we derived from the work of Beck and Klopfer and Kelley.[27] He made both a clinical and a statistical summary for each of the twenty composers who were given the test. (Three composers in the sample were not tested.)

Returning to the problem at hand, the Rorschach summaries for the extreme cases were compared and the differences in personality traits noted. The major difference between VV (commercial) and AA (ivory tower) centers about withdrawal from reality. AA and all other ivory tower composers of similar age in the sample show much in the way of primitive and private reactions to the ink blots, whereas the commercial composer does not reveal these specific tendencies. One might suggest that this trait among the ivory towers is a reaction to their unaccepted state. They are comparatively young, unplayed, and disillusioned (the argument would run). Their withdrawal is a symptom of their protest against a society which will not listen to what they have to say. Alas for such a supposition. AA and his cohorts are among the most frequently played and applauded of all the composers. Their withdrawal, then, probably dates farther back in their life history. Ivory tower tendencies probably existed in these people before they were recruited into the role of composer.

Can one be an ivory tower without showing marked withdrawal symptoms? Three composers who are the oldest of the ivory towers provide interesting evidence as to how it may be done. These men are nearly a generation removed in age from AA. Their backgrounds drip with affluence. One of them considers teaching, not composing, his life's work. Such evidence leads us to suspect that should one grow up in an atmosphere well laden with riches and containing the belief that creative art is a worthwhile vocation or avocation, he may be able to build his ivory tower without pathological accompaniment. The differences between the two generations of ivory towers invites an historical hypothesis which points to a decline of an aristocracy devoted to the arts in America, but it would be difficult to argue that the older men are typical of an earlier generation of composers. The data will not permit it. It is my hunch, however, that American composer recruits with ivory tower tendencies represent a more heterogeneous background now than they did fifty years ago.[28]

We search in vain for the signs of flexibility in the personality that might be presumed to distinguish the composers who represent the extremes of role versatility. Composer S, who has had a highly varied career in and out of music, says that he always adapts himself to whatever the conditions are, but according to the Rorschach record this adaptation is achieved by a personality which tends toward compulsive rigidity. The signs indicate much ego control, a strictly methodical thinking method, and tact related to discernment as the variables which distinguish him from FF, the composer of low role versatility. S's approach to the various roles he has played has been rational, but the Rorschach also indicates considerable emotional expression which is well integrated with the intellectual aspects of his personality. Add discernment of the subtleties of situations, and we begin to see how this particular composer (who has various talents not revealed by the Rorschach) has managed to be so versatile. Composer FF, on the other hand, maintains a precarious control of his personality. Strong affective forces are constantly threatening to throw him and his personal relations into disorder. Though he strives for a methodical approach to situations, his thinking method is nearly irregular. A variety of role situations obviously would be threatening to him.

If a composer must be, or wants to be, highly versatile, there may be other personality styles which enable him to perform at an optimum level, but the data from the sample suggest that a "formula" for approaching various situations is an asset. Of course, the situations may not be very different in their requirements. For example, the roles of conductor, instrumentalist, and composer would seem not to be very inconsistent with one another. If it is true that role versatility in the musical process does not require one to deal with too many inconsistencies, then it would seem that it would be easier, psychologically speaking, to play several roles than to be musically versatile (which means composing in a variety of styles). The composer for motion pictures (or, presumably, television) must be able to produce many different kinds of music according to the occasion. Besides, he usually makes enough money to support him and, perhaps, to assuage any feelings of guilt which may be derived from the inevitable suppression of "self-expression" in this medium.[29] His case, perhaps, serves to explain why there is a tendency for the composers in the sample who show the lowest role versatility to demonstrate considerable musical versatility as judged by my musical informants. Does musical versatility, then, mean commercial music? Not necessarily. It would be premature to suggest that a position near one end of the ivory tower-commercial dimension (say, commercial) tends to be associated with low role versatility. The cases of such well-known public figures as Igor Stravinsky and Leonard Bernstein make one cautious about stating any regular relationship between musical versatility and the other two dimensions of behavior.

The composer's behavior may be looked at from a great many more angles than just the two dimensions mentioned here. For example, one can begin to get down to real musical cases in rating a composer as tending toward absolute or programmatic music and then noting the personality traits involved (reactivity to affective stimuli and the ability to integrate such elements into mental production). But such inquiry verges more and more on the no man's land between art and science into which the social scientist may venture successfully only with the aid of the music expert. By focusing on behavior which is crucial to one's survival as a composer and one's relationship to others in the musical process, this study represents only a cautious beginning to a task which will, I hope, culminate in such fruitful collaboration.

What do the data tell us about the composer's personality? First, they indicate that there are many different personalities who play the role of composer. Some test or technique which uncovers more strictly musical attributes than does the Rorschach might turn up a greater degree of homogeneity in the sample, but we found it very difficult to extract any predictive factors from our use of the Rorschach. But once we know that someone is a successful composer, we can, by using this projective technique, predict where he will fall within that rather broad general area of behavior which comprises the composer's role and which, after all, depends in part on the definitions of various experts as to what a composer of serious music does do, or ought to do.[30] If we think about the composer in the romantic vein as one who listens only to his muses and who does not knuckle under musically to the actions or reactions of others in the musical process, then we have the ivory tower and the personality configuration that goes with it. This is the composer who has something highly personal to say and who is most alienated from the musical process. On the other hand, if we choose to think of the composer as the "compleat" professional musician such as Bach, then the composer of considerable role versatility is our man.

In the process of role recruitment and role playing different kinds of personalities seem to be "selected" for different aspects of the role of serious composer. O. W. Lacy and I are trying to make some statistical sense out of the Rorschach scores for the sample, but unless we find a better key to making generalizations than we have so far, it will be more profitable to speak, in terms of personality, about kinds of composers rather than composers. One thing we can say is this: the composers, taken as a whole, do not like the conditions of their existence; but since the majority (thirteen out of twenty) were judged to be neurotic, borderline psychotic, or out-and-out psychotic, one wonders whether such conditions serve a positive or negative function for them. I would suggest—as others have done before—that *some* of these artists derive a kind of pleasure from being pitted against society, and that this opposition plays a role in their creativity.[31] This probably never could be said about their Balinese counterparts.

The social condition of the composer's role, of course, is not unlike that of other peripheral vocations such as other arts and theoretical science. People working in all of these fields must work out their stance in relation to the world from a position of economic weakness and ill-defined functions. Each role will harbor a range of personalities who have achieved a variety of adjustments with good or bad grace. But the unifying element in all of these separate roles is the postulate that their incumbents should say something. From the social point of view they exist to communicate. In the case of the composer this is done very poorly, if at all. Yet there is no indication that this fact is widely lamented.

VI Implications for Serious Music

If we were to increase magically the amount of shared musical experience of people in the musical process today, what would be the effect on the people who play the composer's role and the kind of music they produce? First, expertise in writing for the various instruments and ensembles undoubtedly would improve. The example of Charles Ives comes to mind. He was an enormously creative composer who anticipated many of the current trends in musical style; but he was not performed much in the early part of his career, and this probably accounts for many of the errors which he made in the realm of technique. Though absolute pitch may be a great help to a composer, most composers agree that hearing one's works performed is indispensable for attaining mastery of the art. However, extensive performance is denied the American composer— especially during the years when he is acquiring the compositional skill. Thus, his craftsmanship suffers, and this in turn may affect his later capacity to get a satisfactory hearing from performers, who are notoriously impatient with an inexpertly prepared manuscript. The Balinese composer, on the other hand, may test, revise, and generally profit from the experience which comes from direct involvement in frequent performances. By way of contrast I would suggest that the artist who does not require performers, for example, the painter, has an easier time in mastering the purely technical aspect of his art.

Performers and others in the musical process who cooperate with the composer to bring his work to performance not only may determine whether a work is heard or not, but also may determine in what form it is heard. William Gibson has said that his drama *Two for the See-Saw* was a far cry from his original when it finally came to performance, and he has documented the various "intervening variables" in the dramatic process which contributed to the change.[32] The composer's situation is analogous to that of the dramatist. Various pressures may stall or change a work as it makes its way down the musical process. How a composer responds to such pressures may be predicted in part from his position on the ivory tower-commercial continuum and the personality configuration that goes with it. To illustrate one kind of encounter and the nature of the pressure involved, here is the report of one composer:

> There occurred in rehearsal a problem between the soprano and the conductor. I knew what was the matter, but I didn't open my yap. No one ever does. I was so beside myself that I went out and got tight, had three martinis, came back, jumped on the stage, and screamed. I showed her exactly what was to be done. I came home and dissolved in tears. Then I called the director up and apologized. He kept the attitude of my staying clear of the work. This display of temperament was very bad for me.

Another takes a firmer stand:

> Of course you have the type of conductor who immediately wants changes. When I am dealing with them, I usually throw a wet blanket over a suggestion pretty quickly. I am writing the thing. I want to be blamed or praised for the entire thing, or not at all.

The trend in the musical process is toward increasing specialization and institutionalization, and since the composer's work is subject to a larger organization in its passage to the audience, the composer will experience greater bureaucratic pressures than will the artist who does not require performance. Large organizations such as the union, concert management, publishing house, and recording company are expanding in the face of an increasing demand for music by the public. Even though the amount of new American music being processed is infinitesimal as compared with the musical total, it still is subject to the same increasingly complex network of roles and organizations which is the musical process today. The composer will experience increasing pressures from large organizations in the future. It will be increasingly difficult for him to achieve an identity outside the pale of such organizations.

There is an interesting gambit being tried by some composers today, which functions to eliminate some of the middlemen in the musical process. This is the development of machine-made or electronic music. By this technique the composer can mix his sounds much the way he wants them and achieve a performance without any performers. The success of this trend would seem to depend mostly upon the need of audiences to identify with performers (as opposed to machines). If the performer goes, where will the music public find its stars? Modern Western history has shown the performer less expendable than the composer. It does not seem, therefore, that this gambit will have much success in the immediate future—even on records.

Leaving the purely technical aspect of the art, let us consider further the implications of the question raised at the beginning of this section. How necessary is communication with others in the musical process for artistic achievement? It would seem to be required insofar as the composer needs a stable membership group for the development of the authentic musical identity which provides the point of view necessary to great art. One frequently hears modern composers criticized for their lack of such a point of view.[33] In this lack they are not alone. The difficulty of achieving an identity in our highly differentiated, rapidly changing society has been remarked.[34] In contrast, the Balinese composer and other composers working under similar social conditions would tend to develop a stable musical identity. Such an identity would be much less difficult to achieve than that of the American composer.

There are some who would argue that the struggle for identity of the modern composer provides a foundation for greatness and that his alienation is the very thing which enables him to cultivate "art for art's sake"—the "highest" form of art. Such an argument is open to serious doubt. Seegar, for example, says it is not possible to judge music according to the degree to which nonmusical factors enter into its construction.[35] No one now seems to deny the greatness of Bach even though he wrote much *Gebrauchmusik*. Nor is it possible to deny the greatness of the many "primitive" composer-poets cited by Radin.[36] It seems probable that if the number of musical resources is considered as a base, then composers in some primitive societies produce compositions which are at least as profound as those created by the most sophisticated composers in America. Yet these composers are not pictured as either alienated or struggling for an identity. Thus, the lack of communication and consequent alienation of the composer is not necessarily a favorable factor for modern music.

It is important to remember that insofar as the composer is engaged in the process of intrinsic symbolization, composition—even in Balinese society—is a private act. In Bali this intrinsic symbolization takes place in terms of some well-defined, broadly shared symbol system. The Balinese composer's private statement is very close to a meaningful public statement. The disparity between the private statement and an acceptable public statement is much greater in modern America. How much the American composer in this situation is committed to his private statement will determine the degree to which his privacy is reinforced. If his needs for self-expression (as compared with communication) are strong, he will eventually become like one of Thomson's and Stein's characters in *Four Saints in Three Acts,* who declaim but do not communicate.

The future for the modern composer who insists on self-expression does not look very bright. Unless government support of the arts is undertaken (and it does not seem likely), there probably will not be many more opportunities of being heard. Just now, foundation support for the production of operas, plus the development of operatic outlets in some large universities, is reviving operatic output by American composers. If such support continues we can look for a greater recruitment of artists who lean toward dramatic music. But the lot of the self-expressive composers, taken as a whole, will not be much better tomorrow than it is today.

Commercially oriented composers, on the other hand, will find increasing opportunities to cater to a homogenized public with increasing leisure time on their hands. Choruses, stamped out of a mold provided by Fred Waring; bands, modeled, perhaps, after the University of Michigan prototype; and children's records are only a few of the mushrooming outlets for new music. Radio and television will offer increasing opportunities only to those who are satisfied with little more than music arranging.

The composer's role, then, will be further commercialized in the future, and it is in this form that it will perform its primary social function—communication. There will be no lack of recruits to carry out this bread-and-butter task. But the opportunity for

self-expression which the role also provides will continue to lure
those musically gifted individuals, many of whom—were it not for
the existence of this peripheral role—might spend their lives working out their disturbances in a much less constructive and dignified
way. Thus, the salvation of human material, not communication,
may prove to be the major function of the composer's role (and
others like it) in our time.[37]

The Alienated Composer

[1] Dennison Nash, "Challenge and Response in the American Composer's
Career," *Journal of Aesthetics and Art Criticism,* Vol. CIV (September, 1955),
pp. 116-122.

[2] See, for example, Suzanne K. Langer, *Feeling and Form in Art* (New York:
Charles Scribner's Sons, 1953).

[3] This functional viewpoint is derived from David Aberle, *et al.,* "The Functional Prerequisites of a Society," *Ethics,* Vol. LX (January 1950), pp. 100-111.

[4] Miguel Covarrubias, *Island of Bali* (New York: Alfred A. Knopf, Inc.,
1942), pp. 163f, p. 209.

[5] *Ibid.,* p. 209.

[6] Leonard Meyer, *Emotion and Meaning in Music* (Chicago: The University
of Chicago Press, 1956), p. 41.

[7] Bruno Nettl, *Music in Primitive Culture* (Cambridge: Harvard University
Press, 1956), p. 10.

[8] Helen Roberts, "Primitive Music," *Encyclopedia of the Social Sciences,*
Vol. XI (1933), p. 150.

[9] In some societies such as our own it is possible to distinguish between
serious and popular music. In others no such distinction is made.

[10] Gustave Reese, *Music in the Middle Ages* (New York: W. W. Norton &
Company, Inc., 1940), pp. 79, 81.

[11] Howard McKinney and William Anderson, *Music in History* (New York:
American Book Company, 1940), p. 129.

[12] *Ibid.,* p. 165.

[13] *Ibid.,* p. 244.

[14] John H. Mueller, *The American Symphony Orchestra* (Bloomington, Ind.:
The University of Indiana Press, 1951), p. 289.

[15] Manfred Bukofzer, *Music in the Baroque Era* (New York: W. W. Norton &
Company, Inc., 1947), p. 404.

[16] Arnold Hauser, *The Social History of Art,* Vol. III (New York: Vintage
Books, 1957), p. 81.

[17] Alfred Einstein, *Music in the Romantic Era* (New York: W. W. Norton &
Company, Inc., 1947), p. 13.

[18] *Ibid.,* p. 16.

[19] In the remainder of the essay I will draw heavily on the study of twenty-
three eminent American-born composers of serious music which was first reported
in Dennison Nash, "The American Composer: A Study in Social Psychology,"

(Doctoral dissertation, The University of Pennsylvania, 1954). See pp. 79-86 for a full analysis of the role of the businessman in the musical process.

[20] John Cage, who has been experimenting with purely rhythmic elements according to an aesthetic of chance, is an example of a particularly "confusing" composer. He has a small and vociferous coterie of admirers and some prestige in art circles, but in 1951-52 most of the eminent composers were unsympathetic to him. There is no indication that his status has changed significantly since then.

[21] Twenty-two of the twenty-three composers in the sample had had teaching positions, and most of them were in colleges and universities. See Nash, *Journal of Aesthetics and Art Criticism,* Vol. CIV, p. 117.

[22] The facts do not support the romantic notion that poverty is essential for artistic success.

[23] From here on I draw heavily on my dissertation, "The American Composer: A Study in Social Psychology." Instead of citing endlessly, I refer the reader to the appropriate part of this work.

[24] Nash, *Journal of Aesthetics and Art Criticism,* Vol. CIV, p. 117.

[25] Virgil Thomson has used the phrase about "operas with horses in them."

[26] The letters used are code designations.

[27] Samuel Beck, *Rorschach's Test,* I (New York: Grune and Stratton, Inc., 1950), II (1951); Bruno Klopfer and Donald Kelley, *The Rorschach Technique* (Yonkers-on-Hudson, N.Y.: The World Book Company, 1946). For a recent authoritative discussion of the Rorschach (which supersedes these volumes), see Bruno Klopfer *et al., Developments in Rorschach Technique,* I and II (New York: Harcourt, Brace & World, Inc., 1954).

[28] There are some data bearing on this point in Dennison Nash, "The Socialization of an Artist: The American Composer," *Social Forces,* Vol. XXXV (May 1957), pp. 308-10.

[29] For a composer's point of view about the composer in movieland see Aaron Copeland, *Our New Music* (New York: McGraw-Hill Book Company, 1941).

[30] See Henry A. Murray's forward in Robert N. Wilson, *Man Made Plain* (Cleveland, Ohio: Howard Allen, Inc., Publishers, 1958). Murray argues that it is very difficult to construct a list of requirements or functional "effects" for the American poet's role. Most people do not care whether the serious poet exists; nor does the work have a discernable effect on his society. It seems to me that it would be only slightly less difficult to construct such a list for the composer of serious music.

[31] Mellers, for example, thinks that adversity played a part in the careers of Elgar, Delius, Holst, and Vaughn Williams. See Wilfrid Mellers, *Music and Society* (London: Dennis Dobson, 1946), p. 109. The life histories of the twenty-three composers who have been mentioned here show that musicality was valued in the homes of most. Only a minority have achieved success despite parental opposition. More important were those factors in the family environments of the majority which "encouraged the development of a personal autonomy which later would be necessary to deal with an hostile or indifferent world." (Nash, *Social Forces,* XXXV, 309-10).

[32] William Gibson, *See Saw Log* (New York: Alfred A. Knopf, Inc., 1959).

[33] Paul Henry Lang, *Music in Western Civilization* (New York: W. W. Norton & Company, Inc., 1941), p. 1028; McKinney and Anderson, *Music in History,* p. 832.

[34] See, for example, Maurice Stein *et al.,* eds., *Identity and Anxiety* (New York: The Free Press of Glencoe, 1960).

The Alienated Composer

[35] Charles Seegar, "Occidental Music," *Encyclopedia of the Social Sciences,* Vol. XI (1933), p. 161.

[36] Paul Radin, "The Literature of Primitive Peoples," *Diogenes,* No. 12 (Winter 1955), pp. 1-28.

[37] This view is more fully developed in Nash, *Social Forces,* XXXV, p. 313.

Three

THE RECRUITMENT
OF THE ARTIST

Both Griff's essay and the succeeding account of student dancers by Carol Pierson Ryser fix our attention on the young artist. They emphasize the pathways of choice in the nascent artistic career and the images creative young people hold of themselves. Both, too, reaffirm the fortitude and vocational faith which were proposed as characteristics of the poet; these durable requisites seem all the more vital to the American artist in the light of the harrowing trials Griff and Mrs. Ryser chart in the beginner's course.

The recruitment process for the Chicago painters Griff studied is extremely complex and instructive. It is apparent that the young artist's career typically hinges on a conjunction of several factors, a network of influence and attraction. Teachers, parents, age-mates, and the art institute are all implicated in the grooming of desire and talent. In contrast to the writer, the aspiring painter has in this instance an institutional framework—the art school with its classes and facilities—which fosters his development in addition to the informal encouragement of his fellows and respected seniors. There is a more or less accepted channel through which these painters pass. It would be of great interest to assess what kinds of influence on the artistic career are exerted by the presence or absence of such established frameworks; one might guess, for instance, that an aspirant to the painter's role has a firmer conception of the professional career than does a young person who envisions himself as poet or novelist.

One of the striking features of the painter's induction is the progressive awareness of the self-as-artist and the way this awareness is initiated by those around the young person and seemingly reaffirmed throughout the school years. The idea (first developed by G. H. Mead, Charles Cooley, and other early social-psychological thinkers) that we come to define ourselves chiefly in terms of the image thrown back to us by our close associates is here tangibly demonstrated. These individuals come very early to think of themselves as painters, and apparently this ideal self is durably implanted; its strength is seen in the determination to persist despite the later family pressures against assuming the full-time vocation of artist.

Griff's discussion of the pointed conflict between fine art and commercial art in the young painter's values emphasizes again the problems of role choice in the artistic career. The aspirant faces an intricate ideological and economic decision, and this must be taken on inadequate evidence; paramount among the unknown contingencies is the fact that the young artist, in whatever milieu, can rarely be certain that his talents are equal to outstanding achievement. Yet he knows that without exceptional performance accompanied by extreme good luck he must forever consign his role as fine artist to the category of avocation. An individual may gain a valued, respected niche in most sectors of the occupational world in the absence of extraordinary gifts, but we do not provide any supporting structures for the journeyman in the arts.

This empirical study enhances our insight into the making of the artist. Its author, however, cautions us that his statements apply strictly to the group of Chicago painters he describes. It would be important to learn how general these patterns may be and whether there are substantial variations by region, city size, social class, and so on. We should also like, in a more comprehensive treatment of the painter's role, to know more about the life styles of mature painters, about the organized complex of art dealers and galleries, about the audience for the creations of fine artists.

THE RECRUITMENT
OF THE ARTIST

Mason Griff

The present paper is a segment of a larger social-psychological study of art students. Its major focus was to discover what motivated individuals to choose art as a career in view of the fact that the chances for conventional "success" are virtually nonexistent. By a career in art we mean the classical picture of the artist who attempted to live exclusively from his paintings. The limited chances for success are demonstrated by the estimate that there are only between five and fifteen American painters who are living exclusively from the sale of their paintings.[1]

This discussion is based on interviews with art students living in the Chicago metropolitan area. Most of these students were attending one large art school located in Chicago. The table below shows the distribution of the sample by year in school and type of course taken at the time.

The column called "drop-outs" refers to individuals who had once attended this school but had left for various reasons. In addition there were various changes from one major field to another. For example, some students switched from a commercial art curriculum to a fine arts course or from fine arts to art education. The problem of where to categorize these individuals was resolved by classifying them under the particular major field to which they had committed themselves at the time of the interviews. Nearly all the

Distribution of Art Students Interviewed by Year in School, Curriculum, Drop-outs, and Sex

Year in school	Division of school			Sex		Total	Drop-outs
	Fine arts	*Commercial art*	*Art education*	*Male*	*Female*		
1	12	5	4	7	14	21	1
2	7	2	1	6	4	10	3
3	1	3	0	3	1	4	0
4	3	1	1	5	0	5	0
5	3	1	3	3	4	7	0
Total	26	12	9	24	23	47	4

interviews were conducted in the respondents' homes. Biographical questions were asked in order to elicit the history of the person's interest in art and how this interest was sustained. Special emphasis was placed on crucial decisions in the person's life which permitted his interest in art to continue, such as the encouragement he received from his parents, his schoolteachers, or his peer group. Or, questions were asked pertaining to the reasons for choosing a particular major field in high school, for example, commercial art rather than fine arts. Most interviews took three hours, some as long as six hours. The generalizations which will be stated in the main body of this paper must be confined to the specific group interviewed.

We plan to describe the main social factors which operate, formally and informally, to select individuals for the art profession. Where feasible, the relationship between informal and formal mechanisms of recruitment has been described. Where the research material permits, the psychological mechanisms will be discussed. Some preliminary comments will sketch the historical role of the artist and the use of recruitment as a sociological concept.

Role and Ideological Considerations of the Artist

The guiding orientation of the painter is that he is the visual interpreter of society. The visual interpretations which he makes are of the fundamental categories of cultural life which are the same in all societies.[2] They consist of such basic elements as "the effort to explore and explain the universe, to understand the meaning of events, to enter into contact with the sacred or to commit sacrilege, to affirm the principles of morality and justice and to deny them, to encounter the unknown, to exalt or denigrate authority, to stir the senses by the control of and response to words, sounds, shapes, and colors."[3] There is less consensus, however, about the artist's method of presenting these basic cultural elements. As Jane Harrison has pointed out,[4] there have been three main theories guiding the role of the artist. The first holds art to be the creation or pursuit of beauty. The second, the "imitation theory," assumes that art either copies nature, or with the natural materials, improves on her. The third is the "expression theory," which conceives the aim of art to be the expression of the emotions and thoughts of the artist. At present the latter theory seems to be in ascendancy and reaches its highest contemporary form in the paintings of such men as Picasso, Paul Klee, and Jackson Pollock. However, each art theory since Plato's time has experienced popularity at the expense of the other two.

Jane Harrison, writing in 1913, noted that the imitation theory was then out of fashion (Plato and Aristotle held it). The imitation theory began to die down with the nineteenth century rise of Romanticism, which stressed the personal, individual emotion of the artist.[5] Miss Harrison believed that the imitation theory of art was killed by the invention of photography. However, she points out that it was impossible for the most insensate not to see that in a work of art there was an element of value not to be found in the exact transcript of a photograph. This allowed the imitation theory to live on, but only in a weakened form of idealization.[6]

The impressionism that dominated the pictorial art of the later years of the nineteenth century was a largely modified and very delicate imitation. It broke with conventions as to how things were supposed to appear, and the impressionistic artist believed that the conventions should be based not on seeing, but on knowing or imagining; the impressionist insisted on purging his vision of veridical physical accuracy and representing things not as they are, but as they seem to be. He imitated nature not in the particular, but as she presented herself to the eyes of the artist. Vincent Van Gogh and Paul Gauguin are two of the best examples of painters who were guided by this ideology.

On the other hand, the more contemporary expressionistic painters have believed that art was not a copying or an idealization of nature or any aspects of nature, but the expression and communication of the artist's emotion. They have believed that life was not simple and therefore the art that expresses our emotions toward modern life cannot be simple. As mentioned previously, it is these later two theories that are in the ascendancy in contemporary times. The artist who is guided by these ideologies creates a painting whose requirements are his own subjective interpretations of any subject matter he chooses. His painting will be displayed where a comparatively small number of people will view it. In most cases the painter does not sell his work until after its completion and in effect sets his own requirements (unlike the commercial artist, who has requirements set by a client).

The artist ocupies an ambivalent position. Supposedly the artist and his work are valued; yet the artist is not rewarded. Consequently his recruitment and his identity involve conflicts within himself and between himself and significant others. There are several questions which are of utmost importance in understanding the recruitment of the contemporary artist: (1) What encouragements and discouragements are made by the larger society to induce people to become artists? (2) What types of people are entering (that is, what social class do they belong to) and at what rate are they entering (that is, how many are entering)? (3) How is the group affected by the particular types of individuals who are recruited into the profession? (4) What are the people who are entering art looking for, or why are they choosing this as their career? [7]

Historical Recruitment of Artists

One of the earliest documents concerning the origins and processes of recruitment of the artist is found in Vasari's *Lives of the Artists*.[8] Throughout his books one finds many references to the apprentice painters. Also it is one of the earliest sources for many of the viewpoints of the early painters.[9] The information available from this source indicates that recruitment has changed considerably since the time Vasari wrote. In his day, individuals became artists by serving an apprenticeship with an established master painter. The individual worked for a master during a stipulated period. His labors included assisting the master with his paintings and also taking care of various household chores. In return, he received a knowledge of the techniques and skills possessed by the master as well as his board and room. The wealthier individuals who could afford to pay the master were exempted from the household duties.[10]

In addition to the apprenticeship system (and many of the great Renaissance painters such as Michelangelo and Leonardo da Vinci came through this system), many artists were trained by their fathers, and they in turn passed their skills on to their children. Neither apprenticeship nor parental succession is today commonly practiced. These have been replaced, except in a few cases in commercial art, by the formal art institutions.[11]

Early American Recruitment

A survey of the early origins and recruitment of American artists shows that many were actually European artists (all of them minor ones) who migrated to the colonies to paint the portraits of the *nouveaux riches*.[12] They were referred to as "traveling artists" since they earned their livelihood by wandering from one section of the country to another painting portraits. Occasionally, when one would stop in a home he would arouse the dormant longing of a boy to become an artist. Speculation and scholarship seem to agree that they were all craftsmen such as tailors, woodcarvers, house painters, stone masons, or, as in New Holland (which reflects the sectional differences) glaziers.

Many of the groping, indigenous young painters were discontented with the taste and patronage of their communities. They wanted to look at other paintings, to see what other artists were doing, and to learn from others the things they desired to know. Consequently, they migrated to the various large cities such as Bos-

ton, Philadelphia, and New York.[13] In these places they found themselves with other individuals who were in similar situations and
were struggling to teach themselves to paint or learn from others and
from the few foreign artists who were available. This situation was
not satisfactory and led to conditions which precipitated the founding of art institutes in America.[14]

Contemporary American Recruitment

The formal recruitment—the main mechanism for formally recruiting art students in this country[15]—is an extensive scholarship
program which is to be found in almost all large communities pos-
sessing an art museum. The program can be divided into two types:
those awarded to incoming full-time students who are entering the
art school for a four-year program, and those awards given to
grammar, junior, and senior high school students. The latter awards
enable students to attend the Saturday morning classes given in most
art institutes. The Saturday morning class scholarships allow young
students to receive professional instruction and also provide the
students with paints and other material.[16]

The underlying theory of the liberal scholarship program is
based on the uncertainty of predicting who will become a master
painter, since the history of painting is filled with instances of
academies and institutes which have initially discouraged great
painters from pursuing an art career, for example, Van Gogh and
Modigliani.

By remitting part or all of the tuition in the form of scholarship, the institute loses little in tuition (which is nominal), gains
recruits and good will for its schools, and most significantly, increases the number of possibilities that one of its students may develop into a master painter. Should this occur, the fame of the master
will reflect on the good judgment of the art institute involved; this,
hopefully, will bring increased endowment and gifts to the school
and the museum.

Particular attention should be paid to the importance of scholarships in recruiting students enrolled at private schools, such as
parochial and ethnically affiliated schools. In most cases these schools

do not have and cannot afford art instruction within the established curriculum.

This raises an important question: if there is no art instruction in the private schools, how does the symbolic attachment to art emerge? When it does, what are the social-psychological mechanisms which generate and reinforce the desire within the individual to the point where he will wish to pursue art as a career? Our evidence points out the important fact that the individual *does* come into contact with art and he does internalize these symbols *before* he enters the private school. The contact and nurturing occurs while the child is attending public grammar school, since it is common for the parents of parochial and ethnically affiliated students to send their children to public school for a few years before sending them to the private school during the more advanced years. In this interval the child's propensity for painting has come to the attention of his teachers, who subsequently have seen to it that he has received a scholarship to the Saturday morning classes.

This appears to eliminate as possible art students, and subsequently as artists, those individuals who have had their entire education in a private institution. Our evidence points to an acceptance of this hypothesis. We found no one entering as an art student who had attended a private school *exclusively*. This certainly must be considered as a result based on the limitations of our sample, since the biographies of many painters show (as I have noted in the section on early American recruitment) that many individuals with a nonpublic school background or without any formal art education are attracted to a career in art. In view of this puzzling result several who had matriculated at these schools were asked how others who had no public school education, and therefore no art instruction, became interested in art. These are a few of their suggestions: the individual may meet a student in the private school who has had previous training in painting and who subsequently interests him in art. He may visit a museum, read a book on art, or come into contact with a painter outside of school. The point is, however, that few are attracted to art in this manner in comparison to the number introduced through a definite educational program which points the student in the direction of the formal art school.

Turning now to the more specific social-psychological mechanisms of recruitment, we see the individual who has had previous art instruction in a unique position in relation to his classmates. His uniqueness is due to his being the only one in his class (in all probability) who has ability or the knowledge of the principles of painting.[17] As a result, this ability attracts the attention of the teacher, who will call upon him to use his talents for various school functions such as painting scenery for school plays, preparing posters for school announcements, or drawing pictures commemorating important religious, ethnic, or national events. This has psychological importance from the standpoint of stimulus and reinforcement theory, since the student's uniqueness or exceptional ability stimulates and reinforces his own interest in art, impelling him in turn to further develop his techniques and ability to handle paint and its accouterments. At the same time, the priest, nun, or lay teacher continues this source of stimulating and reinforcement by constantly calling on him to work in art media because there are few students with this ability. As a result, he will spend a great deal of time working on art forms, becoming more adept at his work, and advancing much further than any other member of his class.

At the same time this is occurring, a second important group, the child's peer group, is functioning in a similar manner. It is in the classroom and school environment that this group plays a crucial part, because it is here that this group continually sees the potential painter working with art forms or perceives the instructor frequently assigning art work to him. Consequently they view him as the only individual among their group who has this ability. They then associate him with the arts and eventually type him as the "artist." This view in turn leads to a constant interactional process between the student and his peer group, which results in their continually reinforcing the student's view of himself as the "artist." The student responds to their conception by perceiving his role to be that of the artist in their eyes, which in turn leads to his eventual internalization and acceptance of this role with its accompanying symbols. As this process continues over time, this role comes to form the core of his self-conception.[18]

The importance of the peer group is especially pertinent in the light of recent developments in social-psychological research. For example, Jean Piaget has shown the importance of the peer group in the child's development from egocentric thought to autonomous thought.[19] David Riesman, in *The Lonely Crowd,* has also shown the importance of the peer group in shaping the character of the individual in what he has called the "other-directed society." [20]

Below are two excerpts from interviews with individuals who attended private schools. They are not unique, but typical of the recruitment of students from these schools. In addition, they indicate two other important aspects of this problem: how an individual changes his goal from commercial to fine arts, and the importance of the Saturday morning classes.[21]

. . . His first interest when leaving high school was in commercial art but he was not well-trained in it. When he first entered the Art Institute he was disappointed because he was not receiving anything pertaining to commercial art. How was the first year? Everything the first year was fine arts. The first month was very discouraging, but as the year went by I discovered I enjoyed fine arts. Not only fine arts but music and many of the other arts. By the time I was in the second year I enjoyed all the fine arts. Before that I had not been interested in them. In high school it was sports, calendar girls, and history. *When did you become interested in art?* It was later on. *Did you go directly into the institute from high school?* Yes, right from high school. *How about your high school teacher's influence?* It was a parochial school and the people there were not interested in art. *Then how did you become interested in commercial art?* From posters and other commercial art work. There were no art courses in the school.

I had come close to art in the Saturday morning classes at the Art Institute. I had gone to public grade schools. The teachers there had encouraged me but just art in general. *. . . If there were no Saturday morning classes do you think that you would have gone into art?* I probably would have gone into something else.

Another interview reveals a comparable experience.

. . . Why were you interested in art if you didn't have a chance to practice it? I went to lecture classes at the Art Institute while I was still in high school. That had something to do with stimulating my interest in art. Also I received a scholarship in the public grammar school, but it

was cancelled when I went to the parochial school. But I did manage to get a scholarship to continue through special arrangement. That is not usually done. This was enough to stimulate and motivate me.

The second type of scholarship program which is instrumental for the recruitment of individuals into the arts is the Saturday morning scholarship program. These scholarships actually have several functions in addition to the nominal one of encouraging and stimulating the interest of children and high school youths in art. The program also reveals to the public and its patrons that the Art Institute is performing an institutional function, that is, it is keeping alive and stimulating the art interest in its particular locality. The program's most important function, however, is in providing children and youths who might not otherwise be able to afford them with techniques, equipment, and instruction relating to the arts.

In this respect the scholarship program's most crucial implication for recruitment is in the later years of high school and after graduation when the individual begins to plan his future. For those in our sample who *consistently* attended the Saturday morning classes, the answer was to attend an art school. We may ask why this is so. What prevented the individuals who had consistently attended these classes from pursuing a different vocation? Our evidence reveals that the students who had attended the Saturday morning classes had either majored in art or had taken a general high school course which precluded other types of educational pursuits, for example, college or business schools. The latter situation may be considered accidental, yet it must be seen as important to recruitment.

In order to understand this phenomenon, we must examine the scholarship recipient in the classroom situation. What we find is a similarity between his experience and those of the talented private school pupil; the teacher and the peer groups play the same role in reinforcing the individual's conception of himself as an artist. For example, the teacher often will call on the skillful art student to perform extra work relating to school plays and posters. Most importantly, the extracurricular activities may remove him from the classroom for various lengths of time with the result that he misses critical academic instruction, especially in those subjects, such as algebra and geometry, which are cumulative and are prerequisites for entrance into many colleges. This situation may result in the artist's having greater difficulty in pursuing his schoolwork than if he had remained continuously in the classroom with the other students.

In this respect the position of the artistically inclined student is unique, especially since the greater his personal ability, the greater will be the demands for his ability. (It should be noted here that these demands extend beyond the school situation and may encompass his religious activities and associations with his friends, relatives, and neighbors. For example, our respondents mention that they have frequently been requested to paint posters for church bazaars or to paint portraits and "pretty pictures" for their relatives and neighbors.) However, the important point to be noted in connection with the classroom situation is the individual's personal reaction to his academic difficulties. Even though he has had less classroom instruction than his schoolmates, he may still feel inadequate toward his schoolwork, and he may not comprehend the underlying reasons. Reflecting upon his difficulties, he may feel that "painting is one thing that I can do better than anyone else." This reaction, in conjunction with those already mentioned, serves to reinforce his self-conception as an artist and to recruit him into the arts.

Thus far the interaction between student and teacher has been discussed from the point of view of the student. Yet the teacher's own perspective also is an important consideration, since by placing demands on the individual's time and artistic ability, the teacher enters and commits himself to an obligatory relationship. This requires him to be lenient toward the academic faults of these students in comparison to the others in the classroom. Combined with the student's loss of time from his studies, this leniency is responsible for lowering the academic grades of the student. Entrance into art school, however, is based not on formal course grades, but on proclivity and potentiality for painting.[22] This means that the possession of talent may seal off other careers from the time the student is awarded a scholarship, even though the scholarship may be won as early as the grammar school years.

The following excerpt illustrates many of the points just mentioned. It also gives insight into the reaction of the individual as he contemplates his future as a painter. The individual quoted here was twenty-five years old and had attended a private school.

... *Do you remember the specific time when you decided to become an artist?* It was in the seventh or eighth grade that I began to seriously think of it. In high school I knew I would become an artist; and I had begun to steel myself to the insecurity of it. *Where did you learn about the insecurity?* I heard about it by hearsay and by reading; also from my father, although initially he and my mother never discouraged me. They took pride in my pictures and showed them to people who visited our home. I did draw at home and in much of my spare time. Also in class the teacher would give me time off from my studies to draw things for the class. They didn't encourage me except to say that I did good work. Many times I used to feel that I was missing out in class work; and I feel that I never did good in math because when I would be doing a lot of drawing for the class, they were having math.

An interview with a girl of twenty-four illustrates a similar experience.

... I remember an incident in high school. The teacher gave two girls and myself all a quarter to just draw on a school project. I was happy over it because it meant that I didn't have to do any other schoolwork.

Another boy mentions that "I was separated in *kindergarten* and left to paint by myself."

The previous discussion centered on the formal mechanisms which were instrumental in recruiting art students. They were designated as formal because they were conscious inducements to interest individuals in becoming artists. We now turn to the informal devices for recruitment, the devices which are not systematically created to induce the individual to become an artist. The most important of these is the high school art instructor.

The art instructor holds a special position in the school system. He is one of the few teachers who does not teach academic subjects and is sometimes the only art teacher in the school. This means that he and the other teachers have comparatively little in common. Also, there is apt to be some suspicion of the artist by the other teachers who, like the general public, hold the stereotyped notion of the artist. This means that they may define him as a deviant from society; and deviancy is one form of behavior which is avoided within an educational institution. Both of these factors may tend to isolate the art teacher from the rest of the institution. To compensate for his isolation he spends more time with his students than do the other teachers. There is thus a greater likelihood for the art teacher to influence his students—especially the ones displaying a propensity for art.

Another important aspect of the teacher's influence on the potential art student is what might be called the attempt to receive reflected glory through his students. The art teacher hopes that the pupils he has given additional encouragement will leave high school and achieve success. If they do, it will reflect the teacher's good judgment in discovering and nurturing young geniuses. This in some ways compensates for the art teacher's own failure to achieve fame.[23]

Art teachers begin to function quite early in the student's art career, usually in grammar school. Impoverished or misguided though their teaching may be, they may introduce the youngster to the satisfactions and delights of drawing and painting. The art classes serve to keep the interest alive throughout the school years, and the teacher bestows approval upon the child—through gestures, singling him out for special honors, placing his work in public view, or assigning him honorific tasks like the decoration of blackboards and borders.

In high school the student continues taking art classes and often has an opportunity to major in art. The art teachers may begin to suggest that he go on to art school—a step that otherwise would not occur to some—and may procure information and even scholarships for their protégés. The high school milieu affords additional prestige sometimes, for the child may win a school, city, or even a national prize or may receive acclaim by decorating stage sets, drawing for the school paper, and other such activities.

The art schools themselves reach down into the public schools in various ways. Their graduates teach the children. Talented students are given scholarships to special children's classes all through the school years and may attend at their own expense with encouragement from their teachers. Art schools and associations sponsor contests and give scholarships. Without this bounty many from poorer families could not receive parental consent to continue schooling and might instead get jobs. Others might go to college. By the time he leaves high school, if he is not yet sure of his bent, the future artist may enter through a way station: the summer school or the night school, whose teachers function to build confidence and encourage the promising.

This appreciation of his own talent does not automatically prepare the youngster to become a professional artist—far from it. Initially, all it signifies is an orientation toward art as something that is "fun." Presumably many talented children never learn to take art seriously. In the conversion from avocation to vocation the art teacher is an indispensable agent, for he may indicate some of the vocational possibilities of art. Rarely does a student report, when interviewed, that a schoolmate, parent, or relative brings home to him any such possibility. The teachers do not seem to function as models of occupational dedication except in some cases of fine arts teachers, which will be discussed subsequently. Of the intricacies of the world into which he is about to enter, the teachers reveal rather little, although they may indicate some of the specialties he will encounter. It may be predicted that the public schools will function increasingly to start the student along the path of occupational specialization, particularly in the larger, better, more advanced urban and suburban schools. What is happening in the visual arts presumably is being paralleled in other fields; and this has prompted one sociologist to venture the guess that recruitment for careers in business, government, and arts, as well as for professions, will occur increasingly through educational channels.[24]

Teachers do not ordinarily build a sense of dedication or mission into the internal psychological structure of the student. However, when they do, this fact is of course instrumental for the type of future career the student pursues.

In this connection one consideration is important. Those teachers with a fine arts orientation who do send pupils to the institute inculcate in students a belief that the fine arts are the only true art. Once students enter the art school they may switch from commercial art courses to fine arts ones; but, as far as our sample indicates, the reverse rarely takes place.

Those with the fine arts orientation may eventually transfer into art education or they may eventually be drawn into commercial art *after* they graduate, but very rarely will they transfer into the commercial art curricula while attending the school. The two fine art majors in the sample who entered commercial art courses were both utilizing the school years as an escape from occupational commitment.[25]

The explanation for this phenomenon is the noncommercial orientation of the fine art student who has been imbued with the notion that there is one art—fine arts—and that other forms, such as commercial art, are *not* art within the context of its true meaning. On the other hand, the commercial art students have never been exposed to a similar orientation in connection with fine arts, that is, they have never been told that there is something inherently distasteful about fine arts. If fine arts has been mentioned, they have been told either that it is something "good," or that it is great art but impractical from a commercial standpoint. These students then can bridge the gap between commercial and fine art, because they have no ideological attachment to commercial art symbols which might serve as a mental block when they contemplate switching from one field to the other, whereas the students who are given a fine arts orientation do have this block and cannot break through it without considerable damage to self-esteem.

Since the symbolic attachment to fine art is so important to these students, one may ask how the teacher conveys an appreciation and feeling for the fine arts to the high school student? The crucial question raised here is: how does the teacher connect the emotional aspects of art with the techniques of painting? The teacher meets this problem by "opening the eyes" of the neophyte fine artist and by teaching him to "feel" and "see" as the artist is supposed to feel and see. Below is part of an interview conducted with a boy who changed his goal from commercial to fine art. It illustrates the methods used for teaching the students the "correct" fine art orientation.

. . . *When did you think about fine arts?* One teacher in my last year of high school was very influential. He was totally different from any of the other teachers I had had. At first every one, including myself, thought him queer because of his attitude toward teaching art. *How did this teacher influence you?* Mr. T. taught us that art was an experience; for example, we collected rocks, and we had to hold them in our hands and had to describe the emotions we felt in doing so. He also brought in the good works for the first time, like Braque, Cézanne, and Picasso. It was the first time any teacher had ever done this. It opened an entirely new field for me. *Were you still interested in commercial art?* Yes, but I was beginning to think about fine arts at this time. . . . In commercial art you are not your own master and do not have control over your own work. . . . After I had made fun of him [the teacher] I realized that he was a good fellow, and I respected him as a person. . . . I thought of him as one person who really enjoyed art rather than the others who took it for granted. He taught us the understanding of art and the philosophy behind it instead of the mechanical aspects of it like the others had done.

A different approach to the problem of learning to convey emotions in one's painting is shown by the interview quoted below.

My teacher told me that you must feel the form of the model as if your pencil were directly on the model and to show how such and such a line was too stiff and in that way he made us see how every line we draw can be made meaningful.

The following excerpt reveals the reaction and conflict engendered in the mind of a student trained as a fine artist when she came into contact with the commercial-oriented individual. She had been attending night school immediately after graduating from high school, and at a later date entered the school as a full-time student.

. . . At first we learned figure drawing. There were many commercial artists there. . . . Their technique wasn't like the fine artist's. They go only to see the model. They just draw the model from the commercial artist's point of view. It's to appeal to the public rather than for art's sake. You ought to see the model and what they do to her features when drawing her. Most of the models are old and ugly bags; but they transform them into beautiful vivacious women with sex personified. They would completely exaggerate the eyebrows and the rest of the anatomy—you know what I mean . . . they were cheapening themselves by distorting what they saw. We used to argue with them about what they were doing. They were always on the defensive side of the argument. I guess they have their place; but it's disgusting to me.

At this point the discussion will turn from the influence exerted by the art instructor in high school and return to the student contemplating art as a profession. It has already been noted elsewhere that the student with artistic inclinations is unique among his fellow students, since he possesses an ability which others do not. It should also be remembered that during high school he is exposed (if his teacher is oriented toward art) to a guiding ideology which has several important features. One of these is that the painter in society is defined as a deviant and that he is the object of ridicule and misunderstanding. Not only does he begin to internalize this conception of the artist, but he *actually perceives and experiences* the public's persecution of the artist. This occurs in several ways. He may be directly ridiculed by his primary groups in the form of his family, relatives, and peer group or indirectly by reading books, newspapers, and magazines. The latter contain numerous stories and illustrations which consistently depict and reiterate the theme that the artist is a social deviant. This creates a paradox; for, although others react to him as a social deviant, they still continue to request that he draw and paint for them. They are therefore partially responsible for his continuing internalization of the ideology of the painter. At the same time that he is being exposed to the negative sanctions, he is selecting these from his immediate milieu as the public's actual definition of the painter; and he eventually reaches the conclusion that it is their true conception of him.

In the interplay of student, school, and art world, the student himself has been shown to be an important factor. It assuredly makes some difference whether the bulk of the art students are following in their fathers' footsteps or are in violent reaction against parental restraint and control. And it certainly is significant whether they come to art school with stars in their eyes or because they cannot think of anything better to do.

In addition to these factors it is also important and makes a difference if the bulk of the students are drawn from one social class rather than another. At the present time, the upper-class segment of society is contributing few individuals to the art profession. Our evidence for this assertion is the fact that only two persons who would remotely come close to being placed in the upper class were interviewed.[26] Having had difficulty in locating members of the upper class, we asked a girl who lived in an upper class neighborhood why there were not more students from this district enrolled in the art school. (It is also interesting to note the social change which has occurred in the recruitment of students into the art school. At one time a large majority of students entering the various institutes were from the upper segments of society, since painting was a sign of "culture.")

> *. . . Why don't more people from X and that area attend the art institute?* X is a wealthy community and people there are "proper." The art institute has a Bohemian reputation and a strangeness about the place, so that not many students go there. Also, there is a strong tradition for everyone to go to college. You know the attitude: "Parents just have to send their children to college!" *Anyone from there go with you to the institute?* Some friends; but only after they had changed from Y University. *Did they ever try to talk you into going to college with them?* Yes. A lot of people recommended college for me, for a few years anyway. They said that I would miss the social life, etc. *Why didn't you go?* I lived on Y campus all my life. I had enough of college life before I left high school. The only point in my going would be the social life; and I had seen how empty it was and what a complete waste of time it was. The art institute was much better than Y's art department. . . . *What do you tell people you are studying when they ask you?* Illustrating. I tell people that when they ask me because you have to tell them something!

Many art students originate in the middle class, whose ethos is the antithesis of the ethos of the fine artist. Middle-class ideology revolves around conformity, respectability, practicality, and security. The ideology of the fine artist stresses individuality, nonconformity, insecurity, and nonutilitarian use of his labor. In addition, the artist has a long tradition of being alienated from society and being the object of society's hostility.[27]

The contradiction of these ideologies works against the recruitment of the artist. Those students who refuse to alter their goals create a crisis within their families. To understand the ensuing situation, one must consider the interaction which occurs in the family between parents, siblings, and the student when the latter announces his intentions of becoming a painter. At the same time, the stereotyped picture of the artist which was described earlier must be kept in mind because the image of the painter held by the public is *also* held by the family of the potential art student. The family is unlikely to have had a background or tradition for the understanding of art; and neither has it had, in most cases, any direct contact with it. Furthermore, as one popular writer has emphasized,

. . . Art needs a proper climate. The average Frenchman is no more artistic than the average American. . . . But the French climate is good for art, because in France an artist isn't expected to earn as much as a stockbroker. He is justified in his existence even if he is a *little* artist. He doesn't have to be a Picasso. He counts as a necessary human factor although he hasn't reached the very top.[28]

During grade school and extending into high school the parents have displayed nothing but admiration for the artistic endeavors of the child. They believe that by some unknown and unexplainable phenomenon their child has been granted a peculiar and strange gift. Yet this gift is never thought of in terms of a future vocation but only as a hobby. These ideas change radically when the child suddenly declares that he wishes to make painting his life's profession and end in precipitating a family crisis. Until this point, the parents have been occupied with other matters and have not seriously considered the future of their child. When he announces his intention of becoming a painter and takes the concrete step of registering at the art institute, the entire family turns on the potential artist in an effort to alter his plans. At this point the parents and members of the family begin to realize for the first time that their son, brother, or sister, wishes to enter a profession that is associated with social deviancy. They now see *their* son drawing nude models and *their* son the object of innumerable jokes in newspapers, magazines, and books. At one time they took part in the joking; but in the present situation a transformation takes place, and they see the whole world now laughing at a member of the immediate family. With this realization comes the belief that the entire family is being indirectly ridiculed. The family, no longer displaying admiration for the painting ability of the student, takes such action as to remove the paintings from the walls where they had been previously displayed in their home; at the same time the entire topic of art is avoided.

While this is taking place, the family may suddenly realize, upon a closer examination of the artist, that he does seem different, that is, he speaks a strange language and associates with peculiar people. The common reaction and resolution of the crisis takes two major forms. The parents may either assume personal responsibility for his defection or place the blame on the student. The resolution is either the individual's being disowned or the parents' concluding that the fault lies with them and that, in somehow failing in the upbringing of their child, they must personally shoulder the blame.

Those parents who take personal responsibility for the child's "deviancy" or realize that the child cannot be persuaded to alter his career accept the situation, often with the mental reservation that somehow they or some unknown intervening force will induce the individual to renounce his unintelligible pursuit. While this crisis is taking place, the parents and other members of the family react to the queries of friends and relatives concerning the future of the artist in several ways: they either lie about the true situation, rationalize the situation, or they tell the truth.

When the truth is told, the family fortifies itself against the ridicule and censure of friends and reluctantly admits failure. At the same time, these constant questions concerning the future of the child generate and add to the embitterment of the family. These inquiries are frequent, for until the time the individual announced his decision to make art his life's work he was the family member with the greatest prestige, due to his unusual gift.

If the family should lie about the true situation, they convey the impression that their son is pursuing the commercial end of art, usually adding: "the respectable aspects (that is, nothing pertaining to pornography) of commercial art"—implying that he is doing work comparable to that performed by Norman Rockwell for national magazines with the commensurate notion that a large salary is accruing. In time they may come to believe that this is the true intent of their child, despite contrary evidence which they witness every day.

If the parents rationalize the intentions of the students, they will do so by telling the truth, but at the same time will point to the past masters and the present day ones who are receiving thousands of dollars, as well as international fame, for individual paintings. At the same time, they avoid mentioning the overwhelming numbers of painters who were and are unsuccessful or who attained success posthumously.[29] In time they may actually believe that this may come true and subsequently may reduce their antagonism toward the artist.

The several interviews which follow illustrate the parental opposition and attitude toward the artist and art. Similar feelings were expressed by the majority of students interviewed.

The first is taken from a girl, eighteen, who had previously attended a commercial art school for one year.

. . . How did your parents feel about your switching from commercial art into fine arts? My mother almost had a nervous breakdown. I went through all kinds of hell, and they almost disowned me. They wanted me to come home so that "mother could take care of me." *How do your parents feel about it now?* My parents are more or less resigned to it now— more so than when I first wanted to stay.

The following interview is taken from a boy, nineteen, whose family is very wealthy and has disowned him.

. . . What else did your relatives tell you? They made silly remarks about starving to death. It didn't impress me. . . . They said all kinds of common talk. They talked about crazy people. I disregarded it at the time. . . . *What would you have done if these conditions were true— that is, the painter starving?* I was actually faced with this situation. My father said that I would either have to go to another school or go to school by myself. He cut me off last quarter, and I went to work on my own. I modeled and washed walls—just about everything. . . . My father thought that I was living in sin in Chicago, having sexual relations with the women at the school and with the models . . . but the funny part about it: I never even discussed art with him at any time. He tended to place money above everything else. He looked at social standing from a financial standpoint. He cut me off last quarter, but it actually did me more good than harm. It was a virtue because it gave me independence; and this is important for an artist. It gives you the necessary freedom to free yourself from any influence that would otherwise affect your art.

The next response is from an art student who was frequently mentioned by his fellow students as the person who came closest to personifying the ideal fine artist of the past. The themes by which they described him concerned dedication, sincerity, and nobility. His remarks also underline the problem of earning a living from art, exemplified by such queries as "What are you going to do with it after school?" or "If you have this talent, why don't you use it in commercial art?"

> *. . . How do your parents feel now about your being an artist?* My parents are convinced after all these years. They now have an idea what can be done in the field. They feel that they can let me alone and that I will make out all right. Then I've had my teacher over for supper and he has talked to them and explained it to them. They have no objections now . . . I've never had any serious doubts about making this my life's work and making a living from it.

Another young student from an upper-middle-class family indicates a positive family attitude toward his artistic ability and at the same time indicates the negative attitudes displayed toward him by his relatives.

> *. . . How do your parents feel about art?* They always let me do what I want to do. I feel that this is a big thing that helps me. They encourage me and try their best to understand. Other people, when I tell them that I'm an artist, expect me to be diseased or lazy. *How about your friends?* I don't have many. They think it is amusing. They don't say anything one way or the other. *How about your relatives?* My uncle thinks I'm crazy. . . . My aunt has changed her mind since she saw my paintings. She is reconciled to having an "abnormal" person in the family.

There is a similarity between art students recruited from the middle and lower classes. Both are confronted by opposition and misunderstanding of art on the part of their parents. They do differ, however, in the way they define and resolve these problems. Goals in the lower class are oriented toward immediate gratification. In addition, income is much more significant for this group than either of the other two classes. An important consideration in this connection is the initial attitude these people take toward allowing their children to have an interest in art. In most instances there is pressure on the student to find employment while still attending high school; and, in many cases, even before he reaches the higher grades. When he attains the required legal age the parents and siblings feel that he should seek employment in order to increase the family income, even though this may mean renouncing a promising future in art.

For the most part, art is viewed as pure nonsense by the lower class (the exceptions will be noted later); and a lower conception of art is held than that of the middle class. Art is thought to be the domain of the wealthy, who, they believe, comprehend it. In most cases, a knowledge of art is entirely absent and incomprehensible to these people. The closest approach to art for them is through pornographic literature. Even the conception, which the middle class holds, of the "pretty picture" is absent. A few may have been influenced by middle-class ideology to the extent of having one or two "pretty pictures" around the home; for example, a calendar or a religious painting. However, the important point for this discussion is that the student of art does not return home with pretty pictures, and even the satisfaction of seeing these is denied them. This means that the family is not only foregoing a source of income, since the student is not employed, but they are also denied a compensatory value which would serve as a partial substitute for the loss of his income. Instead, they see their sacrifices being made for an entirely worthless object. This is especially aggravating since the contemporary trend is toward nonobjective painting. As a matter of fact, the object, in the form of abstract painting, may cause the parents a great deal of anxiety when and if it is brought into the home. There are several reasons for this. The first is that it would expose the family to the sarcasm of their friends; secondly, they would be questioned as to the meaning of the painting—a question which they do not have the knowledge to answer; and finally, they would have to explain why they are allowing their son to engage in this incomprehensible work when he could be working and contributing to the family income.

In addition to the loss of income and embarrassing questions, painters in the lower classes may encounter hostility from their siblings who feel that they are being discriminated against; for while they are engaged in work which frequently involves heavy physical exertion, their brother or sister is dabbling away with paint.

A distinguishing characteristic of the lower class is that the family never totally rejects and disowns the art student, as is sometimes the case with the middle class. The decision to pursue art may engender a family crisis of long duration and be traumatic for the individuals concerned; but the person is never rejected or disowned outright.

An additional distinguishing phenomenon of this class is its attitude toward the individual's ability. In all three classes ability is initially viewed as a unique and unusual gift. As indicated elsewhere in this paper, attitudes change once the individual overtly commits himself to art as his life's work. However, the reaction of the lower class to the phenomenon of the *gift itself* continues, and it is viewed rather mystically, that is, as God-given. This attitude may reflect the parental background of many of the lower-class subjects. Most were offspring of first-generation Americans (Polish and Italian) whose families were very religious.

The mystical reaction has a positive influence in the recruitment from the lower class and partially offsets the negative aspects mentioned previously. This may be accounted for by the parents' pride and the feeling that their child has been divinely chosen to possess a wonderful gift. Closely connected to this reaction is the fact that these people are predominantly Catholic and see the paintings of saints in church. They connect these paintings with their child's gift and conceive of it as an extension of religious ritual. They also feel that they are receiving an additional church blessing and are conforming to church norms and the glorification of God to an extent greater than the other members of the congregation.

A final consideration is the increased pride and support granted the child when the parents perceive him associating with people who appear sophisticated and are members of classes above their own. The common reflection is that their child "is up with the rest of society"; and, in some cases, the child is perceived as being above the upper classes, since his "superiors" *come to their son for advice* and to purchase his paintings.

Closely associated with this is the possibility of social mobility which the parents may see as an outcome of their child's achievement. These factors taken severally add to and reinforce the parental feeling of divine blessing and function to encourage the individual to continue his pursuits.

To conclude this section, several interviews are reported. Each has been selected to illustrate the social factors influencing the lower-class individual either to continue or to renounce his interest in art.

The first is taken from a boy, twenty, who is experiencing difficulty with his oldest brother. It illustrates the importance of birth order. Those who are first-born have much more pressure placed on them to enter an income-producing occupation or a father's business than do the remaining siblings.

    . . . *How does your family feel about art?* I'm from an average family; I've influenced my family to have good taste. *How about your oldest brother?* There isn't any direct influence from him. We argue on the way of thinking—especially about money and business. He's a Philistine. . . . *How do you mean that you influence your family?* I pick out the works to put on the walls. . . . Our family had to strive to get some place after my father died. I hate to think what would have happened if I was in my older brother's shoes and still had the ideas I have now; but that's fate.

The following interview illustrates the relationship with the peer group and its orientation toward income.

    . . . *Did you paint at home at all?* I never did at home. The kids I hung around with didn't encourage me. I didn't talk to them about art. A few thought it was the thing to do . . . others thought it was foolish. They would say I could be working at the X factory and be making Y dollars a week. . . . My parents didn't have any interest in art. My father is a factory laborer.

The excerpt which follows was from a student whose parents held the mystical view toward art.

    . . . My parents thought I was gifted and were very happy over it. They have sort of a mystical feeling about art. *Why?* I don't really know, unless it's the church's influence—I mean the pictures and statues of the saints in church. I think that has something to do with it. . . . They were especially happy over my winning the X scholarship, and then the . . .

87

and other honors. *How about your relatives?* They think that strange people go there and that I should be working to help support the family; but they never tell my parents this.

The concluding interview illustrates the fact that the poorer classes must send their children to work even though many of them have artistic ability.

> . . . *Did you have other interests in addition to art?* It seems that there were no other interests that I had that were as important to me. *Were your friends interested in art?* I had a few friends who were interested in art. However, my classmates in school were all interested in art. They enjoyed it; but none of them continued on in it. Most of them came from poor families. I went to a high school that was not in the district that I am in now. I felt bad about their not going to art school, and still do. . . . So many people I had gone to school with were poor and couldn't go to school yet had a great deal of talent. Yet there at the school there were people who couldn't paint at all, and still they were going. It was a big shock to find this. *You mean that you expected to find something different there?* A lot of people with ability are there, but they weren't of the caliber I had been under the impression I would find. . . . *Do you identify yourself as an artist?* I'm referred to by people as an artist; but I tell them I'm an art student.

Summary and Conclusions

I have described the recruitment of the artist, dividing this process into formal and informal components. The formal attempts were designated as conscious efforts to induce individuals to choose art as a career and an example cited was the liberal scholarship program. The informal components were those which induced interest in art but which were accomplished without conscious intent. An example of this was the typing of the individual as the "artist" by his peer group.

A second classification divided recruitment into positive and negative categories. The positive are those factors that encouraged individuals to enter art—for example, special talent, and the negative ones are those that hindered individuals from entering the field—such as the association of the painter with deviancy.

Implied in these sanctions is a cultural contradiction. On the one hand we encourage and reward creativity, and at the same time the individual responsible for it is penalized. Paralleling this situation has been the encouragement of the individual during his development as an artist from childhood through youth. Yet, when he chooses art as a vocation, the encouragement is withdrawn and negative sanctions substituted. The paradox has led to his rejection by his primary groups and has been followed by his subsequent alienation from society.

This study has revealed the difficulties which face the contemporary art student. It is conceivable that many of the same factors operating in the recruitment of the painter are also operating in the recruitment of other artists, for example, musical composers, poets, and writers. The study has also shown the very important role played by the primary groups and other parts of the social structure in either encouraging or discouraging the individual from a career as an artist.

One of the most pressing problems of the painter and the intelligentsia as a whole is that of financial support. This has been implicitly stated throughout the entire report.[30] In the past a painter, if he were fortunate, could look forward to having a patron to support him. Today patrons have virtually disappeared, and in their places have appeared a new phenomenon—the large, financially secure corporation. Owing to its commercial orientation, many artists have refused support from this source. Instead they have sought employment outside the field or in art education.[31] Either choice has meant that the painter has had to relinquish a large portion of his time and independence and consequently has lowered the level of his work.[32] This has meant that society as a whole has not received the benefits of the artist which we believe should accrue from his labor. Despite recent publicity that the situation is improving, the evidence from my empirical research leads me to conclude that the position of the painter remains financially and morally precarious, and that he must continue to labor outside the field of his chosen profession if he is to survive.

The Recruitment of the Artist

¹ The number is not large in any country.
² Edward Shils, "Mass Society and Its Culture," *Daedalus* (Spring, 1960), 290.
³ Edward Shils, *ibid.*
⁴ Jane Harrison, *Ancient Art and Ritual* (London: Butterworth & Co., Ltd., 1913), pp. 229-33 ff.
⁵ *Ibid.*, p. 230.
⁶ *Ibid.*, p. 231.
⁷ In the following presentation I will not discuss the group of artists who have never attended a formal educational institution but who have been taught by a master painter or otherwise informally schooled. Although they are of the utmost importance, there are few data except biographical on these types of artists.
⁸ Giorgio Vasari, *Lives of the Painters* (London: G. Bell & Sons, Ltd., 1892), *passim.*
⁹ For earlier evidence see the comments of Arnold Hauser in his two volumes on the history of art. Arnold Hauser, *The Social History of Art* (New York: Alfred A. Knopf, Inc., 1951). These all refer to the European artist. For information concerning the origins of artists in non-Western cultures, see Mulk Raj Anand, *The Hindu View of Art* (Bombay: Asia Publishing House, 1957).
¹⁰ For contemporary similarities to the duties of the apprenticeship in Vasari's time, see Mason Griff, "Role Conflict and Career Development of the Commercial Artist" (doctoral dissertation, The University of Chicago, 1958).
¹¹ *Ibid.*, pp. 66-78.
¹² Charlie M. Simon, *Art in the New Land* (New York: E. P. Dutton & Co., Inc., 1945), pp. 15-20. Also see Oliver W. Larkin, *Art and Life in America* (New York: Holt, Rinehart & Winston, Inc., 1949).
¹³ Some, such as Benjamin West and John S. Copley, migrated to Europe.
¹⁴ Charlie M. Simon, *op. cit.*, p. 20.
¹⁵ Implicit in my statements about the art student is that these students graduate and then make up the overwhelming majority of artists treated here as a group. Other countries have different means to recruit students into the field of painting. For example, in some European countries the student is given direct subsidies of money and equipment.
¹⁶ The school will be referred to interchangeably as the art institute, art school, or the institute.
¹⁷ An exception would be the technical school in large cities such as Detroit, where many people with artistic talent are students together. However, these schools are primarily devoted to the teaching of the industrial or applied arts.
¹⁸ Alfred R. Lindesmith and Anselm L. Strauss, *Social Psychology* (New York: The Dryden Press, 1954), pp. 279-82. See especially the quotation from Carl Rogers, the original source of which is in "Some Observations on the Organization of Personality," *American Psychologist*, No. 2 (1947), 358-68.
¹⁹ Jean Piaget, *The Language and Thought of the Child* (London: Routledge & Kegan Paul, Ltd., 1926).
²⁰ David Riesman, Nathan Glazer, and Reuel Denney, *The Lonely Crowd* (New York: Doubleday & Company, Inc., 1953), p. 69.
²¹ Italic type indicates questions or comments by the interviewer.
²² This is usually in the form of a sample of their painting submitted at the

same time as their other credentials. Furthermore, as I have noted, the possession of painting ability has historically not been predictable and consequently has led to a "gentle" admission policy where few applicants are refused. For more on this see Strauss, *Some Aspects of Recruitment Into the Visual Arts,* p. 4.

[23] See Strauss, *Some Aspects of Recruitment Into the Visual Arts,* pp. 5-6, for more information on the importance of the public school teacher.

[24] Theodore Caplow, *The Sociology of Work* (Minneapolis, Minn.: The University of Minnesota Press, 1954), p. 217.

[25] Strauss, *The Art School and Its Students,* p. 16.

[26] These two could only be placed in the upper class on the basis of parents' income and residential location. All other criteria would place them in the lower or middle middle of W. L. Warner's class scheme. See W. L. Warner, Marcia Meeker, and Kenneth Eells, *Social Class in America* (Chicago: Science Research Associates, Inc., 1949). Also W. L. Warner *et al., Democracy in Jonesville* (New York: Harper & Row, Publishers, 1949).

[27] See Mason Griff, "The Alienation of the Artist," in *Arts in Society* (Madison, Wis.: University of Wisconsin Press, Fall 1959), pp. 43-54.

[28] Alexander King, *Mine Enemy Grows Older* (New York: The New American Library, 1960), p. 9.

[29] For an enumeration of what artists are doing for a living, see the McCausland Report. From personal conversations with artists, both during the interviewing of the present report and the interviewing included in a second study of artists, various estimates have been made of the number of full-time American artists earning their livelihood exclusively from their paintings. These range between 10 and 14.

[30] There are two theoretical sources which throw light on the reasons for this nonsupport. The first is Thorstein Veblen, who speaks of the "instinct of workmanship," which always desires to see man laboring at productive work. See his *The Theory of the Leisure Class* (New York: The Viking Press, Inc., 1931), pp. 15-16 and elsewhere. Also see Talcott Parsons, *The Social System* (New York: The Free Press of Glencoe, Inc., 1951), p. 310. Here he is quoting from Durkheim, and he discusses various mechanisms of social control as a protection for society.

[31] See Mason Griff, "The Commercial Artist, A Study in Role Conflict and Career Development."

[32] See Mason Griff, "The Commercial Artist: A Study in Consistent and Changing Identities," in *Identity and Anxiety,* Stein, Vidich, and White, eds. (New York: The Free Press of Glencoe, 1960). The second part of this paper deals with the problems of the fine artists who work in commercial (advertising) art.

Bibliography

BOOKS

Anand, Mulk Raj. *The Hindu View of Art.* Bombay: Asia Publishing House, 1957.

Antal, Frederick. *Florence Painting and Its Social Background.* London: Routledge & Kegan Paul, Ltd., 1947.

Caplow, Theodore. *The Sociology of Work.* Minneapolis: The University of Minnesota Press, 1954.

Duncan, Hugh D. *Language and Literature in Society.* Chicago: The University of Chicago Press, 1953.

Griff, Mason. "The Commercial Artist: A Study in Consistent and Changing Identities" in *Identity and Anxiety.* Stein, Vidich and White (eds.). New York: The Free Press of Glencoe, Inc., 1960.

Harrison, Jane. *Ancient Art and Ritual.* London: Thornton Butterworth Ltd., 1913.

Hauser, Arnold. *The Social History of Art.* New York: Alfred A. Knopf & Co., Inc., 1951. Two volumes, translated by Stanley Godman in collaboration with the author.

Holt, Elizabeth G. *Literary Sources of Art History.* Princeton: Princeton University Press, 1947.

Johnson, Edward G. *Sir Joshua Reynolds Discourses.* Chicago: A. C. McClurg & Co., 1891.

King, Alexander. *Mine Enemy Grows Older.* New York: The New American Library, 1960.

Larkin, Oliver W. *Art and Life in America.* New York: Holt, Rinehart & Winston, Inc., 1949.

Lindesmith, Alfred E. and Anselm L. Strauss. *Social Psychology.* New York: The Dryden Press, 1954.

Mannheim, Karl. *Man and Society.* New York: Harcourt, Brace, & World, Inc., 1941.

McCausland, Elizabeth. *Art Professions in the United States.* New York: Cooper Union Art School, 1950.

―――. *Careers in the Arts.* New York: The John Day Company, 1950.

―――. *Work for Artists.* New York: American Artist Group, Inc., 1947.

Myers, Bernard. *Problems of the Younger American Artists.* New York: The City College Press, 1957.

Parsons, Talcott. *The Social System.* New York: The Free Press of Glencoe, Inc., 1951.

Piaget, Jean. *The Language and Thought of the Child.* London: Routledge & Kegan Paul, Ltd., 1926.

Riesman, David, Nathan Glazer, and Reuel Denney. *The Lonely Crowd.* New York: Doubleday & Co., 1953.

Ruskin, John. *Art and Life.* New York: John Alden Publisher, 1886.

Saint-Gaudens, Homer. *The American Artist and His Times.* New York: Dodd, Mead & Co., 1941.

Simon, Charlie May. *Art in the New Land.* New York: E. P. Dutton & Co., Inc., 1945.

Stranahan, C. H. *A History of French Painting.* New York: Charles Scribner's Sons, 1888.

Van Marle, Raimond. *Italian Schools of Painting,* XI. The Hague: Martinus Nijhoff, 1929.

Vasari, Giorgio. *Lives of the Painters and Sculptors and Architects.* Abridged and edited by Betty Burroughs. New York: Simon and Schuster, Inc., 1946.

———. *Lives of the Artists.* Translated by Mrs. Jonathan Foster. Vol. II. London: George Bell and Sons, 1892.

Veblen, Thorstein. *The Theory of the Leisure Class.* New York: The Viking Press, Inc., 1931.

Warner, W. L. and Associates. *Democracy in Jonesville.* New York: Harper & Row, Publishers, 1949.

Warner, W. L., Marcia Meeker, and Kenneth Eells. *Social Class in America.* Chicago: Science Research Associates, Inc., 1949.

JOURNALS

Crowcroft, Peter. "The Young Artist in Britain," *The New Republic,* Nov. 8, 1954.

Griff, Mason. "The Alienation of the Artist," *Arts in Society.* Madison: The University of Wisconsin Press, Fall 1959.

Martin, W. "The Life of a Dutch Artist in the 17th Century," *The Burlington Magazine,* Vol. VII, Part II.

The New York Times, August 7, 1960.

Rogers, Carl. "Some Observations on the Organization of Personality," *American Psych.* 2, 1947.

Shils, Edward. "Mass Society and Its Culture," *Daedalus,* Spring 1960.

UNPUBLISHED MATERIALS

Griff, Mason. *The Commercial Artist: A Study in Role Conflict and Career Development.* Doctoral Dissertation. Department of Sociology, Chicago: The University of Chicago Press, 1958.

Strauss, Anselm. *The Art School and Its Students: A Study and Interpretation.* Unpublished manuscript.

Strauss, Anselm. *Some Aspects of Recruitment Into the Visual Arts.* Unpublished manuscript.

Four

THE STUDENT DANCER

Alone among the four authors of papers on artistic roles in this book, Mrs. Ryser has herself filled the role she describes (student dancer) and is able to speak confidently from "inside" the universe of discourse. As she points out, this very intimacy with her subject is double edged: it affords her keen knowledge of acquaintance and puts the subjects of inquiry at ease, but may also make it hard for her to maintain the researcher's necessary detachment. The richness of her portrait may well make us feel that the hazards of intimacy are worth taking, that at least in the early exploratory stage of social research in the arts we should prefer to be empathically sensitive rather than methodologically scrupulous.

In many ways the dancer seems very like the poet, composer, or painter; we can recognize consistencies in early career choice, intense desire, economic marginality, and a pronounced divergence from the core values of most American occupational groups. But the dancer is distinguished both by being a performing, rather than creative, artist (although the two are of course not inherently mutually exclusive) and seemingly by the magnitude of his divorce from conventional styles of life. We may perhaps wonder whether the respondents' ease during Mrs. Ryser's interviews and the bond they shared in both being dancers as well as being subject and investigator stimulated a more candid expression of ideological hostility than an "outside" researcher might have elicited.

The fact that these are performers in a strenuous art means active careers tend to be brief; their emphasis on time and age as enemies is probably unique among artists and is more akin to the role of athlete. Do the strain of performance and its perishability mean less satisfaction with one's role here than in the creative arts with durable products? Is the thoroughgoing physical engagement of the dancer allied to a heightened narcissism and a heightened urge to set the self off from other people? Again, does the bodily involvement have special implications for the dancer's identity, and perhaps especially for the homosexual stereotype of the male dancer? Male artists in general have often been suspect in this vein; yet if the poet, let us say, is marked by a more strongly feminine component than the "average" man, he does not exhibit this feature of his personality in the total expressive movement of the dancer on stage.

The theme of adolescent isolation, so clear in the dancers, is not stressed in the accounts of the other arts. Yet many close observers of artistic roles have commented that the artist-to-be may feel separate and lonely during this period of life. Autobiographies, too, often seem to picture the nascent artist as an isolate during the very years when—in American society at any rate—youth at large is most firmly wedded to the community of peers. We do not know whether devotion to art imposes a sense of apartness or whether the lonely young person discovers in art a consolation, a substitute for active social engagement. Presumably both trends may be at work in inducing the complex precipitate of an artistic career. The image of the artist as "doubled," as at once inside and outside the quotidian flux, is reiterated by most persons who are familiar with artists' lives. There is some reason to believe, on the basis of memoirs and psychological theory alike, that the artist has a lifelong (not merely adolescent) problem in balancing the demands of social intercourse against the demands of private craft. The poet Stephen Spender phrases the dilemma clearly:

Meeting people, receiving a large number of letters and invitations, and feeling under an obligation to reply to them, these are perhaps greater dangers to the writer than debauchery. . . .

Social life is all the more dangerous because it is to some extent necessary to him. It is one of his main doors of entrance into the life of other people. . . . He is not protected by having an office and office hours. Unless he fights hard against them he is constantly exposed to interruptions. . . .

I did not want to wear a mask, to exert my will, to choose among people, to judge before I knew them, whom I should see and whom not see; I felt that any such attitude would inevitably result in a kind of hardness from which my work would suffer, and which would be a far more serious sacrifice than the loss of time.

THE STUDENT DANCER[1]

Carol Pierson Ryser

Introduction

This is a study about student dancers. They are in the throes of a rigorous and demanding training which can lead, for a few at least, to the top of the Broadway, television, or concert dance ladder. It is a long and arduous climb. By far the majority will not achieve notable fame; yet they choose to devote their very young lives to the art of dance.

What is the overall picture of dancers and the dance in America today? Only a brief and very general orientation can be given. The dancer is, in many ways, viewed as deviant. He is popularly considered at the least to be apart, strange, and idiosyncratic. The social scientist with his questionnaires and scales hesitates to scrape away the magic which seems to surround this artistic field and to ask the questions he has asked of almost every other class, group, or individual. In hesitating he neglects both a rich source of data and insights into this society afforded by the artistic (nonscientific) point of view. The result of this neglect is a loss for both artist and social scientist.[2] In a very concrete sense the artist and the social scientist are concerned with the same kinds of problems: motivation, meaning, human behavior. Each interprets these problems from a different perspective.

Dance techniques in this country come from many cultural sources. The foreign techniques are in turn changed by the contact with indigenous American ones. Artistically the dance is in an exciting if somewhat tumultuous state. Exponents of ballet, modern dance, Spanish dance, folk dance, to name a few, compete and combine to contribute to the varied scene. While the United States is a nesting place for many techniques, modern dance has evolved into something which is primarily American. As an example, Agnes DeMille brought a whole new approach toward dancing to the Broadway stage; Jerome Robbins did the same for ballet.

If the artistic picture is challenging and bright, the financial picture is challenging and glum. In the United States, in contrast to Europe, where the government sponsors ballet companies, the ballet or modern dance company is forced to survive as best it can through slack seasons and uncostumed debuts. It is the rare dance group that boasts a paying season, a lucky young dancer who is associated with a paying company. For those who love dance, and the number of avid followers is small, the concert audience is composed of familiar faces. From season to season one might almost say hello to most of the members of the audience who mingle in the lobbies at intermission.

As a social scientist I asked what consistencies could be found among this group of young people who choose dance as their art, who realize the economically unrewarding future that awaits them, and who make many personal sacrifices to learn their art and craft. In interviewing these neophytes my specific interest lay in discovering how they see themselves in relation to the dominant middle-class society, whether they constitute an integrated group, and what they consider to be their greatest problems and satisfactions. By asking questions along these very general lines I hoped to evolve an image of the student dancer.

There are at least two major ways of approaching these questions. First, one must ask what the sociological and psychological determinants of their choice are, and second what the consequences of this choice are for them and their expectations of its effect on the world in which they move.

For the first, as many have pointed out,[3] one must look to motives other than those of self-interest and economic gain. These students are not dancers for money or for high social status. To the contrary, they face an existence of relative privation, which *they* do not romanticize if others without experience do. One student expressed it this way:

> You don't think a hungry artist can create, do you? Whatever you might create under those circumstances would be pretty dismal stuff. I live here because it's cheap. I would just as soon live in a penthouse. Artists aren't looking for sacrifices; it's required. Living in a garret may be the romantic stereotype, but I don't like it. You can't really create when you're miserable.

As for the second question, the consequences of this choice, I look to the students' interests, their attitudes toward their colleagues, the meaning of dance to them, and the role they feel dance plays in the larger social network.

In the discussion that follows, there is a heavy reliance on statements by the dancers themselves. If the account seems overburdened with them, it is because I feel that, better than any interpretation or rewriting, the students speak very well for themselves.

There is no single theoretical orientation in this paper. Wherever sociological or psychological concepts aid in explaining the situation under discussion, I refer to them. Until more data are collected, it seems advisable to postpone anything more than tentative theoretical suggestions.

Methodology

The study was conducted in a large metropolitan city. The students were drawn from one dance school. The number of cases on which the findings are based is small—sixteen. Because of this small number any kind of statistical analysis is inappropriate. The aim of the study is to explore several general areas in the hope that professional (that is, nonstudent) dancers can be studied in a more thorough way at a later date. For this reason the interviews were conducted in an informal manner. The questions asked were more nearly exploratory statements designed to elicit reactions than they were actual questions. I was more interested in learning what the students had to say than in securing answers to prepared questions which might well have missed the point.

The students were interviewed in their homes, at the studio, in coffee houses and drugstores—wherever I could catch them between classes or rehearsals. Some did not bother to change out of their leotards for the interview.

It is impossible to say that the students are representative of any given group of dancers or even of the "young American dancer." Their background training had been in various dance disciplines, and they had studied for lengths of time ranging from three to twenty years. Some are with companies or have their own small companies and spend relatively little time in class. Others are virtually full-time students. Recently, all have been subject to the same training, all are aiming at full-time dance careers, and all are residents of the same city. In general, although it is divided in different ways, their time is taken up with the same activities.

One decision that I believe had some influence on the kind of information I obtained in the interviews might be of some interest here. With a number of years of dance training myself, I am well acquainted with the terminology, the major figures in the dance world, and some of the problems that face the students. This was helpful in giving me some kind of orientation in framing the study. The decision made concerned whether or not to tell the students of my experience with dance. If I remained the outsider, the social scientist, the objective observer, the basic tenet of interviewing was not violated. If I revealed my own experience, thereby violating the tenet, I was seen in some sense as being "in the same boat." I decided on the latter alternative, and although time was sacrificed in that the students (and I) were sidetracked in discussions on dance theory, I felt that what might have been a suspicious attitude on their part, was, in most cases, a cooperative one. What was lost in "objectivity" (in the strict sense of the term) was gained in frank answers. It was important that as much "real" information as possible be gained in the interview, as there was only one with each student. It was my impression that the students were used to being stereotyped by the general public, and the answering of questions in accordance with the stereotype rather than their own opinions was a problem I anticipated. I hope this was partly solved by having them identify me as a dancer.

When the interviews were nearly complete, I dropped in to visit several of the classes. Although it was not part of the study, these visits gave me a chance to see some of the students "perform." It was something I wish I had done more often. The picture presented to me in the interview hinged importantly on the student's estimate of his or her ability to dance. In several cases the image presented was slightly glorified with respect to technique, in others underplayed. More insight into the material might have been gained if this kind of observation had been more explicitly incorporated into the study.

In surveying the facts, one is struck by the lack of consistency in the students' backgrounds. One might hope for *the* variable or several explanatory variables that would answer the question of why they chose dance as a career, but the answers do not appear to lie here.

Several factors do tend to be consistent. All but three were born in a major metropolitan area. This is no surprise; the major art centers are there, and the possibility of selecting dance as a career rests in part on exposure to concerts, magazines, dancing schools, and the first taste of performing in recitals and high school shows. Almost all of the students had some performing experience prior to their decision to dance professionally; many of them had extensive experience. The musical comedy theme of the girl from the

101

The Student Dancer

Summary of Personal Data

Age:	16	17	18	19	20	21	22	23	24	25	26	27	28	
No.:	1		3	1	2	1	1	3	1			2	1	Total: 16

Sex:		
	Male	4
	Female	12
		16

Marital status:		
	Single	13
	Married	1
	Divorced	2
		16

Part-time work:		
	Teaching dance	7
	Clerical work	6
	Unskilled work	1
	No outside work	3
	No information	1
		16

Father's education:		
	Grade school	4
	Some high school	3
	Some college	3
	College degree	1
	Graduate school	3
	No information	2
		16

Mother's education:		
	Grade school	1
	High school	7
	Some college	1
	College degree	3
	Graduate school	0
	No information	4
		16

Place of birth:		
	Metropolitan area	12
	Suburban/rural	3
	Foreign/metropolitan	1
		16

Source of school funds:		
	Family	3
	Self	4
	Scholarship/self/family	7
	G.I. Bill	1
	No information	1
		16

102

Father's occupation:	Professional	2
	White collar	6
	Blue collar	
	Skilled	1
	Unskilled	1
	Military	3
	No information	3
		16
Mother's occupation:	Housewife	4
	Secretary	2
	Artist	2
	Teacher	2
	Saleswoman	1
	Nurse	1
	Editor	1
	No information	3
		16
Religious affiliation:	Protestant	3
	Catholic	1
	Jewish	10
	None	2
		16
College training: (students)	Liberal arts	5
	None	5
	No information	6
		16

small town in the Midwest who rises to theatrical heights as a dancer in the big city is virtually nonexistent.

Information on family income was difficult to obtain. It can be noted, however, that nine of the mothers work part-time at paying jobs, although all but two of the fathers could be classified as either professional, white collar, or military workers. Further, all but three of the students were working part-time to pay their way. Although they took about twelve hours of dance class a week, had many hours of rehearsal, and were enrolled in academic courses in some cases, they still had to squeeze in hours to make money. One must consider here that dance is a physically exhausting pursuit, and the common cry was for more time to sleep. Most of them answered the question as to how they spent their leisure time with, "What's that? I don't have any."

There is probably a greater proportion of males in my sample than in the dance world in general. Although for some purposes it might have been ideal to interview an equal number of men and women, there were many fewer men, and it was difficult to arrange interviews with them.

The last thing to note is that over half (ten) of the students are Jewish. I do not know whether this tendency would be found in all the arts or only in dancing. If this proportion were found consistently in other studies, an analysis of the cultural factors involved would be very interesting. No material relevant to such an analysis was gathered in these interviews, however.

Career Selection

These neophyte dancers, young as they are, made a decision to enter the field at a relatively early age. The nature of dance training is such that it is almost necessary to start classes at the late grammar school level. The one apparent exception to this is some modern dancers who start their training at a later age. The popular opinion is that this late start is possible for modern dance but not for ballet—thus the slight disdain with which ballet dancers speak of "modern dance training." Contrasted with other occupations or professions such as medicine or law,[4] the dancer is selected at an early point in the life cycle. One can guess that the factors which influence the choice of dancers are different from those affecting the choice to study medicine or law.

A comparison of the age at which classes were started and the age at which some definite decision was made to dance professionally is presented here:

Age level	First experience in class	Decision of dance career
5-11	8	0
12-14	3	5
15-18	3	5
Over 18	2	6

All but two started their training before they finished high school. One fact should be noted. Of the six who *decided* to dance professionally after the age of eighteen, three are males. (Two of them decided after service stints and the other after several years of college. The difficulties inherent in choosing dance as a career for a man will be discussed later.)

What influence did the parents have on this decision? The image of the mother with ambitions for her daughter in the artistic or theatrical world is a myth according to the students' reports. When asked who had taken the initiative in starting classes (not choosing a career), all but two of the students recalled asking for the classes and in several instances struggling with parental disapproval to get them. If the doting mothers exist who dress their daughters in tutus, it would appear that the daughters drop by the amateur wayside without reaching the status of serious students. In fact, determination from within is probably one of the requisite qualifications for putting up with the long and discouraging apprenticeship.

Another relevant point here is that dance training is a process which continues on through the dancer's career. One never goes through the ceremony of receiving a diploma stamped with "professional dancer" or "ballerina." It is an apprentice system whereby the dancer works his or her way up through the ranks, taking classes, performing in increasingly important roles, and practicing all the time. Some difficulty arose when the students were asked if they considered themselves to be professional dancers. Almost half said yes, although they were enrolled in a rather extensive training program. The criterion of being paid for performing was considered by most to be superficial. As one student put it:

A professional certainly is not a dancer who gets paid. That has nothing to do with it. It's more like someone who performs, does a lot of concerts with a better than average company. When you get to the point where you can establish empathy with the viewer, then you are a professional.

Knowing when you have crossed into the professional world is only one of the uncertainties involved in being a dancer. Without formal *rites de passage* it is an uncertainty that can cause a great deal of anguish. "Professional" means pay and performing, of course, but for these students it also means technique, self-confidence, dramatic ability, and very importantly the ability to convey the meaning of a role to the unknown but much-courted second party, the audience.

What other problems did these students experience in selecting dance as a career? The problems are both internal and external. The internal problem of most consequence is the constant competition with an ideal image of what a good or great dancer is. As one girl put it, "For me [the greatest problem] is to reach the peak I want. I'm a perfectionist and I have a perfectionist's idea of being a dancer; a person and a dancer." Another said:

> I also have the fear that I'm not good enough to achieve the things I desire. You're in such a hectic atmosphere of competition that I feel a great deal of tension about my dancing. The greatest problem is worrying a great deal.

Along with this variety of internal uncertainty and competition with an ideal, there are the more mundane but pervasive problems of money, age, and physical disability. Although not all the students thought all of these were problems (I suggested these as possibilities), most of them saw at least one as a matter of concern.

Discussing age, one student said:

> At the age of almost twenty, I don't feel as if I'll ever have that much technique. A dancer has a limited number of years. You're on the way down by the age of thirty. I was advised not to dance because of my hip. I may have to quit in a year or so, but I'll let things ride for awhile.

Money is the most consistent problem. As stated earlier, almost all of the students work part time. Here is what the students said:

> That's my big problem. My family is very unstable financially. If I come back, I can earn tuition and work during the year. With my present physical problems, it would mean a lot of strain. It depends on the strength of the individual.

As things stand now you can't rehearse, because you have to make money to live, and the dance companies don't put on enough performances to earn a living. At this point my parents are supporting me.

The students deal with these problems in one of two ways. Either they refuse to think about them ("I never think that far ahead"), or perhaps more realistically, they plan to perform for awhile and in the event of disability or advancing age (thirty) retire to teach and choreograph. For the dancer, unlike the musician, the artist, or the writer, time and age are feared enemies, an unwelcome addition to the more usual problem of eating.

The question of marriage is also a problematical one. The majority (nine) of the girls expect to marry and combine marriage with a career. The rest either do not want to marry or would give up a dance career to marry. Unlike other kinds of jobs (at least nonprofessional) the dancer cannot plan on a nine-to-five work day with a wife's responsibilities in the off-hours. Classes, rehearsals, performances, traveling with companies all complicate their solution of combining the two. It was my impression that very few of them were realistic in evaluating the problems and consequences of marrying while pursuing a dance career.

For the men, the problem of marriage is in some ways more difficult. The stereotype of the male dancer in this culture is an effeminate, unmanly, if not homosexual one. Regardless of their behavior, all of the men are faced with the public image. "The public has a perfect right to think it because it's true," one dancer said, and another simply stated, "People associate dancing with effeminacy; it just can't be helped." Within the dance world, the problem is less acute: "Dancers are a great deal more accepting than most." The big city affords both a degree of anonymity and an opportunity to find understanding social contacts. Although the men did define this condition as a problem, they found various ways of accepting it as part of the public image. Though the image does not necessarily impair their dancing, it does have an effect on the scope of their social life.

Attitudes Toward Career Choice

Before attempting to assess the reasons for choosing to dance, let me digress for a moment to consider the prerequisites for dancing. Dancers themselves bewail the fact that dance is "the least of the fine arts." "The arts" means painting, sculpture, composing, writing; it rarely means choreographing, or if it does, few people mention it. In reality, to study dance, all one needs, besides the interest, is a well-coordinated body that is fairly well-proportioned, a sense of rhythm, and perhaps musicality. Almost any athlete can master the beginning of a dance technique. These students have the physical requirements, but so do millions of other city students. What has caused some to make a career choice of dancing?

One might think that artists of one sort or another running in their families might cause young people to choose an artistic career; yet, returning to the data, only one professional artist was noted among the parents and one entertainer among the brothers and sisters. It seems we must look to other kinds of explanation: to family attitudes, to the broader life situation of the person making the decision to dance.

A career in dance, with its connotations of the "evil stage," riotous living, and Bohemianism, might be expected to cause alarm in the students' families. The students expressed feelings very much to the contrary. Two of them said that their families did not particularly object, but they had no understanding of what was involved in being a dancer. Three felt their families were definitely against the decision to dance, but the rest (eleven) felt their families approved the choice. One particularly enthusiastic family reacted this way:

Mom definitely encouraged my going into dancing. She even took dancing classes herself. My sister and brother were attracted by this. The family loved my dancing teachers, and they eventually became close friends with them. My father goes to concerts and is very interested in my dancing.

One student who felt the family did not understand put it this way:

I have two brothers, both married with children; my father is a salesman. Outwardly they said "fine," but I don't think they really understand. Of course my folks never told me what to do. My dad hinted that show business wasn't the greatest, but he's very proud when I send write-ups home.

Along similar lines another student said:

My family were very good about my decision to come here to study. . . . I was always a willful child, and I always did what I wanted to do, so I guess they figured there was no point in arguing. As soon as I learned the value of temper tantrums, I started arguing and won. . . . They were finally encouraging, and I guess now that I'm (a dancer) they feel proud.

Perhaps if I had interviewed the parents, the emerging picture might have been quite different, but in the students' view, there were few real objections. The appealing if simple notion that choosing a career in dance, which is contrary to the prevailing middle-class idea of an appropriate occupation, is in some way an adolescent rebellion is tentatively put aside. Although it may occupy some position in the process of career selection, rebellion does not seem to be in the foreground. What are the alternative explanations?

As important as the family is in the rapidly expanding lives of adolescents, the peer group is an important competing factor. It gives to the adolescent an opportunity to "become himself," test his newly found adulthood, cut loose (or attempt to) the ties that bind him so closely to his family. The feelings of these students toward their contemporaries in high school, and the concomitant self-feelings, prove an interesting avenue of speculation. How did these students fit in with the teen-age culture; how much a part of it did they feel? On this point, with only one exception, there were unanimous clamorings of dissatisfaction in the teen years. In one sense, this question is in the chicken-or-the-egg category. Were these students excluded from the merry if fitful whirl of teen-age social life because of their different interests and talents, or did they develop talents that might otherwise have remained dormant (or at least at the level of a not too serious interest) because of social exclusion? Perhaps the most accurate statement is that between the dance student and the teen-age culture there exists a mutual hostility. As we shall see later, they did not feel much friendlier toward the middle class that spawned them.

One student made no particular mention of the high school dilemma; another said she felt very much a part of the life in high school but qualified this by saying, "I spent most of my life trying to be a good girl. I was sick of not saying what I thought. Now I know where I stand and what I think."

The rest of the students without exception found junior high school or high school a harrowing experience. Most of them felt strange and apart from the rest of the students. Several felt older and more mature. The youthful exuberance, perhaps only stereotypically associated with the average teen-ager, to them seemed silly, childish, or insensitive. These comments are characteristic:

I haven't met many people here who are not connected with music or drama save for the people in high school. . . . I was not much of a thing in high school, yet every evening I would trot over to a house to spend the evening. . . . I felt that I was not so much of a wallflower; I could come out if I wanted to. It didn't bother me, though I wasn't in a clique. . . . Socially, I feel more attuned to the people here. I did feel that I was older than the kids in high school; they were frivolous. I was a deep thinker, not smarter, but more serious minded.

Another student lived through high school in the following way:

The boys would get mad; they called me teachers' pet. I didn't go awfully well with them. My sophomore year I didn't care whether people liked me or not. By my senior year they respected me. I had been a serious student. . . . I was building up a front then. If I came home from school crying my mother would build up my morale so I could keep going.

The examples could be multiplied almost endlessly. It would be unfair as well as incorrect to say that *the* reason dancers are dancers is because high school was something less than a happy or satisfying venture. However, the fact remains that high school was trying, and dancing became more and more time consuming; it became to some extent an effective substitute for the more usual teen-age life.

The Middle Class

Not only did the students remember the high school years with distaste, but when dancing was chosen as a career, middle-class values and the middle-class style of life were rejected in wholesale fashion.[5]

In keeping with the concepts of reference group theory,[6] it seems useful to view the middle class as a negative, nonmembership reference group on the basis of the students' current values. It seems logical that the student would take this view. We have seen him dissatisfied with the life of the middle-class teen-ager, which is in some ways a rehearsal for middle-class adult life. When dance was chosen as a full-time career, a more general rejection of what had previously been frustrating would quite naturally follow. My view is that the general rejection of middle-class culture is a direct consequence of this earlier disappointment and frustration centering around the time of adolescence. Theoretical verification of this point of view is found in those psychologists and psychiatrists who emphasize the importance of later experience in personality functioning and change.[7] This view does not deny the importance of early experience, nor does it attempt to explain why these dancers felt isolated in the first place, but it does emphasize this adolescent crisis as a precipitating factor in career choice. This crisis, in view of the data, might be considered a necessary if not sufficient cause.[8]

With respect to antagonism toward middle-class culture, it must be remembered that we are dealing with a very sharp, two-edged sword. Not only do these students feel unhappy about their adolescence, but their rebellion is reinforced by the attitude of the middle class toward them. They not only feel that the middle class is worthless, but also they believe that the middle class reciprocates their negative feelings. The picture is one which includes the psychological repercussions of a shaky, experimental adolescent world in terms of feelings of isolation and rejection, and the sociological consequences of a reinforced and disagreeable image of middle-class culture in terms of changed values and changed style of life.

Several quotations from the students themselves should be sufficient to indicate their view of the middle class and their perception of the middle class' view of them. For the latter view they said:

> When my high school teachers found out [about taking up dancing], they smirked or grinned. There's nothing in it; many people do. They think it's easy. They feel the people who go into it don't have much in their heads. Dance is becoming more respectable, but it is generally regarded as a low profession.

Another stated:

> . . . too little respect is given to the artist in our society, period! There are too many misconceptions concerning dancers' lives and activities. . . . People feel that dancers lead an easy, glamorous life. This is untrue. . . . They tend to associate dance with vulgarity and sinfulness. The fact of the church's attitude toward this is in some way a reflection. Too little regard is given art on the part of the government. . . . They have a higher regard for literary arts that involve more mental than physical activity.

Their view of the middle class was stated in the following ways:

> There is a great difference between me and middle-class America. I've never been comfortable with middle-class living. I was always different from the people I met in high school.

> I get awfully tired of talking to them. They all got married because it was the thing to do. Before they knew it they were involved in supporting a family and working for a pension. They were doing all the things that kept them from thinking. Now they are lost in a dream world of TV, cars, and payments, and no relationships exist any more between man and wife. Each one is involved in his or her own separate set of worries.

A most emphatic view is represented in the following:

I am both afraid and horrified by the average business types. They have a complete inability to look beyond the city limits. . . . You end by having a great dislike for the nonart appreciators. When forced to associate with a person who is not an artist, you eliminate the possibility of talking about what is most important to you. . . . I'm a big mass-hater. I resent them, and I resent that their taste governs so much of what I have to put up with. There is always a compromise with my standards when I associate with them, but what I have to put up with in the fine arts is not a compromise.

One last opinion:

If they would admit it to themselves; not just look at the superficial things . . . they would see the healthy aspect of art. They would hold us sort of in awe. They don't understand us. I don't think they really mean we're queer. Deep down they respect us, even fear us, because we know what we want to do. As they go on they get caught up in their own lives and they forget. They think only of the ponytails, the sloppy look, the rundown flats. . . . They're afraid to do anything the group doesn't want to do. They live too much the same way in little groups. . . . They are afraid to move away from the group. The outside world thinks you're a little crazy. I get disgusted with the idea.

Clearly, these dancers perceive themselves as misunderstood. They admonish, accuse, defend themselves, and feel superior to the great culturally unwashed middle class. The dancers dislike the life, the goals, and the things that assume great importance in their characterization of the middle class. Is it therefore not reasonable to assume that as both rejected and rejecting, the dancers would form a tight little island of their own to fortify themselves against the onslaught of such kindly meant advice as "give up all this nonsense and settle down, raise a family, and be a woman"? Does the tight little island exist, or are these in reality individual, isolated protests? Disapproving of the middle class, do they necessarily approve of each other?

The answer to the above question is, somewhat strangely, no. Although the students, because of their class and dance company contacts, are required to associate with each other a good many hours of the day, they are far from feeling that dancers form a congenial group or even that dancers, taken singly, make satisfactory friends. If they are bound together as expatriates from middle-class America, they are not overly impressed with the company they keep. Why should this be so?

Again, I believe the relative lack of success with the teen-age culture is pertinent here. If the adjustment to one group of contemporaries is unsatisfactory, there is no reason for thinking that adjustment to another set *will* be satisfactory. Although the content of the relationship has changed (the setting, the subjects of conversation, mannerisms, dress), the form or mode of relating to people remains essentially the same. Looked at from this point of view, it is really not surprising that there are so many complaints about their colleagues; the justifications for dissatisfaction have simply changed. For most of these students there was a short gap of time between the unhappy teen-age experience and the time of the interview; some were still in their teens. I am not thereby discounting the possibility of change, but stating the probability that the mode of relating to people had not substantially changed since the time of the initial crisis. Following this line of reasoning, the lack of a well-integrated dance-student "subculture" is not, from a psychological point of view, illogical.

About half of the students associated with other dancers outside of class. Two of these felt it was necessary. The other half adamantly did *not* associate with them. These data tell only part of the story. The comments they made about other dance students, whether they associated with them or not, are more revealing for purposes of deciding whether dancers constitute an integrated subgroup.

Only two of the students felt that dancers were good company and centered their social lives around them. Several were neutral on the subject, but eleven felt strongly enough to attempt avoiding dancers outside of necessary contacts. (I asked specifically with whom they associated, with whom they spent their leisure, and how they felt in general about other dancers.) Following are some examples of this attitude. I present a number of them because I feel they illustrate an interesting sociological dilemma.

I don't like dancers. I have very few friends who are dancers; as a matter of fact, I have very few friends. . . . Dancers don't talk about anything but dancers. They don't understand what they are doing [here]. Most of them are preparing for Broadway or television, and I think it would be a waste of time if that's all I was preparing for.

Dancers are too narrow. My friends are in folk music, painting, and acting. I feel at one with people who are creating something. I feel like a fish out of water when I'm not with people who are aware.

They [dancers] are so involved in their work they tend to become very narrow minded. They don't read newspapers, they don't know what's going on in the world. This is very depressing. They're very introspective. Themselves, their work, and their progress become all important. They devote so much time thinking about it they consequently all tend to look alike.

The thing that annoys me most about other dancers is the narrow view they have of dancing and of life in general. They know what's right; they won't consider anyone else. This seems to apply generally to any field they talk about. I also hate people that talk nothing but dance; I can't stand to be around dancers all the time.

I have very few dancer friends. I don't like dancers, particularly ballet dancers. Modern dancers know more about what's going on; however, they don't avoid being narrow minded. . . . They are not readers. I thought modern dancers were inclined to be more intellectual, but I find their conversation is almost exclusively dance; not dance as an art or dance as related to the other arts, but how many fouettes someone did in class the other day, or someone else had finally mastered three pirouettes. . . . They know relatively little about their field, and it doesn't seem to concern them.

I would hate to be classified as a typical dancer, the kind that are running around in black tights and long pony tails. Dancers as a whole tend to look as interesting as possible. I think they just want to be noticed as dancers. The tights—the odd make-up—they do all these kinds of things to attract attention. There is a tendency for them to be completely immersed in the field.

The consistency of these opinions I found to be quite overwhelming, especially since they were probably talking about *each other*. Several did mention the "mixed-up" quality of dancers, while others spoke of their indecisiveness and peculiarities. Some preferred to be lone wolves, admitting that people in general didn't interest them much.

One relevant indicator in their comments is that they never refer to dancers as "we" but as "they." Whether they were answering in terms of a stereotype pony-tailed dancer image for my benefit or in terms of their actual social contacts is hard to tell. In any case, considering their intimate contact with dancers, even answering in terms of *their* stereotype is indicative of their lack of identification with dancers as a group in other than competitive or professional terms.

If the inferences are not unwarranted, an interesting sociological situation comes to light. We have a rejection of the middle class in conjunction with a lack of positive identification with dancers as a subgroup. Being against the same thing, and being both against the same thing and integrated as a group with shared norms and values, are two very different situations. J. Milton Yinger has coined the term "contra-culture." [9] He defines this as a group where:

> . . . the normative system of a group contains, as a primary element, a theme of conflict with the values of the total society, where personality variables are directly involved in the development and maintenance of the group's values, and wherever its norms can be understood only by reference to the relationships of the group to a surrounding dominant culture.

A subculture and a contraculture are distinguished by the salience of the conflict element. I think a further distinction must be made if such groups as student dancers are to be taken into account. This further distinction must take into consideration whether the orientation to the contraculture itself is positive or negative. A delinquent gang developing its own norms and values in response to rejection by and dissatisfaction with the dominant middle class is different from the student dancers who have a similar attitude toward the middle class but are essentially bound *only* by this negative orientation. True, they are bound together by their similar professional pursuits, but they remain more an aggregate than a real group. Perhaps this distinction is overrefined, but investigation of, for example, other types of artists or deviant groups might point to whether the distinction is worthwhile.

The last and most general relationship to be discussed here is that of the student's view of the role that dance plays in the arts and in society generally. Devoting so much time, energy, and emotion

to their art, to what purpose do these students work? Are they dancing to convey a message, is dancing seen strictly as a vehicle for performing and entertaining, or do they view dancing as an integral
part of the culture of which they are merely the trained exponents?
What kind of responsibility do they feel to their audience, to their
ideas, to their ability to convey beauty to those with only a talent
for appreciation?

While several of the students were training to be dancers for
educational or entertainment purposes only, by far the majority
were pessimistic about the audience's capacity to understand their
emotion and message and saw their dancing as centering primarily
on their own needs and abilities. The feeling they conveyed to me
was that it was fine if some people in the audience understood what
they tried to say, but if not, the loss was the audience's. They still
had the satisfaction of performing, of saying something well. For
many, the idea of dance (or the arts) having any specific role to play
in the larger social network was totally foreign. How did they state
their case?

One dancer expressed in a very articulate way the salient view
of the role of dance.

Dance for me is purely selfish; it's fulfilling my own needs. You deal
entirely with yourself. Your body is your instrument. You need to communicate and you use your body. A dancer is unique in this way. . . . I
don't think dance can really give anything; except maybe beauty to some
people, but most can't accept it. It's not necessary; they're out of the habit.
People don't think any more. They've lost the capacity for imagining. People are just lazy, I guess. They would rather not have time to think;
they like to have things spelled out to the end. . . . At the same time I
think the dancer has a definite responsibility to his audience.

Another student put it this way:

They [dancers] think everyone knows about dancing, when in reality
the chances of being known are not too great. It doesn't make any difference anyway. The masses won't see enough to acquire a taste for it. I'm
more interested in what I'm doing. I'm neither a promoter nor a martyr;
I don't want to die for any cause. There will always be dancing; it will
never die out. It will go into slumps and it will reach different heights.

. . . I don't consciously go out to say something on a stage right now. I am working through how I feel, and I'll wait to see what happens.

One student saw the reception of dance in this country as a reflection of a broader state of affairs:

Many people have nothing to do with the arts because they're not exposed to them. If there were more education to the arts, then there would be people to create and people to appreciate, and I think they are both important. It is one of the tragedies of modern living that most of the entertainment is of the passive kind. People don't have to think.

These comments parallel those about the middle class, the automaton-like way of life which the students hoped to escape when they made the decision to dance.

While they are concerned with the lack of art appreciation in this country, only six of them were at all interested in teaching. The remainder were interested in performing exclusively or in choreographing and performing in some combination. Three of them proposed to go to foreign countries to establish their own companies, to countries where dance is more integrated with the way of life.

This combination of discouragement with the state of dance appreciation and the felt responsibility to try to convey a message that is both highly personal and artistically comprehensible is a complicated one. The students feel they have something to say but few people to say it to. Small wonder that they emphasize in their own minds what they personally can derive from dancing. The strictly psychological explanations for career selection would not bring this kind of issue to light, although they shed light on other aspects of the problem.[10]

Conclusion

This paper has tried to present several aspects of the student dancer's life: his view of middle-class culture, his opinions about his peers, his view of the role of dance in society, some ideas on his reasons for dancing. Despite the small sample, where there is so little contradictory evidence (as in the case of an adolescent "crisis") it is tempting, and perhaps not unwarranted, to try to make some theoretical sense of the material. I qualify this by saying that I would be much happier with a larger sample. As the purpose of the study was exploratory, I can only make its shortcoming clear and state that the results make the prospect of a more thorough study exciting. Dancers are interesting in themselves; they also raise questions which are very pertinent to sociological and psychological theory. For example, what specific needs are being served by selecting this particular kind of career? What specific social structural strains lead to this choice? Why, given a positive connotation of "creativity," does the society view the artistic group as deviant in some respects?

As I have said before, the dancers also have something to teach us. Their rejection of middle-class culture is not always unproductive; it is a rejection that can lead to critical commentary, and, finally, for some, to creation. What they say is of interest to social science quite apart from theories of personality and social structure.

I will end with a quote which raises questions not dealt with in this paper, questions which point to the complexity of the study of the artist. I find it both hopeful and despairing, a plea and an assertion:

Anyone who can find fulfillment elsewhere should dance as a hobby. Art as a way of life holds too much frustration, and you don't really accomplish anything in the middle-class sense of the word. Unless you *have* to express yourself, it is better not to be an artist. You give up so much. You give up being an accepted member of society; you exist outside the social pattern. You are an outsider . . . however, the only way I can be free is to create something of my own.

The Student Dancer

[1] I wish to thank Professor Alvin D. Zalinger of the Sociology Department, Brandeis University, for his advice and guidance in doing this study. The data were collected in 1958 for a seminar in the Sociology of the Professions at Boston University.

[2] For an expansion of this point of view see R. N. Wilson, "Literature and Sociology," *Alpha Kappa Deltan* (Spring 1960), pp. 32-37.

[3] For example, T. Parsons, "The Professions and the Social Structure," *Essays in Sociological Theory* (New York: The Free Press of Glencoe, 1949), pp. 34-50.

[4] See R. K. Merton *et al., The Student Physician* (Cambridge: Harvard University Press, 1957), Part 2, "Career Decisions."

[5] The vagueness, or perhaps the complexity, of the term "middle class" makes explicit definition difficult. I use it to refer to Class II and Class III in the Hollingshead scheme. The emphasis is on economic security, economic and political activity, extensive community participation, concern with material possessions, and acquiring an education. These seem to be the more general values around which middle-class life revolves. See A. Hollingshead, "Selected Characteristics of Classes in a Middle Western Community," in *Class, Status and Power,* R. Bendix and S. Lipset, eds. (New York: The Free Press of Glencoe, 1953), p. 213 ff.

[6] Robert Merton, *Social Theory and Social Structure* (New York: The Free Press of Glencoe, 1957), p. 225 ff. Specifically, reference group as it pertains to "self-appraisals relative to the group framework . . . such a term as 'reference group' is useful, not because the term itself helps to explain behavior, but because it does not easily allow us to overlook this component in self-appraisals." Thus, the student dancer's self-appraisal is influenced by the surrounding middle class; the relationship is, however, reciprocal; that is, the student dancer's self-appraisal will in turn influence his perception of the middle class. In this case, the perception is more hostile than friendly, and the student perceives the middle class as alien to him.

[7] H. S. Sullivan says: "The fact that the self-system can undergo distinct change early in each of the developmental stages is of very real significance. . . . And it is this capacity for distinct change in the self-system which begins to be almost fantastically important in preadolescence." Sullivan was referring mainly to therapeutic possibilities, but it does not seem to exclude major, prolonged change in the adult situation. *Interpersonal Theory of Psychiatry* (New York: W. W. Norton & Company, Inc., 1953), p. 247.

[8] In discussing the trauma of social isolation and its effects on the adolescent, Sullivan says: "In the juvenile era we see components of what will eventually be loneliness in the need for compeers; and in the later phases of the juvenile era we see it in what I have not previously mentioned by name, but what you can all recognize from your remembered past as the need for acceptance." *Interpersonal Theory of Psychiatry*, p. 261.

[9] J. Milton Yinger, "Subculture and Contraculture," in *American Sociological Review* (September 1960).

[10] Ernst Kris says, "In clinical practice, by rule of thumb, views concerning both specific problems of energy discharge and of ego functions in relation to specific types of creative behavior are taken for granted. Our expectations are significantly limited when we hear that a certain patient is an actor, a dancer, or a cartoonist, or a dress designer . . . In the first instances more definitely—we expect that certain typical conflict constellations will more likely occur than others; the problem of rapidly changing identification may be crucial in the actor, that of coping with exhibition in the dancer . . . ," *Psychoanalytic Explorations in Art* (London: George Allen & Unwin, 1953), p. 28. I don't believe these explanations are contradictory, but complementary. Knowledge of these "typical conflict constellations" give a specific orientation to the social situation in which they are worked out.

120

Bibliography

Hollingshead, August. "Selected Characteristics of Classes in a Middle Western Community," in R. Bendix and S. Lipset, *Class Status & Power.* New York: The Free Press of Glencoe, 1953, p. 213ff.

Kris, Ernst. *Psychoanalytic Explorations in Art.* London: George Allen & Unwin Ltd., 1953. See especially chapters 1 and 2.

Merton, Robert K. *Social Theory and Social Structure.* New York: The Free Press of Glencoe, 1957, p. 225ff.

Merton, Robert K. et al. *The Student Physician.* Cambridge, Mass.: Harvard University Press, 1957, Part II, "Career Decisions."

Parsons, Talcott. "The Professions and the Social Structure" in *Essays in Sociological Theory.* New York: The Free Press of Glencoe, 1949, pp. 34-50.

Sullivan, Harry S. *Interpersonal Theory of Psychiatry.* New York: W. W. Norton & Company, Inc., 1953. See especially chapters 16, 17, 18.

Wilson, Robert N. "Literature and Sociology," *Alpha Kappa Deltan,* xxx (Spring 1960).

Yinger, J. Milton. "Subculture and Contraculture," *American Sociological Review* (September 1960).

Five

THE RECEPTION
OF DOSTOEVSKI'S WORK
IN GERMANY: 1880-1920

We know relatively little in a systematic way about
the critical reaction to a given author, book, or genre.
Literary history tends to give very general impressions
of the nature of critical or audience response, and is
usually limited to recounting the views of a few particularly influential critics. Yet it must be assumed
that critics and newspaper reviewers are central to the
literary process, part of the vast corps of middlemen
who stand in all the contemporary arts between individual creator and anonymous audience.

As Lowenthal notes, his is a pioneer attempt to
specify the major themes of critical evaluation; he then
goes on to interpret these themes in terms of their puta-
tive relation to the ideology of the audience, especially
to political attitudes. One can argue that literature and literary criticism are in some sense "projec-
tions" of their authors' underlying structure of belief
and implicit assumptions about human conduct, although it would be perilous to assert with some reduc-
tionist analysts that this is all the arts, and statements

about them, come to. Thus literary criticism can be taken, as Lowenthal shows, as a set of clues to the covert disposition of the critic. Lowenthal goes a step further: considering the critic to be broadly representative of prevailing climates of opinion in the audience, he infers from critical writings certain dominant moods in entire sectors of the population. The social scientist must question both the magnitude of the inference and the seeming coherence with which critical themes embellish the author's favored observations. At the same time, he must admire Lowenthal's audacity and concede that the essay is firmly anchored in detailed knowledge of this period in German letters and politics.

Some such tracing of dominant themes, whether the specimen be a critical exegesis or a literary work, is central to the growth of a sociology of literature. Only when content can be formulated—categorized and conceptualized—is it then possible to relate that content to social milieu or psychodynamic process. But content analysis is perhaps one of the least explicit and reliable, if most important, of sociological techniques. The problem of content analysis is, as a philospher remarked of metaphysics, "the problem of the categories." In Lowenthal's essay the categories have been erected by a single researcher, and their choice dictated by the researcher's own very articulate ideological posture. His disenchantment with German middle-class views of the social world, with the disinclination of the members of this class to exert themselves for reform and political mastery, shapes his reading of Dostoevski's ,critical reception in obvious ways.

Literary critics' emphasis on Dostoevski's "irrationalism" seems to be, for Lowenthal, the crux. This stress on the mysterious and private in individual lives is seen to parallel and reinforce the middle-class acceptance of the futility of social reform. Further, the author hints that when critics exalt Dostoevski's dark knowledge of the soul's inner regions, his limning of aberrant behavior, they portend the acceptance of mystic violence in National Socialism. The novelist's disillusionment with programs of political action renders him in Lowenthal's judgment "not political." Irving Howe, on the contrary, writing at a later period, contends that: "Dostoevski's truly profound insight into politics . . . cannot be appropriated by any political group, for it has to do with ideology in general."

The hazards of Lowenthal's approach are clear. Many features of his analysis are debatable, including the leap from critical uniformities to middle-class ideology and the reading of Weimar problems into Dostoevski's art. Yet his impatience with attitudes of fatalism and privatization is entirely understandable—indeed, admirable—in the context in which he wrote. He tells us frankly what his biases were, so that we are able to weigh them in the whole. Most important, perhaps, he dares the bold step of teasing out crucial relationships among literature, its several audiences, and a broad social scene.

THE RECEPTION
OF DOSTOEVSKI'S WORK
IN GERMANY: 1880-1920[1]

Leo Lowenthal

The plan of this study was conceived during the last year of the Weimar Republic, and it was during this period that the research data were collected. The study itself was written "in exile" after Hitler had come to power. I make these remarks advisedly in order to warn the reader that the motivation for this piece of work was not so much scholarly interest per se but political or, if you will, moral concern. Working as a sociologist in a German academic context, I became appalled at the increasing political and moral apathy of Germany's lower middle and middle classes beginning in the twenties—an apathy, if not callousness, which was hidden under the veneer of "cultural" pretensions. I was curious to find out whether a method of scientific access could be developed with which to study this constellation of political and moral decay and cultural magniloquence.

Had I known at the time about advanced methods of opinion research and projective psychology, I would probably have never designed this study, for it attempts to accomplish the same ends as these methodologies in a primordial fashion. It assumes that the works of a writer serve as projective devices for the display, through widely published commentaries, of hidden traits and tendencies typical for broad strata of a population. In other words, it studies readers' reactions indirectly through the medium of printed material which is inferred to represent typical group reactions.

The "sample" of this opinion study is very representative as far as it goes. Due to the generous assistance I had as a member of the Institute of Social Research at the University of Frankfurt, I was able to peruse nearly all books, all magazine articles, and even all major newspaper articles ever written on Dostoevski for the time period under investigation. The results of my research, which originally appeared in German, are here presented for the first time in English, in a somewhat abridged form.

During the last two decades of the nineteenth century and the first two decades of the twentieth century, no other modern author received as much literary and critical attention in Germany as Dostoevski. There have been other writers, of course, who have had greater influence or who have achieved more editions, and the curve of the literary preoccupation with Dostoevski shows considerable fluctuation. But not a single year has elapsed since the end of the eighties without some significant addition to the Dostoevski literature. Nor is this literature restricted to the field of aesthetic criticism. Many political, religious, scientific, and philosophic discussions have appeared along with literary essays and critiques. Examination of the complete German bibliography on Dostoevski (approximately 800 items)[2] reveals an unusual number of important names from literary, religious, and philosophic life, distributed among the most diverse schools (only Goethe is comparable in this respect). The same applies to the diffusion of the Dostoevski literature among periodicals and newspapers. Political organs ranging from the conservative through the National-Liberal to the political left, literary periodicals in the strict sense, even scholarly journals devoted to philosophy, law, and medicine have published discussions of Dostoevski.

Such temporal continuity and social diversity suggest certain problems. Are there some particular features which condition this intensity and breadth of interest? Are there specific elements in Dostoevski's works which appeal to a particular social configuration in all its diversity and change?

This paper is not a study of Dostoevski. Certain ideological peculiarities of the German middle- and lower-middle-class reading public clearly do not apply to Dostoevski at all. In fact, the amount of attention which he has received cannot by any means be explained by reference to the content, composition, or language of his novels, by their subject matter or aesthetic qualities alone. The complete answer must lie in fields other than those which the literary historian ordinarily discusses.

I. The Ubiquitous Myth

Studying the written reaction to Dostoevski in all of its multiplicity, one is struck by the fact that the same broad categories of interpretation have been retained throughout. The emphasis varies here and there, to be sure, for the taste for particular works changes in time. Certain aspects, such as the religious significance of the man and his work, for example, did not become important until later. If one looks hard enough, diametrically opposed statements can be found within these categories on many specific points. One conservative critic, for example, stresses the nationalism of Dostoevski,[3] whereas a liberal critic tending toward naturalism emphasizes his humanism.[4] But the common viewpoints are far more apparent than any such differences. Whether examining the commentary of the 1890's or of the 1930's, there are the same typical judgments: Dostoevski is a special kind of psychologist, he preaches the love of man in his own way, he tends to reconcile contradictions among the most divergent theoretical and practical spheres of life, his work expresses the soul of his people, and the like. Our problem is to show the extent to which these judgments contain basic elements of the ideology of the social groups which form the hard core of his readership.

The reception given to Dostoevski, the evaluation of the categories developed in the course of that reception, is positive with a few unimportant exceptions. Dostoevski is acclaimed. One might even say that his popularity is less a matter of literary criticism than of willing and pious adoration. It is significant that there is scarcely one adequate scholarly account of his life and work by a German literary historian, and the few comprehensive treatments which do exist betray their opinionated character by their very design.[5]

From the beginning, Dostoevski is surrounded with an aura of myth. Qualities are added to his personality and works, qualities which transcend verifiable reality and have a super-historical character, and a certain indestructible unity is posited between his life and novels. They are devoid of any connection with the social process, but at the same time they are assumed to make social life meaningful against all historical theory and against every conception of social law.

An examination of mythical speculations in the commentaries on Dostoevski quickly reveals a staggering number of closely related formulations concerning the symbolic nature of the author and his works: "close to primordial conditions," [6] a nature "full of the Devil and full of God," [7] a saint on the road "from Nazareth to Golgotha," [8] a "bottomless pit," [9] "epileptic genius," [10] one who weaves death with life,[11] "reason with madness," [12] chaos with form.[13] Certain common ideas underlie this chaotic abundance.

1. The realm of real being appears in Dostoevski's work, that realm which stands outside mere contingency in human life. With him we approach "the mystical mothers";[14] he "projects for the most part into the new third realm of the human race";[15] "we always carry the abyss with us." [16]

2. Dostoevski's life has a symbolic meaning. It is not molded by manifold experiences; the latter are themselves only stations in an "existence significantly conceived according to a sinister plan," [17] stations on his "dark road." [18] "Mysterious forces, which apparently unseen, rule all the earthly destinies of Dostoevski," brought him to prison.[19] Through illness Dostoevski "was thrust into the darkest

127

abysses of unhappiness and could taste the highest transports of ecstasy." [20] And "He was an epileptic. What does this mean? . . . That he felt a mysterious power within him, the demon, for a brief moment elevating him suddenly, sublimely prostrating him cruelly for days." [21] His death, too, took place under an unearthly sign: "He died like Beethoven in the sacred uproar of the elements, in a storm." [22] If one surveys the development of his personality, one sees that "it grows and is formed from the dark animalic and elementary roots to the highest consummation, and rises to the highest, most radiant peaks of spirituality." [23] Furthermore: "It often seems as if an invisible power presents just that man who is sensitive and receptive above all others with the most terrible of human destinies, so that a man may at length, out of his own experience, show his fellow men how a man of his type can be injured, humiliated, and tortured to death, and nevertheless remain a man. Such mysterious designs guide the destiny of Dostoevski." [24]

Such arbitrariness in the choice of mythical figures, which we meet in Christian and in pagan, in metaphysical and in sentimental form, places public life and the whole of social existence in a context which transcends criticism and dissatisfaction. The enjoyment of works of art casts a veil over reality. Apart from the gratification of the fancy which is achieved by "understanding" the deeper meaning of human life and events in general, one is transported into a sphere in which everyone can experience sublime pleasures. The mechanism which creates ideology also transmutes the lack of a social theory into a profuse wealth of images and fantasies. We shall see again and again that the ideology of the middle class tends to transfigure reality by substituting for it the inner world of the psyche. World history thus becomes private myth.

If myth as super- and prehistoricity serves to bolster the middle class in its relationship to the upper stratum, so also can the life of Dostoevski be interpreted to establish a line of demarcation from the lower classes. The same characteristically private aspect is inherent in the disposition of the life plan of the individual, of the meaning which rules his fate. The glorification of Dostoevski's terrible suffering, his imprisonment, illness, and poverty, in short, every situation to which the propertyless strata are exposed, is in the last analysis an exaltation of passivity. It is absurd to struggle against suffering inflicted by powers which elude every earthly, scientific, or social-reformist effort, and men upon whom such suffering has been imposed acquire a luster of special dignity. Such mechanisms console the middle classes for their own troubles by pointing to still greater ones. By giving full approval to the greater distress and suffering of the lower classes, they also alleviate their anxieties about potential threats from below to middle-class existence.

3. A third mythical factor is represented by the "meeting of opposites." Through the whole history of the reception there runs the motif that Dostoevski the man, the intrinsic quality of his works, the essence of his most important characters, in short, the whole compass of his life and creation, are characterized by a union of factors generally perceived as contradictory. Great pains are taken to show this union of opposites in the most diverse spheres. *Contradictions in Weltanschauung:* Dostoevski is "a conservative writer, yet also a naturalist." [25] The action in the *Brothers Karamazov* encompasses "heaven and hell";[26] "great saintliness and great wickedness" appear in Stavrogin;[27] Dostoevski "is a nihilist and orthodox." [28] *Intellectual contradictions:* we find the author "attaining the highest peak of reason and falling to the lowest depths of the abyss of mysteries." [29] Dostoevski often "undermines his logically constructed world of ideas in order to dash them down to an unfathomable depth." [30] *Moral contrasts:* "The saint and the sinner . . . are never opposites for him." [31] His countenance bears witness to "diseased passions and endless compassion";[32] the religious fanatic is steeped in guilt and the prostitute is pure.[33] *Contrasts of character:* "We must solve the apparent contradictions . . . in the greatness of his genius and of his heart, and look upon them in the same way as we look upon the contradictions in nature." [34] He "was an epileptic, a man in whom extremes of dullness and lucidity coalesced." [35] His countenance is "half the face of a Russian peasant, half that of a criminal." [36] Finally, there are contradictions which cannot be subsumed under fixed categories: "Every person . . . is only a bit of his immeasurable, indistinct personality . . . the sharply outlined details, the naturalistic element which we think we perceive, are blurred. . . . It is the abyss in which mists brew . . . abyss and level ground are the same." [37] "We hesitate to

use the formalistic hackneyed word, harmony of an author who permits the experience of all manner of blessedness and deviltry with cold-bloodedness." [38] His world is "full of heights and depths, narrow places and spacious extents, abysses and prospects." [39] "Chaos constantly takes on form . . . but at once the form grows soft and melts away. . . ." [40]

This mythological element illustrates a central factor in the construction of every ideology, namely, the glorification of existing social contradictions. This is the essence of the mechanism. All other factors are more or less subsidiary and may grow out of the socio-psychological peculiarity of the groups concerned, they may receive their emphasis from the historical situation involved, or they may be determined by material or cultural traditions. But the one constant is the glorification and embellishment of social contradictions.

In the first type of myth, the realm of real Being, concrete reality is removed from sight. In the second, the role of the individual within the social process is isolated and overestimated; but in the third, the meeting of opposites goes straight to the social contradictions themselves. The ideological mechanism is developed in such a way that the antagonistic character of a given social order is denied more or less indirectly; an image of harmony within established order is created. The meeting of opposites assumes a unique position within the context of such ideological mechanisms. It does not deny the existence of contradictions in the most diverse spheres of culture and life; yet it justifies the contradictions metaphysically.

The following sentence could stand as a motto for this essay: "Political and social problems were transformed for him [Dostoevski] into problems of soul and faith." [41] Anti-intellectualism could hardly be manifested in more pregnant fashion. It is not a question of carrying out an idea, of admitting a sentiment, of respecting an ethical or political position as the only possible one, but of attributing equal validity to the antithetical idea, to a contrary sentiment, to a completely different position. It is never a question of anything very precise or certain; the diversity of life, its alleged depth and inexhaustibility, gives it its peculiar attraction. This expresses the fantasy life of social groups who cannot derive pleasure from a rational analysis of the external world. By reading fiction, however, they can enjoy the apparent diversity of life and resolve its social contradictions irrationally.

4. The national or folk myth assumes the most varied forms in the Dostoevski reception. "His literature is Asia . . . and even the impossible is entirely possible for him. . . . In the last analysis Russian mysticism is . . . yearning and fulfillment at the same time." [42] Or it is simply announced that "theory and life are one and the same to the Russian." [43] The historian Heinrich Friedjung makes a particularly open confession of his acceptance of this national mythology when he refers to Dostoevski's creed of the Russian soul: "If one applies the rules of logic to the religious and political views of Dostoevski, they crumble into contradictions. Here, too, the elementary is more powerful than the mere rational. . . ." [44] This statement recalls another typical element of the national myth, the ever-repeated assurance that Dostoevski is "one of the greatest manifestations of the Russian folk spirit," [45] that "in him . . . the Russian soul has found its most powerful and at the same time most intimate expression," [46] that "in Dostoevski we learn to understand the Russian and through him the Russian people." [47]

Closer inquiry into the nature of this Russian nation leaves us in somewhat of a quandary. We learn of the "Russian soul which splits its thirst for God into earthly pleasure and negating reverie." [48] We are told that there is no other nation "which is so religious in every stratum as the Russian," [49] that the soul of the Russian manifests "itself more directly, more impetuously, more unreservedly than ours." [50] Apart from such vague and intangible characterizations, however, we must be satisfied with the knowledge that Dostoevski and his work offer us "a solution of the problem of Russia," [51] that he "depicts with particular purity the essence of the Russian people, wondrously rich in strength and weakness, riddles and contradictions," [52] in short, that he leads us into the "secret of the national existence." [53]

The most important documentation of this national mythology is to be found in the writings of Moeller van den Bruck, who edited the most widely circulated German editions of Dostoevski's works. Forerunner of German National Socialism, his comments represent a classical example of the social interpretation of the national myths of today. At the beginning of his introduction to *The Pos-*

sessed, van den Bruck speaks of the Russian soul, for which "man himself is a dark yearning after intuition and knowledge." [54] In contrast to the German, the "born carrier of ideas" who can often enough "return as Plato or Kant," the Slavs are "born heralds of faith." "If some day evening comes to Western humanity and the German is at rest, only a Slavic mother could again bear Buddha or Jesus out of the Eastern world." [55] The Russian *Weltanschauung* was transformed into great literary art for the first time in Dostoevski. "The expression of Russian madness, of the tragedy in Slavdom, the incarnation of all its mystical internalizations and hectic tension," [56] he gave Russia its proper mythology of the soul. Russian life is determined by the "overly particularistic, constantly decentralizing racial developments," and on the other hand by the Russian national character—dreamy, sentimental, and resigned to fate, not active and determined. This internalized Russian nature finds expression everywhere, "even when it is unfolded in mad, and even atrocious, deeds."

Dostoevski, van den Bruck continues, was one of the very few novelists of the nineteenth century to say something new, more than Balzac, Flaubert, Zola, or de Maupassant. Only Goethe is comparable. Goethe "imbedded realism further in the spiritual and eternal by giving it a foundation of nature and the rising natural science." [57] Dostoevski went still further and, as "a complete naturalist, showed how modern life too has its mysticism and phantasies." He apprehended life "in its inner demonism . . . with its new beauties and ugliness, its new moralities and immoralities . . . and, instead of degrading naturalism into a mere copy, he again resolved it into a vision." [58] *The Possessed* reveals the demonism in the Russian conception of state and history, which, in view of degenerate social conditions, feverishly drives Russian youth to politics.

The year 1906, in which this introduction to *The Possessed* appeared, marked a definite stage in growth of monopoly, industrial and political, and the essay itself is a symptom of this ideology. If giant economic and political structures were to be accepted by the people, the ideal of competition among men through the development of reason and will had to be replaced by veneration of nonrational ideals removed from the forum of critical verification. It is one of the inherent contradictions of modern society that the growing dominance of rational planning in the economic and political structures should be accompanied by increasing suppression of rational and critical elements in the social consciousness.

Van den Bruck's essay on Dostoevski prepared the way for the development of a false legend about the nineteenth century. This is particularly clear in his oversimplification of the concept of naturalism. He extends it into a visionary, artistic conception of the world, a distortion which has been widely perpetuated, often with the help of references to the widely circulated introduction to *The Possessed*.[59] Van den Bruck denies the relationship of Dostoevski to the great tradition of European, and particularly French, realism and naturalism, and postulates an untenable connection with Goethe. Dostoevski is thus torn out of the real context of the human qualities which the nineteenth century developed, in a succession of artistic figures from Balzac to Zola, all of whom Moeller van den Bruck summarily dismisses. Realism and naturalism in the novel, which acknowledged the necessity for taking an unequivocal stand on the social conflicts, was one of the most important achievements of the nineteenth century. The artistic products of this naturalism, precisely because they strive to reflect real life, constitute an appeal for change.

But for Moeller van den Bruck the decisive element to be gleaned from the traditions and products of the nineteenth century appear under the vague title of "national mythologies." It is no longer history when he asserts that Dostoevski "encompasses in a thousand new answers not only the whole of Russia, but also the whole Slavdom in all its various nationalities, castes, and types, from the simple *mujik* to the Petersburg aristocrat, from the nihilist to the bureaucrat, from the criminal to the saint. . . ."[60] There is not the slightest scientific or even rational ground for asserting that the German is a "born carrier of ideas" (even though Plato is reckoned among the Germans), that the Slavic soul can, in its dark, yearning fashion, create a Buddha or a Jesus, or that the Russian national character is dreamy, sentimental, and submissive to fate rather than active and determined. More recently, such ideologies flourished in the powerful ideologies of totalitarian cultures.

The concept of the mythical, especially the myth of the community, comprises the most essential feature of the Dostoevski reception in Germany. But the material also affords concrete expression for several other basic factors of the social consciousness of the middle class. We shall first examine a factor which may be called *passivity*. This stance reflects the growing impotence of the middle class, and it is expressed in the glorification of the concept of duty and suffering, in the renunciation of any moral action which might be directed against social abuses. Here one comes much closer to social praxis than in the mythical, and the fact that important elements are most noticeable by their absence should not be cause for wonder. Specifically, it is the sphere of activity, and especially moral and political activity, which is missing or, at best, devaluated.

Dostoevski is used as an intellectual weapon against efforts to reorganize society. When his political doctrines are discussed, a malicious or uneasy voice is frequently heard applauding the opponent of revolutions and revolutionaries, the man who warned against political upheavals which bring distress, illness, and unnaturalness in their train. Political action is either condemned as a sin against the universal duty to submit, or transformed into mere inner exaltation, which is declared to be the essence of man. Dostoevski is a prophet of darkness, it is repeatedly said, who "foresaw the nihilist assassinations." [61] It was after the revolution of 1905 and after the publication of the German translation of *The Possessed* in 1906, that his "baleful prophecy" revealed the future of Russia most strikingly.[62] "Many scenes from *The Possessed* are conceived as prophetically as if they were written during the revolution and today." [63] The point is repeatedly made that he "stood up so passionately and relentlessly against socialism." [64] Or: "Socialist Utopias were not only foreign to his nature, but directly counter to it. What inspired him . . . to the strongest loathing for socialism . . . was the moral materialism of this doctrine." [65]

It might be argued that one must not expect an activist approach from the apostle of love and compassion for mankind. Nearly all the literary critiques of Dostoevski do, in fact, revolve about the theme of love and compassion—in elegant formulations such as the "surpassing calm, through which only a sort of deeply secret sorrow vibrates, an endless compassion . . .",[66] or in painfully popular statements, such as "his heart trembles with sympathy, compassion." [67] Or censoriously, "His predilection for the oppressed and the depraved gradually assumes the morbid form of . . . 'Russian compassion,' that compassion which excludes all upright, honest working men, and extends only to prostitutes, murderers, drunkards, and similar blossoms on the tree of mankind." [68]

This statement may be crude, but it underscores the fact that in Dostoevski's work love remains a weak disposition of the soul. We have here a situation similar to the meeting of opposites. The demand for love and compassion could mean a realization of the existence of social contradictions and the need for change; it could lead to the recognition of the value of justice. But the idea of action cannot enter into the consciousness of persons in a relatively impotent social stratum, any more than they can accept a principle of justice which destroys their solidarity with the upper class and points to their common interests with the masses.

It has often been said that Dostoevski had no inner relation to politics, that he was really no political theorist.[69] But how rarely has it been pointed out that the demand for social justice is never proclaimed in his political writings.[70] The irrelevance of this category, a category which finds powerful expression in the outstanding works of European naturalism, that is to say in the most advanced artistic camp, is a clear sign of the reactionary attitude of Dostoevski, and it is still more characteristic of social groups which approve this silence.

II. Ubiquitous Psychology

The most frequent of all attributes of Dostoevski, acknowledged in his reception in Germany before World War I at least, is that of psychologist. The "most learned psychologists" could "take lessons from him." [71] He was a "most subtle psychologist," [72] and "all the psychological skill of the world" pales before Raskolnikov.[73] *The Possessed* penetrates with "overwhelming genius into all the depths of the human soul and its demonism." [74] There are three answers to the question of the precise nature of these extraordinary psychological accomplishments.

1. Dostoevski brings new, hitherto secret and dark psychological facts to light. He knows "the most secret psychic movements of the

human soul." [75] He has an extraordinary talent for revealing "un-perceived stirrings of the soul." [76] He "divines . . . all the uncon-scious, atavistic, and brute forces which stir the dark depths of faltering souls." [77]

2. Dostoevski is a specialist on diseases of the soul, an incom-parable "master of pathological psychology." [78] Some of his works are all "psychological pathology." [79] A theologian claims that Dos-toevski has "depicted the gradual outbreak of a mental illness more accurately" than any other novelist.[80] The same sentiment is ex-pressed by a specialist: "a better expert in the sick psyche, a greater psycho-pathologist, than Dostoevski" has probably never existed among novelists.[81]

3. Dostoevski provides a "unique psychology of crime." [82] Once again we find a specialist saying that in "Dostoevski's works we possess quite a complete, faithful description of diseased mental states and criminal types." [83]

The extent to which Dostoevski may actually have enriched psychological knowledge is a separate question. Like all great novel-ists, he is passionately interested in psychological problems, and many of his characterizations are masterpieces even when consid-ered against the more highly developed knowledge of today. What is important is that Dostoevski as psychologist reinforces the interest of the middle class in psychological problems. This interest has its own significant history. Before the middle-class revolutions in France and Germany, when there were sharp cleavages between the economic mechanism and the forms of political domination and between the intellectual maturity of the bourgeoisie and the feudal cultural apparatus, the protest of the bourgeoisie was expressed in literature as a fiery profession of faith in great passions and the importance of the independent life of the soul. This glorification of passion is, for example, clearly manifest in Goethe's *Werther*. It was a progressive attitude toward life, yet it was incapable of adequate social concretization. The security of feudal economy and its regu-lated market had disappeared, and a well-developed psychology was a necessary presupposition for a liberal economic system. One must know one's business partner; one must know with whom one is dealing. The producer, now opposed by other producers, merchants, and consumers, must know them, must be fully acquainted with their psychology, in order to calculate their possible reactions to himself and his enterprise. This is one of the social origins of the important role played by conversation and discussion in the modern novel and drama. Conversation is one indication of the psychological knowledge which competing individuals in a modern society possess. He who is rationally superior, more adroit, and more dexterous because of his knowledge of the ways in which his conversational partners react, has at his command one of the necessary conditions of economic success.

What was true in the period of middle-class absolutism is being repeated, to a certain extent, in a later phase of German society. Broad strata are again turning to the inner life for satisfaction, particularly in Germany, where liberalism never really gained control because of the merger between the feudal political power and the industrial bourgeoisie. It is an ideological consolation for the middle classes to indulge in psychological "discoveries" (a pleasure limited to the inner life) in precisely the same way as they enjoy the splendor of the German empire and, more recently, the Third Reich—as a satisfaction of imagination.

Pleasure in psychology fits this picture. The restriction of pleasure to one's own inner life acquires luster the more one loses oneself in an orgy of psychological interpretations. In this connection, the enjoyment of psychopathology and criminal psychology has an ideological significance of still another sort. The middle class cannot question the existing social organization as a whole, but must accept and approve it. This system, therefore, is "healthy." Crime and disease are overheads which are inevitable in the operation of the organism, but they are the exceptions of a temporary or peripheral nature which prove the rule, that is, the benign state of the whole.

The study of the reception of works of fiction thus becomes important from a new point of view. It contributes to the study of those factors which, over and above the mere power apparatus, exercise a socially conservative and retarding function through their psychological power. Desires do not disappear entirely, but they must be diverted, and art may help to transform the instincts. The effects of such conversion, the satisfaction of the fancy which the work of art gives, remain enclosed within the sphere of the inner life.

The German commentary on the writings of Dostoevski reveals the following psychological factors.

1. As a psychologist, Dostoevski proceeds "with the cold-bloodedness of an anatomist." [84] "The so-called psychology of Dostoevski reminds one of a mighty laboratory with the finest, most precise tools and machines for the measurement, investigation, and testing of the human soul." [85] This "anatomization of human souls" [86] is "almost gruesome" [87] and "exceedingly cruel." [88] No "corner of the soul" [89] escapes him.

2. From the beginning, attention was directed to the "naked realism and naturalism," [90] the scrupulous fidelity with which Dostoevski portrays the most "depraved characters" and the "most ghastly scenes." [91] His genius gives him insight into the "cesspools of mankind." [92] There is something tawdry about society in all his books. "They contain nothing but usurers, liars, double-crossers, grovelling upstarts, bloated fools, drunkards, and gamblers." [93] In his "repulsive images of dissolute fancy," and in his "splendidly realistic portrayal of national types of criminal and moral monsters," [94] Dostoevski always "sees the soul naked before him in its anxiety and its agitation." [95]

3. An early critic remarks that *Crime and Punishment* lays "an incubus on the breast" of the reader by its "portrayal of a soul burdened with guilt," [96] and this motif of being "breathlessly" clutched by "wild visions" [97] has been maintained throughout. The precise formulations vary, so that one writer states "that a cruel delight permits Dostoevski to torture his reader," [98] another confesses "a very peculiar desire to creep on all fours" after reading Dostoevski,[99] still another experiences "genuine Gothic humility," [100] and to a fourth it signifies that "the horrible possibility of the fall often lives in our dreams. This abyss is Dostoevski." [101] Through all these variations, however, one thing always remains true of Dostoevski and his success—the atmosphere "oppresses the heart and racks the brain." [102]

The picture of the cruel, torturing anatomist, with a predilection for the unclean and the forbidden, appeals to impulses which take pleasure in hurting and tormenting. It also reveals a peculiar contradiction in the reception. The mythical spell cast over the world, the emphasis upon its enigmatic character and upon the "irrationality of the human soul which no knowledge and no culture can set straight," [103] cannot be reconciled with the picture of the anatomist who seeks clarity in the darkest corners. This contradiction symbolizes the contradictory social situation under discussion. The tendencies which transcend reality by making it the symbol of a higher meaning oppose the tendencies which create a sense of imagined power by permitting the experience of aggressions which have no real significance. This contradiction expresses the interrelation of the feelings of resignation and rage.

The social basis of the hymn of overflowing love and endless compassion in Dostoevski now becomes clear. These emotions are not associated with any desire to transform reality, but remain mere inner experiences. Men love or feel compassion, but no consequences are drawn. Such feelings neither remedy a deficiency, nor demand a remedy. Ideal nobility of the soul becomes the reflection of social impotence. It contributes to the satisfaction of the fancy of social groups who have been driven to the wall by reality. Love and compassion are mere social illusions in this context.

Our discussion of the mechanisms of psychological mediation is not complete. We have merely shown how certain impulses and needs are transformed and achieve satisfaction in fancy. These elements of the Dostoevski reception, however, and especially the combination of anatomist and painter of the impure meet with the restraints raised by the Freudian censor. Their nature is such that they are threatened with complete repression by the requirements of morality and conscience. In the make-up of the individual, prohibitions against the satisfaction of impulses may lead to neurosis. This neurosis can be quite typical for specific social strata, and to that extent, it is meaningless to speak of illness. A large section of the middle class has just such neuroses. But the art form of the novel, its social position, is, as it were, the reward for getting around the restraints of the censor. The formal elements in fiction corrupt the conscience, and, in the garb of fancy, permit the satisfaction of impulses which would be unthinkable outside the protective covering of aesthetic value.

Other psychological factors are also at work in the Dostoevski reception to permit the vicarious enjoyment of censored impulses.[104] Sadism acquires still greater luster if it is supposed to contribute to the fulfillment of worthwhile human impulses. If it is crime, prostitution, and the perversions associated with them that present an opportunity to practice love and compassion, then they have been legitimized. The difficulty still remains, however, that, despite all rationalization, novels afford a vicarious enjoyment of the unclean and the repugnant. The final justification for speaking of such things at all lies in the fact that the common, unclean, and loathsome are assigned to declassed outsiders. In this way, pleasure in degradation can be satisfied in the fancy, and this satisfaction and glorification appears in the sphere of politics today. In the political ideologies which are widely accepted by the lower middle class, great emphasis is laid on dragging the dirty linen of one's opponent into the light so that its "stench" may no longer defile the air of a particular social circle. These opponents are characterized as unclean criminal elements, as riff-raff who shun the light of day.

III. Ubiquitous Reception

Our discussion of the reception of Dostoevski into the ideology of the middle classes requires at least a reference to the reception by other groups. We shall illustrate the Dostoevski reception outside the middle classes by examining the attitudes of three critics of Dostoevski: 1) Rollard, contributor to a widely circulated middle-class family journal;[105] 2) the anonymous author of a postscript to the *Brothers Karamazov*,[106] employed by a rather progressive bourgeois publishing house; 3) Zabel,[107] contributor to one of the leading bourgeois political journals (which was working for a unification of all conservative and right-liberal forces),[108] a member of the upper bourgeoisie by his whole demeanor and social consciousness (in 1914 he still designated himself as National-Liberal).[109]

The culture represented by Rollard remains within the framework of simple family life when he restricts himself to the observation that Dostoevski "was the most faithful portrayer of his contemporaries and of the present conditions of his fatherland"; and that "a thorough study of Dostoevski might perhaps be more appropriate for shedding light on Russian conditions . . . which is in

140

many respects quite unlike the conditions of the rest of Europe." Rollard speaks of Russia almost as if it were a wild tribe.

The anonymous author of the postscript to the *Brothers Kara-mazov* has a more enlightened and highly developed interest. He links the book to the Panslavic movement, and even adduces it for an understanding of the *Dreikaiserbund*. Though he regrets that Dostoevski left us in doubt "about the main lines which he had in view for the future organization of the nation," he believes that after the assassination of Alexander II "ideas made headway among the Slavophiles to which Dostoevski, the most illustrious of all the Panslavists and Slavophiles, gave living expression in his *Brothers Karamazov*." This political approach reflects a social conviction that learning can bring profit.

Zabel's approach to Dostoevski as a source of knowledge is still more ingenious and adequate. He ranks Dostoevski as "a highly significant phenomenon in modern literature and a completely indispensable tool for judging the Russian mind." The "recent terrorist movement has shown us how youth takes recourse to assassination." In *Crime and Punishment,* written in 1867, "Dostoevski introduces us to the beginnings of this movement," and provides "an important document for the history of our time" which "must arouse the interest of every cultured person." Here the attitude shows decided partisanship. A spokesman for the upper classes discovers a friend, so to speak, whose "life force and originality" can be praised, whose characters "are properly crammed full of real life." Even Zabel's stylistic tools (like this particular expression, "crammed full"), his emphasis upon the "living element," and his recognition of the "extraordinary force of his fancy and his power of description," of his grasp "of the complete life of man," of his "fully matured artistic nature," lead to a completely different social atmosphere. It is ruled by the possibility of great enjoyment, not limited by the need for regression into more primitive, purely illusory psychic pleasures, nor by weak and irresolute efforts to struggle upward, as expressed in the perpetual accumulation of knowledge. Zabel is the first German who gives the impression that he has read Dostoevski very carefully. And it is precisely this atten-tiveness, with its feeling for nuances, with its accurate understanding of what can be accepted and what must be rejected, in short, an attitude which, unlike the great mass of the reception, is without psychic inhibitions and which grasps and judges things as they are, that is characteristic of the social consciousness of the ruling strata. Zabel finds conditions in his own country entirely sound, and though he shares with the rest of the critics the stock phrases about Dostoevski's "endless sympathy for the oppressed and demonic hatred of the oppressors," the conditions which arouse these feelings in Dostoevski are for him historically and nationally determined. He refers to the "horrible cruelty of Russian justice," to the "Panslavic bias, the provoking insistence upon Russian manner and custom." It is noteworthy that not a single reference can be found in Zabel's essay to the whole sphere of mythical ideology.

This example of reception by the upper class finds its counterpart at the other extreme, in proletarian circles. At first, the literary spokesmen of the proletariat remained quite faithful to the conventional bourgeois picture. Rosus, for example, in his article in the *Neue Zeit* for 1884, has a purely didactic approach and uses the traditional literary categories. Apart from his remark that Dostoevski portrayed the Russian Socialists and Communists as mere "babblers and numbskulls," Rosus repeats the stock phrases, "cold-bloodedness of the anatomist," "case history of disease," "naked realism." The theoretical understanding of proletarian writers had to reach a higher level before they could formulate a clear and correct statement of the Dostoevski problem.

When we turn to Korn's essay in the *Neue Zeit* for 1908,[110] we find that all ideological character has vanished. From a proletarian position, Korn gives a better class analysis of Dostoevski than Zabel, with his upper bourgeois attitude. He calls *The Possessed* a "reactionary poisoner" (with all due recognition of "Dostoevski the novelist and *Weltanschauung*-visionary"). It is absurd to look to this work of Dostoevski for an understanding of the Russian Revolution of 1905, since there was no "revolutionary, *i.e.*, class conscious proletariat" in the book (nor did such a proletariat exist in Russia at that time), but only "declassed nobility and petty bourgeoisie, a rabble between the classes." Korn perceives the deeper ideology-forming factors in this novel, and he notes "the paradox, bewildering at first sight, that an ideology, which in its original form may

142

have been an accurate reflection of the economic and political situation of Russia in the '50s and '60s, is experiencing a rebirth in monopoly capitalist Germany of the twentieth century." He realizes how little Dostoevski's novel contributes to a real knowledge of historical and social relationships, how little the treatment reflects even the prerevolutionary social conditions, and how its atmosphere is "pure intellectual and ethical chaos." It is precisely those blurred tones in the development, motivation, and style of the book which give it its ideological value for the bourgeois German public: "What the literary spokesmen of our bourgeoisie have recently proclaimed as a discovery, namely, that it is not man's consciousness but his subconscious which is important, that everything worthwhile in the soul begins where the mind ends and the 'depths' open up—that was, in fact, the programmatic psychology, the *Weltanschauung* of Dostoevski fifty years before." It must be remembered that Korn is not attacking the scientific activities of psychoanalysis, which was itself subject to the unanimous opposition of the official scientific world; he is attacking the anti-intellectual currents which appear in the myth of the demonism of the soul, in the enchantment of personalization of reality.

In the post-World War I reception of Dostoevski we find the same ideological factors as before the war, with even more abundant documentation. Immediately after the war, the myth of the inner life was predominant because of the general breakdown of social organization in Germany and, more specifically, because of the final dispossession of the middle class. More recently, however, the national myth has come to the fore as a model for the growing heroic-racial ideology. The radical tendencies of Dostoevski, though badly distorted in his writings, exercised a measure of influence upon the young German intellectuals immediately after the war, but this was an influence for socio-political radicalization only where other more powerful forces had already set in. The great mass of these intellectuals were confined to middle-class conceptions, and Dostoevski could perform a particular ideological service for them. Since he was labeled a product of the Russian nature and since the study of his works was supposed to give a clear insight into that nature, it followed that the key to the understanding of Bolshevism had also been found. Dostoevski can be put to extensive use in providing an

imaginary solution whereby such middle-class groups can avoid a
real analysis of the problem of transforming the social system, by
satisfying anal-sadistic drives in the fancy and, at the same time,
condemning them with the help of rationalizations buried in Dostoevski's writings.

The post-World War I phase of the reception points in two
directions: 1) Dostoevski was placed in the intellectual context of
Kierkegaard, Karl Barth, and the whole of dialectical theology.
Indifference to earthly things, glorification of the individual, his
inner world, and his relation to God, thus acquire extraordinary
importance. This view is bound up with a social consciousness which
hopes for nothing more from the present; it belongs to the circle
of resigned strata. 2) The other tendency represents the politically
dominant groups. It endorsed the national element in Dostoevski,
but with limits imposed by the prevailing German ideology of
Dostoevski's "racial" inadequacy.

The Reception of Dostoevski's Work in Germany: 1880-1920

[1] Comprehensive documentation limited to the period ending 1918.

[2] Good but incomplete bibliographical references are to be found in The-
oderich Kampmann, *Dostojewski in Deutschland* (Münster: 1931, first published
in 1930 as a dissertation).

[3] Franz Sandvoss, "F. M. Dostojewski," *Preussische Jahrbuecher*, XCII (1899),
pp. 330-41.

[4] Hermann Conradi, "F. M. Dostojewski," *Die Gesellschaft*, V (1889), pp.
520-30.

[5] See, for example, the chapter headings in R. Guardini, *Der Mensch und
der Glaube; Versuche uber die religiöse Existenz in Dostojewskis grossen
Romanen* (Leipzig: 1933): "The People and Its Way to Holiness," "Silence and
the Great Acceptance," "Ecclesiastics," "The Cherub," "Revolt," "Godlessness,"
"A Symbol of Christ." Cf. titles like "Faith as the Will to Spirit," "The Experience of Being Real for Man: in His Relation to the Whole Disegoistic You: to
God," in K. Nötzel, *Das Leben Dostojewskis* (Leipzig: 1925).

[6] K. Weiss, review of several of Dostoevski's novels, *Hochland*, VI (1908), p.
364.

[7] O. J. Bierbaum, "Dostojewski," *Die Zukunft*, XVIII (1909), p. 186.

[8] O. Kaus, "Dostojewskis Briefe," *Die weissen Blatter*, I (1913/14), p. 1353.

[9] L. Beer, "Quo vadis," *Die Nations*, XVIII (1900/01), p. 793; and K. H.
Strobl, "Dostojewski, Russland und die Revolution," *Die Gegenwart*, XXXVI
(1907), p. 87.

[10] Georg Brandes, *Dostojewski, ein Essay* (Berlin: 1889), p. 3; cf. Strobl, *op.
cit.* and Bierbaum, *op. cit.*

The Reception of Dostoevski's Work in Germany: 1880-1920

[11] H. Coralnik, *Das Russenbuch* (Strassburg: 1914), p. 20.
[12] W. Scholz, "Dostojewski," *Westermanns Monatshefte*, XXXIII (1888/89), p. 766.
[13] Hermann Bahr in Bahr, D. Mereschkowski, and O. J. Bierbaum, *Dostojewski: 3 Essays* (München, 1914), p. 15.
[14] Bierbaum, *op. cit,.* p. 197.
[15] Leo Berg, *Der Übermensch in der modernen Literatur* (Leipzig: 1898), p. 111.
[16] Strobl, *op. cit.*
[17] O. Stossl, "Die Briefe von Dostojewski," *Der neue Merkur*, I (1914), p. 499.
[18] Adolf Stern, *Geschichte der neuen Literatur* (Leipzig: 1885), VII, p. 550.
[19] Mereschkowski, *Tolstoi and Dostojewski als Mensch und als Künstler* (Leipzig: 1903), p. 39.
[20] Frieda Freiin von Bülow, "Dostojewski in Deutschland," *Das Literarische Echo*, IX (1906), p. 204.
[21] Bierbaum, *op. cit.*
[22] Stefan Zweig, "Dostojewski, Die Tragödie seines Lebens," *Der Merkur*, V (1914), p. 106.
[23] Mereschkowski, *op. cit.*, p. 222.
[24] K. Nötzel, "Dostojewski," *März*, V (1911), p. 301.
[25] Stern, *Geschichte der neuen Literatur*, VII, p. 550.
[26] M. Necker, "Dostojewski," *Die Grenzboten*, XLIV (1885), p. 349.
[27] Mereschkowski, *Tolstoi und Dostojewski*, p. 92.
[28] Strobl, *Die Gezenwart*, XXXVI, p. 87.
[29] R. Saitschik, *Die Weltanschauung Dostojewskis und Tolstois* (Halle: 1901), p. 9.
[30] *Ibid.*, p. 2.
[31] Coralnik, *Das Russenbuch*, p. 20.
[32] Brandes, *Dostojewski, ein Essay*, p. 3.
[33] Kurt Eisner, "Raskolnikov," *Sozialistische Monatshefte*, V (1901), p. 52.
[34] N. Hoffmann, *Dostojewski, eine biographische Studie* (Berlin: 1899), p. 2.
[35] F. Servaes, "Dostojewski," *Die Zukunft*, XXXI (1900), p. 258.
[36] Brandes, *op. cit.*
[37] Strobl, *op. cit.*
[38] Weiss, *Hochland*, VI, p. 364.
[39] Bierbaum, *Die Zukunft*, XVIII, p. 196.
[40] Bahr, *Dostojewski: 3 Essays*, p. 15.
[41] Hoffmann, *op. cit.*
[42] Strobl, *Die Gegenwart*, XXXVI, p. 87.
[43] Joseph Müller, *Dostojewski—ein Charakterbild* (München: 1903), p. 183.
[44] Heinrich Friedjung, *Das Zeitalter des Imperialismus* (Berlin: 1922), III, p. 142.
[45] Joseph Melnik, introduction to A. S. Wolynski, *Buch vom grossen Zorn* (Frankfurt: 1905), p. v.
[46] Theodor Heuss, "Dostojewskis Revolutionsroman," *Die Hilfe*, XII (1906), p. 9.
[47] M. Schian, "Dostojewski," *Die christliche Welt*, XXVI (1912), p. 205.
[48] Hoffmann, *Dostojewski*, p. 425.
[49] Müller, *op. cit.*
[50] Bülow, *Das Literarische Echo*, IX, p. 204.
[51] Weiss, *Hochland*, VI, p. 364.

[52] Bülow, *op. cit.*

[53] Melnik, *op. cit.*

[54] Moeller van den Bruck, introduction to Dostoevski, *The Possessed*, Piper-Verlag edition (München, (1906), reprinted in *Die Zukunft*, XIV (1906), p. 66; we shall cite the article in *Die Zukunft*.

[55] Moeller van den Bruck, *Die Zukunft, loc. cit.*

[56] Moeller van den Bruck, *Die Zukunft, loc. cit.*

[57] Moeller van den Bruck, *op. cit.*, p. 68.

[58] Moeller van den Bruck, *Die Zukunft, loc. cit.*

[59] Thus Heuss, *Die Hilte*, XII, p. 9, speaks of the "spiritual character" of Dostoevski's naturalism. Strobl, *Die Gegenwart*, XXXVI, p. 87, says that naturalism is transformed into mysticism in Dostoevski: "The naturalistic . . . becomes phantomlike as soon as we seek to focus our eyes upon it."

[60] Moeller van den Bruck, *op. cit.*

[61] A. von Reinholdt, *Geschichte der russischen Literatur* (Leipzig: 1886), p. 695.

[62] L. Brehm, "Dostojewskis 'Dämonen,'" *Der Deutsche*, V (1906), p. 342.

[63] Weiss, Hochland, VI, p. 364.

[64] Müller, *Dostojewski*, p. 131.

[65] Mereschkowski, *Dostojewski: 3 Essays*, p. 33.

[66] Conradi, *Die Gesellschaft*, p. 528.

[67] Brehm, *op. cit.*, p. 346.

[68] C. Busse, *Geschichte der Weltliteratur* (Bielfeld and Leipzig; 1913), II, p. 595.

[69] Cf. Thomas Mann, *Betrachtungen eines Unpolitischen* (Berlin; 1920), pp. 532-44.

[70] In the *Politische Schriften* (München, 1917), the word "just" occurs only once, if I am not mistaken—and then in a quotation from Tolstoi (Cf. pp. 232 and 234). Belief in "the solidarity of men" also appears but once—and then it is a matter of establishing that "peace brutalizes much more than war" (pp. 415-16). A plea for "active love" is also made—but when it is put into concrete form, it never rises above the level of vague exhortations: "Be but straightforward and sincere" (p. 247).

[71] E. Brausewetter, "Der Idiot," *Die Gegenwart*, XXXVI (1889), p. 73.

[72] O. Hauser, *Der Roman des Auslands seit 1800* (Leipzig: 1913), p. 165.

[73] Emil Lucka, "Das Problem Raskolnikows," *Das Literarische Echo*, XVI (1913/14), p. 1099.

[74] Johann Schlaf, in *Buchbesprechungen des Piper-Verlags* (1914)—appendix to Bahr, Mereschkowski, and Bierbaum, *Dostojewski: 3 Essays*.

[75] P. von Wiskowatow, *Geschichte der russischen Literatur* (Dorpat and Fellin: 1881), p. 44.

[76] Stern, *Geschichte der neuen Literatur*, p. 550.

[77] E. Hennequin, "Dostojewski," *Die Gesellschaft*, XVI (1900), p. 337.

[78] W. Henckel, "Dostojewski," *Das Magazin für die Literatur*, LI (1882), p. 78.

[79] G. Malkowski, "Der Hahnrei," *Die Gegenwart*, XXXIII (1888), p. 408.

[80] J. Leipoldt, *Vom Jesusbild der Gegenwart* (Leipzig: 1913), p. 339.

[81] F. Münzer, "Dostojewski als Psychopathologe," *Berliner Klinische Wochenschrift*, XXVII (1914), p. 1943.

[82] Necker, *Die Grenzboten*, XLIV, p. 344.

[83] W. von Tschish, "Die Verbrechertypen in Dostojewskis Schriften," *Die*

Umschau, V (1901), p. 961. Cf. J. Stern, "Über den Wert der dichterischen Behandlung des Verbrechens für die Strafrechtswissenschaft," *Zeitschrift für die gesamte Strafrechtswissenschaft*, XXVI (1906), p. 163.

[84] Rosus, "Ein russischer Roman," *Die neue Zeit*, II (1884), pp. 2-12.

[85] Mereschkowski, *Tolstoi und Dostojewski*, p. 236.

[86] Scholz, *Westermanns Monatshefte*, XXXIII, p. 766.

[87] Saitschik, *Die Weltanschauung*, p. 9.

[88] Bülow, *Das Literarische Echo*, IX, p. 204.

[89] Münzer, *Berliner Klinische Wochenschrift*, XXVII, p. 1945.

[90] For example, J. J. Honegger, *Russische Literatur und Kultur* (Leipzig: 1880), p. 146. Rosus, *op. cit.*, p. 2.

[91] *Magazin für die Literatur des Auslands*, XXXVI (1867), p. 317.

[92] Brandes, *Dostojewski*, p. 7.

[93] Brausewetter, *Die Gegenwart, XXXVI*, p. 73.

[94] Reinholdt, *Geschichte der russischen Literatur*, p. 693.

[95] R. M. Meyer, "Das russische Dreigestirn," *Oesterreichische Rundschau*, XVI (1908), p. 39.

[96] Henckel, *Das Magazin*, LI, p. 73.

[97] Brausewetter, *op. cit.*, p. 72.

[98] A. Garbell, "Ein Dostojewski-Gedenktag," *Das Magazin*, LXV (1898), p. 183.

[99] Max Harden, *Literature and Theater* (Berlin: 1896), p. 80.

[100] Nötzel, *März*, V, p. 309. Cf. Bierbaum, *Dostojewski: 3 Essays*, p. 192.

[101] Strobl, *Die Gegenwart*.

[102] G. Malkowsky, "Die Besessenen," *Die Gegenwart*, XXXIII (1888), p. 42.

[103] Hoffmann, *Dostojewski*, p. 398.

[104] See Freud, "Mourning and Melancholia," *Collected Papers*, trans. supervised by Joan Riviere (London: 1924-25), IV, pp. 152-70.

[105] G. Rollard, "Dostojewskis Roman 'Raskolnikow,'" *Das Magazin für die Literatur*, LI (1882), pp. 291-92.

[106] "Dostojewski," in *Brüder Karamazov* (Leipzig: Grunow-Verlag, 1884), IV, 328-31.

[107] E. Zabel, "F. M. Dostojewski," *Die Gegenwart*, XXV (1884), p. 307 ff. reprinted, characteristically enough, in the extreme upper bourgeois *Deutsche Rundschau*, LIX (1889), pp. 361-91. For a discussion of the social role of the latter journal, see *Zeitschrift für Sozialforschung*, II (1933), pp. 59-62.

[108] Cf. Erich Leupold, *Die Aussenpolitik in den bedeutendsten politischen Zeitschriften Deutschlands 1890-1909* (Leipzig: 1933), especially pp. 9-10.

[109] *Wer ist's?* (Berlin: 1914), p. 1900; note the list of his extensive travels.

[110] E. Korn, book review of *Die Dämonen*, in *Die neue Zeit*, XXVI, (1907/08), I, pp. 503-4.

Six

"ROBINSON CRUSOE"
AS A MYTH

Watt's examination of the meanings of *Robinson Cru-soe* is an admirable example of that sophistication in sociological approach for which he argues abstractly in Chapter 11 ("Literature and Society"). He presents us with an extraordinary exercise in content analysis based on two primary techniques: a close, subtle, perceptive reading of the novel; and a detailed contextual study which relates *Robinson Crusoe* to the history of ideas, to the audiences of its era—and of ours. Although Watt's own profession is literature rather than social science, his awareness of the social framework of capitalism and its myths renders his work equally valuable to the sociologist and the literary critic.

Perhaps the most striking theme of the essay is the demonstration that readers have bent the substance of Defoe's creation to fit their own ideological contours. Whether deliberately or not, Watt shows that society—or at least some articulate critics—has made of *Crusoe* "only what its unconscious needs

148

dictate." He raises an exceedingly important question about the relations between an author's intent, his text as given, and the audience's responsive inclinations. He builds a strong case for the proposition that this story has been subject to systematic distortion in the service of preferred myth. The popular view of the book illustrates that selective perception embodied in Tomlinson's aphorism, ". . . we see things not as they are, but as we are." Like Lowenthal's discussion of Dostoevski in the previous chapter, Watt's account views literature as being in some sense a "projective test" for the company of readers, an ambiguous manifold of stimuli upon which the audience may trace its heart's desire. When the authors of *1066 And All That* caution us that "history is not what you thought, but what you can remember," they point to the fact that the influence of art on society depends as much on the nature of the audience and its chosen distortions or emphases as on the manifest content of art itself.

On the figure of Crusoe society erected a favored image of economic man, an archetype of the individual entrepreneur. In a curious way we find Crusoe a solitary hero, a socially isolated man who is at the same time psychologically secure because he has a stolid inner determination and acts precisely as the absent society would supposedly have him act. Is he David Riesman's "inner-directed" individual incarnate? Crusoe might be compared with the solitary hero of the modern novel, with Stephen Daedalus or Eugene Gant, the man immersed in society but psychologically alone. If the contemporary hero is also inner-directed, he lacks Crusoe's self-assurance and Crusoe's confidence that economic rationality is a worthy means, as profit is a worthy and comprehensive goal. But the contrast should not be overdrawn; Watt notes Defoe's lack of realism in preserving his hero from the physical and mental terrors of isolation, and social psychology affirms that intercourse with others is the essence of becoming and remaining human.

Watt elaborates the classical interpretations of *Robinson Crusoe,* placing the myth properly in the mainstream of the spirit of capitalism and individualism. Since the myth lives on, it might be entertaining to assess the response of contemporary naïve readers. If changes in the audience shape the *effective* content of a work of art, what is the meaning of *Crusoe* to schoolchildren of the mid twentieth century? Their responses across classes and cultures could be the basis of a revealing study in social change—or perhaps in social sameness.

"ROBINSON CRUSOE"
AS A MYTH

Ian Watt

We do not usually think of *Robinson Crusoe* as a novel. Defoe's first full-length work of fiction seems to fall more naturally into place with *Faust, Don Juan,* and *Don Quixote,* the great myths of our civilization. What these myths are about it is fairly easy to say. Their basic plots, their enduring images, all exhibit a single-minded pursuit by the protagonist of one of the characteristic aspirations of Western man. Each of their heroes embodies an *arete* and a *hubris,* an exceptional prowess and a vitiating excess, in spheres of action that are peculiarly important in our culture. Don Quixote, the impetuous generosity and the limiting blindness of chivalric idealism; Don Juan, pursuing and at the same time tormented by the idea of boundless experience of women; Faustus, the great knower, whose curiosity, always unsatisfied, causes him to be damned.

Crusoe does not at first seem a likely companion for these other culture heroes. They lose the world for an idea; he, for gain. Their aspirations are conscious and defiant, so that when retribution comes it is half expected and already understood; whereas Robinson Crusoe disclaims either heroism or pride; he stolidly insists that he is no more than he seems, that you would do it too in the circumstances.

From *Essays in Criticism: a Quarterly Journal of Literary Criticism* (April 1951), pp. 95-119. Reprinted by permission of the publisher and author.

Yet of his apotheosis there can be no doubt. By the end of the nineteenth century, *Crusoe* had appeared in at least seven hundred editions, translations, and imitations, not to mention a popular eighteenth-century pantomime and an opera by Offenbach.[1] There are other more picturesque examples of his fame. In 1848 an enterprising French industrialist started a restaurant up a tree, a particularly fine chestnut in a wood near Paris: he called it "Robinson," and now restaurateurs vie for the title in a village of that name.[2] In France, again, "un robinson" has become a popular term for a large umbrella.

Nor, as Virginia Woolf has pointed out,[3] is Robinson Crusoe usually thought of as a hero of fiction. Instead, partly because of Defoe's verisimilitude and partly for deeper reasons, his author's name has been forgotten, while he himself has acquired a kind of semihistorical status, like the traditional heroes of myth. When his story appeared it is reported to have been "universally received and credited as a genuine history";[4] and we today can surely apply to it Malinowski's description of primitive myths: "It is not of the nature of fiction, such as we read today in a novel, but it is a living reality, believed to have once happened in primeval times, and continuing ever since to influence the world and human destinies."[5]

Almost universally known, almost universally thought of as at least half real, he cannot be refused the status of myth. But the myth of what?

It is at first difficult to answer, especially if we take into account the later portions of the Crusoe trilogy. For Defoe at once cashed in on the success of the *Strange and Surprising Adventures of Robinson Crusoe* with two other books, the *Farther Adventures* and the *Serious Reflections.* They complicate the answer because, though the character is the same, he is no longer on the island. But perhaps there is no need to consider them in detail. Myth always tends in transmission to be whittled down to a single, significant situation. Hardly anyone knows the later books of the trilogy; the stark facts of the hero's island existence occupy almost all our attention, and the rest is largely forgotten or plays a very secondary role. Even the other portions of the first volume of the trilogy, comprising the early adventures and the eventual return to civilization, though better known, are hardly part of the myth, which retains only the

151

island episode. But even if we ask what is the essential social meaning of that one episode, that solitude, many answers suggest themselves.

Defoe himself gives two main explanations for Crusoe's solitude. At times Crusoe feels he is being punished for irreligion;[6] at
others for his filial disobedience in leaving home—in the *Farther
Adventures* he even accuses himself of having "killed his father."[7]
But Crusoe as a man isolated from God, or as a modern Oedipus,
is not our subject here. For the myth as it has taken shape in our
minds is surely not primarily about religious or psychological
alienation, nor even about solitude as such. Crusoe lives in the
imagination mainly as a triumph of human achievement and enterprise, and as a favorite example of the elementary processes of
political economy. So, in our attempt to understand the causes for
Crusoe's apotheosis, we will look first at the relationship of his
story to some of the enduring traits of our social and economic history.

It is easy to see that *Robinson Crusoe* is related to three essential themes of modern civilization—which we can briefly desig-
nate as "Back to Nature," "The Dignity of Labor," and "Economic
Man." Robinson Crusoe seems to have become a kind of culture
hero representing all three of these related but not wholly con-
gruent ideas. It is true that if we examine what Defoe actually
wrote and what he may be thought to have intended, it appears that
Robinson Crusoe hardly supports some of the symbolic uses to
which the pressure of the needs of our society has made it serve. But
this, of course, is in keeping with the status of *Robinson Crusoe* as
a myth, for we learn as much from the varied shapes that a myth
takes in men's minds as from the form in which it first arose. It is
not an author but a society that metamorphoses a story into a myth,
by retaining only what its unconscious needs dictate and forgetting
everything else.

I

The term "Back to Nature" covers the many and varied forms
of primitivism, of revulsion from the contemporary complexities of

civilization into a simpler and more "natural" order. The movement necessarily features two forms of regress: technological and
topographical; a simpler economic structure and its associated rural
setting. Both are involved in *Robinson Crusoe,* and it is interesting
to see that Rousseau, the great prophet of both these trends, was the
first to see in it something which far transcended the status of a
mere adventure story. The book played an important role in his
imaginative experience, and he frequently referred to it. The most
famous reference occurs in *Émile.*[8] There, after announcing that in
principle "he hates books" and that he is determined to correct the
predominantly bookish tendency of traditional methods of education, Rousseau solemnly proclaims an exception. One book exists
which teaches all that books can teach. It is "the first that my Émile
will read; it will for a long time be the whole contents of his library;
and it will always hold an honoured place there. . . . What then is
this marvelous book? Is it Aristotle? Is it Pliny? Is it Buffon? No,
it is *Robinson Crusoe.*"

The hero, alone on his island, deprived of all assistance from
his fellows, and nevertheless able to look after himself, is obviously
a figure that will enthral readers of all ages. The book's consequent
entertainment value renders palatable the moral and philosophical
teachings which are Rousseau's main concern. We cannot here give
a full account of them, but two are particularly relevant. One is
based on the descriptions of Crusoe's labors: they will fire Émile's
imagination with the practical, natural, and manual education to
which he is destined. Bacon, Comenius, and Locke had urged this
change of emphasis, but Rousseau takes it very much further; Defoe's story, a box of tools, and the philosopher of Geneva, these will
suffice Émile: anything more would be superfluous, nay vicious.

But the pattern which Émile must imitate is not only that of
the simple life of toil. Crusoe also stands for another of Rousseau's
favorite ideas—radical individualism. To attain this way of life,
Rousseau believes that "the surest way to raise oneself above
prejudices and to order one's judgment on the real relationship between things, is to put oneself in the place of an isolated man, and
to judge of everything as that man would judge them, according to
their actual usefulness."[9] Hence, again, the pre-eminent utility of

Robinson Crusoe as a basic text: for the hero's life is its demonstration.

The book as Defoe wrote it (strictly speaking, the *Life and Strange Surprising Adventures* as Saint Hyacinthe and Van Effen transposed it into the more formal French literary tradition)[10] is not perfect. So Rousseau proposes a version freed of all "fatras";[11] one which was in fact that of the myth. The story was to begin with the shipwreck and to end with the rescue: Émile's book would be less instructive if it ended in the way Defoe's actually does—with a return to civilization.

Defoe, of course, would have been surprised at this canonization of his story. His surprise would have been increased by Rousseau's other references where Crusoe becomes a sort of John the Baptist, who in his solitude made straight the ways of the final incarnation of the extravagancies of romantic individualism. For Crusoe is after all a *"solitaire malgré lui,"* as Paul Nourrison points out in his *Jean-Jacques Rousseau et Robinson Crusoë.*[12] He is an involuntary and unappreciative prisoner of the beauties of nature. Rousseau was a botanist but Crusoe is a seed merchant: and the moral of his activities is quite different from that which Rousseau extracts. Indeed, if we, perhaps unwisely, attempt to draw any general conclusions from Crusoe's life on the island, it must surely be that out of humanity's repertoire of conceivable designs for living, rational economic behavior alone is entitled to ontological status. Crusoe "returns to nature" only according to Defoe's characteristic definition of that accommodating word: in his newspaper, the *Review,* Defoe had written that "Nothing follows the course of Nature more than Trade. There Causes and Consequences follow as directly as day and night." [13] So in the island the nature of the universe is most importantly manifested in the rationality of the processes of economic life. There are the "real relationships between things" which Crusoe discovers, relationships whose value and interest come from the way they help man to secure the maximum utility from his environment.

Defoe's "nature" appeals not for adoration but for exploitation: the island solitude is an exceptional occasion not for undisturbed self-communion, but for strenuous efforts at self-help. Inspired with this belief, Crusoe observes nature, not with the eyes of a pantheist primitive, but with the calculating gaze of colonial capitalism; wherever he looks he sees acres that cry out for improvement, and as he settles down to the task he glows, not with noble savagery, but purposive possession.

The interest of Rousseau and Defoe in a "state of nature" has only one motive in common: it and it alone will allow them to realize without interference their own thwarted vocations. The island offers exemplary opportunities for total laissez faire: or perhaps we should say, for *laisse-moi faire*—to put the doctrine in psychological terms, terms which help to explain its appeal to Rousseau.

But the vocations are different, and indeed contradictory. The primitive setting of the island which is Rousseau's goal is only a starting point for Crusoe. He finds himself on a desert island, but he has no intention of letting it remain as such. Rousseau wanted to flee the complication and corruptions of the town, to take refuge in a solitary pastoral retreat: Defoe's solution of the dilemma is much more deeply representative of our culture. If the pace gets too fast at home, go overseas—not to pastoral retreats but to colonies. There the imagination is fired by a splendid prospect which shows the true and necessary conclusion of the ancient conflict between urban and rural ways of life. That conflict can only be resolved in one way —by the urbanization of the countryside. The new culture hero's task is done only when he has taken possession of his colony and stocked it with an adequate labor force; presumably Rousseau did not read *The Farther Adventures of Robinson Crusoe,* where his favorite hero rejoices that "never was there such a little city in a wood." [14] But this is the ultimate message of Defoe's story. The most desolate island cannot retain its natural order; wherever the white man brings his rational technology there can only be manmade order, and the jungle itself must succumb to the irresistible teleology of capitalism.

II

That is the direction which Defoe gives his story. It is fundamentally antiprimitivist. If many readers have interpreted it as a "back to nature" story, they have done so to satisfy their own needs, and have interpreted quite contrary to Defoe's general development of his theme. The implications of *Robinson Crusoe* are equally equivocal as regards "the dignity of labor": but the immediate justification for seeing in it a panegyric of work is a good deal stronger.

Rousseau saw Defoe's story as an object lesson in the educational virtues of manual labor; and Crusoe does indeed draw the correct moral from this activity:

By stating and squaring everything by reason, and by making the most rational judgment of things, every man may be in time master of every mechanic art. I had never handled a tool in my life, and yet in time, by labour, application and contrivance, I found at last that I wanted nothing but I could have made it, especially if I had had tools.[15]

The pleasures of this discovery to Crusoe and his readers are largely the result of the *division of labor*. The term is Adam Smith's, but he was to a large extent anticipated by Defoe's contemporary, Bernard Mandeville.[16] The process to which the term refers, and which, of course, began very early in human history, was at that time as far advanced in England as anywhere. This advanced development of the division of labor is an important condition of the creation and immediate success of *Robinson Crusoe,* just as the later accelerated development of the process is a condition of the subsequent triumph of the myth. For the main processes by which man secures food, clothing, and shelter are only likely to become interesting when they have become alien to his common, everyday experience. To enjoy the description of the elementary productive processes reveals a sophisticated taste. Obviously, primitive peoples can never forget for a day what Crusoe announces with the tones of one making a discovery: "It might be truly said that now I began to work for my bread. 'Tis a little wonderful, and what I believe few people have thought much upon, viz., the strange multitude of little things necessary in the providing, producing, curing, dressing, making and finishing this one article of bread." [17] The account continues for seven pages, and each detail is new or at least unfamiliar, and reminds us of the vast ignorance that separated production and consumption in the London of Defoe's day, an ignorance that has inevitably increased since then, and that surely explains much of the fascination we find in reading the detailed descriptions of Crusoe's island labors.

Rousseau was very much aware of these factors. In his political and economic writings the development of the arts and sciences past the stage of patriarchal simplicity, and the consequent growth of the division of labor, urbanization, and the political state, are the villains.[18] One deplorable result is to separate manual from mental labor. For Rousseau's purposes, therefore, *Robinson Crusoe* was a valuable corrective to the unnatural intellectualism which society inflicts upon the middle class.

Progressive education and the arts and crafts movement owe a good deal to Rousseau's pages on *Robinson Crusoe* in *Émile*. Educationalists try to rectify many of the results of the division of labor and of urbanization by including in the curriculum many of the practical and manual activities which Crusoe pursued on the island and which Rousseau recommended for his pupil. In the adult sphere, many reformers have attempted to bridge the gap between the allegedly inventive, satisfying, and humanizing processes of primitive methods of production and the dehumanizing effects of most economic activities under capitalism. The Arts and Crafts movement, for example, and the cult of the rough edge, are two of the most obvious attempts to remedy the social and esthetic effects of the division of labor in industrial capitalism with an artificial primitivism in technique and way of life. The same attempted diagnosis and remedy—in which one can often detect a residue of moral and religious overtones—can be traced in many of the modern forms of leisure activity. It seems typical of our civilization to try to palliate the distortions of specialization by reintroducing the basic economic processes in the guise of recreations. In school, and in later life, it is suggested, by such pursuits as gardening, home weaving, woodwork, the keeping of pets, we can all partake of Crusoe's character-forming satisfactions.

There are other aspects of the glorification of labor which are relevant to the function of *Robinson Crusoe* as a myth. Many political reformers since Rousseau have been occupied with the idea of rectifying the effects of the division of labor in the whole of the economic and political system. Both on the right and the left they

157

have tried to realize in practice, by new social arrangements, the ideal of the dignity of labor.

For Marx, man and man's universe are the products of work. Marx's political system was designed with the idea that human labor under changed conditions could undo the contemporary estrangement of most men from their labor and recreate a society where all economic activities would increase each individual's moral stature. William Morris and the Guild Socialists in advocating a return to a simpler communal economy suggested a different road: but they were trying to achieve the same moral end, and accepted, in the main, Marx's analysis of the real conditions of human labor in the society of their day. And on the right, Samuel Smiles, for example, was also trying to persuade us that hard work even in the present state of society is the key to all: that *labor omnia vincit*.[19] Much of Carlyle's political theory and moral teaching derives from his idea that the great lesson is "Know what thou canst work at." All these and many others—educationalists, moralists, social and political reformers, publicists, economic theorists—seem to base themselves upon a dogma which finds its supreme narrative realization on Crusoe's island.

The reader's ignorance of the basic processes of production is not the only source of the appeal of Crusoe's island labors. He is also affected by the obscure ethical and religious overtones which pervade Defoe's intense concentration upon each stage of Crusoe's exertions. Eventually, they fasten upon our imaginative life a picture of the human lot as heroic only when productive, and of man as capable of redemption only through untiring labor. As we read we share in an inspiring and yet wholly credible demonstration of the vitality and interest of all the basic economic pursuits. If we draw a moral, it can only be that for all the ailments of man and his society, Defoe confidently prescribes the therapy of work.

The extent both of Defoe's concern with labor, and that of the whole ideology of our culture, is certainly unprecedented. Older cultural traditions would probably have seen *Robinson Crusoe* as a glorification of the purely contingent (if not wholly deplorable) aspects of human experience. Certainly most of their myths, the Golden Fleece, Midas, and the Rheingold are concerned, not with the process by which people ordinarily manage to subsist, but with

158

the sudden magical seizure of wealth: ultimately, they are inspired by the prospect of never having to work again.

Defoe's interest in labor is part of the ideology of a new and vast historical process. The dignity of labor is the central creed of the religion of capitalism. In this religion Marx figures as the arch-schismatic who—like all heretics—became so by taking one part of the creed too seriously and trying to apply it universally and inconveniently.

It is impossible to deal summarily with this creed. But some attention to that part of it which is directly related to the creation of *Robinson Crusoe* seems necessary.

It is no accident that the idea of the dignity of labor sounds typical of the Victorian Age, for it was then that the new ideology was most publicly and variously established. But actually, of course, the "gospel of work" was by no means new even in 1719. In ancient Greece, Cynics and Stoics had opposed the denigration of manual labor which is a necessary part of a slave-owning society's scale of values. In the Christian tradition labor had never been a dishonorable estate. In the sixteenth century, Protestantism, in harmony with the obscure needs of social and economic change, revived and expanded an old belief until it loomed much larger in the total picture of the human lot. The Biblical view that labor was a curse for Adam's disobedience was displaced by the idea that hard work —untiring stewardship of the gifts of God—was a paramount ethical obligation.

The extent of this shift of values can be measured by comparing Defoe's attitude to work with that of Sir Thomas More. In More's *Utopia* hours of work are limited to six, and all surpluses of production are redistributed in the form of extra holidays.[20] Defoe, in *The Complete Tradesman,* proposes very long hours and insists that leisure activities, even an inordinate craving for sermons, must be kept in check.[21] The same tendency can be observed in the practice of Robinson Crusoe, to whom More's ideal would have seemed moral laxness. For Crusoe hard work seems to be a condition of life itself, and we notice that the arrival of Friday is a signal, not for increased leisure, but for expanded production.

One of the reasons for the canonization of *Robinson Crusoe* is certainly its consonance with the modern view that labor is both

159

the most valuable form of human activity in itself, and at the same time the only reliable way of developing one's spiritual biceps. Defoe's version of this attitude is at times overtly religious in tone. Crusoe's successful improvisations, his perfectly controlled economy, foreshadow his ultimate standing in the divine design. From his own Dissenting milieu Defoe has taken an idea, now familiar to us from the writings of Weber, Troeltsch, and Tawney, and given it a fascinating narrative form.

The combination of this aspect of the ideology of Ascetic Protestantism, or Puritanism, with a kind of return to nature, is particularly happy. Defoe thereby embodies in the same story two historically associated aspirations of the bourgeois class with whom he and his hero have been long and justly identified. In his epic of individual enterprise he bequeathed them both a program of further economic action and a figure on whom to project a quasi-religious mystique which retained from the ebbing fervors of Calvinism its essential social and economic teaching. The program of action is Empire: and it includes, as we have seen, temporary submission to primitivism, or at least to the lure of the wide open places. The mystique is one which distracts attention from the enormous and rapidly growing differences between the kinds of work and their economic rewards, by lumping them together under the one word "labor" and erecting a creed which bestows the same high "dignity" on *all* forms of activity which are subsumed under that one word.

That the mystique of the dignity of labor helped to ensure the later success of *Robinson Crusoe* as a myth seems certain. It needed a gospel. But much of what Defoe actually wrote had to be overlooked. This may seem surprising, since Defoe, the complacent apologist of nascent industrial capitalism, certainly approved of the new ideology. But as a writer his eye was so keenly on the object, and second thoughts so rarely checked the flow of his pen, that he reported, not his wishes, but the plausible image of the moment, what he knew people would actually do. So it is that he tells us much which, if analyzed, questions not only the simple message of the myth, but even some of his own cherished beliefs. And as these details do not protrude, we must consider them a little more closely.

On the desert island Robinson Crusoe turns his forsaken estate into a triumph. This is a flagrant unreality. Other castaways in the past, including Defoe's main model, Alexander Selkirk, were reduced to an extremely primitive condition, and in the space of a few years.[22] Harassed by fear, dogged by ecological degradation, they sank more and more to the level of animals: in some authentic cases they forgot the use of speech, went mad, or died of inanition. One book which Defoe had almost certainly read, *The Voyages and Travels of J. Albert de Mandelso,* tells of two such cases: of a Frenchman who, after two years of solitude on Mauritius, tore his clothing to pieces in a fit of madness brought on by a diet of raw tortoise;[23] and of a Dutch seaman on St. Helena who disinterred the body of a buried comrade and set out to sea in the coffin.[24]

Defoe's readers, perhaps, from their own ordinary experiences of solitude, may suspect as much, even if in a less dramatic form. But as they read *Robinson Crusoe* they forget that isolation can be painful or boring, that it tends in their own lives toward apathetic animality and mental derangement. Instead, they rejoice to find that isolation can be the beginning of a new realization of the potentialities of the individual. Their inertias are cheered by a vicarious participation in Crusoe's twenty-three years of lonely and triumphant struggle. They imagine themselves to be sharing each representative step in his conquest of the environment and perform with him a heartening recapitulation of humanity's success story.

To all who feel isolated or who get tired of their jobs—and who at times does not?—the story has a deep appeal and sends our critical faculties asleep. Inspired by the theme, and blinded, perhaps, by our wishes and dreams, we forget the subtle ways by which a consolatory unreality has been made to appear real.

The psychological unreality has its complement in the material one. The normal economic picture—that known to most of Defoe's readers—has been tampered with, unobtrusively but decisively. Defoe's hero—unlike most of us—has been endowed with the basic necessities for the successful exercise of free enterprise. He is not actually a primitive or a proletarian or even a professional man, but a capitalist. He owns, freehold, an estate which is rich, though unimproved. It is not a desert island in the geographical sense—it is merely barren of owners or competitors; and, above all, the very event which brings him there, the shipwreck, which is supposed to be a retributive disaster, is in fact a miraculous present of the means of production, a present rendered particularly felicitous by the death of all the other passengers. Crusoe complains that he is "reduced to a state of nature"; in fact he secures from the wreck "the biggest magazine of all kinds . . . that ever was laid out . . . for one man." [25]

The possession of this original stock, which Defoe's imitators usually retain, usually on a more lavish and less utilitarian scale, is the major practical unreality overlooked by many of his admirers of the classic idyll of individual enterprise. Yet it alone is enough to controvert the myth's wishful affirmation of a flagrant economic naïveté—the idea that anyone has ever attained comfort and security entirely by his own efforts.

The myth demanded that the storm be presented as a tragic peripety, although it is really the *deus ex machina* which makes its message plausible. Some such legerdemain was necessary before solitary labor could even appear to be not an alternative to a death sentence, but a solution to the perplexities of economic and social reality.

The dignity of labor is salvaged, then, under the most apparently adverse conditions, mainly because Crusoe has been lucky with capital stock. One wonders whether his "instinct of workmanship" would have been of any avail if he had really begun from scratch. Certainly Johann Heinrich Campe, the head master of the *Philanthropium* at Dessau, felt that there was a logical objection here which should be countered. He acted on Rousseau's suggestion that only the island episode was improving, and produced a *Nouveau Robinson* for the young which superseded Defoe's original version both in France and Germany. In it, the stock of tools was omitted.[26]

This version imposes a severe strain on our credulity, at least on that of anyone who does not live in a *Philanthropium*. But even if we grant the possibility of an isolated man reaching a high technological level unaided, there remain other more drastic difficulties in interpreting *Robinson Crusoe* as a myth of autarchic individual enterprise—difficulties based on the fact that the island is, after all, an island, and that whatever happens there is exceptional and does not seem to happen anywhere else.

On the island there is—with one exception to which we shall return—only real wealth. The perplexities of money and the price mechanism do not exist. There is there, as perhaps nowhere else, a direct relation between production and consumption. That is one obvious reason why we should not argue from it to our society; another follows from the fact that Crusoe did not want to go to the island, and once there, doesn't want to stay. The fact that he is forced to be a model of industry does not mean that he likes work. Actually, in the total setting of the trilogy, it becomes clear that Crusoe regards his little profits on the island as only a consolation prize. What he wanted (and later obtained) were unearned increments from the labor of others. In Brazil he had soon tired even of the tasks of a sugar plantation owner, and it was his quest of the more spectacular rewards of the slave trade which took him to the island.[27] To use Max Weber's distinction, he preferred the speculative rewards of "adventurer's capitalism" to the uneventful, though regular, increments which are typical of the modern economic order.[28] And after Crusoe leaves the island, he again succumbs to the lure of foreign trade, which at that time gave the highest and quickest returns on capital.[29] It is only on his island that Crusoe shows the regulated diligence combined with accurate planning and stocktaking which is so important in modern economic organization. Defoe knew this theoretically; he dealt with such matters in his economic manuals. But he himself had not been able to carry out his economic ideals into practice. They were to be realized only on Crusoe's "island of despair" which is actually a utopia, though of a new and peculiar kind.

Most utopias have been based upon the ideal of a more harmonious relationship among men. Those of Plato and More are wholly social in inspiration. They, and many later utopias, are also characterized by a certain static quality, and by the fact that people seem to do much less work and get much more for it than in the real world. But this new utopia is the answer, not to the easy and expansive yearnings of the heart for individual happiness and social harmony, nor even to Crusoe's acquisitive instincts; it is the answer only to a very rigorous conception of what kind of life Defoe feels is good for other people.

Crusoe, in fact, has been stranded in the utopia of the Protestant Ethic. There temptation, whether economic or moral, is wholly absent. Crusoe's energies cannot be deflected, either by the picnic promises of pastoral utopias, or by the relaxing and un-economic piety of the hermits and mystics who are the heroes of an earlier form of Christianity, heroes whose faith is measured by their certainty that "God will provide." On Crusoe's island, un-remitting toil is obligatory; there, and only there, it is instinct with both moral value and calculable personal reward.

If we look further afield for economic motivation in Defoe, if we leave the island, we find a very different picture. The other ad-ventures of Robinson Crusoe, and the lives of Defoe's other heroes and heroines do not point in the direction of the dignity of labor. Defoe knew very well that the normal social conditions of his time caused very different adjustments to the environment. Moll Flan-ders, Roxana, and Colonel Jacque satisfy their needs in ways which no one would propose for imitation. Indeed, their exploits demon-strate quite another type of political economy, and point the moral that—to those outside Crusoe's island, and without his heaven-bestowed capital—La propriété, c'est le vol.[30]

Defoe, then, is a realist about the individual and his economic environment. He has no illusions about the dignity of the labors of most people in the England of his day. He expressed their lot in a moving passage which William Morris used as epigraph to his lecture on "The Art of the People": "And the men of labour spend their strength in daily struggling for bread to maintain the vital strength they labour with: so living in a daily circulation of sorrow, living but to work, and working but to live, as if daily bread were the only end of a wearisome life, and a wearisome life the only occasion of daily bread."

If we wish to trace in Defoe any universal and overriding idea, it is certainly not that of the dignity of labor as a social fact or even as a moral dogma. The key to the basic motivation of his characters and the hypothesis that best explains their history both apply to Crusoe. For he is only a special case of economic man. Just as the doctrine of the dignity of labor can be understood as the optimistic and deluding myth which hides the realities involved in the division of labor, so the fortitude of Defoe's isolated man withdraws from general attention the true lineaments of that lonely and unlovely archetype of our civilization, *homo economicus,* who is also mirrored in *Robinson Crusoe.*

III

Homo economicus is, of course, a fiction. There has long been a conflict about the utility of the abstraction. Briefly, the classical political economists found in the idea of Robinson Crusoe, the solitary individual on a desert island, a splendid example for their system building. On the other hand, their critics who, like Marx, were concerned to prove that economics can be a guide to reality only when it is a historical and a social science, have denied the relevance of Robinson Crusoe to any realistic economic thinking.

Marx began his polemic against classical political economy by insisting on the social nature of production. He, therefore, attacked the starting points of Adam Smith and Ricardo—the isolated hunters and fishers, who were, he said, "Robinsonades," and belonged to "the insipid illusions of the Eighteenth Century." [31] Later, in *Capital,* he appropriated Crusoe to support his own theory of value. For Crusoe, "in spite of the variety of his work . . . knows that his labour whatever its form, is but the activity of one and the same Robinson, and consequently, that it consists of nothing but different modes of human labor. . . . All the relations between Robinson and the objects that form this wealth of his own creation, are here so simple and clear as to be intelligible without exertion." [32] But it is only on the island that the value of any object is directly proportional to the quantity of labor expended upon it. In Western capitalism the rewards of labor and the price of commodities are subject to market considerations which are capricious and unjust, especially to labor.[33] The use of Crusoe as an example therefore distracts attention from the dark realities of the economic system as it is.

Marx does not make the useful polemic point which Crusoe's fortunate acquisition of capital might have afforded him. Nor does he mention the extent to which his personality embodies the moral evils which he ascribed to capitalism. This is no doubt because he is using Crusoe only as an example of one particular theme, and not for any general purpose. For actually Crusoe exemplifies another aspect of Marx's thought; the process of alienation by which capitalism tends to convert man's relationships with his fellows, and even to his own personality, into commodities to be manipulated.

This view of economic man is not, of course, limited to Marx. Max Weber's idea that the Protestant Ethic involves a thorough systematization of behavior according to rational norms of personal profit is very similar,[34] and so is Tawney's picture of the acquisitive society composed of individuals pursuing their individual interests without any recognition of social or moral solidarity.[35] But these theoretical formulations had long before been anticipated by literary realization. For, as an ironic commentary upon the myth, the book of *Robinson Crusoe* depicts in its casual reports of the hero's behavior and of his occasional parenthetic reflections, the shameless and pervasive impact of the cash nexus upon the character and personal relationships of the archetypal economic man. Defoe has supplied the antidote to the myth of his unwitting creation—not only in the already mentioned incidental unrealities of the plot, but also in the somber touches which are an overt part of his picture of the personality of the protagonist.

Crusoe treats his personal relationships in terms of their commodity value. The Moorish boy, Xury, for example, helps him to escape from slavery, and on another occasion offers to prove his devotion by sacrificing his own life. Crusoe very properly resolves "to love him ever after," [36] and promises "to make him a great man." But when chance leads them to the Portuguese trader, and its captain offers Crusoe sixty pieces of eight—twice Judas's figure —he cannot resist the bargain and sells Xury into slavery. He has momentary scruples at the betrayal, it is true, but they are soon economically satisfied by securing from the captain a promise "to set him free in ten years if he turn Christian." [37] Remorse later supervenes, but only when the tasks of his island existence renew his need for a slave.[38]

Slaves, of course, were his original objective in the voyage which brought him to the island. And eventually Providence and his own exertions provide him with Man Friday, who answers his prayers by "swearing to be my slave for ever." [39] The unsolicited promise is as prophetic as the development of the relationship is instructive. Crusoe does not ask Friday his name, he gives him one; and there is throughout a remarkable lack of interest in Friday as a person, as someone worth trying to understand or converse with. Even in language—the medium whereby human beings may achieve something more than animal relationships with each other—Crusoe is a strict utilitarian. "I likewise taught him to say yes and no," [40] he tells us, though, as Defoe's contemporary critic Gildon not unjustly remarked,[41] Friday still speaks pidgin English at the end of their long association.

Yet Crusoe regards the relationship as ideal. In the period alone with Friday he was "perfectly and completely happy, if any such thing as complete happiness can be found in a sublunary state." [42] A functional silence, apparently, adds to the charms of the idyll, broken only by an occasional "No, Friday" or an abject "Yes, Master." Man's social nature is wholly satisfied by the righteous bestowal, or grateful receipt, of benevolent but not undemanding patronage.[43]

Only one doubt ruffles Crusoe's proprietary equanimity. He becomes obsessed with the fear that Friday may be harboring an ungrateful wish to return to his father and his tribe. But the fear proves groundless, and they leave the island together. Crusoe later avoids any possible qualms about keeping Friday in servitude by the deferred altruism of a resolution "to do something considerable for him, if he outlived me." [44] Fortunately, no such sacrifice is called for, as Friday dies at sea, faithful to the end, and rewarded only by a brief word of obituary compassion.

Crusoe's attitude to women is also marked by an extreme inhibition of what we now consider to be normal human feelings. There are, of course, none on the island, and their absence is not deplored. When Crusoe does notice the lack of "society," he prays for company, but it is for that of a male slave. With Friday he is fully satisfied by an idyll without benefit of woman. It is an interesting break from the traditional expectations aroused by desert islands, from the *Odyssey* to the *New Yorker*.

Defoe's view of the individual was too completely dominated by the rational pursuit of material self-interest to allow any scope either for natural instinct or for higher emotional needs. Even when Crusoe returns to civilization, sex is strictly subordinated to business. Only after his financial position has been fully secured by a further voyage does he marry, "and that not either to my disadvantage or dissatisfaction." [45]

Some of Crusoe's colonists have the same attitude. He tells how they draw lots for five women, and he strongly approves of the outcome: "He that drew to choose first . . . took her that was reckoned the homeliest and eldest of the five, which made mirth enough among the rest . . . but the fellow considered better than any of them, that it was application and business that they were to expect assistance in as much as anything else; and she proved the best wife of all the parcel." [46]

The conflict is put very much in Weber's terms.[47] Sex is seen as a dangerously irrational factor in life which interferes with the pursuit of rational self-interest: and economic and moral worth in the male does not guarantee him a profitable matrimonial investment. On his colony "as it often happens in the world (what the wise ends of God's Providence are in such a disposition of things I cannot say), the two honest fellows had the two worst wives; and the three reprobates, that were scarce worth hanging, . . . had three clever, diligent, careful and ingenious wives." [48] It is therefore no accident that love plays a very minor part in Crusoe's own life, and is eliminated from the scene of his greatest triumphs.

IV

One could illustrate the ideology of *homo economicus* at much greater length from *Robinson Crusoe*. Everything is measured from the rational, asocial, and antitraditional standards of individual self-interest, and some of the results are not pleasant. But these results are surely the lamentable, but necessary, corollaries of the social process which the story reflects; and the common tendency to overlook them in the hero must be attributed to the obscure forces that guard the idols of our society and shape its myths.

Malinowski has said that "myth is . . . an indispensable ingredient of all culture." [49] It would indeed appear to be so, but I have no wish to be numbered among those who would prove our common humanity by putting us back on a level with the Trobriand islanders. The aim of this essay is rather to do something they don't do; that is, scrutinize one small item of our cultural repertoire in the hope of clarifying its role in the past and present of our society.

Much has had to be omitted—the appeal of the adventure in itself, for example, and the theological aspect of the story, which modifies the picture considerably. Some of the social and economic matters have been treated somewhat cavalierly. The case of Robinson Crusoe as *homo economicus* has been somewhat oversimplified. For Defoe does suggest on at least one occasion (the famous episode when Crusoe comes across a hoard of gold on the island and, after declaiming on its uselessness, "upon second thoughts" takes it away)[50] the irrationality of the goals which shape the character of economic man and which affect his actions more powerfully than his own understanding of his real needs. And, of course, in a wintry sort of way, Crusoe has his pleasures. He does not, as Selkirk had done, dance with the goats, but he does at least occasionally supplement occupational by recreational therapy. Still, it seems true to say that the reality of Defoe's masterpiece, its ultimate referent, is economic man. So that if we seek a general meaning for his solitude it must be the social atomization which *homo economicus* brings in his train. That, surely, is the main historical basis of this metaphor of human solitude which has haunted the Western consciousness. And the need to obscure the regrettable social and psychological corollaries of the rise of economic individualism must explain much of the very general disinclination to see the darker side of Defoe's hero.

It is certainly curious to observe how all but universal has been the reluctance to challenge Crusoe as a model for imitation and inspiration. In some cases there may be other explanations for this. The myth of national character, for example. Some foreign commentators have had ulterior motives in presenting Robinson Crusoe as the typical Englishman. Marx calls him a "true-born Briton";[51] and Dibelius echoes the impeachment of a nation of shopkeepers with more obvious venom.[52] For France, de Vogüé, in his study of what he calls *"Le livre anglais,"* though more polite, is equally disparaging by implication.[53] What is curious is to find that most English writers, too, have tended to accept Crusoe as the typical

Englishman, apparently undeterred by any of his antisocial idio-
syncrasies.

There have been occasional dissentients. Dickens, for example,
was revolted by Crusoe's attitudes toward the death of Friday, and
to women generally; and he wrote in a letter that Defoe must have
been a "precious dry and disagreeable article himself." [54] Ruskin—
another critic of the mentality of industrial capitalism—uses the
phrase "a very small, perky, contented, conceited, Cock-Robinson-
Crusoe, sort of life." [55] Yet on the whole, Crusoe has been accepted
as the typical Englishman by his fellow countrymen, although, as
it happens, Defoe made Crusoe's father "a foreigner of Bremen."

In some ways, of course, the character of Robinson Crusoe is a
national one. Courage, practical intelligence, not making a fuss,
these are not the least of the virtues, and their combination in
Crusoe does seem to be according to an English pattern. But these
virtues cannot be regarded as exemplary and sufficient. Dickens
wrote of *Robinson Crusoe* that it is "the only instance of a universally popular book that could make no one laugh and no one
cry." [56] This suggests the major flaw. Defoe's epic of the stiff upper
lip does not propose a wholly satisfactory ideal. For Crusoe's merits
are combined with a stolid and inhibited self-sufficiency which is
disastrous both for the individual and for society. That is Crusoe's
hubris—a defect not unlike Rousseau's *hypertrophie du moi*.

There is, even on Crusoe's own showing, very little content or
peace in this way of life. Pascal said that the misery of man can be
traced from a single fact, his inability to stay still in his own room.
Crusoe can never stay still. His brisk and businesslike exterior
cannot wholly conceal the deadening compulsion of an alienation
which is assuaged only by ceaseless economic activity. He is modern
economic man putting a poker face on the fate that Pascal found
intolerable. "Nothing else offering, and finding that really stirring
about and trading, the profit being so great, and, as I may say, certain, had more pleasure in it, and more satisfaction to the mind,
than sitting still, which, to me especially, was the unhappiest part
of life. . . ." So, in the *Farther Adventures,* he sets out on yet
another lucrative Odyssey.

His author, deeply implicated in the character that Walter de
la Mare has called Defoe's "Elective Affinity," [57] appears to ap-

prove. But he certainly does not see his work in an optimistic vein: "Nothing else offering . . ." suggests why. Defoe wrestles with the meanings of his creation in the essay "On Solitude," which begins the *Serious Reflections*. The essay is inconclusive, and there are several different strands of thought in it. But the bitterness of isolation as the primordial fact repeatedly moves Defoe to a great fervor of communication. One of the passages seems a particularly moving commentary on the isolation which the pursuit of individual self-interest creates in the human spirit.

What are the sorrows of other men to us, and what their joy? Sometimes we may be touched indeed by the power of sympathy, and a secret turn of the affections; but all the solid reflection is directed to ourselves. Our meditations are all solitude in perfection; our passions are all exercised in retirement; we love, we hate, we covet, we enjoy, all in privacy and solitude. All that we communicate of those things to any other is but for their assistance in the pursuit of our desires; the end is at home; the enjoyment, the contemplation, is all solitude and retirement; it is for ourselves we enjoy, and for ourselves we suffer.[58]

The loneliness of economic man was a tragic fact. Many Stoic or Christian thinkers might have said "We love, we hate . . . all in privacy and solitude." But "we covet, we enjoy" is characteristic of a later ideology. To the solitude of the soul which so many have expressed, Defoe adds "all we communicate of those things to any other is but for their assistance in the pursuit of our desires." A rationally conceived self-interest makes a mockery of speech, and suggests silence.

So, although *Robinson Crusoe* is a mutation of a very ancient theme, its specific cause and nature are wholly modern. And now that it is possible to see fairly clearly the realities of which Crusoe is the menacing symbol, we must surely question his desirability as an ideal prototype. What has happened in the last two hundred years has shown that where Defoe's new culture hero is admitted into the pantheon of myth, he soon crowds out or subjugates the other figures, whether comic or tragic, round whom have gathered those more generous aspirations that occasionally mitigate the bitterness of history.

Robinson Crusoe as a Myth

[1] For a survey of the work done on this subject, with very full references, see Philip Babcock Gove, *The Imaginary Voyage in Prose Fiction* (New York: 1941). The study of *Robinsonaden* is particularly connected with the name of Hermann Ullrich, author of *Robinson und Robinsonaden* (Weimar: 1898), and *Defoes Robinson Crusoe, Geschichte eines Weltbuches* (Leipzig: 1924). H. C. Hutchins has studied the early editions of *Robinson Crusoe* in his *Robinson Crusoe and Its Printing* (New York: 1925), and William-Edward Mann is responsible for a useful study of *Robinson Crusoë en France* (Paris: 1916).

[2] René Pottier, *Histoire d'un Village* (Paris: 1941), pp. 171-74.

[3] Daniel Defoe, *The Common Reader*, first series (London: 1925).

[4] Max Günther, *Entstehungsgeschichte von Defoes Robinson Crusoe* (Griefswald: 1909), p. 29.

[5] Bronislaw Malinowski, *Myth in Primitive Psychology* (London: 1926), pp. 18-19.

[6] *The Life and Strange Surprising Adventures of Robinson Crusoe*, George A. Aitken, ed. (London: 1902), pp. 41-43, 95-100, and *passim*.

[7] *The Farther Adventures of Robinson Crusoe*, G. A. Aitken, ed. (London: 1902), pp. 149-50. Also *Life and Strange Surprising Adventures*, p. 216.

[8] *Émile, ou De L'Éducation*, F. and P. Richard, eds. (Paris: 1939), pp. 210-14.

[9] *Ibid.*, p. 211.

[10] See Gove, *The Imaginary Voyage*, p. 36; Mann, *Robinson Crusoë en France*, pp. 51-55 and 102; W. J. B. Pienaar, *English Influences in Dutch Literature and Justus Van Effen as Intermediary* (Cambridge: 1929), pp. 248-49.

[11] *Émile*, p. 211.

[12] (Paris: 1931), p. 30. This hostile and somewhat exaggerated polemic discusses Rousseau's other references to *Robinson Crusoe*.

[13] *Review*, II, 26; *cit.*, Walter Wilson, *Memoirs of the Life and Times of Daniel Defoe* (London: 1830), II, p. 319.

[14] P. 118.

[15] *Life and Strange Surprising Adventures*, p. 74.

[16] *The Fable of the Bees*, F. B. Kaye, ed. (Oxford: 1924), I, cxxxiv-cxxxv; II, 142 *n.*

[17] *Life and Strange Surprising Adventures*, p. 130.

[18] See Arthur Lovejoy, "The Supposed Primitivism of Rousseau's *Discourse on Inequality*," *Essays in the History of Ideas* (Baltimore: 1948).

[19] Smiles gives this epigraph to his delightfully entitled *Life and Labour or Characteristics of Men of Industry, Culture and Genius*, attributing it to Virgil. Virgil actually wrote, of the coming of the Age of Iron:

> *labor omnia vicit*
> *improbus et duris urgens in rebus egestas.*
> (*Georgics*, I, 145-46)

The time-hallowed misquotation is an interesting example of the forces which have made *Robinson Crusoe* into a myth. That labor does and always will conquer all is a modern view which cannot be derived from Virgil. There seems no reason to consider *vicit* as a gnomic perfect: Conington remarks that "the poet is narrating, not uttering a sentiment," although he approves of the general characterization of the *Georgics* as a "glorification of labour." (P. *Vergili Maronis Opera* . . . (London: 1881), I, 151-55). F. Plessis and P. Lejay comment acidly: "*Le poëte n'éxalte pas le travail pour lui-même, ce qui est une affectation toute moderne, une idée d'Encyclopédiste, mais pour ses résultats.*" (*Œuvres* (Paris: 1945), p. 29). L. P. Wilkinson, in a recent article, writes, "The text of Virgil's Gospel of Work was not *laborare et orare*, as some have suggested, but *laborare et vivere.*" ("The Intention of Virgil's *Georgics*," *Greece and Rome*, XVIII (1950), 24.) Virgil's interpretation of the end of the Golden Age bears obvious resemblances to the Christian, and especially Protestant, welcome to the loss of Eden; as Adam says in *Paradise Lost*, "Idleness had been worse." See also A. Lovejoy and G. Boas, *Primitivism and Related Ideas in Antiquity* (Baltimore: 1935), p. 370.

[20] *Ideal Commonwealths*, H. Morley, ed. (London: 1899), pp. 97, 101.

[21] *The Complete English Tradesman* (Oxford: 1841), I, 32-34. See also, A. E. Levett, "Daniel Defoe," *Social and Political Ideas of Some English Thinkers of the Augustan Age*, F. J. C. Hearnshaw, ed. (London: 1928), p. 180.

[22] A. W. Secord, *Studies in the Narrative Method of Defoe* (Urbana, Illinois: 1924), p. 26.

[23] *Ibid.*, p. 28.

[24] *Ibid.*

[25] *Life and Strange Surprising Adventures*, p. 60.

[26] See Mann, *Robinson Crusoë en France*, pp. 85-101. It was this version which H. H. Gossen used in deriving economic laws from *Crusoe* (W. Stark, *The Ideal Foundations of Economic Thought* [London: 1948], p. 159): and was probably that of Frédéric Bastiat in his *Harmonies Économiques* (Brussels: 1850), pp. 99f., 214f.

[27] *Life and Strange Surprising Adventures*, pp. 40-42. See also, *Farther Adventures*, p. 66, where Defoe shows his awareness of the dangers of this type of enterprise by attributing it to idle ne'er-do-wells.

[28] Weber, *The Protestant Ethic and the Spirit of Capitalism*, trans. T. Parsons (London: 1930), pp. 21, 74-78; and *The Theory of Economic and Social Organization*, trans. T. Parsons and A. M. Henderson (New York: 1947), pp 50-52, 279ff.

[29] A. L. Merson, "The Revolution and the British Empire," *The Modern Quarterly*, IV (1949), p. 152.

[30] J. Sutherland points out that on the island, although stealing is impossible, the satisfactory emotions of successful theft are suggested by the looting of the wreck. *Defoe* (London: 1937), p. 232.

[31] *A Contribution to the Critique of Political Economy* (1st edition, 1859; New York: 1904), pp. 265-66.

[32] Chap. 1, sec. iv.

[33] Defoe had experienced this for himself. His bookseller, Taylor, owned the whole share of all three parts of *Robinson Crusoe* and is said to have made his fortune by it. (Hutchins, *Robinson Crusoe and its Printing*, p. 185.) Defoe worked indefatigably for most of his seventy years of life, and though he was at times rich, he died alone, hiding from a creditor. (Sutherland, *Defoe*, pp. 269-74).

[34] Weber, *Theory of Economic and Social Organization,* pp. 191-249 *et passim.*
[35] R. H. Tawney, *The Acquisitive Society* (London: 1921), p. 32.
[36] *Life and Strange Surprising Adventures,* p. 27.
[37] *Ibid.,* p. 36.
[38] *Ibid.,* p. 164.
[39] *Ibid.,* p. 226.
[40] *Ibid.,* p. 229.
[41] *Robinson Crusoe Examin'd and Criticis'd;* P. Dottin, ed. (London and Paris: 1923), pp. 70, 78, 118.
[42] *Life and Strange Surprising Adventures,* pp. 245-46.
[43] The Crusoe-Friday relationship is representative in many other ways, not least in showing how the quest for the white man's burden tends to end in the discovery of the perfect porter.
[44] *Farther Adventures,* p. 133.
[45] *Life and Strange Surprising Adventures,* p. 341.
[46] *Farther Adventures,* p. 77.
[47] Max Weber, *Essays in Sociology,* trans. H. H. Gerth and C. Wright Mills (New York: 1946), p. 350.
[48] *Farther Adventures,* p. 78.
[49] *Myth in Primitive Psychology,* p. 125.
[50] *Life and Strange Surprising Adventures,* p. 62.
[51] *Capital,* chap. 1, sec. vi.
[52] *Englische Romankunst* (Berlin: 1910), I, p. 36.
[53] *Revue des deux Mondes* (October 1, 1895), as is Jean Giraudoux in *Suzanne et le Pacifique* (Paris: 1921), pp. 228-33.
[54] John Forster, *Life of Charles Dickens,* rev. by J. W. T. Ley (London, 1928), p. 611.
[55] Peter Quennell, *John Ruskin* (London: 1949), p. 15.
[56] Forster, loc. cit.
[57] *Desert Islands and Robinson Crusoe* (London: 1930), p. 7.
[58] *Serious Reflections of Robinson Crusoe,* G. A. Aitken, ed. (London: 1902), pp. 2-3.

Seven

JOHN DEWEY'S SOCIAL ART
AND THE SOCIOLOGY OF ART

Among philosophers of art, John Dewey is unquestion-
ably the thinker who would most readily be termed
"sociological" in the common use of that adjective. He
was insistently concerned with the various ways in
which artistic creativity and artistic appreciation are
bound up with the mundane phenomena of social life.
He was, in a sense, obsessed with showing us how
"normal" art is, how much a part of common experience and how little merely a rarefied, unique region
of life. Dewey is firmly rooted in the American social
psychological tradition of the early years of this century, especially in his emphasis on the central significance of communication in human conduct. Thus he
gives one of the clearest expositions of art as essentially
an act of communication, a relational event:

Language exists only when it is listened to as well as spoken.
The hearer is an indispensable partner. The work of art is

complete only as it works in the experience of others than the one who created it. Thus language involves what logicians call a triadic relation. There is the speaker, the thing said, and the one spoken to. The external object, the product of art, is the connecting link between artist and audience. Even when the artist works in solitude all three terms are present.

If Dewey then grounds art in social time and space, in the fundamental interactions among men, he obviously helps prepare the way for a sociology of art. Yet as Graña so incisively contends, his thesis has the grave faults of its virtues: in making art a universal experience, he renders it too prosaic; in fitting it to the framework of pragmatic thought, he oversimplifies intricate aesthetic problems; in stressing the social nature of art, he blunts our apprehension of individual psychological depths in creator and in appreciator. Dewey's rough, commonsensical approach, which is so salutary a counterweight to aesthetic dandyism, tends to take for granted relationships which are problematic.

Graña notes, for instance, Dewey's easy assumption of a vague "correspondence" between a total culture and one of its specific art products. Although Victor Hugo claimed that a perceptive observer could read the spirit of an age in the details of a doorknocker, we are far from being able to explicate how he should go about his reading: from what universe of doorknockers must he draw his specimen, and how precisely must he relate it to varieties of artisans and householders?

Perhaps most vital is Dewey's neglect, to which Graña also points, of what one might call the diabolic and the lonely features of art—and especially of the creative process itself. In his vision of harmony and sweet reason, both within the artist and in the transactions with the audience, there scarcely seems to be room for a Rimbaud or a Dean Swift or even for a Dylan Thomas. The violent psychological disorder that may lie behind artistic order is glossed over. So too, if we agree with Dewey, as we must, that the artist is imbedded in his society, we must also recognize the mood evoked by the first four essays in this volume: his frequent and deep sense of alienation and isolation. The artist is that paradoxical creature who is both at one with his society and fundamentally at odds with it. Yeats said that poetry is the social act of a solitary being. As his art binds him to his fellows, the creative work commends (and condemns?) him to the reaches of solitude.

JOHN DEWEY'S SOCIAL ART
AND THE SOCIOLOGY OF ART

César Graña

The most general statement that can be made about Dewey's philosophy is to say that for him life was experience, and experience was two things: a vision of man as an organism which was creative and responsive in its relations with nature, and a vision of society as part of the natural surroundings of man.

It was through individuals, of course, that experience became actuality, the substance of life's events. But always with the understanding that for Dewey the individual was the marshalling point of social realities, a gathering fold in which collective demands, intimations, and challenges were thrown into the machinery of articulation, and returned to the historical environment as specific acts, as distinct exhibits of social agreement and purpose.[1] In 1934 Dewey published *Art as Experience,* a work at once embraced by one critic, not only as the greatest American contribution to aesthetic theory, but as a summation of Dewey's entire philosophical message.[2] We meet again in this book Dewey's never-relaxed advocacy of empiricism and social realism, and while, of course, this is to be expected, it is difficult to suppress a first and conventionally patronizing surprise. In what way, or even by what right, could the pragmatic mind concern itself with something so gilded, so regally nonsecular as art? If, as Dewey said, art, however refined or force-

---

Reprinted from the *Journal of Aesthetics and Art Criticism,* Vol. XX, No. 4 (Summer 1962).

ful in its form, was rooted in "the everyday doings and sufferings universally recognized to constitute experience," [3] where did one find the passage from the ordinary to the extraordinary, from the homely predicaments of existence to art's singular imagination and skill?

The answer, we might think, lay in the search for those day-to-day meanings to which art lends a peculiar voice and eloquence. In reality it went much beyond that. For Dewey the greatest obstacle to aesthetic understanding was the accepted classification of art as objects made by professionals, possessed by institutions, or bought and sold under the rules of the cultural market. Instead, in a pointedly chosen contrast, he turned at the beginning of his book to workaday events:

the fire engine rushing by; the machines excavating enormous holes in the earth; the human fly climbing the steeple-side; the men perched high on girders, throwing and catching red-hot bolts; . . . the tense grace of the ball-player; . . . the delight of the housewife in tending her plants. [4]

Like others of us, Dewey experienced a sense of welcome and ardent admiration at the psychological and dramatic decisiveness of such acts; at the courage, verve, precision, elegance, and articulation that men brought to them. But he also knew that, though we may call them "beautiful," our views of high culture would not consent to their being "artistic." It was Dewey's intention to convince us that the daily language of our aesthetic emotions held a truth far deeper than that of any lofty conventions, that aesthetic meaning was not a property of things but a parcel of experience, and that no real borderline existed between the quality of art and the content of life.

It is quite accurate to regard *Art as Experience* as a primer of Dewey's ideas, for what he has to say in this book about aesthetic events is only an extensive illustration of his general philosophy of human acts. As he so tirelessly repeated, man was a *live* creature, an organism linked to the surroundings by relations of dominance over it, defense against it, or acquiescence with it. Even ideological issues were discussed by him in the language of organic adjustment. Intelligence was the capability to restore on the plane of meaning that union of the sense of need, impulse, and action which marked the living being. Sensitivity was the gauge of man's well-tuned response to the solicitations of the environment. Not, of course, that man and reality stood always poised in felicitous balance. Strain occurred, as did discord, but when they did, intelligence and sensitivity were at once mobilized to restore organic comfort and fulfillment. Art, too, was for him an act which, while involving intellection and imagination, stood basically as a symbol of organic conformity and control. Explaining the transformation of ordinary emotion into artistic expression he says in *Art as Experience*:

Irritation may be let go like an arrow directed at the charge and produce some change in the outer world. But having an outer effect is something very different from ordered use of objective conditions in order to give objective fulfillment to emotion. The latter alone is an expression, and the motion that attaches itself to, or is interpreted by, the resulting object is esthetic. If the person in question puts his room to rights as a matter of routine he is anesthetic. But if the original emotion of impatient irritation has been ordered and tranquilized by what he has done, the orderly room reflects back to him the change that has taken place in himself. He feels not that he has accomplished a needed chore but that he has done something emotionally fulfilling. His emotion as thus "objectified" is esthetic.[5]

All of Dewey's writings are, in a sense, episodes out of great struggle against the traditional image of human thought as something surveying the world from a detached eminence of its own, the "spectator" theory of the mind which Dewey attributed to the historic connection between intellectual pursuits and aristocratic leisure. What he saw instead was a resourceful organism, dwelling in the midst of reality and forever redefining itself as it gauged the character and demands of oncoming events. Most sociologists looking at such a philosophical prospect would find nothing in it to alienate their relativistic and secular standards. As an instrument for investigation, on the other hand, they might find it, as they do most philosophies, either too schematic or too grand. After all, it is the particular badge of sociological theories of the mind that they place the mind's work within a collective situation to be understood in its concrete complexity. It is, however, unlikely that Dewey

179

would have acknowledged this as an argument counting him out of the sociological camp. In many cases the social emphasis of his work was contained chiefly in the admonition that education and the arts of thinking should train men for cooperative tasks, and not merely enrich and adorn the person, as the traditions of honorific individualism demanded. But the social teacher did not exclude the social theorist. In a language which almost duplicates William Sumner in *Folkways and Mores,* Dewey upheld the reality of social customs as facts whose force was "comparable to the momentum of physical objects once they are set in motion, and the resistance to movement possessed by the same object once they are at rest." [6] And, in the best anthropological manner, he based this belief on the assumption of a changing human nature capable of hardening into structure around any given body of social inheritance. It is from this psychology of custom, aided perhaps by the influence of cultural historians like Spengler, that Dewey may have derived his explanation of the specific social characteristics of art. At the beginning of *Art as Experience* Dewey's attack on handed-down aesthetic judgment insists only on the link between aesthetics and experience. Later Dewey adds that art is, in the largest sense, a social phenomenon, and that men should understand it as a manifestation of their *collective* spirit. Whole societies, and not individuals alone, could be the agents of experience in his sense. Such terms as Negro, Gothic, Chinese, or Greek art, were not simple labeling distinctions. They stood for the "veridical significance" of culture as a collective individuality capable of producing art forms.[7]

As with others of his books, Dewey's *Art as Experience* is written in a taxing style, tangled by superfluous devices, and always moving with stubborn and meticulous artlessness. Yet, it is Dewey's peculiar paradox that, like all of his work, this book is dedicated to "warranted assertability" and the dismissal of aprioristic and hierarchical theories of knowledge, in short, to philosophical plain talk. In this respect *Art as Experience* is not only a professional treatise but a cultural document; an expression of intellectual preferences by a man who, like others of his time, wanted to find a poetic, moral, and psychological language for the deep historical strain of American pragmatism. For, even from the distance of its professorial prose, Dewey's admiration for the hardy glamor of makers and doers inevitably suggests the utilitarian rhetoric of Carl Sandburg's *Chicago,* just as his rejection of the leisure-class tradition recalls Thorstein Veblen's belief in the inner law of craftsmanship, and the righteousness of efficiency and engineering.

However, it is one thing to speak of Dewey as the philosopher of the workaday world—or, perhaps, as the American aesthetician of democratic productivity and its inner life—and another to evaluate his work as a method for the analysis of art. Convinced as he was that aesthetics was an expression of society, Dewey employed all of his philosophical industry to bring it from heaven to earth, and in this sense *Art as Experience* can be considered a declaration against solemnity and snobbery, and the treatment of art as a kind of ideological narcissism ("the beauty parlor of civilization"). It is obvious, on the other hand, that there is very little analytical profit to be derived from something so sketchy and overextended as Dewey's view of culture. No one who spends a moment remembering that the sheltered intellectuality and orderliness of Raphael's art was produced in an age of dazzling political ruthlessness will be able to speak confidently of the "veridical significance" of the Renaissance as a seamless historical event. The same is true of the rest of Dewey's cultural sampler: Gothic, Mohammedanism, Ancient Greece, the South Seas, which is to say anything from architectural styles to social-religious movements, historical periods, and "culture areas." Only great haste would take these bluntly miscellaneous illustrations as similar instances of the kind of reality upon which art is thought to stand, and one can only puzzle at the promptness of the great empiricist in giving way to academic habit and embracing as facts what he should have regarded as intellectual conventions.

A sound sociology of cultural life requires first an accountable view of the social element itself. It should be imaginative and resourceful but, obviously, precise and circumspect. For centuries European literature rested on the narrowest of cultural foundations, aristocratic patronage. But, though literary creations of these times are stamped with their origins, they are not easily or manifestly labeled. The hand of aristocratic favor did not turn all of literature into a series of gestures of class adulation. Some writers looked at princes and noblemen as creatures with a capacity for moral concern and moral resolution immeasurably beyond the spiritual powers of most humans; to great men great duties and great sorrows. But others devoted themselves to that formalized sentimentalization of the game of love which provided so much of the reading of fashionable *salons*. The essential feature of aristocratic literature was something more general. It was, de Tocqueville said, the link between traditional power and artistic craftsmanship, and the way in which this alliance made possible the perpetuation of certain concerns of taste and imagination. One of these concerns was the careful regulation of style by an audience with leisure enough to nurse artistic perfectionism. Another was the promotion of what de Tocqueville calls, in a particular sense, poetic, that is the suggestion of things marvelous and remote flowing from two social characteristics of the aristocracy: an inscrutable reverence for the past, and the aristocrat's awe-inspiring personal and spiritual distance from the rest of men.[8]

It is not only the content of art that challenges the sociologist, but the very nature of artistic expression. Art and literature may be reportorial, propagandistic, "subjective," "objective," explicit, implicit, personal, or social. But what makes them different from philosophical disquisition, economic doctrine, political papers, and the observations of psychologists, anthropologists, and sociologists, is that they are, in a literal sense, creative, and aim to bring into existence as concrete presence, a world like life itself. The paradox is that this very intention of art as an act of expression makes of its analysis a constant intellectual gamble. Our need for a seen and felt sense of reality conspires only too easily with the convincing power of artistic creation to go beyond interpretation to passionate and ingenious misinterpretation.

The provocative ambivalence of this predicament will be made clearer by this quotation from Henry Berenger's *L'Aristocratie Intellectuelle*. "Men of genius," says Berenger, "listen to the millions of little souls around them, then they themselves speak, and their voices are heard through the silence of history." [9] This is, of course, a mythological statement, however flattering to the intellectual's occupational fondness for the presumed powers of the mind. Still, we must recognize the inverted truth hidden in it. Creative intelligence does furnish the voices heard in history because of its overriding wish to reveal, to affirm, and, above all, to cast understanding into an unmistakable legacy of expression. We are, therefore, perennially beset by the fact that what we assume to be the meaning of the lives of most people comes to us from the words and the images of the few. The others, those whom artists paint and write about, are the voiceless ones. We choose to think that they are voiceless *because* they cannot tell us what they are, and that the artist speaks *because* he can tell us about others what they cannot themselves say. In other words, we concede to the act of communication itself the title of reality.[10]

This is in many ways an unavoidable decision. It is also a sensitive question, and another example of the kinds of problems that cannot be met by any of Dewey's methods. Panoramic conceptualizations about culture will only reduce the social element of creativity to a simplified romance between the "people" and "their" art, and works of art to the stature of ideological posters. Needlessly, too, it denies art much of its real autonomy, even at the price of confusion since, as we shall see, a forced choice between the aesthetic and the social meaning of art may be, not only false, but sociologically misleading. For instance, speaking of the Parthenon, Dewey tells us that we might better understand this monument by turning away from the building itself to look at the "bustling, arguing, acutely sensitive Athenians with civic pride identified with civic religion," who built it, he says, "not as a work of art but as a civic commemoration." [11] This is a statement that wavers between the deceptive and the erroneous. Of course Athenian religion was civic. But if the Parthenon was intended as a public gesture and no more, why did Pericles and the Athenian assembly entrust it to a notable architect and a famous sculptor? The answer is simple and denies nothing to the pride and sensitivity of the Athenian citizen. The Parthenon tells us something about the Athenians, not aside from its being a work of art but *because* of it. Which is to say that we understand the Athenians better when we know that they wanted their civic temples to be monuments of great beauty.

In a general way Dewey acknowledges that to speak of art as a representation of reality is not simple. Photographic reproduction in painting is not art, he says, nor is tramping through a museum art appreciation. These statements are true. How could they *not* be?

For unless Dewey is attacking simple-minded "realism," or the unthinking hunting expeditions of sight-seers and culture-vultures, they say nothing that a sensible person would not easily take for granted. The same is true of his remark that an artist does not approach a subject with an empty mind but through subtle affinities between the subject and his own experience as a "live creature," which cause line and color to assume one pattern rather than another. Since experience teaches us that different artists work differently, the statement is both unimpeachable and unrevealing. Whether the artist approaches his subject with or without an "empty mind," however, is a matter which may be simply beyond our reach. For nothing would seem harder to reconstruct than the specific psychological history of a work of art, that is, the sequence of intellectual and emotional promptings (deliberate and unconscious) leading to its creation.

If there is an issue here, it is to be found in the meaning of the familiar expression "live creature." Does it mean that we must put aside a purely spiritualistic view of art, or avoid a capricious and empty mannerism in our tastes? And would not the men guilty of these tendencies be live creatures all the same? In short, what human being that is breathing and moving is not a "live creature"? The only answer seems to be that this term, like "experience," is not neutral but what Dewey himself calls "emotional," that is to say, a term presented as descriptive but really pledged to some subsurface preference. Dewey argues for a wholeness in man's intellectual, moral, and aesthetic experience, recalling the Greek view that good conduct was graceful, and graceful conduct good. Our morality, he says, is the product of dogmatic artifices and induced anxiety, and, for that reason, inharmonious, struggling, ragged or, in one word, ugly. But, however we may decide on the intellectual comforts of proper conduct, the application of such a view to art would mean that anything is artistic that creates well-being, is the product of well-being, or is capable of "conflict-resolution." This would be a difficult theory to document indeed. Mozart sometimes knelt in supplication for creative strength. He also had a bawdy sense of humor. But his music flows with a feeling of unchecked ease and purity, wholly and perfectly "composed." And, looking at the other side of the matter, we might ask into what realm of comfort and balance is the mind cradled by Goya's sketches, or by the paintings of Hyeronimous Bosch, bristling with mystifying fears and laden with the rot of human venality? For, what is a resolution of conflict to the artist, in the sense that he finds the form to state the problem, may be the beginning of conflict for the viewer, who finds himself challenged by the power of the artist's statement.

It is nevertheless Dewey's intention to judge artistic success as part of a symbolic accommodation to the surroundings, including, of course, the social surroundings. "Inner harmony," he says, "is attained only when, by some means, terms are made with the environment." [12] And reading further and more closely we find that, in a social sense, the significant terms of the environment are not just events, the inescapable conditions of human life or, in a large sense, experience. They are "the normal processes of living," and what is "characteristically valuable in the things of everyday enjoyment." [13] Meaningful aesthetic expression, Dewey adds, depends on the development and accentuation of a continuity between these realities and art. The answer to what the artist as a "live creature" might be is, then, clear. He is someone who makes creative use of the characteristically valued and enjoyed normal processes of living.

Curiously, when Dewey discusses form as such he contradicts some of the things he says when he discusses social content. He quotes Henri Matisse on the emergence of form through the building of balanced relationships of color. He also recalls an illustration from Max Eastman's *The Enjoyment of Poetry*, which runs more or less as follows: A number of men are riding the ferry-boat between New Jersey and New York City. Some of them must go into New York and pass the time of the trip as best they can. One man, a real estate agent, tries to calculate the value of the land from the height of the buildings. Another, who is on his first journey to the city, is excited but bewildered. Somewhere on that boat one man may be looking at the buildings as colored and lighted masses in relation to one another. He, says Dewey, sees aesthetically, "as a painter might see." [14]

This rings a note of unexpected and remarkable aesthetic purism. Dewey says nothing about civic or public character, as he did in the case of the Parthenon, or about the social or institutional significance of the buildings. For that matter it does not occur to him that art has *also* been created to express excitement, sudden experience, and the glorification of wealth. The reason is that Dewey is engaged here in showing that form, as "an operation of forces that carry the experience of an event, object, scene, and situation to its own integral fulfillment," is true of art as it is true of all experience. Form makes experience possible, because it gives experience structure, articulation, and a point of resolution. It also determines the basis of expressive adequacy. "If the matter is of a jolly sort, the form that would be fitting to pathetic matter is impossible. . . . In comedy a man at work laying bricks while dressed in evening clothes is appropriate; the form fits the matter. The same subject matter would bring the movement of another experience to disaster." [15]

These generalizations show Dewey's unwittingly stubborn tendency to simplify art for the sake of a point of theory. Of his statement about the overdressed bricklayer as an alternative form of expression one can say that it is genuinely incomprehensible. What *else* does Dewey have in mind that can be expressed by a man in formal clothes laying bricks? What *is* the subject that would upset another experience? Comicity as such? The man laying bricks in a frockcoat? The scene is not the formal expression of a funny subject matter. *It* is funny. In another sense Dewey does not seem to realize the complexity of his own suggestion. Is the funny always "funny"? Dewey's little fiction evokes Chaplin, but with Chaplin such a situation would pantomime the spectacle of desperate straits and absurd pride, which is more than comicity or, at least, any easy notion of it. Are Watteau's clowns self-effacing, accusing, or just innocent fools? They are certainly wistful, which might mean all three. Dewey says that if the matter is jolly it could not take a pathetic form, and he would no doubt maintain the opposite as well. But, obviously, neither is true. Oddly, Dewey writes as if there were no such thing as irony. The very greatness of *Don Quixote*, as a work of art and of thought, depends on our inability to separate the comical from the tragic. What makes Kafka so depressing is that he regarded what he had to say about the human condition as a joke.

Dewey's arguments about form are inseparable from his attacks on the nineteenth-century concept of sensation. In an early article on the theory of stimulus and response he showed how the character of an observed object, and the character of the action towards it, were one with the nature of the complete experience. Or, as he put it, that impulse is not just discharge but must have medium and form to become expression.[16] These are important observations in the sense that they dispel systematically a false proposition. They are also a demonstration of the power of precise intellectual schemes, like the stimulus and response theory, to confound the testimony of reality, since all experience, social, aesthetic, and intellectual, shows that human acts are inseparable from a condition of quality and a means of expression.

"Perceptions fall into the brain rather as seed into the furrowed field. . . . Each image breeds a hundred more." These words of Santayana, quoted by Dewey, are not only true but inescapably true. And Dewey should certainly have assumed this of art, for if art is not an expressive medium and an act of form, it is nothing. Dewey was right in insisting on the aesthetic quality of daily acts (we should happily concede that good pitching is a beautiful thing). But the essential point left undecided is whether there is no distinction between the aesthetic and the artistic. The distinction is important because of Dewey's unspoken assumption that the closer one is to a direct aesthetic experience the more social that experience is, and that the more social an aesthetic experience, the closer it is to artistic expression and form. If one is thinking of the aesthetic aspects of a collective ritual, such as tribal singing and dancing, aesthetic feeling is, of course, indistinguishable from social feeling. But Dewey might have recognized that even popular aesthetic traditions of our society, such as the contemplation of nature, may be cultural properties and private practices which depend for their meaning on the individual's belief that he is the subject of a solitary experience. It is true that Emile Durkheim, who described so well the rituals of collective feeling in *The Elementary Forms of Religious Life,* thought that even the supreme act of loneliness, suicide, had social causes. But Durkheim did not deny the reality of individual emotions as a concrete experience. To deny this would be to deny in life, and in art, the presence of intimacy, fantasy, or personal sensuousness, anger, and love. Dewey ignores this possibility because he tends to think that all psychological energy, at least all meaningful and real psychological energy, flows towards the environmental "others." This makes it difficult to imagine examples of art based on common experience which, according to his formula, would not result in some form of popular or folk piousness. Would Ernest Hemingway, Mark Twain, or Ring Lardner be instances of the social artist? They all turned to popular life, and Hemingway was, if nothing else, concerned with Experience. Yet Hemingway is fundamentally a romantic writer whose fishermen, boxers, and bullfighters are really heroes of transcendental daring for its own sake. As for Twain and Lardner, one wonders what in them would have been the social *function* of literature, since they were both native-grown iconoclasts, unmoved by the edifying preoccupations which dominated Dewey.[17]

If we cannot accept that experience is always, in Dewey's particular sense, social, what will make it so? The answer would seem to be art, which, by removing aesthetic emotion from the realm of direct experience, and giving it formal expression, makes it communicable, that is, social in a true sense. Not only that. Contrary to what Dewey assumes, art is also capable of giving aesthetic values (in his sense of a meaningful life-experience which resolves a human question) to something that is not aesthetic in actuality. To have to listen to the barbershop conversation in Lardner's *The Haircut* would make anyone desperate with boredom. But reading it we feel the boredom only as a structured and synthetic image-idea, that is, as a symbol. We know that both the teller of the story, the barber, and his subject, the town's practical joker, are insufferable bores. But we are not ourselves bored because of the formal powers of expression of the artist.

Dewey's psychological populism seems a notably well-meaning view today if we consider the worldwide surfacing of the masses' capacity for the glossy, the ingeniously fraudulent, the stereotyped, and the transient, or the post-traditional wave of philistinism in changing societies whose passionate goal seems to be to embrace the consumption tastes of industrial societies, no matter how frivolous or how ephemeral. Neither can one forget that among the art forms dedicated to the "things of everyday enjoyment" none are more conspicuous than the anecdotal prints and reproductions hanging in countless living rooms. This might seem to invite an unfair inference, since Dewey intended his philosophy as a technique for *dealing* with problems, and the avoidance of problems is the first canon of *kitsch* and sentimentalism. Besides, someone will say, there is plenty of art which is topical and also great. To the first the answer is that, while no one will want to accuse Dewey of advocating calendar scenes as aesthetic models, his persistent talk about "normal processes of living" happens not to be the strongest argument against them. To the second one can only say that great descriptive art, great in a formal sense *and* as an expression of a "life-experience," has been created under an infinite variety of personal and social circumstances, normal and "abnormal," if for no other reason than that art is precisely what Dewey said philosophy ought to be: an endeavor dedicated to the apprehension of meaning rather than the discovery of "truth." [18]

John Dewey's Social Art and the Sociology of Art

[1] John Dewey, *Human Nature and Conduct* (New York: Holt, Rinehart & Winston, Inc., 1932); especially Introduction and Part I, sections 1-5. For the relation of Dewey's social view to education and philosophy, see among others: *Democracy and Education* (New York: The Macmillan Company, 1916) and *Reconstruction in Philosophy* (New York: 1920).

[2] Horace Gregory, *The New York Herald Tribune*, May 6, 1934.

[3] John Dewey, *Art as Experience* (New York: G. P. Putnam's Sons, 1934), p. 3.

[4] *Ibid.*, pp. 4-5.

[5] *Ibid.*, p. 78.

[6] John Dewey, *Problems of Men* (New York: Philosophical Library, Inc., 1946), p. 178.

[7] *Art as Experience*, pp. 330 ff.

[8] Alexis de Tocqueville, *Democracy in America* (New York: Alfred A. Knopf, Inc., 1945). Two volumes. Vol. II, pp. 71ff.

[9] Henry Berenger, *L'Aristocratie Intellectuelle* (Paris: 1895), p. 166.

[10] Though hardly sociological in an age of mass polls, questionnaires, and interviews, this statement is still true in two important ways. Historically, because our information of the social past comes from the testimony of its articulate men; and generally, as a description of social imagination, because the commonplace portrayal which a given public has of its society tends largely to be derived from literary and artistic creation, both good and bad.

[11] *Art as Experience*, p. 87.

[12] *Ibid.*, p. 87.

[13] *Ibid.*, p. 87.

[14] *Ibid.*, pp. 135, 136.

[15] *Ibid.*, p. 137.

[16] John Dewey, *Philosophy and Civilization* (New York-London: G. P. Putnam's Sons, 1931), pp. 233-48.

[17] It would also be well to remember that in genuine folk and popular art, as in the great artists of folk and popular inspiration, from Villon to García Lorca, one finds lyrical sadness, lyrical sensuousness, human fellowship, human cynicism, and bawdy good spirits, not just some form of wholesome and organic "democratic" feeling. "Genuine" folk and popular art is taken here to mean the significant art of which people are capable outside of formal sponsorship and the tutoring of "high culture." In this sense it stands for the opposite of the manufactured popular art of today and its mass acceptance. As the concluding paragraph of this article makes clear, people are also capable of surrendering their autonomous traditions, and developing the psychological characteristics required by the mass market, both in art and otherwise.

[18] *Philosophy and Civilization*, pp. 2-5.

Eight

A WOMAN NAMED COURAGE

In his absorbing analysis of a writer little known to English readers, Hans Speier exemplifies the merits and limitations of the case study. He explores in depth, with precise and telling detail, what kind of artist Grimmelshausen was and how his creations articulate with the society of seventeenth century Europe. The vivid historical focus and the dense texture of narrative let us see the writer and his time with a richness absent from most essays in the sociology of literature.

As any case study, *A Woman Named Courage* implies at least two very difficult questions for the social scientist. The first is, how can one generalize from this convincing portrait of Grimmelshausen to state something universal about the relation of literature to society? The second is the question implied by most selections in this volume and rehearsed by Dornbusch in his concluding reflections on method: how can the author's insights be "verified" by other observers, especially when, as in this instance, his analysis rests on a singular configuration of talents for translation, historical study, literary criticism, and sociological scholarship?

At the same time, the peculiar merits of the case approach are explicitly displayed. Speier's fine-grained historical report, his marvelous sensitivity to the shadings of a literary work and its total social context, his probing discussion of Grimmelshausen's personality, all serve as a brake on easy speculation. We are shown plainly how complicated is the interweaving of artistic intent with the shaping forces of personal and social circumstance. We are shown, too, how careful must be the sociologist's reading of a literary text. Further, of course, Speier reveals much of value in itself—much that satisfies an intrinsic interest in the artist and his period. Such a clinical emphasis is clearly a legitimate technique of literary criticism; it is perhaps less clearly a sociological technique, although one might aver that many of the investigations treasured by the social scientist have been rooted in deep examination of very specific milieux, from Freud's consulting room to William Foote Whyte's street corner.

One of the notable features of *A Woman Named Courage* is its extraordinary exercise in the sociology of knowledge. Speier is not content to assign Grimmelshausen's style or his themes to some oversimplified personality characteristic or to his socio-economic background. Instead, he illuminates the complexity of the causal chain, limns a delicate tracery of antecedent and result, and keeps the conscious effort of the novelist in the forefront of attention.

At the heart of Speier's study lies the person of Courage herself. She is brought before us as an exciting, amoral creature, suffused with life and animated by heroic energies. In her freedom from hypocrisy and her obdurate selfishness she might be seen as cruelly refreshing. Is Courage an "existential" heroine, perpetuating the force of life in a meaningless universe from which God is absent and in which ideology offers no recourse?

A WOMAN NAMED COURAGE

Hans Speier

The Simplician Writings

In 1668 the catalogue of the Frankfurt Book Fair announced the publication of a new novel with the title *Der Abenteuerliche Simplicissimus Teutsch. The Adventurous Simplicissimus, that is, True Description of the Life of a Strange Vagabond, named Melchior Sternfels von Fuchshaim,* was published in 1669. It contained the grim story of a deceptively simple man during the Thirty Years' War, or, to be exact, from 1622 to 1650, two years after the conclusion of the Peace of Westphalia. The editor of Fuchshaim's alleged autobiography, which consisted of five parts or books, called himself German Schleifheim von Sulsfort. In the same year, 1669, a *Continuatio* or conclusion of this work was published both separately and as the sixth book of *The Adventurous Simplicissimus.* This *Continuatio* was signed by another editor with the initials H.J.C.V.G.; he declared that the story of Simplicissimus was not an autobiography, but a piece of fiction written by Sulsfort, partly in his youth "when he was still a musketeer" in the Thirty Years' War. According to H.J.C.V.G., Sulsfort's true name was Samuel Greifnson vom Hirschfeld, a name that he had concealed by transposing its letters to make up the anagram Melchior Sternfels von Fuchshaim (Fugshaim).

But H.J.C.V.G. were not the initials of an editor who pretended to know and reveal the identity of the author; instead, they were the initials of the true author, Hans Jacob Christoffel von Grimmelshausen. In his youth he had indeed been a musketeer in the long war, and it was established later that various passages in his novel reflected actual experiences in his life. Samuel Greifnson vom Hirschfeld was merely another anagram of the author's true name, just as German Schleifheim von Sulsfort and Melchior Sternfels von Fuchshaim were such anagrams. In the course of his literary career Grimmelshausen used no less than seven other pen names. Only three of his works were published under his real name, namely two conventional novels, *Dietwald und Amelinde,* 1670, and *Proximus und Lympida,* 1672, and a small, unimportant, anti-Machiavellian treatise, *Ratio Status,* 1670.

Grimmelshausen's identity was re-established in 1837, one hundred sixty-one years after his death.[1] When Goethe and Lessing read *The Adventurous Simplicissimus* they did not know that its author was Grimmelshausen, and in a learned edition of 1836 authorship was still attributed to Samuel Greifnson. And yet, Grimmelshausen not only had hinted at his identity through the initials H.J.C.V.G., but also had prevailed upon three poets, Sylvander, Perikles, and Urban, to praise him under his true name as the author of novels that he had published or was going to publish under some pseudonym. To complete the masquerade, these poetic commendations of Grimmelshausen and of his Simplician writings appeared in the prefatory material of the two novels which the author published under his own name, and much later it was discovered that Sylvander, Perikles, and Urban were all one person: Grimmelshausen himself!

When he wrote commendatory poems on his own behalf he followed, as it were, the advice laughingly given by the friend to whom Cervantes complained about his misfortune in not having an illustrious poet to help *Don Quixote* on its way: "Your difficulty, respecting the want of sonnets, epigrams, or panegyrics by high and titled authors, may at once be removed simply by taking the trouble to compose them yourself, and then baptizing them by whatever name you please."[2] Probably, Grimmelshausen panegyrized himself because he had no trusted friend among the literati to render him this service. His praise was so fulsome, however, that there can be little doubt of his interest in satirizing the complimentary style of commendatory poetry while at the same time blowing his horn for his own works.[3]

The Adventurous Simplicissimus was an instantaneous and

great success. Within a few years several editions were published. Other authors used the name Simplicissimus in the title of their books, presenting further adventures of the picaresque character, who quickly became a folk figure in Germany like Till Eulenspiegel or Dr. Faustus.

Grimmelshausen himself not only made Simplicissimus the main character of his work, but also had him reappear in several other novels, treatises, and almanacs. Moreover, he often treated him as though Simplicissimus were the author of these books so that Grimmelshausen and the legendary figure he had created seemed to merge.

The resulting equivocation may mislead the unwary reader. It is not safe to attribute a particular view to Grimmelshausen merely because Simplicissimus can be shown to have held it at some time in his life. If the author resembled the main character in his works he must have been capable of many different things: solemnity and laughter, veracity and dissembling, moral preaching and cynicism, compliance with the demands of the Church and something close to blasphemy. By accepting the hero's views uncritically as those of the author, one merely raises the question as to what kind of man Grimmelshausen really was.

Simplicissimus grows older and less foolish in the course of the Simplician writings. The views he holds in his youth differ from those which he expounds as a mature man; evidently, the latter more than the former are likely to represent the author's own opinions. Except for the early part of *The Adventurous Simplicissimus,* all Simplician writings were composed when Grimmelshausen was in his late forties and early fifties. He was at that time a mature man, if it is right, as Aristotle suggests in his *Rhetoric,* that man reaches the prime of his mind "about the age of forty-nine."

The attempt to infer Grimmelshausen's convictions from the actions of the mature Simplicissimus is not without hazards either. For example, at the end of *The Adventurous Simplicissimus* the hero renounces the world, lives as a recluse on a remote island, and refuses to return to civilization, but in the sequels to the book he again moves about in this world as though he had never bid adieu to its troubles and follies. Thus, the renunciation has to be taken with a grain of salt. In the three major sequels Simplicissimus is no longer the main character; sometimes he does not seem to act at all but rather to observe, and comment on, the actions of others. Evidently, in this role he approaches the mature author most closely.

Grimmelshausen wrote three additional brief continuations and a *Zugab: Simplicissimus als Arzt* (*Addendum: Simplicissimus as Physician*), all of which he included as "side stories" in the 1670 edition of *The Adventurous Simplicissimus*,[4] and three other important novels: *Die Landstörzerin Courasche* (*The Story of Courage, The Archscoundrel and Vagabond*), 1670, *Der seltsame Springinsfeld* (*The Strange Skipinthefield*), 1670, and *Das wunderbarliche Vogelnest* (*The Enchanted Bird's-nest*), Part I, 1672, and Part II, 1675. Together with *The Adventurous Simplicissimus*, which consists of six books, these novels form a larger unit—the Simplician cycle (comprising ten books), Grimmelshausen's main literary achievement.

We also encounter Simplicissimus as a fictitious author or as a character in several other writings by Grimmelshausen, for example, in various didactic treatises dealing with the art of growing rich, with the reform of the German language, with certain superstitions, and with other matters. Simplicissimus is also the fictitious author of *Ewigwährender Kalender* (*The Everlasting Almanac*), published in 1670. Even in the briefest account of Grimmelshausen's large *opus*, which astonishingly enough was published in one decade, the last of his life, mention must finally be made of his earliest literary efforts, *Der satyrische Pilgram* (*The Satirical Pilgrim*), published in 1666, and a Biblical novel, *Der keusche Joseph* (*The Chaste Joseph*), which appeared a year later. *The Satirical Pilgrim* is completely dependent on other moralists of the time and without any originality. *The Chaste Joseph*, of which Grimmelshausen remained strangely proud even after he had greater attainments to his credit, was imitated and surpassed in literary quality by Philipp von Zesen, Grimmelshausen's contemporary, in his novel, *Assenat*.

Thus Grimmelshausen treated in his writings the most varied subjects, or as he put it, "high and low things": concerning "high things" he wrote rather poorly, in the taste prevailing at the courts and among the acknowledged literati, but he wrote very good popular stories.[5] The "low things," that is, above all, the Simplician writings, have survived, while Grimmelshausen's attempts at more refined writing are happily forgotten by everyone today excepting certain specialists in literary history.

Court and Tavern

The Thirty Years' War crippled German political and cultural life for several generations. During the war Germany had lost perhaps one third of her population. In 1648, when the Peace of Westphalia was concluded, she was left with about thirteen and a half million inhabitants. Only a very small fraction—perhaps five per cent—of this staggering loss had resulted from violence in battle. The relatively low rate of battle casualties—1000 to 1500 per year on the average—was testimony to the inefficiency of firearms. Bullets weighed ten to the pound, their penetrating power was low, and many of them missed their aim. This state of technology sustained the belief, so widely held in the seventeenth century and indeed well into the eighteenth century, that invulnerability could be acquired by magic and overcome only by magic bullets (or weapons other than firearms). Famous generals employed workers to manufacture such bullets of silver or glass.[6]

As was true of war until the second half of the nineteenth century, the biggest toll in lives was taken by epidemic diseases. In the Thirty Years' War other contributing factors to the awesome loss in life were local famines and marauding bands, many of which were composed of deserters from the armies.

While the long war was a total war in its time, its destructive power was shallow, making some rapid recovery possible. Stone and brick buildings survived even in those cities which were sacked, and wooden houses were quickly rebuilt. But owing to the shortage of capital and the low degree of administrative efficiency, demobilizing the troops was a painful process taking several years. Many mutinies occurred. In certain districts soldiers formed outlaw bands so that "for many years after the war merchants preferred to travel in great companies and well guarded." [7]

While the war had led to some mixture of races, it had failed

197

to open new routes of social advancement. "The social hierarchy emerged from the war as rigid as before." [8] The war produced a landless aristocracy, strengthened the importance of the peasant in relation to the rest of society, and contributed to the further decline of the burgher. When peace finally came, the privileged classes attempted to fortify their social position. The landed gentry succeeded in having feudal restrictions reimposed, so that in many districts peasants were no longer allowed to leave their village or to pursue any home industry. Many experienced middle-class secretaries and councillors were replaced in the service of princes "by a swarm of young place-hunters of noble birth whom the peace had deprived of their proper employment, and whose pride was only equalled by their incapacity." [9]

The influence of the commercial class had been declining prior to the outbreak of the Thirty Years' War, and the outcome of the war weakened its position further. When peace was concluded, industry and trade were hampered by innumerable tolls and taxes, a bewildering variety of weights and measures, and a multiplicity of laws regarding trade. For example, goods shipped from Strasbourg to the frontier of Holland had to pass no less than thirty different customs stations.[10] For a long time to come the middle class in Germany was to be composed of dependent officials rather than of entrepreneurs and merchants.

As Miss Wedgwood has pointed out, "the breakdown of social order, the perpetual changing of authority and religion in so many districts, contributed to the disintegration of society which was more fundamentally serious than the immediate damages of war." [11] The common people lived in fear of the devil and of witches, and not only the common people listened eagerly to reports of apocalyptic visions of the end of the world.[12] Many of these beliefs were taken seriously by both Christian and Jewish theologians; nor were the ties between science and magic as yet entirely cut.

Germany as a whole was divided into three hundred principalities. She had neither a political nor a cultural center like Paris. At the court in Vienna, Latin and Italian were spoken, and Vienna, like Munich, was a site of Jesuit, rather than German, culture. Political life in Germany was provincial in character. Absolutism lacked the scope and luster that it attained in contemporary France. The German courts enjoyed the ephemeral splendor and celebration of power rather than its substance. Nor did Germany have the salon as a social institution in which *bienséance* was developed and pedantry shunned. Instead, bombastic dignity was valued more than true elegance; heroic gestures, like all theatricality—whether in fireworks or opera, in masquerades, or in public displays—were applauded. And all this rarefied, illusory, expensive culture was entirely removed from the mainstream of society. The distance from the courts to the people was farther than that from the monarch to Heaven.

German literature was dependent upon achievements in Italy, Holland, England, and, above all, France and Spain. Especially the German novel—whether heroic, pastoral, picaresque, historical-political, or comical—consisted almost exclusively of translations, adaptations, and imitations of foreign works. There was a deep gulf between the educated minority and the uneducated mass of society. Since the authors valued scholarship, they did not write for wide public approval.

Popularity meant for an author that he had failed to produce a work of art. Poets banned from their collected works songs that had had the misfortune of reaching the common people. The poets were ashamed of having written such poetry.[13] Similarly, in serious baroque music popular taste was given no consideration. Complaints that the common people failed to understand the elaborate church music of the age were disregarded by the composers. In his *Psalmodia Christiana* (1665), H. Mithobius took note that the common people were unable to follow "all tricks and artifices of the musician," but in his view it was sufficient for them to know that they were listening to a sacred tune. Instead of suggesting that contrapuntal complexity be abandoned to bring the music within the grasp of the untrained, Mithobius held that "God cannot be praised artificially enough" and that the people should rise to an understanding of music by "exercise." [14]

The historical-political novel was fully intelligible only to the aristocracy, because only they could understand the many allusions it contained to contemporary events and personages. It was not rooted in the life and imagination of the people,[15] but written for a socially exclusive audience whose life and manners it idealized. Anton Ulrich, Duke of Brunswick, anonymous author of *The Syrian Aramena* (1669-73) and *The Roman Octavia* (1676), was one of the foremost writers in this genre. Goethe thought highly of his style, and some German critics regard him still today as the greatest German baroque novelist.[16]

Anton Ulrich's *Aramena* contains a long *Voransprache,* a preface addressing "the noble reader," in which the social theory of what we shall call the conventional novel is fully developed. Claiming that the historical-political novel, like Barclay's *Argenis* (originally written in Latin), d'Urfé's *Astrée,* or the Duke's *Aramena,* contain more truth than do historical yearbooks, the author of the preface proudly presents the conventional novel as a mirror of princes. "Such novels are real schools for the court and the nobility, which ennoble the soul, the mind, and the manners and teach refined, courteous speech." [17] Similarly, the publisher (Esaias Fellgiebel) of some of Daniel Casper von Lohenstein's tragedies recommended the author's novel *Arminius and Thusnelda* (1689) to "princes, noblemen and persons in the service of the state in peace time as well as war": they would be both pleased and instructed by it.[18] Lohenstein, a patrician, wrote for noblemen who, different from the country squires, were educated to assume positions in the higher bureaucracy of the absolutist states.[19]

The conventional novel dealt with matters of state in an exemplary and representative fashion. Its main characters were members of ruling houses, and since the interest of state coincided with the fate of the ruling families, their affairs of the heart and their intrigues had political significance. Of *Aramena* it was said in the preface that "it had grown at the court and not in the dust of the schools. It is not covered with the dust of the vulgar, but speaks of the history of princes with great politeness and in quite princely a fashion." The alleged purpose of the novel was to rid the aristocracy of its common opinions and to ennoble their minds through examples of virtue and true wisdom. In order to accomplish this aim, the august characters were placed in situations of conflict in which reason gained the ascendancy over passion, the interest of state triumphed over love, and constancy and dignity prevailed.

In all conventional novels of the period history was merely a façade for staging the moral problems of contemporary aristocratic life. Whether Roman, as in La Calprenède's *Cléopatre* or Anton Ulrich's *Octavia*; Teutonic, as in La Calprenède's *Faramond*, Lohenstein's *Arminius,* and Buchholz's *Herkules*; or Asiatic, as in La Calprenède's *Cassandre,* Anton Ulrich's *Aramena,* and Zigler's *Asiatische Banise,* history was always a fountainhead of virtue and wisdom. Since nothing new happened in history, lessons for modern use could be gleaned from ancient events.[20]

The conventional novel also offered models of polite conversation on a variety of topics, which permits insight into the manners at court. For example, Anton Ulrich's *Aramena* contains a conversation on the question of whether it is possible for a disappointed lover to love a second time, and in Lohenstein's *Arminius* a discussion is held in the company of distinguished ladies on whether it is a lesser misfortune to be blinded or to be castrated.[21]

All conventional novels demonstrate through the behavior of the main characters the importance of dissimulation in guarding oneself against false friends, rivals, and evil intrigues. Dissimulation is associated not only with the pervasive distrust which governs all human relations in high places, including those among lovers and friends, but also with the demands of dignity and courtesy. In the conventional novel, as in life at court, the distance between two persons is never closed.[22] Even friends and lovers remain ultimately strangers, who at the slightest turn of fortune are at once inclined to believe that they have been mutually betrayed or deceived.[23] Never is unshakeable confidence placed blindly in a friend or a lover. In these circumstances the ability to suppress emotion is both necessary for insuring survival in an intensely dangerous milieu and praiseworthy as a sign of dignity that no misfortune can undermine. Lohenstein in his *Arminius* repeats almost verbatim a rule of conduct contained in Gracian's *Art of Worldly Wisdom* (which he translated into German) to the effect that neither fortune nor misfortune should affect the facial expression of the hero. The hero's perfection becomes visible when he receives the news of being condemned to death, and neither his voice nor the expression of his smiling mouth changes: he continues playing chess.[24]

In this moral climate silence is often pregnant with meaning.

Anton Ulrich at one time explains a moment of silence as the result of both grief and the desire not to annoy society by complaints. The personal and the intimate are suppressed. Everything is representational and public. Even Zesen, whose ethos is more bourgeois than that of Anton Ulrich, says in his *Assenat* of Joseph and his bride that it would be unseemly to divulge their conversation.[25] In the conventional novel only the villains display unbridled passion. Heroes and heroines attain mastery over nature by silence, dissimulation, patience, and stoical equanimity.

The authors of the historical-political novel were ". . . mostly either distinguished members of the titled nobility and other aristocrats or people acquainted with such persons."[26] For poets and writers who were not of aristocratic descent few avenues to social recognition were open. Perhaps the most important one was membership in a language society where intellectually distinguished commoners met aristocrats with an interest in literature.[27] Another way of attaining social distinction was through panegyrical poetry and prose praising other authors and, above all, some personage at the summit of political power.[28]

Grimmelshausen remained throughout his life a child of the lower middle class. He was at home in taverns rather than at court. He knew beggars and soldiers but no great merchants or important officials; he was familiar with peasants and lowly people in small towns and villages, with camp followers and jugglers, but only with a few members of the aristocracy. His relations with polite society were tenuous; nor did he belong to any literary clique or society. His wide knowledge was acquired autodidactically, mainly with the help of compendiums. He did not travel abroad and did not speak any foreign language.

The kind of people Grimmelshausen knew best appear in his Simplician tales. The relation of these tales to the conventional novel resembles that of comedy to tragedy. Martin Opitz's description of comedy fits the Simplician writings well, though not perfectly. In his *Book on German Poetry,* he said that "comedy consists of low (*schlecht*) things and persons; it deals with weddings, festivities, gambling, fraud and roguery of knaves and vainglorious soldiers, with love affairs, the frivolity of youth, the miserliness of the aged, with procuring and other matters that occur every day among common people." [29]

Grimmelshausen's main characters in the Simplician writings are not heroes. They are socially undistinguished—soldiers, camp followers, highwaymen, and the like. Their actions have no political consequences whatever. In their adventures they are ensnared by the physical needs of the body, by passion, and by evil. They do not love but fear their neighbors, much as the courtier in the conventional novel fears his rival, and they see the hand of the devil in everything unexpected that happens. They are concerned not with dignity but with survival.

The difference between the Simplician writings and the conventional novels of the baroque era is also manifest in the use of language. The Simplician writings abound with proverbial expressions and colloquialisms of the lower classes, whereas the language of high or learned society is formal and precludes proverbs; even Grimmelshausen's own two conventional novels are virtually free of proverbs. Because of the use of earthy expressions, colloquialisms, and dialect, Grimmelshausen's Simplician writings have an extraordinarily rich vocabulary; his German was richer than Luther's.[30]

The liberal use of proverbs is one of many features which Grimmelshausen's Simplician writings have in common with the popular literature of the folk books. There are also the same descriptive chapter headings and the "oral style" of delivery, originally born of the custom of having the folk book read out loud. The oral style is most evident in Grimmelshausen when the narrator, who tells his tale in the first person, interrupts himself to inform the reader directly that he should listen to the next adventure. This device, which Grimmelshausen employs very frequently in *The Story of Courage,* creates an illusion of the almost physical presence of listeners sitting around the storyteller. The novel begins with an imaginative conversation between the author and her former lovers. Then she addresses herself to Simplicissimus, and when she reaches the point in her story where she finally relates an adventure involving him, she writes—or rather says—"but now, Simplicius, I must finally tell you what a sound rating I gave you. For this reason I will no longer talk to you but to the reader. You may just as well listen, and if you think I am lying, don't hesitate to interrupt me." [31] As in all folk books and folk tales, Courage's and thus Grimmelshausen's "public" seems to be listeners who hear a story they are being told.

Some critics have said that Grimmelshausen's "grossness" has no parallel in any Spanish novel and that his realism "knows no subdual of detail." [32] This opinion is incorrect on both counts. His so-called realism slights or suppresses whole regions of reality—landscapes, architecture, family life, all of upper-class life and large sectors of the life of the lower classes, including work. Grimmelshausen does not describe seventeenth century society. He is as little realistic as are the authors of the picaresque tales in Spain.[33] His realism, such as it is, is exaggerated, burlesque, and obscene for the purpose of throwing his fantasies and his moral concerns into relief.

The impression of grossness and "realism" is perhaps created in large part by the prominence of scatological imagery in Grimmelshausen's writings. In order not to misinterpret this aspect of his work, it must first be understood that the inclusion of such material violated no moral taboo. Scatological topics were vulgar and hence comical. They appear not only in many folk books, but also in comedies of the period written by distinguished poets like Gryphius[34] and seen by the same audience that attended performances of tragic plays by the same authors. All satirical, comical, and picaresque writings emphasize the physical functions of man and abound with such imagery. Examples can be found in ample profusion in Quevedo's *Buscon,* if not in Aleman's *Guzman,* in Sorel's *Francion,* and in English tales of roguery.

In Grimmelshausen, and in the picaresque novel as well, scatological incidents furnish the most powerful scenes of humiliation. It seems that they do more than merely ridicule social distinction by pointing to common human frailties and natural functions that all men share alike. The victim in such scatological scenes is frequently reduced to a primitive state of helplessness. He is dragged through excrements, and in this regard the fiercely aggressive function of seventeenth century comical literature leaves nothing to the imagination. Everything is presented in the most blatant directness to the senses: excrement is smelled, felt, heard, and even tasted. When it is felt, it is often by the face as if the noblest part of the human body is the preferred target of degradation.[35]

It is only in a social environment in which the demands of Christian morality do not interdict erotic pleasures that these scatological interests recede. Most writers who deal with erotic subjects do not indulge in descriptions of vomiting, flatulence, and soiling oneself or others. For example, the Renaissance novella, which explored the erotic sphere freely, shunned, on the whole, the scatological realm.[36]

Grimmelshausen's novels seem to be filled with Christian condemnation of sex as sin. His description of sexual adventures and, more broadly, of all natural functions of the body fit the image of man as an animal that but for the power and grace of God would be devoid of spiritual life. At the same time, this spiritual life has an ethereal and synthetic quality in the Simplician tales, as though it could well be a superstitious delusion, whereas these same tales make it quite clear that there is nothing illusory about eating, vomiting, flatulence, defecating, and fornication. The pain of childbirth is the reality which remains of the woman's belief that she will give birth to the Messiah; dreams of peace on earth vanish in an itch that is caused by vermin; theological discussions end abruptly with a narrow escape from death; beauty is disfigured by syphilis; plans of marriage are thwarted by sudden loss of testicles or by unexpected threats of murder.

Grimmelshausen was, of course, neither an atheist nor a torchbearer of enlightenment. In many regards, the spirit of his Simplician tales points back, rather than forward, to religious skepticism and political disaffection in earlier times. It is related in spirit to *Reynke de Voss,* which Goethe called an unholy Bible of the world, and to *Till Eulenspiegel,* who, asked by her on his deathbed for a last word of wisdom, gave his mother the most cynical advice that ever came from the mouth of a dying man.[37]

Grimmelshausen was cool toward the organized religion of the Christian churches and seems to have had nothing but smiles for various facets of Christian theological doctrine which conflicted with the observation of nature, with common sense, and self-interest. A certain measure of such folk-blasphemy, as it were, has lived through the ages in proverb, song, and euphemism. On a few matters of great relevance to Christian theological doctrine, Grimmelshausen's views bordered on blasphemy. This fact is concealed from plain sight by a cloak of orthodoxy.

Grimmelshausen often played with blasphemy in his Simplician writings, but the three most striking instances are: the central tale in *The Adventurous Simplicissimus* concerning the madman who calls himself Jove, who wants to punish the world and hopes to establish eternal peace; the story about the false Jewish Messiah in *The Enchanted Bird's-nest*, Part II; and *The Story of Courage*.[38]

If a moral doctrine were distilled from Grimmelshausen's Simplician tales, it would be rigorously Christian in character, but the moral rigor of the man was tempered by grim laughter and by the fascination that natural, rather than moral, behavior, exerted upon him. He wrote about man as he naturally is.

Grimmelshausen was no Christian moralist who peevishly lamented temptation, rebuked man for his trespasses, and sat in judgment over his sins. The same writer, who quoted Guevara's fiery, ascetic words to conclude the fifth book of *The Adventurous Simplicissimus* with a grand and somber, if borrowed, renunciation of this world, found words of his own in praise of folly—and words of no lesser eloquence.

I think there is no one in the world who does not carry a fool around with him, for we are all alike, and looking at my own pears I can tell when others ripen.—"Hey, coxcomb," you may say to me, "do you think that just because you are a fool, others must be foolish, too?"—No, I don't say that; it would be saying too much. But I maintain that some people hide their folly better than others. No one becomes a fool merely because he has foolish whims, for in youth all of us have the like. But whoever lets them run loose is held to be a fool, because many people do not let their fool be seen at all or conceal him half way; those who suppress him altogether are simply peevish. Those who let him stick his ears out from time to time so that he can breathe some air and won't be choked, I hold to be the best and wisest men.[39]

Grimmelshausen conceived of "high and low things" as opposites, but he contrasted the Simplician or comical (*lustig*) style not with the style of the conventional baroque novel but with the theological style, that is, with the form and content of sermons and serious devotional books. Young Simplicissimus "becomes pale" when he sees a parson read "his" book, *The Chaste Joseph,* and is reproached by him for having treated at such length the alluring beauty of Potiphar's wife. But Grimmelshausen feels no compunction in introducing the aged Courage, a former camp follower, into the company of Secundatus, a nobleman, who presides over the conversation in his *Rathsstübel Plutonis (The Council Chamber of Pluto),* and this nobleman admits freely to having read the scandalous story of her life. The difference between Grimmelshausen's conventional novels and his Simplician writings is more clearly visible in subject matter and style than it is in the social status of his readers.

While it is extremely difficult to gain reliable insight into the social composition of Grimmelshausen's audience, it is almost certain that the author wished to have among the readers of his Simplician writings members of the aristocracy and of the learned. Some instances of such readership can be definitely proved. Thus the Duchess Sophie of Hannover wrote to her brother Karl Ludwig, an Elector of the Palatinate, that she had someone read to her *Simplicissimus;* she found its beginning very pious in character. She was also pleased with *The Story of Courage.* Nor did all learned readers reject the Simplician tales because they contained so many moral admonitions or because they were "vulgar." Such objections were raised by some of Grimmelshausen's literary colleagues who enjoyed social respectability (and did not hesitate as Protestants to write panegyrical poetry in praise of Catholic rulers). By contrast, men of freer spirit, like Leibniz, found *The Adventurous Simplicissimus* delightful reading. He wrote to the Duchess of Hannover that the work approached the genius of Charles Sorel's *Histoire Comique de Francion.*[40] This is high praise indeed, both because of the intelligence of the critic and because of the comparison he made.

Grimmelshausen began his literary career with extraordinary self-consciousness. In an age when poets were proud to be scholars, he seems to have been keenly aware of his lack of erudition, and may have feared criticism and ridicule. Thus, perhaps in order to protect himself, he not only masked the authorship of his first book, *The Satirical Pilgrim,* but also criticized his own writing in the first preface to that work. Then in a second preface, entitled "The

Author's Rebuttal," he proceeded to attack the imaginary critic on behalf of his readers, characterizing them as "simple-minded people like myself"; this second preface also contained a defiant statement to the effect that he had not written his book for gain: "otherwise I would have dedicated it to someone." [41]

His conventional novels were published under his own name. Grimmelshausen dedicated them to aristocrats, though with less than customary obsequiousness. Thus there is at least this much and possibly some additional evidence[42] that Grimmelshausen placed some value on his connections with the aristocracy.

He masked the authorship of all his tales written in the earthy and popular Simplician style; but with mounting literary success he gained self-assurance and hinted obliquely at his real name. At the same time he insisted that his Simplician works were not merely written to entertain and instruct the vulgar but to benefit everyone, regardless of social status.

Grimmelshausen's understanding of himself will always remain a matter of conjecture, but writing *The Third Continuatio* of *The Adventurous Simplicissimus* may have been a moment of self-recognition for him. "If my critics say so loudly that I am an ignoramus, why don't they leaf through my *Everlasting Almanac* and many other thoughtful little treatises remembering how often a philosopher wears an uncouth cloak. Similarly, it happens sometimes that under a simple sounding name and behind the printed words that deal with insignificant things something else is hidden which evades discovery by many a reader." [43]

Life

Grimmelshausen was born in Gelnhausen at the foot of the Spessart Mountains, probably in 1621 or 1622. He was a small child when his father died; his mother remarried in Frankfort am Main in April 1627. Her child grew up, virtually without parents, in the care of his grandfather Melchior Christoff, a stern Lutheran and a harsh man, who had lived in Gelnhausen as a baker and tavern keeper at least since 1588. In 1613 he was involved as a radical on the side of the burghers against the suppression of their civil rights by the councilmen of the town. He accused one of them of having homosexually abused his young son, Grimmelshausen's father.[44] It is not known whether Grimmelshausen ever learned about the incident; but since his grandfather testified before a commission that had been appointed by the Elector Johann Wilhelm to settle the civic conflict, this possibility cannot be dismissed. Nor is anything known about Grimmelshausen's relations with his grandfather, unless one wants to attribute special meaning to the fact that as an author he liked the name Melchior and used it often.

Perhaps because of his occupation, perhaps because of his political views, the grandfather had dropped the claim to nobility in his name in 1597, using his middle name Christoff as a surname. Caspar Christoff (von Grimmelshausen), for a long time held to be the older brother of the author but now almost certainly identified as his uncle, also used Christoff as his family name. Only for 1648, eight years after his grandfather's death, do we have the first documentary evidence of Hans Jacob Christoff's having reclaimed the family name, H. J. C. von Grimmelshausen. Until the age of twenty-six or twenty-seven he had been a commoner.

The circumstances of his early life were shaped by the Thirty Years' War. When he was still a small boy, in September 1634, Croat soldiers sacked Gelnhausen, and he was drawn into the maelstrom of the endless war. It is likely that he was taken away as a boy by the Croats and not much later captured by Hessian soldiers.

In 1639 Grimmelshausen became a musketeer in the regiment of Baron Hans Reinhard von Schauenburg in Offenburg, Baden, and beginning in 1645 he held a clerical job in that regiment for three years. From then on to the end of his life, Grimmelshausen lived in the Black Forest area in Germany within narrowly restricted boundaries, although his creation, Simplicissimus, traveled through all of Europe, Russia, to the Middle East, and to remote islands.

In 1648 Grimmelshausen advanced to the position of a regimental secretary when he joined another regiment, that of Schauenburg's brother-in-law, Johann Burkhard von Elter, but in that year peace was finally concluded, and the young man, now with a fuller and more distinguished name, became a steward for various members of the Schauenburg family. In this job he gained insight into the legal and economic affairs of his masters. These provincial experiences with local lords in Southern Germany were the closest Grimmelshausen ever came in his life to the upper reaches of European society, a long way indeed from its summits of power and splendor.

Apparently the steward of Baron von Schauenburg could barely manage to eke out a living for his growing family; he had married in 1649 and was to have many children. He collected taxes from the peasants, and brought recalcitrant debtors to court. For a while he also acted as host in a local tavern that belonged to one of the barons, and he sold horses to add to his income. In keeping books on his transactions for the baron, he committed irregularities which aroused the displeasure of Carl von Schauenburg.[45] In 1655 the steward was about to be discharged, but Baron Hans Reinhard gave him another chance, though under stricter supervision. When Grimmelshausen quit his job in 1660, he was in debt to the Schauenburg family for land bought with their funds. Thus at the age of about forty, von Grimmelshausen, the father of a large family, after many years of military and civil employment in the service of provincial noblemen that outranked him, had failed in preserving his honesty as well as in attaining security.

A year later he was employed for a while as steward of a castle belonging to a rich physician, Dr. Johannes Rüffer, who had a prosperous practice in Strasbourg. The doctor was an admirer of the arts, a friend and patron of important writers and poets like Moscherosch and Rompler, a member of the influential Tannengesellschaft in Strasbourg (a language society), and a poet, of sorts, himself. Grimmelshausen might have benefited from this association, if only because it gave him easy access to books and acknowledged writers. But again, he failed. He did not get along at all with Dr. Rüffer. The association lasted only until the spring of 1665, although Grimmelshausen was involved in legal quarrels stemming from this employment until 1672.

If the viciously satirical portrait of Dr. Canard in *The Adventurous Simplicissimus* was inspired by Dr. Rüffer, Grimmelshausen resented the social aspirations of the man and hated him deeply. In order to ingratiate himself with his noble and rich clientele, Dr. Canard, who is socially ambitious in the extreme, tastes the stool of his patients and defends this practice to Simplicissimus as a means to success and wealth. Even allowing for the freedom with which many seventeenth century authors used scatological imagery, Grimmelshausen could hardly have expressed his hatred and contempt more strongly and more characteristically.

Nor did he establish closer contacts with the other members of the language society in Strasbourg. Throughout his literary career he lacked any friends among the respected writers of his time, and he took furious issue with those among them, like Christian Weise and Philipp von Zesen, who criticized his works.

For the next two years Grimmelshausen was again a tavern keeper in Gaisbach. His house was small. The tavern on the first floor consisted of a guest room with a table and four benches and a kitchen. On the two upper floors were bedrooms, small chambers, and another kitchen. The small room in which the tavern keeper did his writing was located on the third floor. The yard contained a barn for cows and pigs.

In the spring of 1667 Grimmelshausen was appointed bailiff of Renchen, a small place in the Black Forest area, after his father-in-law had put up the required security for him. He now was under the jurisdiction of the Bishop of Strasbourg, although his immediate superior was the chief bailiff at Oberkirch. Thus Grimmelshausen finally reached a position that freed him of financial worries and gave him at the same time enough leisure to write. His income consisted in large part of a share in the revenues from Renchen, and much of the payment was made in kind.

Not long before his death on August 17, 1676, Grimmelshausen was drawn once more into a war, the war between the French, the Dutch, and the Germans; he probably re-entered military service in circumstances of which nothing is known. In January 1674 an imperial horse regiment took quarters in Renchen, and since the burghers were not reimbursed for their expenses they refused to pay taxes. Grimmelshausen must have been hard pressed like everybody else: one of his functions was to collect the taxes. But worse was to come. In June the whole army of Lorraine was stationed near Renchen, and many people fled in panic. Later that year an imperial army replaced the French and after an unsuccessful winter campaign in Alsace made Oberkirch its headquarters. In May 1675

Renchen was in the midst of the theater of war; in the battle at nearby Sasbach the French Marshal Turenne lost his life. At the time of Grimmelshausen's death, Renchen was virtually depopulated, and the roads were again as unsafe as they had been in the Thirty Years' War. Grimmelshausen was survived by nine children and by his wife, who died seven years later.

Grimmelshausen changed not only his name but also his religion. Some time between 1638, the first year which he spent in a strictly Catholic environment on the Upper Rhine, and 1649, the year of his marriage, he left the Lutheran Church. Neither the exact date nor the reasons for his conversion to Catholicism are known, but from the church records in Offenburg it is certain that he was a Catholic at the time of his marriage to Catherina Henninger, the daughter of a lieutenant of the guard. It does not seem prudent to attribute too much importance to this conversion.

Grimmelshausen's religious beliefs have been the subject of much controversy.[46] Some have considered his work to be inspired by Protestant thought, many other critics have read him as a Catholic whose works are filled with the spirit of the Counter Reformation.[47] In one excellent study, the influence of Pelagianism has been detected in the Simplician writings, and Grimmelshausen has even been called a nihilist,[48] whereas another eminent critic has found in his works "irenical understanding for the equal value of all faiths." [49] One student has taken Grimmelshausen for a man who, like the lower classes of his epoch, was still engrossed in medieval ideas of the world as a realm of the devil, of a united Christendom, and of Christian zeal to convert the infidels.[50] Still another student has stressed his progressiveness, saying that among all German satirists of the seventeenth century Grimmelshausen was the only one who looked forward to the unification of the Christian churches.[51] This meant attributing to him a spirit somehow akin to that of men like Calixtus[52] and Leibniz instead of seeing him as a superannuated crusader.

His work contains several striking passages in which the quarrels between the Christian churches are ridiculed. One of these passages occurs at the very end of the Simplician cycle. On a journey up the Rhine, a Catholic priest and a Protestant minister join forces in an attempt to convert a Jew who accompanies them. "Although this fellow had studied a lot and was well informed, he did not really want to argue. He said that the Christians should glue their own schisms together before trying to convert to their religion the Jews who were united. For even if one of them wanted to become a Christian, he would not know which Christian he should turn to, since each claimed to be best." [53]

There is almost general agreement that Grimmelshausen had little use for the established churches. His concern was with men's moral and immoral behavior. If anything, he regarded the hermit, rather than the priest or the monk, as a true Christian. Neither priests nor monks are presented in his work as venerable characters. With apparent approval he quotes a popular saying that preachers scold the people if they have nothing else in their heads,[54] and at one point old Simplicissimus angrily exclaims that he would rather have his son become a soldier than see him enter a monastery.[55]

The Christians whom Grimmelshausen admired most were not those who belonged to any of the established churches, but were the Hutterian Brethren, an anabaptist sect founded in Switzerland in 1525, which suffered much persecution until well into the eighteenth century. Some members of the original "Church of the Brethren" fled to Holland to escape Zwinglian persecution, and through their leader Simon Menno became later known as Mennonites. Other members of the church went to live in Moravia, then a haven of religious tolerance. Their faith forbade them to bear arms, private property was abolished in their community, the sexes were separated, and they developed a communistic system of rearing children. Later, these religious communities suffered the most cruel treatment from Turks and Jesuits alike, partly for religious reasons, partly because of their wealth. The patient brethren were dispersed to other lands—Russia, England, and North America.

Grimmelshausen described the life and institutions of the "Hungarian" Hutterites in loving detail and with astonishing accuracy.[56] It has been suggested that his information may have come from an itinerant member of the sect.[57] There can be no question that Grimmelshausen admired these anabaptists deeply. Simplicissimus declared that their heretical life, which he called "seemingly Christian," "excelled the monastic one." As the most learned critic of Grimmelshausen's views on this subject has said, his references to heresy and the mere appearance of Christianity among these anabaptists were probably made *"pro Ecclesia et Pontifice."* [58] Simplicissimus declared that he would have liked to live like a Hutterite if it could only be done "under the protection of the authorities," adding that as one of its members he would gladly have surrendered all his worldly possessions to such a community. But his stepfather, a peasant, warned him that he would never succeed in getting enough people to join!

More than any other passage in Grimmelshausen's writings, the chapter in *The Adventurous Simplicissimus* which describes the life of the Hungarian anabaptists is convincing testimony of the author's attachment to Christian moral teaching, but even this chapter proves nothing about Grimmelshausen's beliefs in any Christian dogma. His admiration is confined to matters of practical conduct. In all his Simplician writings, Grimmelshausen has little to say about God's mercy or justice and nothing to say about the Holy Trinity, the revelation of truth, the sacraments, or about the power of faith. He wrote as though acts of God cannot be anything but disaster rather than causes of joy, like the song of the nightingale or a good meal.

Whatever he says seriously about religion is pale and dry compared with the lively colors to be found in his humorous anecdotes. Consider this jest—if it is a jest—from *The Everlasting Almanac:*[59] "There was a fellow in his company who was very melancholy and sometimes troubled by his spleen. He was never more reverent than when he was in a state of drunkenness. Simplicissimus said about him that the man had every reason to ask of God to be called by Him when drunk; and if St. Paul himself were still alive and his shepherd, he could not admonish him in good conscience to stay sober."

Names and Identity

In considering Grimmelshausen's astonishingly frequent change of name as an author, it must be borne in mind that anagrams were a favorite sport in the baroque era. So were chronograms of various designs, for example, that of substituting for the date of publication at the bottom of the title page a few lines of verse or prose in which the letter symbols of Roman numbers added up to the desired year. Any verbal, numerical, allegorical, heraldic, or hieroglyphic expression that was enigmatic and in which secret meaning could be concealed exerted a peculiar fascination on the minds of men. Martin Opitz, the seventeenth century mentor of modern German literature, reminded his readers that poetry itself was "at the beginning nothing but a hidden theology and a doctrine of wisdom and heavenly things" concealed by wise men in the garb of rhyme and parable for the vulgar.[60]

Related to the concealment of names in anagrams was the passion for reading secret meanings into an ordinary word through rearranging its letters, just as the art of composing chronograms was related to interests in number symbolism and in numerical composition of literary works. In their search for hidden truth, poets and scholars studied gematria and other cabalistic teachings.[61]

Some of the tricks to which baroque authors took a fancy strike us as pedantic today. For example, Georg Philip Harsdörffer pointed to the affinity of money and death in a poem which exploited the possibility of transposing two letters of the German word for money so that its meaning becomes that of the word "lays"; the first line of the poem reads, "Money lays many a man into his grave" (*"Gelt legt manchen in das Grab"*).[62] Similarly, Friedrich von Logau, writing an epigram playing upon the anagram *Alter* (age)—*Taler* (money) began with the words, *"Ein Alter liebt die Taler . . ."* ("The old love money"); Logau's poetry is replete with anagrams. Abraham a Sancta Clara used the association of sound, assonance, and anagram to produce ever new meanings. He called *acht* the best number because it warned people to be careful (*acht geben*); similarly, *Diener* (servant) reminded him of *nieder* (below), since the servant is *"nie der für den er sich ausgibt"* ("never the one he pretends to be"); or *Esel* (donkey) suggested *Lese* (read), and *Corpus,* Porcus.[63] At one time Abraham managed to transpose the letters of the beginning of the "Ave Maria" no less than forty-seven times in such a way that each time a different meaning emerged.[64]

Grimmelshausen was a child of his age in that he, too, liked to play with words and numbers. An accomplished punster, like Rabelais and Shakespeare, he was fascinated by double meanings that were or could be locked into words. Sometimes he seemed merely to amuse himself. For example, as author of *The Enchanted Bird's-nest,* Part II, he gave himself an unpronounceable name composed of the letters of his true name, rearranged in alphabetical order: "Aceeeffghhiillmmnnoorrssstuu"; it almost looked like a printer's oversight. At other times, he seemed to be playful, while in fact he was serious.

An illustration of the serious use of "concealed writing" is Soon-Different's offer to teach Simplicissimus "the art of conversing with things that are dumb by nature, such as chairs and benches, pots and saucepans, and so forth." Soon-Different writes down the following words:

Manoha, gilos, timad, isaser, sale, lacob, salet, enni nacob idil dadele neuavv ide eges Eli neme meodi eledid emonatan desi negogag editor goga naneg eriden, hohe ritatan auilac, hohe ilamen eriden diledi sisac usur soladed auar, amu salif ononor macheli retoran; Vlidon dad amu ossosson, Gedal amu bede neuavv, alijs, dilede ronodavv agnoh regnoh eni tatae hyn lamini celotah, isis, tolosttabas aronatah asasis tobulu, Vviera saladid agrivi nanon aegar rimini sisac, heliosole Ramelu onoror vvindelishi timinituz, bagage gagoe hananor elimitat.[65]

After changing into a bird, Soon-Different flies away. Simplicissimus then sits down in the grass, gazing at the incomprehensible message. For fear of conjuring up some evil spirit he does not dare to pronounce the words in front of him, but the more he stares at them the more he wants to know their meaning. He goes on to say that "all boasting aside, I am pretty good at this art of deciphering" and claims to be able to understand "the meaning of concealed writing" even more difficult than the *Steganographia Trythemii,* that is, a secret code invented by an abbot named Johannes Tritheim (1462-1516). Suddenly Simplicissimus realizes that Soon-Different had given him an answer "with more candor than I thought he possessed." The solution to the riddle is withheld from the reader. He must find it himself, but the meaning of the message emerges easily enough. If all but the first and last letters of each word are discarded, the message reads:

Magst Dir selbst einbilden wie es einem jeden Ding ergangen; hernach einen Discurs daraus formirn; und davon glauben was der Wahrheit aehnlich ist; so hastu was dein naerrischer Vorwitz begehret.

Why don't you imagine how all things fare, put this into the words of a discourse and believe that which resembles the truth; then you will have what your foolish curiosity desires.

H. M. Moscherosch, as a satirical writer a forerunner of Grimmelshausen, mentions similarly coded, if less important, messages in his *Soldaten-Leben*—a French one written in Greek letters and another one in which vowels and liquid sounds are changed; for example, *Liebe* becomes "Riobo" and *wird* is changed into "wild." [66]

Neither the baroque fad of anagrams, however, nor Grimmelshausen's possible reluctance to claim authorship of his Simplician writings under his own name can fully explain the mystifying playing with his name. Why did he use so large a number of anagrams and at the same time make it possible for contemporary readers to discover his true name? At least two critics have expressed the opinion that Grimmelshausen's use of anagrams was more than mere play. One of them has suggested that the author's frequent transpositions of the letters of his name were "for him a symbol of the changeability of everything mundane." [67] The other has intimated that Grimmelshausen "was still alive to the ancient magical relationship between person and name." [68] Both suggestions have merit.

By thinking of ever new anagrams, Grimmelshausen did not entirely deny his identity, since all anagrams are made up of the letters contained in the same true name. Thus like Simplicissimus, Grimmelshausen may be said to change in appearance, but "never to be lost" in reality: as a person he is *"doch nit verlorn."* [69] Different from the use of other pseudonyms, resorting to anagrams may even be said to indicate *attachment* to the true name, as a symbol of personal identity, although the frequent rearrangement of the letters suggests no close attachment and perhaps a weakened sense of identity.

If the suggestion that Grimmelshausen still had a feeling for the magical relationship between person and name is applied to himself (and not merely to characters in his novels), his use of so

217

many different anagrams would suggest further that he was *uncertain* of his identity. In the truly magical relationship between person and name, the existence of the former depends on the latter; life and death are affected by naming.

Perhaps Grimmelshausen's playing with his own name bore a certain resemblance with the interest of adolescents in changing their given names or the spelling of these names. In adolescence such activities are expressive of the striving for independence and self-possession, of the effort to attain self-recognition as one who is not dependent upon others such as elders but instead exists decidedly of his own. When not the self, but only the name is as yet fully "given," casting away that given name and exchanging it for a new one of one's own free choice is more than an act of liberation: it is self-identification, an act of creation by truly magical means.

Little is known about Grimmelshausen's life, but it appears that he was indeed a man intrigued by the question of his identity, perhaps in no less than three different respects. He struggled for recognition not only as a writer but also as a member of an aristocratic family; it is even possible that he had doubts about his origin: who were his parents, and did he owe his existence to God or to nature? Finally, he seems to have been curious about bisexualism and to have had ambivalent feelings toward women.

The Cycle of Simplician Novels

Although each of the four main novels of the Simplician cycle is an independent unit that can be read and appreciated without knowledge of the other three, Grimmelshausen himself stated explicitly in the second preface to *The Enchanted Bird's-nest,* Part II, that the four novels or ten books formed a unit and that only those readers would understand his work who were familiar with the whole cycle. This statement has been variously interpreted by those critics who have taken it seriously.

The four novels are interlocked in the sense that Simplicissimus, Courage, and Skipinthefield appear in several books of the cycle, and not only in the novels which carry their names in the titles. For example, Courage, a woman more adventurous, more evil, and considerably more interesting than Defoe's Moll Flanders or Brecht's Mother Courage, is introduced to the reader first in a minor episode of *The Adventurous Simplicissimus,* when the hero, at a watering place in the Black Forest, meets a lady who pretends to be a noblewoman. He is attracted by her, but soon she strikes him as "more mobile than noble," [70] since for due payment she readily grants him the favors he seeks. Finally he leaves her to marry a young peasant girl. Not long thereafter he finds a new-born son of his abandoned on his doorstep.

The Story of Courage, the seventh book of the Simplician cycle, is the autobiography of the wily harlot whom Simplicissimus met at the watering place. She discloses her whole adventurous and dissolute life allegedly for the sole purpose of taking revenge on her lover, for she has never forgiven him (although her name was not mentioned in his tale). The original German title of her story begins with the words *"Trutz Simplex . . ."* ("To Spite Simplex . . ."), Simplex being a short colloquial version of the name Simplicius Simplicissimus. Courage reaches the height of her furious triumph when she reveals the true identity of the baby that she had ordered her maid to leave on Simplicissimus' doorstep. The baby was not the son of her lover, nor even her own child, but a bastard born by her maidservant. In her malice Courage wanted not only to cause trouble between Simplicissimus and his wife, but also to force him to bring up a bastard as his own son.

In *The Strange Skipinthefield,* the eighth book of the cycle, Courage's story is developed further. A young Swiss clerk to whom, it now turns out, she dictated the story of her life reminisces about the beautiful, evil woman who had taken revenge on Simplicissimus. The Swiss tells the story in an inn with the aged Simplicissimus and Skipinthefield, an old veteran maimed in the war, listening to his tale. Readers of the preceding books of the cycle remember Skipinthefield as he was in his younger days, a reckless comrade of young Simplicissimus in the war. They recall also that, like his famous companion, he, too, once loved Courage.

When Simplicissimus learns from the Swiss of Courage's base revenge by forcing a bastard child upon him, he replies calmly that the woman failed: the deceiver was deceived. For at the time when Simplicissimus had known Courage he had in fact seen less of her than of her maidservant, and the child left on his doorstep was, unbeknownst to Courage, his own son after all. Thus familiarity with various books in the cycle is necessary to reach a full understanding of the plot and of the individual events and actions that occur in any one of them.

The conventional baroque novel presented the world as enigmatic,[71] conveying this notion by unexpected reunions, incidents based on disguise and mistaken identity, startling disclosures of unexpected blood relationships, and many other devices. The "comic" novels of Grimmelshausen reverberate with echoes from the conventional baroque world. The origins of both Simplicissimus and Courage are at first obscure to the reader and disclosed only slowly to him. Disguises and mistaken identity play a prominent role, especially in the first sexual experiences of the two characters. Intricate interlocking of the various parts of a long work in order to cast a different light on past events from a new vantage point was a standard compositional practice in all baroque novels, including Grimmelshausen's works.

It is not only with reference to such literary techniques that the ten books of the Simplician cycle may be said to form a unit. They are held together also by a theme mentioned first at the beginning of the first book and recurring in the preface to the tenth. In both places Grimmelshausen remarks that the end of the world may be near. Several critics have taken these references as indications of Grimmelshausen's deep concern with Christian beliefs, the alleged focus of his entire work. This is not necessarily sound. Apocalyptic notions were widespread among both Christians and Jews in the seventeenth century; the times were full of portents and prophecies.[72] In all his works Grimmelshausen made literary use of widely held beliefs, particularly beliefs in the devil and various other superstitions.

In the first sentence of the cycle Grimmelshausen merely says in parenthesis about the present time that the end of the world "is held to be near"—"*diese(r) unsere(r) Zeit (von welcher man glaubt/dass es die letzte seye)*"—just as in the tenth book he mentions very briefly that the end of the wretched world "perhaps" is near—"*in jetzigen elenden, vielleicht letzten Zeiten.*"[73] In neither place does Grimmelshausen, who chose his words with care, contend that the end of the world "is" near. This idea was in conflict with Grimmelshausen's belief in continuous change and in transformation, for which he used the prominent symbol of the Phoenix and the allegory of Baldanders (Soon-Different), a popular version of the Renaissance idea of *fortuna*.[74] Nevertheless, the reference in the tenth book does point back to the beginning of the cycle and helps the reader to understand the work as a unit.

In further support of Grimmelshausen's claim that the cycle of novels is a unit, it might be said that no single book, but only the cycle as a whole, discloses the author's full view of the nature of man and of his life in this world. In order to understand the nature of man, the nature of woman must be considered, and an important aspect of the latter subject is a central theme only in *The Story of Courage*, the seventh book of the cycle. Similarly, in order to understand the nature of life in this world, both peace and war must be represented, and apart from the sixth book of *The Adventurous Simplicissimus*, only the two parts of *The Enchanted Bird's-nest* deal with life in peacetime; all other books of the cycle are put in a war setting. Finally, and most importantly, the meaning and consequences of Simplicissimus' two renunciations of the world, occurring at the end of the fifth book, and again at the end of the sixth, are bound to be misunderstood unless the sequels are read.

At least one scholar, Siegfried Streller, has attempted to show that Grimmelshausen wrote the whole Simplician cycle most carefully according to principles of number composition, so that the specific number of chapters into which the author divided his novels and the allocation of certain topics to positionally and numerically important chapters were to convey certain secret meanings.[75] This interpretation, which extends an earlier inquiry into the structural balance of *The Adventurous Simplicissimus*[76] to an extreme, suffers from certain intrinsic implausibilities, and in consequence of severe criticism has in the meantime been almost entirely withdrawn.[77]

For reasons other than those advanced in the controversy, Streller's original view is probably false. According to Streller, Grimmelshausen was an orthodox Catholic. All important numerical symbols in his work called for an interpretation in the tradition of Christian number symbolism, and Streller's original interpretation indeed relied heavily on St. Augustine. But the orthodoxy of Grimmelshausen's Christian faith is questionable. The Simplician writings contain many heretical and blasphemous allusions. To accept Streller's original view one would have not to disregard, but to dismiss as irrelevant, the meaning and double meaning of Grimmelshausen's words in many of his tales, both in the Simplician cycle of novels and in the Simplician *Everlasting Almanac*.

The Naming of Courage

Many characters appearing in Grimmelshausen's novels have significant names that are changed often. The development of Simplicissimus toward manhood is marked by various names, each appropriate to the respective stage of his career: "boy," Simplicius, "the Calf," Simplicius Simplicissimus, the Huntsman, Beau Alman; in the end he remains forever Simplicissimus, the most simple man. The meaning of the name Heartsbrother, Simplicissimus' friend, is apparent.

The extraordinary marriage contract between Courage and the musketeer who later is named "Skipinthefield" contains the stipulation that her husband answer forever to a name to be derived from the first command she gives him. Courage orders him to "skip into the field" so that in his absence she can enjoy herself with another man.[78]

These and other instances of significant names in Grimmelshausen's work are well known, but the shocking double meaning of two names has been overlooked. In the story of the false Jewish Messiah, Grimmelshausen's greatest novella,[79] Esther, a Jewish girl in Amsterdam, gives birth to a child nine months after what the Jews falsely believe to be an immaculate conception. The divine baby happens to be a girl. When Esther and her baby are baptized later, the child acquires the name of Eugenia—the literal meaning of Eugenia being "the well-born one"—and the mother is now called Mary. The names in the Simplician writings are indeed filled with pregnant meaning.

In *The Story of Courage* Libuschka (the young girl), while

dressed like a boy, is called Janco. In her adolescence she acquires the name Courage. Grimmelshausen's account of the naming of the great harlot is both daring and masterful. While Janco, the girl in boy's clothing, is a captain's servant, she gets into a fight with another boy at the sutler's. "When we were in the thick of it," she says, "this fellow grabbed me between the legs, because he wanted to get hold of my tool that I did not have." She prevails over him. Later in his quarters the captain asks Janco, whom he still takes for a boy, why she had beaten up her opponent so terribly. She replies, "Because he tried to grasp my courage which no other man has ever touched with his hand." [80] Then she confides in the young captain that she is a girl who disguised herself as a boy merely to escape abuse by the soldiers. She begs him to protect her honor, and he promises to do so but to her delight does not keep his word.

When the captain understands the meaning of the word "courage," with which the girl had "so colorfully described the emblem of her sex," he cannot help laughing at her and calls her Courage. Try as she will to rid herself of that name, it clings to her forever. Perhaps an important detail should be added here. In the story of her life the reminiscing woman explains that she used the word "courage" in her talk with the captain for reasons of seemliness: she wanted to avoid using a lewd word that would have hinted without sense of shame at her *female* sex organ. The name "Courage," then, stands for what Grimmelshausen regarded as the physiological site of vitality, bravery, and godlessness.

The Wild Virago

On the title page of *The Story of Courage,* Grimmelshausen indicates that in this novel the reader will find the account of a descending life. As a young woman, Courage is the wife of a cavalry captain, then she marries a captain of foot-soldiers, then a lieutenant, thereafter she becomes a sutler-woman, next the wife of a musketeer, and finally a gypsy.

Different from the heroes of the picaresque novel, who proceed from one adventure to the next without change in character, Courage does change under the influence of experiences. In the early part of the novel she is not the evil woman into which she later turns. To be sure, in part it is her native endowment that makes her a lustful creature, envious, greedy, and vindictive, but in part the evil in her emerges from senseless misfortune and in response to the cruelty of men.

Courage's exploits equal or excel those of men. In battle she is more valiant than her male companions, on a marauding expedition more daring, as a thief more resourceful and cunning. In most of her enterprises she is mistress, rather than helper; often she directs men to assist her. Her vitality is inexhaustible. When at the end of her career she has reached the status of an outcaste, she remains a queen, if only of the gypsies, aged, but still beautiful in appearance, her spirit unbroken and her skill unrivaled.

Whenever she fights men, whether with her fists as a young girl, with sword and pistol in battle later, with a cudgel after one of her many wedding nights, with a knife in the woods, or with wit, false tears, and pretty words—she almost always wins. Almost without exception men who oppose her are beaten up or humiliated, taken prisoner, killed, duped, or exploited by her. Courage is as much an Amazon as a harlot.

Indeed, she has many of the qualities of the heroines in the idealistic novels of the baroque era. Like them, she is a manlike, vigorous creature, a virago in the sense in which Pope still used this word:

> To arms, to arms the fierce virago cries
> And swift as lightening to combat flies.

The virago was an ideal of the Renaissance, fashioned after illustrious ancient models. Viragos appear not only in Ariosto's and Bojardo's heroic poetry, but also in life: women like Caterina Sforza—*"prima donna d'Italia"* to her contemporaries—or Isabella d'Este, the wife of Marchese Francesco Gonzaga, were admired for both their beauty and their courage in meeting the formidable risks of their careers.[81] The third book of Castiglione's *Cortegiano* contains the portrait of the perfect lady at court and the Renaissance tribute to the civilizing influence that women exerted on men, but it also presents many great ladies in contemporary Italy, as well as in antiquity, who showed "virtue and prowess" in "the stormes of fortune." [82]

In the German idealistic novel of the seventeenth century, this Renaissance ideal is still potent: many heroines are Amazons.[83] Even the middle-class Protestant, Andreas Heinrich Buchholtz, shows Valisca, his heroine, to be the equal of man in the fields of science and music, as well as in battle. Disguised as a beautiful young man on a journey to Prague, she "does miracles" fighting off the highwaymen who assault her. At the Persian court, again in men's clothing, she shines in the arts of fencing and shooting with bow and arrow. She cruelly kills three Persian servants, defends her honor against the attack of a lover by thrusting her "bread knife" into his heart, and slays robbers with lightning speed. She fights gloriously as a general in battle, her beautiful hair falling down to her shoulders, a precious sword and a quiver of arrows at her side. In Buchholtz's novel, not only is Valisca a virago, but also Herkules himself has female qualities: for all his manliness, he is beautiful like a young girl, dances daintily, and sometimes fights clad in the garb of an Amazon.

Viragos appear also in the novels of Anton Ulrich and D. C. von Lohenstein. Aramena is a royal personage and hence, on the whole, dignified rather than heroic: the wisest and most learned men seek her company even in her childhood in order to converse with her "about the most difficult things." And yet, the author shows her also as a warrior going to battle, with an expression "as majestic as benevolent, and as sensible as pious." At one time, she goes to the field leading a group of her female court attendants, "a marvelous host of the most beautiful ladies in the world."

But the most extraordinary viragos were created by Lohenstein. His princesses, Thusnelda, Ismene, and Erato are all fighting, duelling Amazons. Lohenstein uses the generally favored technique of showing an unidentified cavalier triumphant in extreme danger, without revealing at first that it is a woman who behaves so heroically. Then he lets the reader share the thrill of the loving hero at discovering that it is a beautiful woman, an Amazon, that has aroused his admiration.

"Amazon" is a word reserved in all these books for use in bestowing the highest possible praise upon a woman. Lohenstein gave this description of Thusnelda through the eyes of Marbod, who loves her: "The day before Marbod had looked admiringly at Thusnelda only [!] as a woman, but this day he saw her on horse-back as a valiant heroine. He had honored her as a half-divine being, now he was compelled to worship her as a goddess, for she sat astride her horse as a true amazon; in the race and in the shoot-ing contest she did better than all, and she slew twice as much game as anyone else. For no stag was too swift for her, no bear too cruel, no lynx too terrible." [84]

Anton Ulrich's second great novel, *Die Römische Oktavia,* H. A. von Zigler's *Asiatische Banise,* and Philipp von Zesen's novels do not present anything comparable: the Amazon motif recedes in these works. So it does in the writings of Johann Beer, whose realistic tales abandon the heroic, idealistic mood and discover new subjects of everyday life for literary treatment. But even in Beer's works Amazons do reappear, though with less bombast and fanfare. For example, in one of Beer's major works "a strange cavalier," his visor closed, suddenly appears to help the noble friends who fight the villain and his evil companions. The stranger wounds and captures the wicked man, and when the friends, rejoicing about their victory, want to thank the stranger, he lifts his visor. Then, the friends all grow pale. They behold "the beautiful Amalia, dis-guised in knightly armor." Needless to say, beautiful Amalia is loved by one of the cavaliers whose valor she excelled so impres-sively in the fight.[85]

If the modern reader is amused by all of this theatrical display of heroism, just as he might be amused by the theatricality of the heroes and heroines in distress—when they pray with tears stream-ing down their cheeks or lift their eyes up to the Heavenly Father in martyrdom—he is in a mood which Grimmelshausen seems to have shared. For Courage is at least as much a caricature and mockery of the Amazons to be found in the conventional baroque novel as she is a picaresque character. Her relation to the ideal virago resembles that of Don Quixote to the knightly code. Like the once much-admired ladies who populate the idealistic novel, Courage is an Amazon, but as a counter-heroine. She displays the qualities of a wild virago, in the modern sense of that term, while still retaining all the physical features of the ideal, in particular radiant beauty, physical prowess, and manlike energy. Like the Amazons in the conventional novel, she is also highly intelligent and indestructible in trial and misfortune. But in three respects she is a counter-heroine.

First, despite her noble, if somewhat tainted origin, she moves in a socially undistinguished milieu, resembling in this regard all of Grimmelshausen's main characters. She is never at court, and when she meets an ambassador, spends some short time at a nobleman's castle, or lives for a while like a woman of means in town, it is for her sexual enjoyment and the amassing of a fortune.

Second, it is not virtues that are put to test after test in Courage's life, as is true of the heroic careers in the conventional novel. If anything is tried, it is her ability to survive as a victim of a blind and impenetrable destiny. A plaything of senseless fate, which tosses her up and down in quick and violent motion, Courage is flung back and forth from the heights of prosperity to the depths of poverty, from health and beauty to disfiguring illness, from safety and comfort to hunger and humiliation. Thus, in Chapter 11 of her story, we find her happily married and prosperous; then her husband is killed in the war—an event told in one sentence. In the next chapter she is captured by the enemy, and a fiendish, revengeful officer thrusts her into an abyss of rape and sadistic torture. At the end of this chapter a very young nobleman rescues her, and she is treated like a little princess in his castle, but before long, some servants of the young nobleman's parents abduct her under false pretenses. Expecting to be married by her noble lover in Hamburg, she is abandoned and threatened with murder. In the meantime, all her savings, too, have been lost. So again, within the confines of a single chapter, the princess turns into a woman forced to earn her living at night. Pitting her wit and vitality against misfortune, she becomes in the end an outcaste, because neither man nor woman can win in a world which is more surely of the devil than of God: God is silent. But she survives and, like Simplicissimus, lives forever.

Finally, by all ordinary standards of Christian morality, which Grimmelshausen himself reasserts continuously, if only in the interstices of his tale, Courage is corrupt and wicked, whereas the heroines of the idealistic novel remain of untarnished virtue, no matter how often and how cruelly this virtue is put into thrilling jeopardy. Courage does not want to be virtuous. She has wild, insatiable appetites for men and riches, but no conscience. Her moral character owes nothing either to religious teaching or to Descartes' theory of passion, but almost everything to Galen's views of the human temperament. "I cannot take out my gall," she says, "as the butcher turns the pig's stomach inside out to cleanse it." She is full of lust and avarice and envy, and most easily aroused to fierce anger; she is evil, although it should be stressed that she never inflicts pain on others without provocation. But she is natural, and this cannot be said of the heroines whose Christian conscience she in fact defies and denies with every fiber of her existence.

Revenge

It was not Grimmelshausen's main intention in *The Story of Courage* to parody the conventional literary motif of the Amazon. While he succeeded in doing that, he had a still more important purpose in mind. Nor did he primarily want to show the corrupting influence of a long war on human character,[86] since the fact that life is corrupt had more weight with him than the fact that war is corrupting. Grimmelshausen stated his intention clearly through the mouth of Courage in the grand opening chapter of the novel. There Courage explains why she has decided to tell the story of her shameful, adventurous life. The sole motive of her confession, she says, is revenge. She wants to avenge herself on Simplicissimus, one of her many lovers, who had spoken ill of her. She laughs derisively at the idea that her monstrous confession might be taken as an act of penitence: her vengefulness involves not only Simplicissimus, but God himself. She defies both.

Her soul is entirely untroubled by the dissolute life she has led. If she confesses anything it is her godlessness. She fears God as little as men. She loves life and is not afraid of death. Thoughts of punishment and damnation, of divine justice and hell-fire, never curb her worldly passion. She loves money but not her neighbors, and she says so. Her life is exuberantly evil. Nature has made her so, and neither the magistrate nor the priests, neither man nor God, is able to change it. By telling her story in order to avenge herself, she makes a mockery of the act of confession in the Christian sense.

Courage's spite and revengefulness are aroused by small provocations. At one time she avenges herself on a young woman merely because in church a gallant pays more attention to this lady than to her. At another time she believes that someone has played a practical joke on her, and her fury knows no bounds. When her competitors make some gains which she thinks would be hers, if it were not for them, she must "repay" them. When she fears that one of her lovers may be influenced by his drinking companions to get hold of her money and wrest from her the power that she wields over him, she bides her time to rid herself of him and gives him a magical bauble as a good-bye present that nearly sends him straight into hell.

She knows herself perfectly well: "I stole not from necessity or want, but mostly in order to avenge myself on those I found hateful." [87] And again, "My heart was vengeful and unrelenting whenever I felt that the least offense or wrong had been done to me." [88] The intensity of her feeling is conveyed by Grimmelshausen not only by a whole series of rogueries in which revenge is the main motive but also, with startling force, by Courage's observation that her heart is like her body: when hurt, it takes a long time to heal.

Nor is the motive of revenge merely a trait of Courage's character. It reappears in other characters of the novel and in other works of Grimmelshausen. One of the officers whom Courage has taken prisoner happens to capture her some time later in battle. Not because he is attracted to her, but merely in order to avenge his humiliation on having been captured by her, a woman, he abuses her sexually and encourages other men to do the same. He acts in furious rage rather than under the impulse of unbridled sexual desires, and so his hatred and inability to forget the injury that was once inflicted upon him lead to the most brutally sadistic scene of the novel.

There are many other incidents in the Simplician writings which suggest Grimmelshausen's preoccupation with brutal revenge. The young Simplicius almost becomes the victim of a terribly vengeful man who is his master. Disguised as a girl, young

Simplicius arouses the sexual appetites of three persons at once, his
master, his master's wife, and his master's servant. When the master
believes that the servant is more successful in his advances than
he has been, he immediately calls Simplicius "a bloody whore" and
turns "her" over to the stable boys for sexual abuse. The master
acts according to a maxim whose truth seems to have been so self-
evident to Grimmelshausen, and possibly to many of his readers,
that he treated it casually, like a proverb. As Simplicissimus puts
it, when he is disappointed by the character of his second wife,
"since I found myself so betrayed, I thought to betray the trai-
tress." [89]

The Strange Skipinthefield, the eighth book of the cycle, is
written so that Simplicissimus and his old comrade will get even
again with the spiteful harlot, and *The Enchanted Bird's-nest,* Part
II, contains a novella on the theme of revenge.

Grimmelshausen's interest in the subject is so intense and
abiding that one begins to wonder whether he himself was a vengeful man. Given the sorry state of information on the author's life,
it is impossible to be sure. Furthermore, we do not know how much
to attribute to the torture of Grimmelshausen's soul and how much
to the tradition which required of him as a satirical writer that he
present and condemn pride and envy and anger as well as all other
vices. So we are left with a surmise.

It seems that Grimmelshausen was proud of his aristocratic
origin and struggled, not too successfully, for recognition as an
author among members of the higher aristocracy. He never stooped
down to the obsequious deference that other writers paid their
betters for patronage. It is almost certain that he hated the wealthy
Dr. Rüffer and took literary revenge on him in the vicious portrait
he painted of Dr. Canard. He seems to have resented the criticism
of literati who, more erudite than himself, found his work wanting
in style and taste. Grimmelshausen struck back at them in his works
and seems to have avoided their company.

There is, finally, another seemingly trivial point that needs to
be made in this connection. It is known that Grimmelshausen was
derisively called "the red steward" (*"der rote Schaffner"*) by a colleague in the employ of the Schauenburg family. Grimmelshausen
had red hair, which according to a very old and widespread super-

stition was regarded as a sign of evil character. Since superstition holds especially the lower classes of society in its grip, it is likely that Grimmelshausen was exposed to the full force of this prejudice in the army camps and taverns, the countryside and villages, where he spent most of his life.

Already Martial had said that Zoilus was to be avoided because of the red color of his hair; the Latin satirist held red hair to be as bad a portent as a club foot.[90] In Christian civilization, red hair was ascribed to Judas and the devil. In German proverbs the red haired are knaves marked by God.[91] A Russian proverb says, "There never has been a red-haired saint," [92] and a Spanish proverb, "Red hair on the head—treachery in the soul." [93] Commenting on this proverb, Werner Krauss mentions a sixteenth century collection of anecdotes which contains the story of a man who was flogged because of a miscarriage of justice. When the judge noticed the error he remarked, "If he has not committed his crime, he is going to do so, since he has red hair." [94]

In Quevedo's *Historia de la vida del Buscon,* 1626, the despicable Cabra, a clergyman who is "generous only in height," has red hair, and the author adds significantly, "Need anything further be said?" [95] In Philipp von Zesen's *Simson,* 1679, the hero's evil father-in-law has red hair,[96] and in H. A. von Zigler's *Die asiatische Banise,* 1668, Prince Balacin says of reddish hair that it betrays not infrequently evil intentions.[97]

Perhaps, it is not only a literary curiosity, but a psychologically significant fact that Grimmelshausen wrote a grimly humorous pamphlet in defense of red beards, *Bart-Krieg* ("The War of Beards").[98] It contains further evidence, drawn from proverbs and other sources, on the prejudice from which he seems to have suffered, and an attack on the "physiognomists" who infer moral qualities from physical characteristics. As was his habit, Grimmelshausen took much of his historical material—for example, on Martial—and some of his arguments from Garzoni, but this makes the choice of subject no less significant.

At least one perceptive literary historian, Walther Muschg, has suggested that Grimmelshausen must have regarded his red hair as a misfortune, since he wrote his "The War of Beards" in defense of the red haired.[99] Muschg has mentioned in this connection a number of writers who may have felt their physical deformity as a stigma; their work may have been influenced by the cripple's hatred of the healthy and by feelings fluctuating between "horror of themselves, extreme sensitivity and cynical conceit." He points out that "many great satirists and polemicists had such a stigma." [100] Excluding from Muschg's list those writers who were repulsively ugly, there remain the cripples: Aesop, Thomas Murner, Scarron, Pope, Lichtenberg, Gottfried Keller, Kierkegaard. The name of Quevedo may be added: he was lame.

Love and Sex

Among the main concerns of the conventional historical novel of the baroque era were the dignity and equanimity of persons of rank. The test of such virtue in vicissitudes of intrigue and misunderstanding and in the most adverse turns of fortune took precedence over the exploration of love. All human feeling was represented as exemplary and thus free of uniqueness and intimacy. There is no parallel in seventeenth century German literature to Madame de Lafayette's *La Princesse de Clèves* (1678); even in France it took about fifty years until the sensitive and lucid analysis of love in this extraordinary novel was matched.

In comical baroque tales the physical needs and passions of persons who lacked political significance and social distinction were given a great deal of attention. In fact, because of fierce opposition to the moral idealization of man, this natural sphere of life was grotesquely enlarged.

In Grimmelshausen's Simplician writings, as in the works of other satirists of the age, love is presented with on uncompromising antifeminism, which is Christian and middle class in origin. Love appears to be either utterly sinful or utterly ridiculous. Sexual activity is inevitable rather than enjoyable, even as the woman is indispensable for the propagation of the race, whereas love is nothing but rape, debauchery, filth, a carrier of disease, and the root of inconstancy and many other vices. Thus, "The heroic-gallant novel never reaches love because of too much virtue, the naturalistic novel never does because of too much vice." [101]

232

Nor does the baroque novel deal with the family as a social institution. The woman in her role as wife or mother and the family exist as little as does romantic love. The only feelings of close human attachment that Grimmelshausen describes are those prevailing between father and son and between two young men. And in this respect, as a writer on friendship, Grimmelshausen is unique among the novelists of the seventeenth century. When he speaks of the friendship between Simplicissimus and Heartsbrother, he finds words expressing deep emotion, whereas all his words on heterosexual love are detached or cynical and arouse either disgust or raucous laughter.

In this connection Grimmelshausen's choice of Courage as a picaresque character for one of his main works invites some further speculation. Today, it is considered unlikely that *The Story of Courage* owes much to Francisco de Ubeda's *Picara Justina* (1603), although Grimmelshausen may have been familiar with the long-winded German translation of that work. Ubeda's novel was an avowed imitation of *The Celestina* (1449)[102] and other picaresque Spanish tales, whereas Grimmelshausen's *Story of Courage*, like *The Celestina*, is a masterpiece in its own right. Even if there were close dependence on *Picara Justina*, however, the question would still remain why Grimmelshausen's imagination was captured by a female picaro. Why did he, despite all his ostensible contempt for love and women, create such an extraordinarily vivid picture of a manly woman whose beauty and vitality excelled the evil in her? No one who has read *The Story of Courage* will escape the conclusion that Grimmelshausen was fascinated by Courage. He admired her.[103] While condemning sex in all his writings, in this novel he managed to present at the same time the portrait of an irresistible woman, who after she has been abused by men, reacts with lusty sexual abandon and revenge and yet remains human and powerful.

Let us pursue this subject one step further. Courage is a tom-boy in her youth and by force of circumstances passes for a boy. Later, she repeatedly speaks of her burning desire to wear men's clothing and to be in every way like a man. As a grown woman she remains barren, and she behaves like a man not only in battle and as a forager, but also in some of her marriages. At one time she establishes superiority over her husband after the wedding night in a physical fight with him. In her relations with Skipinthefield, the social sex roles are completely and formally reversed.

It is striking that both Simplicius and Courage have their first sexual experiences in homosexual situations. It also appears that Grimmelshausen had a keen interest in hermaphrodites and in the changing of sex. References to hermaphrodites occur in several of his works. In the tale which deals with the birth of a false Jewish messiah, the child turns out to be a girl. When the gullible Jews in Amsterdam believe that God may change this girl into a young man at the age of maturity, Grimmelshausen points out that it would be no miracle for a female child to develop male sex characteristics.[104]

Finally, there is a most curious description of Skipinthefield's distress shortly before the blasphemous marriage arrangement is made. Tortured by his love for Courage, Skipinthefield enters the woman's tent under the pretense of wanting a pot of wine. Grimmelshausen describes his appearance as seen through Courage's eyes as follows: "He looked so pale and disconsolate then as though he had just gotten a child without having or knowing its father, and without having either milk or meal-pap for it." [105] This sentence is strangely ambiguous. The musketeer cannot be imagined to have given birth to a child, but if his appearance resembled that of a *father* who is pale and disconsolate merely because he has no means of feeding his newborn child, why does Grimmelshausen associate the misery of the man with the absence of a father, rather than a mother? It is just possible that the ambiguity is intended to suggest Courage's feeling toward the musketeer, who is so weakened by his love that he appears contemptibly womanish to her. Or else we are left with the possibility that the sentence contains a slip of the pen. (Taken as such, it does not carry the weight of the curious birth certificate of Herman Melville's son, on which the writer entered his name and, by mistake, that of his own mother as parents of the child,[106] but the description of the poor musketeer's condition remains strangely ambiguous.)

Along with everything else that has been said, the strange sentence might lend support to the suggestion that Grimmelshausen had ambivalent feelings toward women and sex. Perhaps he felt even dimly anxious or uncertain about his own sexual wishes. In his fantasies, "the red steward" may have come close to identifying himself with this golden haired Amazon who defied God.[107]

But these are speculations. There are few baroque authors who do not invite similar speculations. In many conventional baroque novels, as in comedy and farce, disguise and confusion of the sexes are common. Homosexual allusions are far more prominent in Callot's engravings than in Grimmelshausen's Simplician writings, and other writers of the period were intrigued by homosexuality as well.

Harsdörffer shared Grimmelshausen's interest in hermaphrodites. The Catholic convert Anton Ulrich was much concerned with incest as an involvement that puts virtue to a thrilling test. In one of Lohenstein's tragedies a corpse is unearthed and covered with passionate kisses. About Buchholtz it has been said that while "the Christian element, which he strongly emphasizes is for him identical with the world of superintendants and *Konsistorialräte* from which he sprang," his scenes of martyrdom are so depicted that before the imagination of this conciliatory and mild man "the fantasy of the Marquis de Sade fades into paleness." [108] Buchholtz presented the relations between man and woman so crudely that only a few years after the publication of his novels he had to be defended against the accusation of pornography.[109]

Courage and Moll Flanders

Defoe's Mrs. Flanders, as well as Grimmelshausen's Courage, is a challenge to morality, but Moll Flanders belongs already to the age in which virtue began to be identified largely with chastity in women. She is a middle-class heroine. By contrast, Courage boldly calls virtue in the older, broader, sense into question; in the account of her life she rocks even the Christian foundation of virtue. Moll Flanders has many children and finishes her dissolute life as a dowager, who has become respectable through remorse and wealth. Grimmelshausen created Courage barren, and he was aware of it. Childless, Courage is more of a man, as it were, without becoming any less desirable as a woman in the eyes of men. In the end,

Courage prefers the life of a gypsy to that of a respectable widow, and so perhaps did Grimmelshausen. While Moll Flanders in her reckless life has only three principal sources of income—needlework, men as husbands and lovers, and theft—Courage adds to these booty in war, which she gains sword in hand. There is, of course, nothing manly about Mrs. Flanders, and the risks she takes lack any grandeur.

The gulf separating Courage and Moll Flanders can perhaps best be shown by the involuntary, physical expression of their feelings. For all her wickedness Moll Flanders cries and blushes and faints hardly less often than her female, middle-class readers were prone to do. Her sickly femininity easily falls prey to lingering fevers when she receives a piece of news adversely affecting her life. This woman, whom Defoe gives "that unmusical, harsh-sounding title of whore," cries on every possible occasion, including the hour in which fear of being hanged overcomes her.

Courage, too, cries, especially in the early part of her career, but almost always in order to deceive men. She cries by design, her tears are a trick that never fails her. One of the little poems inserted in Grimmelshausen's novel deals with the tears women shed so easily, saying that such tears do not come from heartache but flow at will to capture men. Characteristically, the only instance of careless writing in the novel is the use of this sarcastic verse on two different occasions (with only a minor change in wording): evidently, the thought it expressed was much on the author's mind.

Only twice does Courage cry to express despair, the first time when she is among troops who are forced to surrender to the enemy and again after she has been utterly debased, humiliated, beaten, and cruelly abused many times by a mob of drunken, brutal officers and servants for several nights in succession. Courage never faints or blushes, and yet, despite her insatiable sexual appetite and her excessive abandon, at the end of her enormous tale she appears to the reader as a radiantly beautiful woman of rare natural power, unquenchable zest for life, and inexhaustible vital resources. Courage is her just name in the extraordinary equivocation of meaning that Grimmelshausen in a master stroke of genius and humor bestowed upon it. The words by Izaak Walton about Donne's poems

This book (dry emblem) which begins
With love; but ends with tears or sighs for sins[110]

do not apply to *The Story of Courage*.

Grimmelshausen's novel is cruder and coarser than Defoe's, but paradoxically, less lascivious. The most shocking episode in *Moll Flanders* is the marriage of the heroine to a man who, unbeknownst to her, is her brother. One of Mrs. Flanders' many children is the fruit of this incestuous relationship. But in the end her brother conveniently dies, giving Mrs. Flanders a chance at social respectability, which she presumably deserves by her riches, her enterprising commercial talent, and the confession and repentance of her sins in Newgate Prison. In prison she despairs because the hangman is waiting for her, and thus she opens her trembling heart to a priest who saves her life by intervening on her behalf. He is moved by the intensity of her remorse, although her repentance does not extend to her bigamy or to that escapade in her life which legally constitutes incest. Defoe does not dwell on this trifle, being rather preoccupied with her thefts, the crimes against private property. Nor does the priest urge the contrite and lachrymose sinner to give her ill-gotten wealth to the poor, if she cannot restore it to the rightful owners. It seems that for Defoe wealth is wealth, no matter how it was acquired, as long as the law of the land no longer prevents its enjoyment. This kind of morality reaches its climax when Mrs. Flanders, now safely in Virginia, presents one of her stolen gold watches to her son begotten by her brother. In Defoe's novel this sentimental scene crowns the sweet reunion of Mother and Son and evidently is to be taken seriously by the reader.

Nothing as scandalous as that occurs in *The Story of Courage*. It is inconceivable that Grimmelshausen could have stooped to thrill his readers with the cheap pornography of inadvertent incest. Grimmelshausen borrowed from Bandello a shocking scatological story, in which a man takes revenge in the filthiest possible manner on his unfaithful wife, but he did not borrow from him, as he could have, the story of an incestuous relationship, a tale that in plot and elegant execution far exceeds Defoe's prurient adventure.

The most shocking incidents in the life of Courage are not those in which refined tastes or affectations are offended, but rather

237

those in which religious propriety is flaunted. The supreme instance is the extraordinary contract in which Courage makes a mockery of the sacrament of marriage. The musketeer who becomes her man under conditions stipulated in this contract must not only pledge submission to her in all affairs of the household, but also grant her the right to remain a whore, in order to get the phantom of a spouse. This perversion of Christian marriage results in the utter degradation of the musketeer to the status of a servant, thief, and mock husband. The woman whom he must treat as his wife insists on his own cockoldom in the marriage contract. Moreover, Courage exercises her right to give him a name of her own choosing that marks him forever. The burlesque humor of this marriage arrangement cannot hide its fierce, shocking assault on the religious sanction of the relation between the sexes. Nothing like it occurs in Moll Flanders.

It is evident that Grimmelshausen was fully aware of the boldness of his conceit. He carefully prepared the reader for the dry description of the incredible contract by dwelling first in detail upon the infatuation of the musketeer and the manner in which Courage cunningly exploits it for her purposes. In these passages of the book Grimmelshausen displays great power as a satirist of polite conversation. When the acceptance of the contract by the wretched musketeer is thus made credible, Grimmelshausen interrupts his narrative to insert a pious warning to "honest Christians" not to follow Courage's example!

Grimmelshausen's novels abound with such pious moralizing and Christian warnings. They occur in prefaces and postscripts and as reflective insertions in all his works. Since the use of such apologetic material is traditional among satirists[111] to justify their colorful depiction of that which is disapproved in society on moral, political, or religious grounds, Grimmelshausen's effort to dissociate himself by pious words from the evil he describes with so much gusto and humor should not distract the attention of the critical reader from the content of his tales. In *The Story of Courage* moral and religious protestations appear with particular insistence just prior to the description of the blasphemous marriage contract and in "The Author's Postscript," which concludes the novel. This postscript is taken almost literally from *Piazza Universale* by

Tomaso Garzoni and thus is written in borrowed prose, like the sonorously Christian ending of the fifth book of *The Adventurous Simplicissimus,* which is taken verbatim from Guevara. As one critic put it, the curiosity of Grimmelshausen's reader "is legitimized by a moral superstructure [provided by the author (H. S.)] which pacifies his conscience and thus leaves him free to enjoy pure adventure";[112] and, we may add, which protects the author from the wrath of censorious readers, who lack his impious humor. Simplicissimus, who laughs often, says at one time that Christ never laughed.[113]

Grimmelshausen and Bertolt Brecht

To the modern reader Bertolt Brecht's *Mother Courage and Her Children,* written in 1939 and first published in English in 1941, is better known than Grimmelshausen's Simplician novels, from which Brecht took the milieu of the Thirty Years' War for his play and the name of its main character. But Brecht's play has very little to do with *The Story of Courage* or, for that matter, with *The Adventurous Simplicissimus.*

In Brecht's play the main character is Anna Fierling, a mother of three illegitimate children whom she loses one by one in the cruel war. The name Courage clings to her because she keeps trying to make a miserable living by pulling her cart and selling her wares to the soldiers, although misfortune after misfortune befalls her. In a sense, her name is that of all those downtrodden but undaunted who go on living despite their misery. "The way you run your business and always come through," says the chaplain in the play, "is highly commendable, Mother Courage—I see how you got your name." To which Mother Courage replies, "The poor need courage. Why? They're lost. That they even get up in the morning is something—in *their* plight. Or that they plow a field —in war time. Even their bringing children into the world shows they have courage, for they have no prospects. They have to hang each other one by one and slaughter each other in the lump, so if they want to look each other in the face once in a while, well, it takes courage. That they put up with an Emperor and a Pope, that takes an unnatural amount of courage, for they cost you your life." [114]

Brecht did not name Courage properly: he thought her stupid rather than brave. He failed to convey the meaning that he intended to convey in his play. Mother Courage was to teach the spectator that a woman who carries on her trade despite the loss of her three children and continues to try in this way to profit from war deserves no sympathy. Brecht wanted the spectator to be indignant about Mother Courage rather than feel compassion for her suffering.[115] He blamed lack of political comprehension on the part of his audiences, both in Zurich, where his play was first performed in 1946, and in East Berlin in 1949, for the misunderstanding of his propaganda. In his *Versuche* he noted that unlike his audiences he was not interested in the "moving vitality of the mother-animal," and had only scorn for those who took pity on Mother Courage as a modern Niobe.[116] He wanted her to be understood as "a hyena of the battlefield." The success the play had must therefore be attributed to a misunderstanding on the part of the audience and to the author's failure to express his intention clearly: the play aroused sentiments among the spectators which he condemned.

Communist authorities in the Soviet Zone of Germany proposed to Brecht that he add a speech by Mother Courage to the play in which she would admit her error and announce her resolution to fight all warmongers from now on. Brecht did not make these changes, but he made others in order to stress what he considered to be the negative qualities of Mother Courage's character; nevertheless he failed.

Grimmelshausen and Brecht only seem to talk about the same historic events in their works. Grimmelshausen knew the Thirty Years' War from his own experience. *The Adventurous Simplicissimus* was published more than twenty years after the long war had run its course. Brecht wrote *Mother Courage* about twenty years after the end of World War I in which he had taken part as a medic in 1918. His experiences at the age of twenty in an army hospital in Augsburg shocked him deeply and inspired some of his most powerful antiwar ballads in the early twenties. Two decades later, in *Mother Courage*, Brecht expressed no more and no less than the views of war held by young German left-wing intellectuals in the early years of the Weimar Republic.

This is particularly true of the notion that the underprivileged are exploited by the military class and that the members of that class prefer war to peace. For example, in the opening scene of the play the sergeant utters opinions that sound distinctly, if anachronistically, like the militaristic views attributed by the political left to the Prussian officers' corps in the Kaiser Reich. "Peace, that is merely a mess, war makes for order." [117] Similarly, later in the play, the chaplain speaks of the "final victory," the *"Endsieg,"* [118] a word that in German has the ring of World War I political usage.

Brecht presented the wretched life of Mother Courage and her three children in a setting that was historically remote and hence seemingly timeless, but the author's sentiments remained confined to the radicalism of his early manhood in Germany. Grimmelshausen, who knew more than Brecht about the brutalities and miseries of war from his own experience as a soldier, wrote about the Thirty Years' War, the total war of his lifetime, in the natural, coarse tongue of the common people. But *The Story of Courage* as well as *The Adventurous Simplicissimus* reach beyond the specific events of the war, because Grimmelshausen held all war to be a poignant expression of the human condition, rather than a state of affairs for which a particular social class was responsible.

War and Utopia .

In his war novels Grimmelshausen describes many acts of wanton cruelty, which the soldiers commit against the peasants and the peasants commit against the soldiers. All of these atrocities are known from other evidence to have indeed occurred at some time or other in the Thirty Years' War. Pouring liquid filth into the mouth of a victim became known in Europe as the Swedish drink. Incidents in which peasants were roasted over a fire or in an oven are reported in other sources as well. So are the use of pistols for thumbscrews and many other hideous tortures, not to mention rape and mutilations. Stripping a slain enemy of his clothes was common practice and considered to be as permissible as taking his weapons, horse, or money. At one time Simplicissimus remarks quite incidentally that at the conclusion of an encounter he did not plunder the dead; the emphasis is not on the moral worth of his conduct, but merely on the fact that he had "no time" to do otherwise.[119] Skipinthefield re-equips himself twice by means of murder.

Nevertheless, Grimmelshausen's Simplician writings can be used as source material by historians only at their own risk. They must remember that the author's treatment of reality was highly selective. Compared with the writers of conventional novels, in which common people were "the vulgar" or at best shepherds, Grimmelshausen was a "realist," but he gave undue prominence to lawlessness, cruelty, and filth, to the weird and the wretched, to soldiers, beggars, whores, and highwaymen, neglecting many moral and social aspects of reality.

Grimmelshausen can be cited in support of the orthodox opinion that war is a scourge sent by God to punish sin, but he knew that in war the innocent suffer with the guilty. The dynastic interests in the Thirty Years' War did not concern him. In his view, it was "an internal war and a conflict between brothers";[120] even many years after the Peace of Westphalia was concluded he seems to have been of the opinion that the rivalry among the Christian churches stood in the way of lasting peace. This is at least the argument which Simplicissimus offers to the mad character who thinks of himself as Jove and has come to establish eternal peace.

Grimmelshausen presented many of his general views on war, as on other subjects, in the form of proverbs. This includes the saying, "Young soldiers—old beggars," also to be found in *The Pentameron;*[121] it is the main lesson contained in the life of *The Strange Skipinthefield.* Again, "boys who fail to obey father and mother follow the drummer, if not the hangman";[122] an elaboration of this theme is *Der stolze Melcher (The Proud Melchior),* one of Grimmelshausen's last writings, in which he equated turning soldier with joining a gang of loud-mouthed, hard-drinking gamblers, robbers, and seducers of maidens. Grimmelshausen was of the opinion that war attracts especially the rotten elements in society. They drift into the armies. "Oh, Jove," says Simplicissimus, "if you send a war, all the evil fellows and daredevils will join it and torment the peace-loving, pious people." [123]

"In war," Courage observes, "most people become worse rather than better," [124] and she attributes this fact to the company which soldiers and camp followers keep. The point is worth noting. Grimmelshausen was not of the opinion that any abstract conditions account for human vice and depravity. It is quite concretely the example given by other men—what they do to you and others—that is corrupting. Such corruption—by bad example, by temptation, and as in the case of Courage, by humiliation—cannot occur without corruptibility, a general quality of human nature. Precisely for this reason man should avoid bad company. "Avoid bad company" is one of the three pieces of advice given by the hermit to his son Simplicius, the young, ignorant boy. War, to Grimmelshausen, meant above all, a tempting opportunity for young people to keep especially bad company.

Grimmelshausen depicted the disorder and corruption of the world, in peacetime as well as in war. He showed man in his blindness, his cruelty and suffering, and as a liar to both others and himself. He plumbed the depths of man's terror in this world. But time and again in his work, Grimmelshausen presented also fantasies of a good moral order. Sometimes such a dream emerges from the satirical depiction of the real, corrupted world. An example is the grand speech at the end of *The Council Chamber of Pluto*, in which Simplicissimus condemns the luxury, ostentation, and wastefulness at the courts.[125] At first glance this speech may seem to be but a high point of moralizing ardor, but the significance of the passage is thrown into relief by the absence of similar criticism in the conventional novels of the period. For example, Zesen, in his *Assenat,* the story of Joseph, praised as exemplary statesmanship the usurious exploitation of the middle and lower strata of society during the seven lean years.

Sometimes the image of the good order emerges from the ironical ascription to the various professions of virtues they do not possess, as in the account of life on earth that Simplicissimus gives to the king of the submarine beings who inhabit the Mummelsee:[126] no priest is given to lust, all theologians resemble Hieronymus or

Bede, the merchant is free of avarice, the innkeeper serves selflessly those who suffer hunger and thirst, the physician never seeks profit but only the restoration of his patients' health, the craftsman is honest, the soldier does not rob and ruin the people but protects the fatherland, etc.

What is the nature of the good order? At one time, when Simplicissimus comes to Switzerland, he holds the mere state of peace to be "paradise on earth," [127] but Grimmelshausen was deeply convinced that the good order is utopian, because man is beyond reform. His evil nature asserts itself inexorably in peacetime as well as in war. This can be seen perhaps most clearly in the sixth book of *The Adventurous Simplicissimus,* which tells of the hero's life after the Westphalian peace of 1648 and in *The Enchanted Birds-nest,* which depicts life in society after the war. In no respect does man in these three books of the Simplician cycle appear more contented than in the other books, where everything happens in the setting of the Thirty Years' War. Of course, peace is preferable to war, but life is not essentially different, because man is not better in peacetime than he is in war. It is this "pessimism" which gives to Grimmelshausen's portrait of man and to his picture of war a perspective that eludes the children of the age of enlightenment, like Bertold Brecht, however much their writing may be indebted to stimulation by the baroque author.

When the captain of a Dutch ship discovers Simplicissimus on his paradisaical island and urges him to sail back to civilization, Simplicissimus, calling himself "a free person not subject to anyone," [128] refuses to return to Europe. "Here is peace, there is war," he says, and embarks upon an eloquent denunciation of civilized life. It becomes clear from this passage that Grimmelshausen presented the difference between peace and war in two different ways. Simplicissimus, the recluse, does not juxtapose the peace of the island with war in Europe, but with civilized life in general, whether in times of war or of peace: from the vantage point on the island, even peace in civilized or real life is a form of war. He says,

When I still lived in Europe . . . everything was full of war, fire, murder, robbery, looting, raping of women and girls. But when God in his goodness took away these scourges along with the terrible pestilence and the cruel hunger, giving to the poor hard-pressed people noble peace, all the vices of lust made their appearance, such as eating, drinking, and gambling, whoring, sodomy, and adultery, and they brought on the whole swarm of the other vices until finally a condition was reached in which everyone publicly tried to become great by suppressing someone else, and no ruse, no fraud, no political artifice were spared; nor have I mentioned the worst: no hope for things to turn better remained. . . .[129]

Grimmelshausen was of the opinion that man's nature makes the realization of the good order impossible. No other view of his work can be seriously entertained.

Grimmelshausen admired the moral order which the Anabaptists had established in their communities. But so preoccupied was he with the corruption of the world in which these islands of morality existed that he was able to portray their moral perfection only in negative terms. Reminiscent of Gonzalo's dream of a good political order in Shakespeare's *The Tempest*—"I would by contraries execute all things" [130]—Simplicissimus says of the heretical Anabaptists that in their community "there was no wrath, no zeal, no revengefulness, no envy, no enmity, no care for the temporal, no pride, no remorse. . . ." [131]

A Woman Named Courage

[1] Another major figure of seventeenth-century German literature, Johann Beer, was even more successful in hiding his name behind a large number of pseudonyms. His identity was rediscovered only two hundred thirty-two years after the author's death by Richard Alewyn in his *Johann Beer, Studien zum Roman des 17. Jahrhunderts* (Leipzig: Mayer and Müller, G.m.b.H., 1932).

[2] Miguel de Cervantes, *Adventures of Don Quixote*, trans. Charles Jarvis (New York: John Wurtele Lovell, n.d.), p. 5.

[3] Cf. Hans Ehrenzeller, *Studien zur Romanvorrede von Grimmelshausen bis Jean Paul* (Bern: Basler Studien, 16, 1955), pp. 99-106.

[4] These three additional continuations were also published separately in annual almanacs entitled *Simplicianischer Wundergeschichten Kalender (Simplician Almanac of Curious Stories)* for the years 1670, 1671, and 1672 respectively. Interestingly enough, this almanac continued to appear well into the nineteenth century.

[5] Grimmelshausen's popular writings include a beautiful fairy tale, *Der Erste Beernhäuter (The First Sluggard)*, published under the pen name "Illiteratio Ignorantio, also called Idiota." The story is generally known as Grimm's fairy-tale of "Bearskin;" Grimm took it almost verbatim from Grimmelshausen.

[6] A. T. S. Goodrick in his introduction to his (incomplete) English translation of *The Adventurous Simplicissimus,* published in a limited edition (London: 1912) and reprinted in a paperbound edition (Lincoln: University of Nebraska Press, 1962), p. xvi.

[7] C. V. Wedgwood, *The Thirty Years War* (New Haven: Yale University Press, 1949), p. 509.

[8] *Ibid.,* p. 517.

[9] A. T. S. Goodrick, *op. cit.,* p. x.

[10] Robert Ergang, *The Myth of the All-Destructive Fury of the Thirty Years' War* (Pocono Pines, Pa.: The Craftsmen, 1956), p. 33.

[11] C. V. Wedgwood, *op. cit.,* p. 516.

[12] Cf. Marianne Beyer-Fröhlich, ed., *Selbstzeugnisse aus dem Dreissigjährigen Krieg und dem Barock* (Leipzig: Philip Reclam Jun., 1930); Abba Hillel Silver, *A History of Messianic Speculation in Israel* (Boston: Beacon Press, 1959), chap. 7, and preface.

[13] Martha Lenschau, *Grimmelshausens Sprichwörter und Redensarten* (Frankfurt am Main: 1924), p. 11.

[14] Quoted by Manfred F. Bukofzer, *Music in the Baroque Era* (New York: W. W. Norton & Company, 1947), p. 411.

[15] Richard Alewyn, *op. cit.,* p. 122.

[16] Especially Günther Müller in many of his works, such as his "Barockromane und Barockroman," *Literaturwissenschaftliches Jahrbuch der Görresgesellschaft (Barock,* IV), ed. Günther Müller (Freiburg: 1929), pp. 1-29.

[17] Anton Ulrich von Braunschweig, in the preface to *Die durchleuchtige Syrerinn Aramena* (Nürnberg: Johann Hofmann, 1678-80). On Anton Ulrich and La Calprenède's influence on him, cf. the excellent dissertation by Carola Paulsen, *"Die durchleuchtigste Syrerin Aramena" des Herzogs Anton Ulrich von Braunschweig und "La Cléopatre" des Gautier Coste de La Calprenède. Ein Vergleich.* Bonn: typed.

[18] Daniel Casper von Lohenstein, *Römische Trauerspiele,* ed. Klaus Günther Just (Stuttgart: Anton Hiersemann, 1955), p. 143.

[19] Paul Hankamer, *Deutsche Gegenreformation und deutsches Barock,* 2nd ed. (Stuttgart: I. B. Metzler, 1947), p. 441.

[20] Max Wehrli, *Das barocke Geschichtsbild in Lohenstein's Arminius. Wege zur Dichtung.* Zürcher Schriften zur Literaturwissenschaft, ed. Emil Ermatinger (Frauenfeld/Leipzig: Huber & Co., 1938), xxxi.

[21] Cited by Max Wehrli, *op. cit.,* p. 77.

[22] Günther Müller, "Höfische Kultur der Barockzeit," in H. Naumann and G. Müller, *Höfische Kultur* (Halle: Max Neimeyer, 1929), p. 135.

[23] Cf. Clemens Lugowski, *Wirklichkeit und Dichtung* (Frankfurt am Main: 1936); and Herbert Singer, "Joseph in Aegypten," *Euphorion,* 48 (1954), p. 267.

[24] Cf. Luise Laporte, *Lohenstein's "Arminius"* (Berlin: Germanische Studien, 48, 1927), p. 41.

[25] H. H. Borcherdt, *Geschichte des Romans und der Novelle in Deutschland* (Leipzig: 1926), p. 219.

[26] Anton Ulrich, preface to *op. cit.*

[27] One of the most influential societies of this kind, the Fruchtbringende Gesellschaft, was founded by Prince Ludwig of Anhalt-Cöthen in 1617. It existed until 1680. According to a contemporary source, until 1662 its members consisted of one king, three electors in the German Empire, forty-nine dukes, four

margraves, ten landgraves, eight Pfalzgrafen, nineteen princes, sixty counts, thirty-five barons, and six hundred "noblemen, scholars, and other distinguished persons of bourgeoise standing, who had acquired great merit in Germany through the sword as well as the pen." (Neumark [anonymous], *Der neusprossende Teutsche Palmbaum . . .* (Weimar: 1668), p. 34, cited by Ernst Manheim, *Die Träger der öffentlichen Meinung* (Leipzig: 1933), p. 81, note 2). On the language societies in general, cf. Carl Viëtor, *Probleme der deutschen Barockliteratur* (Leipzig: 1928), pp. 63-72. On Grimmelshausen's relation to them, cf. Felix Scholz, "Grimmelshausen's Verhältnis zu den Sprachgesellschaften und sein 'Teutscher Michel,'" *Euphorion,* Ergänzungsheft 17 (1924), pp. 79-96.

[28] Curt von Faber du Faur, "Monarch, Patron, and Poet," *The Germanic Review,* 24 (1949), pp. 249-64.

[29] Martin Opitz, *Buch von der deutschen Poeterei* (1624), ed. Wilhelm Braune (Tübingen: Max Niemeyer, 1954), p. 20.

[30] Friedrich Gundolf, "Grimmelshausen und der Simplicissimus," *Vierteljahrsschrift für Literaturwissenschaft und Geistesgeschichte,* 1 (1923), p. 346.

[31] *Die Landstörzerin Courasche,* ed. J. H. Scholte (Halle: Max Niemeyer 1923), chap. 23. Hereafter cited as *Courage.*

[32] Frank Wadleigh Chandler, *The Literature of Roguery* (1907), reprinted (New York: Burt Franklin, 1958), I, p. 30.

[33] The point that Grimmelshausen's Simplician writings are not "realistic" has been made most convincingly by Richard Alewyn, *op. cit.,* pp. 208ff. On the difference between the picaresque and the realistic novel, cf. also Antoine Adam, *Histoire de la Littérature Française au XVIIe Siècle* (Paris: Editions Domat, 1956), I, pp. 138ff. He says, *"par plusieurs de ses aspects les plus importants, le roman picaresque n'est pas réaliste."* Nor are the *histoires comiques* realistic. Richard Alewyn, in *op. cit.,* has also pointed out the difference between the picaresque novels and Grimmelshausen's Simplician novels. In the picaresque novel characters other than the picaro himself are strictly episodic. Simplicissimus is flanked by at least two important characters, Heartsbrother and Olivier. The typical picaro goes from one adventure to the next without any development of character. Courage's character changes.

[34] Andreas Gryphius, *Horribilicribrifax,* in *Der deutsche Barockkomödie,* ed. W. Flemming (Leipzig: Philip Reclam, jun., 1931). On the use of scatological humor, in Gryphius, cf. also the Introduction by W. Flemming, p. 18.

[35] See, for example, *Courage,* chap. 17; *Des wunderbarlichen Vogelnests zweiter Teil,* in *Grimmelshausens Werke,* ed. H. H. Borcherdt (Berlin, Leipzig, Vienna, Stuttgart: Deutsches Verlagshaus Bong & Co., 1922), 3, chap. 7 (hereafter cited as *Bird's-nest II*); cf. also Francisco de Quevedo, *The Life and Adventures of Don Pablos the Sharper,* trans. Mack Hendricks Singleton and others, in *Masterpieces of the Spanish Golden Age,* ed. Angel Flores (New York: Holt, Rinehart & Winston, Inc., 1957), p. 112; and Gryphius, *op. cit.*

[36] In his comments on Johann Beer's *Das Narrenspital,* 1681 (Hamburg: Rowohlt, 1957), Richard Alewyn discusses the relationship between scatological humor "from the later Middle Ages to the end of the baroque" and "repressed sexuality" (p. 147). The "hero" in *Das Narrenspital* may claim unique distinction by an unsurpassed performance in breaking wind. The point on repressed sexuality as an explanation of scatological humor was also made previously by Richard Alewyn in *Johann Beer,* pp. 174-75.

[37] *"Die muter sprach ach lieber sun gib mir dein süss ler da ich dein bei*

gedenken mag. Ulenspiegel sagt ia liebe muter wan du wilt deins gemachs thon, so ker den ars von dem wind so gat dir der gestank nit in die nass." (*Till Ulenspiegel*, 1515, ed. Herman Knust (Halle: Max Niemeyer, 1884), p. 140.)

[38] For the encounter with Jove see *Grimmelshausens Simplicissimus Teutsch*, ed. J. H. Scholte (Tübingen: Max Niemeyer, 1954), III, chaps. 3-6 (hereafter cited as *Simplicissimus*). The three most important discussions of this episode, which has been studied very carefully, are Julius Petersen, "Grimmelshausen's 'Teutscher Held'," *Euphorion*, (1924), 17. Ergänzungsheft, pp. 1-30; Günther Weydt, "Don Quijote Teutsch. Studien zur Herkunft des Simplicianischen Jupiter," *Euphorion* 51 (1957), pp. 250-70; and Manfred Koschlig, "Das Lob des 'Francion' bei Grimmelshausen," *Jahrbuch der deutschen Schillergesellschaft*, 1 (Stuttgart: 1957), pp. 30-73. Cf. also James Franklin Hyde, *The Religious Thought of Johann Jacob Christoffel von Grimmelshausen as Expressed in the Simplicianische Schriften*. (Dissertation Indiana University, 1960). [typescript]. On the story of the false messiah, cf. still Otto Weinreich, *Der Trug des Nektanebos*, Berlin and Leipzig: 1911; and Hans Speier, "Grimmelshausen's Laughter," *Ancients and Moderns. Essays on the Tradition of Political Philosophy, in Honor of Leo Strauss*, ed. Joseph Cropsey (New York: Basic Books) [forthcoming].

[39] *Simplicissimus*, III, chap. 17.

[40] On *Simplicissimus* and *Courage* being read by the Duchess Sophie of Hannover, cf. J. H. Scholte, *Der Simplicissimus und sein Dichter* (Tübingen: Max Niemeyer, 1950), p. 144; the relevant passage in Leibniz's letter to her (of April 1688) is quoted by Manfred Koschlig, *op. cit.*, pp. 33-34. Attacking the older view that Grimmelshausen's *Simplicissimus* was influenced by Spanish picaresque models in German translation, Koschlig tried to show the debt Grimmelshausen owed to the comical novel by Charles Sorel. By contrast, Günther Weydt, in *op. cit*, and before that in his essay "Zur Entstehung barocker Erzählkunst. Harsdörffer und Grimmelshausen," *Wirkendes Wort*, 1, Sonderheft (1952), proved Grimmelshausen's indirect indebtedness to Cervantes by way of various intermediaries, of whom Harsdörffer, the industrious translator and adaptor of picaresque and other foreign tales, was especially important as a literary source. Koschlig correctly assesses the common function of Grimmelshausen's and Sorel's humor, but seems to overstate the influence of Francion on the character of Grimmelshausen's Jove. Koschlig also failed to comment on the significant differences between the French and the German work. Sorel dealt with the upper classes as well as university life and the lowly elements in society. Both the social scope of his observation was larger and the fervor of his early nonconformism greater than Grimmelshausen's. Sorel wanted to teach people "to live like Gods." (Charles Sorel, *Histoire Comique de Francion;* 5ᵉ livre, ed. Emile Roy (Paris: Librairie Tachette, 1926), II, p. 123.)

[41] The prefaces of the *Satirical Pilgrim* have been reprinted in Hans Ehrenzeller, *op. cit.*, pp. 203-7.

[42] Cf. especially Manfred Koschlig, " 'Edler Herr von Grimmelshausen.' Neue Funde zur Selbstdeutung des Dichters," *Jahrbuch der deutschen Schillergesellschaft*, IV (1960), pp. 198-224.

[43] *Grimmelshausens Simpliciana*, ed. J. H. Scholte (Halle: 1943), p. 43. Hereafter cited as *Simpliciana*.

[44] Gustav Könnecke, *Quellen und Forschungen zur Lebensgeschichte Grimmelshausens* (Weimar. 1926), I, pp. 110-11.

[45] *Ibid.*, II, pp. 152ff.

[46] "Curiously, the works of this poet do not permit a clear understanding of his own position, and the attempts to answer the question of his faith, have led to surprisingly different contradictory results." (Maria Mostert, "Ueber Grimmelshausens Konfession," *Literaturwissenschaftliches Jahrbuch der Görresgesellschaft*, 4 (1929), p. 143.

[47] Jakob Grimm (1785-1863) held the view that Grimmelshausen's views were Protestant. J. H. Scholte and many others are of the opinion that his writings reflect the Catholic spirit of the Counter Reformation.

[48] Paul Gutzwiller, *Der Narr bei Grimmelshausen* (Bern: Francke Verlag, 1959), p. 90. On Pelagianism, p. 106: "kein wirklich religiöser Geist. . . . nur äusserlich christlich;" on nihilism, p. 108: "Fast immer steht hinter dem Lachen das Nichts."

[49] Friedrich Gundolf, *op. cit.*, p. 354. About irenical tendencies of Gryphius, cf. Carl Viëtor, *op. cit.*, p. 30; of Harsdörffer, *ibid.*, p. 47.

[50] Siegfried Streller, *Grimmelshausens Simplicianische Schriften* ([East] Berlin: Rütten & Loening, 1957).

[51] Hildegarde Wichert, *Johann Balthasar Schupp and the Baroque Satire in Germany* (New York: King's Crown Press, Columbia University, 1952), p. 112.

[52] Julius Petersen, *op. cit.* On Calixtus, cf. Ernst Ludwig Th. Henke, *Georg Calixtus und seine Zeit* (Halle: 1853).

[53] *Bird's-nest II*, chap. 27.

[54] *Der stolze Melcher (The Proud Melchior)*, in *Grimmelshausens Werke*, ed. H. H. Borcherdt, IV, p. 337.

[55] *Bird's-nest I*, ed. J. H. Scholte (Halle: Max Niemeyer, 1931), p. 111.

[56] *Simplicissimus*, V, chap. 19.

[57] A. J. F. Zieglschmid, "Die ungarischen Wiedertäufer bei Grimmelshausen," *Zeitschrift für Kirchengeschichte*, 59 (1941), pp. 352-87.

[58] *Ibid.*, p. 386.

[59] *Ewigwährender Kalender*, ed. Engelbert Hegaur (Munich: Albert Langen Verlag, 1925), p. 208.

[60] Martin Opitz, *op. cit.*, p. 7.

[61] On the interest of German baroque authors in the cabala, cf. Carl Viëtor, *op. cit.*, pp. 58ff. Grimmelshausen knew about the cabala at least as much as he could find in Tomaso Garzoni's *Piazza Universale*, translated into German in 1659. In *Der teutsche Michel (The German Michael)*, incidentally one of the three of his books containing a chronogram on the title page, he mentions the symbolic meanings that were traditionally attributed to certain numbers and opposes the modernization of German spelling with the argument that the secret and sacred significance of words to be found in the Scriptures would be destroyed thereby.

[62] Georg Philip Harsdörffer, *Grosser Schauplatz jämmerlicher Mordgeschichten*, 1693 (7th printing), p. 153.

[63] Hildegarde Wichert, *op. cit.*, p. 38.

[64] Abraham a Sancta Clara, *Aus dem handschriftlichen Nachlass* (Vienna: Akademie der Wissenschaften, 1945), III, p. 401.

[65] *Continuatio*, ed. J. H. Scholte (Halle: Max Niemeyer, 1939), chap. 9.

[66] H. M. Moscherosch, *Gesichte Philanders von Sittewald* (1642-43), ed. Felix Bobertag (Berlin and Stuttgart: Spemann, 1883), pp. 259 and 267.

[67] J. H. Scholte, *Der Simplicissimus und sein Dichter*, p. 9.

[68] Hans Ehrenzeller, *op. cit.*, p. 58. Cf. also discussion on pp. 185ff.

[69] The frontispiece to *Simplicissimus* has at the bottom a poem in which

Simplicissimus is compared with the Phoenix, "born through fire, flying through the air, and yet not lost."

[70] *Simplicissimus*, V, chap. 6.

[71] The "enigmatic" character of human relations in the baroque novel (*"Verrätselung"*) has been discussed in the brilliant book by Clemens Lugowski, *op. cit.*

[72] Cf. note 12.

[73] Cf. note 12.

[73] *Bird's-nest II.*

[74] "Soon-Different" is so called after an allegorical figure in a poem by Hans Sachs. Cf. his *Werke*, ed. A. V. Keller and E. Goetze (Tübingen: Litterarischer Verein, 1870-1908), V, pp. 310ff.

[75] Siegfried Streller, *op. cit.*

[76] Johannes Alt, *Grimmelshausen und der Simplicissimus* (Munich: C. H. Becksche Verlagsbuchhandlung, 1936).

[77] Cf. Horst Hartmann, "Bemerkungen zu Siegfried Strellers Theorie der Zahlenkomposition," *Zeitschrift für deutsche Literaturgeschichte*, V (1959), pp. 428-36; and Siegfried Streller's reply, "Spiel oder Forschungsgegenstand" in the same journal, pp. 437-40.

[78] *Courage*, chap. 15. For this reason the German *"Springinsfeld"* must be translated literally as "Jump-i'-th'-field" or "Skipinthefield," in order to do justice to the author's intention. Mr. Walter Wallich's imaginative choice of "Happy-Go-Lucky" as an English equivalent for the German *"Springinsfeld"* in his new translation of *The Adventurous Simplicissimus* (under the title, *The Adventures of a Simpleton*, London: The New English Library Ltd., 1962) does not deserve the unqualified praise it received from the reviewer in *The Times Literary Supplement* of Novmber 9, 1962. The translation is even less complete than Mr. Goodrick's (cf. note 6) and not based on the original *Simplicissimus* edited by J. H. Scholte.

[79] This novella is part of *Bird's-nest II*, taking up nine of its twenty-seven chapters.

[80] *Courage*, chap. 3.

[81] Jacob Burckhardt, *Die Kultur der Renaissance in Italien*, 14th ed., ed. Walter Goetz (Leipzig: Kröner Verlag, 1925), p. 271.

[82] Baldassare Castiglione, *The Book of the Courtier*, Done into English by Sir Thomas Hoby, anno. 1561, Everyman's Library, p. 218.

[83] For the following discussion, cf. Antoine Claire Jungkunz, *Menschendarstellung im deutschen höfischen Roman des Barock* (Berlin: Germanische Studien, 1937), pp. 42, 78-90, 189, 220.

[84] Quoted in *op. cit.*, p. 88.

[85] Johann Beer, *Kurtzweilige Sommer-Täge*, 1683, ed. Wolfgang Schmidt (Halle: Max Niemeyer, 1958), p. 116.

[86] This is G. Weydt's view of Grimmelshausen in his monograph, "Der deutsche Roman vom 15. bis 17. Jahrhundert," *Deutsche Philologie im Aufriss*, 2nd ed., ed. Wolfgang Stammler (Berlin: E. Schmidt, 1952), II, p. 1256. This study is perhaps the best modern introduction to the history of the picaresque novel and Grimmelshausen's place in it.

[87] *Courage*, chap. 20.

[88] *Ibid.*

[89] *Simplicissimus*, V, chap. 8.

[90] *Crine ruber, niger ore, brevis pede, lumine laesus, rem magnam praestas,*

Zoile, si bonus es. Of red hair, swarthy of face, short of foot, of eye blear, you show yourself to be a portent, Zoilus, if you are virtuous. (Martial, *Epigrams,* XII, 45. [Loeb Classical Library, II, p. 356].)

[91] Friedrich Seiler, *Deutsche Sprichwörterkunde* (Munich: C. H. Becksche Verlagsbuchhandlung, 1922), pp. 401-2.

[92] Andrew Guerschron, *Certain Aspects of Russian Proverbs* (London: F. Muller Ltd., 1941), p. 155. See also Iwan Klimenko, *Das russische Sprichwort* (Bern: A. Francke, 1946), p. 27.

[93] Werner Krauss, *Die Welt im spanischen Sprichwort* (Wiesbaden: Limes Verlag, 1946), p. 45.

[94] *Ibid.,* p. 53.

[95] Francisco de Quevedo, *op. cit.,* p. 94.

[96] Cf. Jungkunz, *op. cit.,* p. 37.

[97] *Ibid.,* p. 75.

[98] The title of Grimmelshausen's pamphlet is "Bart-Krieg." Grimmelshausen's authorship of this pamphlet was proved only in 1940 by Manfred Koschlig, "Der Bart-Krieg—Ein Werk Grimmelshausens," *Neophilologus,* XXXIV (1938-39), pp. 42ff. "Der Bart-Krieg" is included in *Simpliciana* pp. 128-48.

[99] Walther Muschg, *Tragische Literaturgeschichte* (Bern: A. Francke, 1948), pp. 265-66.

[100] *Ibid.*

[101] Richard Alewyn, *op. cit.,* p. 172.

[102] A good English translation of *Tragi-Comediade Calisto y Melibar,* popularly known as *The Celestina* (after the character of the procuress in the play), was made by Lesley Byrd Simpson (Berkeley and Los Angeles: University of California Press, 1955, paperbound edition, 1959).

[103] The point that Grimmelshausen admired Courage is also made by Siegfried Streller, *op. cit.,* p. 195. Streller speaks of Grimmelshausen's "unconfessed sympathies for this hated and loved character" and refers to the magnificent description of Courage (then already sixty-six years old) by the Swiss clerk in *Grimmelshausens Springinsfeld,* ed. J. H. Scholte (Halle: Max Niemeyer, 1928), chap. 4 (hereafter cited as *Skipinthefield*).

[104] *Bird's-nest II,* chap 18. Cf. also the story of Aemilia, who after twelve years of marriage changes her sex and becomes Aemilius (*Everlasting Almanac,* pp. 396-7).

[105] Er "sahe so bleich und trostlos aus, als wann er kürzlich ein Kind bekommen und keinen Vatter, Meel noch Milch darzu gehabt oder gewüsst hätte." (*Courage,* chap. 15).

[106] Henry A. Murray in his introduction to Herman Melville's *Pierre* (New York: Farrar, Strauss & Cudahy, Inc., 1949), note, p. xxxvii.

[107] Courage has blond hair (*Skipinthefield,* chap. 4). So do the heroines in the conventional baroque novels, even if they are of Roman or oriental descent. This shade of hair, also to be found on women painted by Rubens, signifies the purity of the heroine, a convention that dates back to the Greek erotic novel and to Greek and Roman lyrical poetry. (Cf. Jungkunz, *op. cit.,* p. 33.)

[108] Curt von Faber du Faur, *German Baroque Literature: A catalogue of the collection in the Yale University Library* (New Haven: Yale University Press, 1958), p. 213.

[109] Paul Hankamer, *op. cit.,* p. 418.

[110] In an edition of Donne's poetry of 1635.

[111] Cf. Hans Ehrenzeller, *op. cit.*

[112] Hildegarde Wichert, *op. cit.,* p. 140.

[113] *Skipinthefield,* chap. 3.

[114] Bertolt Brecht, *Mother Courage and Her Children: A Chronicle of the Thirty Years' War* (New York: Grove Press, Inc., 1963), pp. 75-76. English version by Eric Bentley. Copyright © 1955, 1959, 1961, 1962, 1963, by Erich Bentley.

[115] Martin Esslin, *Brecht* (Frankfurt am Main and Bonn: Athenäum Verlag, 1962), pp. 312ff.

[116] Esslin, *op. cit.,* p. 314.

[117] *"Frieden, das ist nur Schlamperei, erst der Krieg schafft Ordnung."* (Bertolt Brecht, *Mutter Courage und ihre Kinder* [1939, but first published in German only in 1949]. Paperbound edition [Berlin: Suhrkamp Verlag, 1960], p. 7). Mr. Bentley translates, "You know what the trouble with peace is? No organization. And when do you get organization? In a war." (*Op. cit.,* p. 13).

[118] Bertolt Brecht, *op. cit.,* p. 77.

[119] *Simplicissimus,* III, chap. 7.

[120] *Simplicissimus,* I, chap. 18.

[121] *Simplicissimus,* III, chap. 19. Basile, *The Pentameron,* trans. Sir Richard Burton (London: William Kimber, 1952), p. 96.

[122] *Simplicissimi Galgenmännlin,* in *Werke,* ed. H. H. Borcherdt, IV, p. 305.

[123] *Simplicissimus,* III, chap. 3.

[124] *Courage,* chap. 9.

[125] *The Council Chamber of Pluto, Simpliciana,* pp. 114-26.

[126] *Simplicissimus,* V, chap. 15.

[127] *Simplicissimus,* V, chap. 1.

[128] *Continuatio,* chap. 26.

[129] *Continuatio,* chap. 27.

[130] Shakespeare, *The Tempest,* Act II, Sc. 1.

[131] *Simplicissimus,* V, chap. 19.

Nine

INSTITUTIONAL CHANGE IN
THE FRENCH PAINTING WORLD

Sociologists have often been remarkably insensitive to the uses of history. Yet here, in the past as laboratory, we can see social experiments performed in all their complex natural detail. History is perhaps especially pertinent to the study of the arts, since the arts have been characteristically human enterprises over very long time periods; they bear in themselves an intrinsically rich historical pattern. Moreover, because art is in some important respects noncumulative, all artists are to a degree contemporaries of one another. They are alike immersed in a tradition whose eras exert mutual import, so that a work of art lifted from its context is only slightly comprehensible in isolation.

What the Whites have done in the present essay is to demonstrate how artistic careers are affected by a dense texture of social organization. We see the painter shaped not only by his psychological dynamism and individual talent, but by the structure of opportunities offered by a particular environment. In a society which was interested in painting and had fostered an institutional framework to enclose and regularize its pursuit, the Whites chart the implications of that framework for the professional career. Most importantly, we are given a picture of social and artistic change; the involved interaction of social forms and creative endeavors impresses us with how much art and sociology can contribute to one another.

In this analysis, which begins from the institutional system rather than from the perspective of the individual painter's role, several themes of the studies of role earlier in this book are re-iterated. For instance, there is again the stress on a shift from some version of patronage toward a more nearly open market; there is the increasingly sharp distinction between fine and commercial art, or artist and artisan. Overall we see the consistencies of change in art and artist as the general contours of Western society changed from traditional, hierarchical, closed systems to more nearly democratic, mass, open societies—or perhaps better, from early industrial to mature industrial societies.

There are two crucial features of the Whites' concluding remarks. The first is their notably cautious claim for the explanatory power of this institutional analysis. Having clearly traced a configuration of social determinants in the development of French painting, they remind us that even such a complicated web of influence cannot be assumed to be the whole story of why artists lived and created as they did. Noting the "inner logic" of style, they abjure an easy explanation and point instead to a sophisticated Gestalt of influence: the formal immanence of stylistic evolution joined to a congeries of social forces. Too often the social scientist in his approach to art fails to grant this complex symbolic pattern its measure of autonomy, despite the fact that one of the most persuasive exponents of immanent change is an anthropologist, A. L. Kroeber, whose *Configurations of Culture Growth* affords convincing evidence of intrinsic exfoliation in artistic form.

The second, related emphasis on the possibilities of comparative study of the arts in different societies is equally heartening. Generalizations about the sociology of the arts on any broad and enduring basis will probably depend on series of just such admirably detailed histories as this one.

INSTITUTIONAL CHANGE
IN THE FRENCH PAINTING WORLD

Cynthia White
Harrison White

We have no brief for any social and economic determinism of art. Rather, we are interested in the changing organizational context in which styles and "movements" in painting are created. To sociologists this problem can be of intrinsic interest as social change. To art historians, it can be a supplement and perhaps an enrichment of work already done.

Looking backward from the explosive era of the 1880's, we seek a pattern to explain the limited social world in which French painters were trained, worked, and made their reputations. We assume that, as with other professions, there is at most times a more-or-less coherent social structure, an institutional system of organizations, rules, and customs centering around the painter's career. These social institutions are shaped by all painters, good, bad, and indifferent, famous or forgotten, who pass through them. So that, in addition to the common information about the few great painters of the century, we must know more about the condition of the run-

We would like to thank Robert N. Wilson for generous encouragement over a six-year period, and Messrs. John C. Sloane and John Rewald for criticisms of earlier manuscripts. A detailed report of our work will be published as a monograph, *Canvases and Careers*, by John Wiley and Sons, Inc. It is impossible to include adequate documentation for an interpretation of a long and complex period in the compass of a short chapter; so we refer the reader to our book for bibliography, specific citations, and detailed accounts of the procedures by which we made the various estimates that follow. Financial assistance from the Social Science Research Committee of the University of Chicago is gratefully acknowledged.

of-the-mill painter. As far as the nineteenth century is concerned, many painters then considered great are now thought run-of-the-mill; and the converse is also true.

We could find no estimates of how many professional painters there were living, working, and competing for recognition at any given time in France. But accurate biographical records of all painters who exhibited at least two or three times at the annual Paris salons are found in the most complete dictionary of French painters, the *Dictionnaire Général des Artistes de L'École Française,* by E. Bellier de la Chavignérie and Louis Auvray, published in 1882. In this source we counted by a sampling procedure those whose major work was in painting. The number per decade showed a strong growth. For example, there were eighty-five per cent more painters born in the two decades 1815-1834 than there were in the two decades 1785-1804. In the year 1863 there were between 3000 and 3600 living male professional painters in the Parisian art world. They exhibited in the Salon over a span of eighteen years on the average.

How many painters were there who worked exclusively in the provinces, who are not included in Bellier and Auvray's dictionary? We used the only two good dictionaries of provincial painters, those for the regions of Lyonnaise (centering around Lyon) and Franche-Comté (Dijon-Besançon). Extrapolating to all provinces on the basis of government data on faculty size in all the various local art schools, we estimate that there were about 1100 provincial professional painters alive around 1863. Another 1200 painters sufficiently identified with a locality to be in a provincial dictionary are also included in the Parisian orbit. (And the remaining third of provincial entries had too little training and too few exhibitions and/or awards to be considered professional).

All in all, we have a total of at least 4000 male professional French painters alive in 1863.˙ Now, what is the point of all this? Four thousand is not a staggering number of painters to encompass in a decentralized institutional system. But in this case 3000 men were in one lump, at the core of the institutional system centered on Paris: the Academy and the supporting government art bureaucracy. Pressure from this greatly expanding number of professional painters on an organizational and economic framework designed to handle a few hundred painters was the steadily increasing force for change. Why did the population of painters in Paris grow so strikingly? The academic institutional system was itself responsible, to some extent.

The old Royal Academy had directed and stimulated, by its prestigious example, the establishment of many provincial academies which trained young painters in the rudiments and then sent them on to Paris. By 1786 there were thirty-three of these provincial establishments, their greatest growth having taken place in the latter half of the eighteenth century. The maximum rewards of Paris were high—nothing in the provinces could compare with them. And with nineteenth century Salons open to all who could pass the jury, with a proliferation of awards and nationwide publicity, more and more painters were drawn into the Parisian orbit. Records of the careers of provincial painters show that few artists could be famous, even in their own region, without entering and competing in the Parisian art world.

It may be, indeed, that there were not so many more artists, but that there were more who aspired to be "fine artists," that is, painters exclusively. The painter's high status as a man of learning with a noble calling is a continuing theme from the Italian academies of the late Renaissance to the nineteenth century descendant of the original French Académie Royale of Charles Lebrun (1648). The other side of this theme is the downgrading of the artisan painter or applied artist. This academic view of the painter implied that he was middle class. Such was the assumption and aspiration of most nineteenth century painters.

Here is another clue to the growth in numbers of painters. A respectable profession with nationally known rewards and state-supported training was a great drawing card to a young man of talent. Methods of advancement in the painter's training were as prescribed, in principle, as those of Saint-Cyr; so that bourgeois fathers grew more willing to trust their sons to what seemed a consistent official painting system where application and perseverance could produce a public record of attainment. Yet, in reality, there was no monopoly on training; a bewildering variety of schools and ateliers, partly or wholly independent, confronted the young novice in Paris.

257

There are several important themes here: the centralization of the art world and the academic system in Paris. Concentration on one type of artistic activity—painting. Rejection of the artisan role. The expectation of a middle-class standard of life for the painter. Unregulated growth in numbers. These themes are woven from the historical fabric of the official system; they also fit into the pattern of its decline. Let us consider the structure of that system at the start of the nineteenth century. There were inherent instabilities in the way it was set up.

The eighteenth century Academy had been a professional society with a membership of around one hundred fifty. On the whole, it seems to have been a flexible organization, capable of absorbing varied sorts of talent and resolving internal conflicts. A distinctly baroque sort of organization, it had many ranks and kinds of members.

The nineteenth century Academy was telescoped into a small "official" elite of fourteen, all of equal rank, the "immortals" in gold-laced green uniforms. As one historian has put it: "The old Academy was a hierarchy with a base which sustained it and was sustained by it. The new (Academy) was that hierarchy without its base. It was not . . . in contact with the whole body of artists so as to have them constantly en route towards and certain of a share in its honors, and having always a place for talent worthy of admission." The Academy became almost a subsidiary of the government and its connections with the rest of the centralized art bureaucracy were highly formalized. At the very time when it was necessary to broaden membership and decentralize the structure, the academic system took the opposite course, and yet the Academy clung to its role as arbiter of the worth of all painters. Although the government bureaucracy gradually usurped most of the Academy's prerogatives, it did not change the basic form of the semiofficial system until late in the century.

A related instability was the lack of economic jurisdiction or any regulatory powers over the number and careers of practicing artists. These powers of the mediaeval guilds were exactly what the original Royal Academy had so bitterly opposed. In the century and a half after the Academy's establishment, the modified guild had lost such powers, but it remained as a rival institution, a gadfly forcing academic flexibility, until the Revolution. Now, in the nineteenth century no such rival institution remained. Economically, the art world had been laissez faire for some time, but the Academy claimed a sole authority not compatible with its disavowal of responsibility.

There was a need felt for regulation and protection of artists' interests. Numerous attempts to form artists' syndicates and mutual aid and pension societies testify to it. The nineteenth century Academy could have entered this field. It failed to do so, as it also failed to concern itself directly with the careers of applied artists or marginal painters. Broadening its activities and including many types of artistic careers under its aegis might have allowed the academic system to cope with the flood of painters. However, the structure remained centralized with a small elite at the top dominating training, the single annual exhibition, and the elaborate obstacle course of awards.

For a very small number, the rules of this game worked smoothly. There were twenty-one winners of the Prix de Rome from 1840-1860. (After a weeding-out process in which preliminary drawings were submitted, the finalists were shut up *en loge* for about two months to paint a set subject. The Grand Prize winner was ceremoniously crowned with laurel and sent to the French Academy in Rome for four to five years' study.)

Eighteen of these winners were alumni of the official École des Beaux-Arts. Three quarters of them were coached by the academicians Picot or Drolling—in some cases, when the pupil was taking no chances, by both. Let us compare the fortunes of the Prix de Rome winners with the careers of all professional painters of the first six decades of the nineteenth century.

The median age of the prize winners at their first Salon exhibition was twenty-three, much below that for all Salon exhibitors.

Nineteen of the winners received Salon medals, usually high ones, the first medal at a median age of only thirty-four. A medal was received by one fourth of the total male professional painters.

Over half of the twenty-one winners had pictures purchased by the Luxembourg (*the* national museum for contemporary art) as well as for provincial museums, whereas only a third of all professional painters received any official commission or purchase at all.

By 1882 fifteen of the twenty-one had been made members of the Legion of Honor. Less than a fifth of all painters attained this distinction. And finally, one out of the twenty-one was elected to the Academy by 1882. Only one in a hundred made it from the total group of painters.

Not only does a rather small minority receive any official distinction or financial support, but the different kinds of honors and support are not spread around to different men. The rich get richer; but in reputation, not in money. Even the favored few could hardly live on state commissions and purchases; and there were not enough official sinecures to pay very many steady salaries to painters. For the great majority of professional painters, actions of the Salon jury and related State purchases were clearly not pervasive enough. Their effect was less and less decisive, either as negative control or positive reward.

Two contradictory but avowed purposes were contained in the institution of the Salon. It was intended as the main instrument for review, reward, and control of painters seeking official recognition. In this professional aspect, it continued that obstacle course of contests, the training system. At the same time, the Salon was a vast show of thousands of paintings put on for the public in the spirit of an Age of Expositions.

On the one hand, the judgments of the official elite were considered sacred to the welfare of the profession and the upholding of its standards. On the other hand, there was a strong faith in the judgments of the public. Again, historical background is reflected in this dual character. The Salons of the Académie Royale were open only to members and were juried only from 1748. The precedent of a "democratic" Salon open to all competitors was created during the Revolution. At this time, also, an unjuried Salon for all painters was held (1791) and "free" Salons recurred several times, in various forms, during the succeeding century.

To fulfill the purpose of presenting works for public judgment, the most sensible thing to do might have been to proliferate Salons, holding several annually, perhaps by specialty. This was, in effect, what eventually happened late in the century in a new institutional context. A contrary solution could have been to cut drastically the number of applicants to the Salon, going back, in essence, to the

Royal Academy rules. The number of *works* to be submitted from each painter was cut to three, then two; but these measures did not begin to solve the problem of size. Instead, pressure from the growing number of painters forced the jury to raise the number of admissions in pace with the rising number of pictures submitted. Thus, pretty consistently, about half the applicants to juried Salons were admitted. The number excluded was large, but even in years of maximum protest at harsh juries at least forty per cent of the paintings submitted were accepted.

It is exceedingly difficult to evaluate large numbers of objects, using a single centralized organization, when the objects are culturally defined as being unique. From the 1840's on, this was the jury's main problem. It had, annually, to consider 4000 to 5000 paintings, and in a limited period of time. The masterwork, the single painting, had been the emphasis of the academic system. Training, competitions, and Salons were so set up that the judgment of an artist's work hinged, at any time in his career, upon the single painting. Of course, a good deal of log-rolling went on in jury sessions. It was a picture-for-picture exchange, encouraged by the impossibility of seriously considering the type and quality of each of 5000 paintings. In a world of fewer artists and smaller Salons, general familiarity with each painter's work, as represented in the picture at hand, could have been assumed. In the overcrowded nineteenth century art world, knowledge of and communication about the whole body of each artist's work was impossible.

Neither could the salon be an effective market place for its bewildering sea of paintings. The artist's career and the security of his living do not depend on a single painting bought off the Salon's walls, but on the reputation and saleability of his work as a whole. Ingres, neoclassicist purist, himself an academician who believed that the Academy betrayed its heritage, disgustedly labeled the salon "a picture shop." It is ironic that picture shops eventually became, in effect, the Salons.

So far, we have analyzed some of the internal instabilities of the academic system and described the pressures brought to bear on it. As a national art machine to recruit painters and dignify painting, it was certainly successful; as an organization to support, oversee, and direct professional painting careers, it fell far short. The majority of aspiring artists, talented and mediocre, were channeled exclusively into the prestigious career of painting. The system provided no escape hatch, via alternative art careers.

As the pressure of overloading became greater, other gaps appeared in the system and widened. Informal sponsor-protégé relations among painters became more and more attenuated. There was no provision, beyond drop-in-the-bucket official rewards, for the continuing economic and social needs even of the recognized painters. Communication on practical and painterly matters was no longer adequate in flow or dispersion. Professional evaluation of painters' works and the related reputation making could not be adequately handled in the face of such multitudes. Lacking economic functions, the academic system could not develop and cultivate a variety of markets for painters, nor effectively identify individuals with a given public or group of buyers.

For all this, the academic system remained legitimate and powerful in the eyes of painters. There was hardly a one, even among the celebrated rebels, who did not desire its official approval and sponsorship. The Salon was evidently a highly unsatisfactory institution, yet pictures kept coming in by the carload each year. Storms of protest were directed against specific rules and policies— but usually not against the system in principle.

We must look at the other side of the coin and see how an institutional system developing around art dealers and critics took on more and more of the functions of the old system and eventually usurped its legitimacy. Dealers and critics had long been subsidiaries of the academic system. Journalistic art criticism was, in fact, a direct product of the Royal Salons, originating in the mid eighteenth century. Dealers moved to a large-scale interest in current art mainly as a result of the prestige of contemporary painting generated by the nineteenth century academic system. Otherwise, they might have remained in the service of old masters, rather than living painters.

We could find no evidence of any big art dealers operating in the first thirty years or so of the nineteenth century in Paris. (A satisfactory history of trade in art in nineteenth century France has yet to be compiled.) Antique dealers, jewelers, print sellers and color-and-canvas shops often handled pictures on the side. But "galleries" dealing exclusively on a large scale in contemporary art are a phenomenon of the second half of the century. They are a response to a need on the part of painters and the growth of a potential market. Let us consider this market, the requirements of the painter, and the type of painting involved.

Paintings are unique objects, by present cultural definition. In principle each is considered individual, almost mystically different from any other. A painting is also piecework and was paid for, generally, on a piecework basis. In fact painters were professionals who, though middle class, operated on a manual, piecework basis. A painter has to supply his own materials as well. The nineteenth century French painter needed a steady income not only for the middle-class way of life that he expected, but also for continuous outlay on the materials and other overhead of his trade. Not occasional high prices, but the steady sale of a fair proportion of his work was what he needed. And the number of commissioned paintings declined, if anything—anticlericalism decreased government support of church decoration for one thing, and portraiture probably fell off; so the artist was in the quandary of seeking steady income from work produced on speculation.

What did this mean in terms of the market needed by the growing numbers of artists? How many paintings were being produced? The minimum estimate for the number of painters was 4000 around 1863. Available complete catalogues for individual painters show that ten paintings a year is a low rate for most painters during the main part of their careers. But let us be conservative and cut this to five paintings annually. So, it seems reasonable to say that, after midcentury, 200,000 paintings must have been produced per decade, by professional French painters.

The increase in sheer numbers of pictures is related to some changes in procedure, technique, and size in painting as well as to trends in taste. New color preparations, thicker and more manipulable paints, were sold in tin tubes easy to preserve and handy to use. "Ready-made" canvas, as well as paints, simplified preparation and stimulated the use of fast painting techniques. The typical academic procedure, as generally taught, was "planned" painting: a work was carefully built up, stage by stage, from the groundwork of the original drawing. With the easy new materials the concurrent interest in painting done completely outdoors could attract adherents.

Swift brush techniques developed, and the trend was all toward small pictures and more of them. Many of these could be finished in the time it would have taken to produce one large "planned" picture. Now few painters were needed or used to devote their time to routine chores of preparation and background as assistants to a master; all could produce many paintings solo.

The prevailing taste also was for small paintings. There was a growing interest in landscape. But the bulk of paintings being produced were those known as "genre." And here, taste seems to play the main role, rather than technology; for many genre paintings were executed with procedure and technique as meticulous as that of a large "planned" painting.

A genre painting was usually anecdotal, most often showing a setting from the imagined life of the lower classes, another historical era, or an exotic place. The Impressionists, it should be noted, are really genre painters who portray scenes from the real middle-class life of the times in a disturbingly new style. Herein lies the real shock of their innovations.

In the academic scheme of things, which ranked paintings in order of significant subject matter rather than style, genre takes a middle place, lower than the noble themes of "history" painting and higher than landscape (because the latter subordinated or left out the human figure). The central struggle, as seen by the art world of the time and reflected in the critical writings, was that of elevated history painting with its patriotic, classical, and Biblical subjects, versus genre, often of a saccharine and anecdotal variety. Genre painting won. Ernest Meissonier, delineator of highly finished genre scenes in wondrously small sizes, was elected to the Academy in 1861.

Attempting to find a steadier, more secure career, many genre painters specialized, taking a popular subject and capitalizing on it. Paintings of rural scenes were especially popular. There were the fabulously successful Rosa Bonheur, specializing in farm horses and cattle, and the painter Troyon, who was at one point so pressed for his pictures of grazing cows that he hired Eugene Boudin (one of the fathers of Impressionism) to brush in some landscape backgrounds in a hurry. There were painters of picturesque military scenes, like Detaille, a pupil of Meissonnier. There were those who specialized in cutting the heroic orientalism of Delacroix down to genre size.

Thus, to some degree, the painter was imitating mass production and cutting down the factor of uniqueness. A buyer is attracted to any Troyon rural scene—if he likes cows!

Small genre paintings—and portraits—had, in fact, made up the bulk of Salons from as far back as 1740. The rage for Dutch "little master" pictures had been a strong influence. And demand for small-scale decorative canvases was a continuing factor. For this "move-able decoration" is what best fits the style, mobility, and time span of a bourgeois family. The influence of the bourgeoisie is no new phenomenon in the nineteenth century; French class structure had already shifted long before the Revolution. There was, however, a broadening of the middle class, especially after 1848. Here lay a greater potential market for art if it could be tapped.

To return, then, to the dealers: viewing this potential market, they were anxious to expand their clientele. They saw a chance to develop circles of buyers around a focus on specific groups of painters who followed the trend in size and subject matter.

At the same time art critics in a growing and fiercely competitive journalistic world wanted to expand their readership and make their reputations as influential intellectuals. Close identification with specific painters could make a critic stand out amongst the throng of writers. The academic system could not ignore critics, for during the 1800's published criticism became essential to communication in the swollen art world in supplying information needed to evaluate painters and paintings. Indeed, bribes by dealers and painters were not uncommon.

To most buyers, however, the academic seal of approval, in the form of Salon exhibition or a Salon prize, was what made a painter and painting saleable. And the most common stock-in-trade for both dealers and critics was the works of Salon painters, for whom they accomplished the detailed task of creating a circle of buyers for a painter's output.

To combat the academic imprimatur, protesting painters together with the dealers and critics who backed them had gradually created an ideology of their own. It was that legacy of Romanticism,

265

the "unknown genius" idea. When critics publicized and lauded an unrecognized painter, they were urging a speculation in taste. Writers like Zola said, "In twenty years, the works of this man will be considered masterpieces!", the implied corollary being that a critic with such prescience deserved recognition as a gifted intellectual. And dealers joined in the refrain: "In twenty years these paintings will be worth a fortune!" In pushing the works of "unrecognized genius," both of individuals and groups, dealers took advantage of the speculative fever pervading French economic life, especially during the 1850's and 1860's.

Paintings of past centuries had long been considered as a safe investment with growth potential suitable for international exchange. But changes in value were usually too slow to warrant the term "speculation." In any case, the buyers of such paintings operated at a higher financial level than most buyers of contemporary art. Present prestige and value were the prime concerns of most of the latter. And initial prices for "medaled" Salon favorites were so high that they could hardly be looked to for short-term speculation. So the dealer was developing a way of attracting short-term speculators.

But if a dealer were to speculate, he needed to own enough of a painter's works to make that speculation rational. Something of a monopoly was necessary. Here, the growing custom of dealer-painter contracts could benefit both parties. These were usually gentlemen's agreements rather than signed contracts, although late in the century signed agreements became more common. There were various forms: a cash advance on specific promised works, a steady monthly "salary" or a sort of unwritten agreement where the dealer acted as "banker" for the artist, paying his rent, food, and paint bills as they came in.

In a sense, the dealer recreates an old role, that of the patron in earlier centuries. He works from different motives and a different economic base. But in emotional and social tone, the relationship is very different from the state patronage of the academic system. An artist had someone of whom he could demand support and recognition. The flavor is best conveyed by a few quotes from the famous letters of Impressionists to their dealer-patron Durand-Ruel:

You are not going to believe that I doubt you. No, I know your courage and your energy . . . are you certain that you can give me some money today . . . send your reply by the bearer (of this letter), it irritates me to come continually to the shop to importune you. . . . Here it is a month and a half since your departure and not a word from you, not a penny from your son. I don't know what you think I'm living on, but I remain amazed by your indifference.

I see myself forced to sell, if possible, a few paintings. I greatly regret being obliged to come to this, for necessarily the prices on my pictures will be lowered, but I have no choice, having many debts. . . . Have the goodness to tell me, my dear M. Durand-Ruel, what I should do.

I have been surprised and a bit pained, I must say, by your silence; and if Boussod had not given me an advance, and without the Petit exhibition, I would doubtless have found myself in difficulties.

Painters soon learned the technique of playing one dealer off against another, as in earlier times the artist threatened to leave one patron to glorify another. The dealer-patron, in principle, can be regarded as a device which coagulated a chaotic free market into a few competing nuclei, stable enough to serve as effective substitutes for government patronage. It was natural for both dealers and critics to emphasize the career of the painter and his total works. The single current painting as an isolated item in trade is too fugitive to serve as focus for a sales or publicity system. The new pattern emerged more and more clearly from the 1840's, when Durand-Ruel backed the group of landscapists known as the Barbizon School, on to the Impressionists, and beyond to later movements in art.

Group exhibitions, a joint creation of painters, critics, and dealers, were a phase in the launching of painters and the build-up of their individual careers. The publicity splash of a group show eventually forced even conservative Salon critics to cover the event. Thus the public was made more and more aware of these alternatives to the Salon, and it became fashionable to at least look in on them.

Critics served not only as publicists but as theorists, explaining to the public how to look at a painting. Their instruction was less and less in terms of subject matter, the traditional academic touchstone, and rather in terms of style and technique. This was not only because of the rate of stylistic innovation and the trend toward smaller, more decorative paintings. Painters showing in a group need a stylistic identity and, when a large chunk of a painter's work is shown at one time, it is the more important to emphasize stylistic development. It does not seem accidental that Salon criticism throughout the century leaned heavily on subject matter as a mode of discussing the paintings exhibited. (Most Salon critics even followed the academic rank order of subjects, grouping paintings accordingly in their articles.)

By the late 1880's, one-man shows of living artists, sponsored by dealers in their "galleries," were common. The painter's total works and developing style were again emphasized. At the same time, the "series" painting, especially as developed by Monet in his "Haystacks," "Water-Lilies," and "Cathedrals" made its appearance. This is the ultimate in stylistic variations on a theme, as the artist builds up, picture by picture, his interpretation of nature. Today, it is often customary for an artist simply to number his works in a series. The individual work of art takes on a different meaning, one that is increasingly complicated and difficult because it is only a piece of a meaning.

Thus, the buyer's demand for small, decorative pictures, the dealer's development of various social and financial techniques, the critic's roles as publicist and theorist combine with the needs of the painter and his own chosen forms and techniques to generate by a rather complex process the new institutional system that emerged in the late nineteenth century.

The academic system is more the victim than the villain in this process. As we have seen, many of the conditions for its decline —and for the rise of a new social framework—were generated by its creative successes. The irony is that the official system could not adapt to function effectively at the size inherent in its own goals.

Flexibility and specialized clienteles were the strength of the dealer-critic system. Yet it lacked formal structure. Only the centralization of the art world in Paris, an international art city with a rich and varied cosmopolitan clientele, allowed a skeleton-less system like that of dealers and critics to come to power. And its whole development owed much to the drama of conflict with the prestige of that ancient edifice, the academic system.

Now all this makes a rather neat pattern of a very complicated piece of history. Neither the data nor its interpretation are complete. But from this starting point, it should be possible, by looking at some comparative cases, to find what questions to ask next. In art history, two comparisons especially come to mind as subjects for research.

Dutch painting during the seventeenth century displays some of the same institutional characteristics that we have seen in the French art world of the nineteenth century. There were large numbers of painters, decorative easel painting predominated, specialization was common, and dealers and painters entered into some of the same contractual relationships. Holland had no academies of art to speak of; yet our interpretation of the French case leant heavily on the dynamic social situation created by the Academy's rise and decline. On the other hand, French painting and its social institutions continued to develop and bear fruit, whereas Dutch painting seems to have declined in the eighteenth century.

Another comparison with a totally different framework is suggested by the English art world. Here, as is perhaps typical, no violent changes occurred in the social institutions. The Royal Academy, a creation of the eighteenth century, sailed along through the nineteenth with rather unruffled calm. It always maintained independence from the State. England showed an early concern with applied art training and seems to have been far ahead of France in making provisions for it. There was a great popular interest in cheap engravings; many painters worked directly with the object of having their painting bought and engraved by a specific print publisher. A wider audience for art seems to have been achieved in this way rather than by great Salon shows. There were inexpensive "subscription plans" to suit even the lower-middle-class pocket. And some English academicians are to be found unabashedly selling their art to the greater glory of Pear's soap advertisements.

Can the approach we take lead to a fuller understanding of art: for example, what does this paper tell us of the meaning and development of Impressionism? Or are we looking at the art world simply for more case studies of social change? Impressionism was not "produced" by social changes in the French art world. One must know the inner logics of stylistic development in order to begin the explanation of why other movements in style (or subject matter!) did not develop and why those that did were stillborn. They were stillborn from the perspective of much later, of course; for a problem quite different from the development both of institutions and of art later accepted as a part of the great tradition is the relative popularity of contemporaneous painting. Yet immediate social pressures are a necessary component of any explanation of the presence or absence of various possible changes in art. These pressures limit the range of developments that can take place and the paths by which they take place. On the base of comparative historical studies we can build theories of what these limits are and how they vary; eventually these theories must be tested in the complexities of contemporary developments in art.

Ten

F. SCOTT FITZGERALD:
PERSONALITY AND CULTURE

This essay is most nearly comparable, in the present collection, to Watt's analysis (Chapter 6) of *Robinson Crusoe,* although the latter is couched at a higher level of generality and distinguished by a richer mold of historical allusion. Like most of the articles on individual figures in this book, it raises implicitly the question of the value of case studies to the sociology of literature. A well-fashioned study of the single case may clearly contribute to one possible aim: enhanced appreciation and understanding of an author or an art product. And perhaps this is reason enough for concentration in depth, provided that the object of attention is deemed significant. (Presumably, though, the judgment as to what is "significant," hence meriting detailed study, takes place at least partly in terms of aesthetic—not social-psychological—criteria.) Even at the level of case analysis, however, the distinctive increment supplied by the sociologist is at issue: what can the professional social scientist add to our awareness that is not afforded as well or better by a learned, perceptive literary critic like Kenneth Burke, Lionel Trilling, Edmund Wilson, Malcolm Cowley, or Ian Watt?

Let us suppose in the case of Fitzgerald that we really gain here a sharper insight into his personality, his values, and the content of his novels and short stories. What does this insight imply for the student of human behavior who is primarily interested in broadly applicable generalizations about individual psychic structure, social interaction, or cultural pattern? Or what, indeed, for the sociologist of literature who may be principally concerned with the meaning of a literary era in its social framework or with the impact of art on audience?

Part of the answer to such pertinent but embarrassing queries hinges on the representativeness of the chosen case. Here Watt, with Defoe, is on much firmer ground than Wilson with Fitzgerald; it now seems highly unlikely that *Robinson Crusoe* and Defoe's influence on the novel's development will ever be judged negligible, shunted aside in favor of some more salient work. Yet Fitzgerald is a figure from the very recent American past, about whom we can have no guarantee of either centrality or staying power. Perhaps all one can contend is that he is an exceedingly interesting writer and that he has been accorded a measure of aesthetic sensibility. Many critics have taken him, partly on the basis of his own somewhat reluctant evaluation, as representative of important features of the 1920's, and Malcolm Cowley avers that he "represents the human spirit in one of its permanent forms."

To the social scientist, this essay maintains, Fitzgerald offers an especially striking example of a personality structure termed the "Icarus complex." We do not know how pervasive this structure may be in any given population, although there is reason to suspect that it is closely akin to certain features of American character. There is at least a possibility that the documenting of Icarian modes in Fitzgerald could aid in the refinement of clinical thinking about personality types. Fitzgerald is also seen as a cultural exemplar because of his vivid incorporation of American value orientations in life and work, and his absorption in the maze of social stratification. He is of course not a "typical" American, whatever that mythic creature might be; what he *may* be is a heightened version of some important successes and failures in the way we live our lives as a people. If Fitzgerald was a failed writer and a failed man, his courageous and sombre self-appraisal is instructive. He teaches a culture that is dedicated to success—how to win with exuberance—but there is something more: his crack-up and its aftermath teach us how to lose with a certain ironic dignity.

F. SCOTT FITZGERALD:
PERSONALITY AND CULTURE

Robert N. Wilson

I. Fitzgerald as Icarus

> Fitzgerald was perhaps the last notable writer to affirm the Romantic fantasy, descended from the Renaissance, of personal ambition and heroism, of life committed to, or thrown away for, some ideal of self.
>
> ——Lionel Trilling, *The Liberal Imagination*

The relation between the artist's personality and his work, while obviously intimate, can never be made wholly explicit. Creativity is too elusive, too fundamentally mysterious, to afford a point-by-point correspondence between the man and the art. Yet the artist's role has shifted historically on the question of the individual's degree of identification with his books or paintings or music. From the anonymous art of the Middle Ages, dedicated to the glory of God, one may trace a movement toward ever greater concern with the artist as a person, toward a highly individualized art dedicated to

First published in *The Antioch Review* (Winter 1957-58), and reprinted in *Americana* (1958) [Japanese translation]. Excerpts from F. Scott Fitzgerald's *This Side of Paradise, The Great Gatsby, The Last Tycoon*, "The Rich Boy," and "Winter Dreams" are reprinted by permission of Charles Scribner's Sons.

the glory of self. In some instances this tendency has resulted in a relative disregard of the work, its overshadowing by the symbolic importance of the artist's person. Rimbaud, for example, has perhaps been more influential as the prototype of a role—the alienated, rebellious writer at odds with society—than as a poet to be read for his poetry.

As Trilling notes in the preceding passage, F. Scott Fitzgerald may stand as an exemplar of self-exploitation in the novel. His life and work were so interwoven that the distinction between them blurs; in a sense, he imagined and created his life and lived in his fictional protagonists. The quiet life of the conscientious artisan, the poet whom Milton counseled to drink plain water from a wooden bowl, was utterly foreign to Fitzgerald's conception of the writer's role. Rather, the author must live as his characters live, must make their style his and his theirs. In living up to a dream, an ideal of dramatic selfhood, Fitzgerald merged both his personality and the society in which he lived into his artistic representations. It would be as true to say that his life was a novel in progress—and, like his last novel, unfinished—as that his novels are autobiographical. As Malcolm Cowley says, "Sometimes the heroes started as very different persons and were transformed imperceptibly, as he worked over them, into an image of the author."

When he strove toward an ideal of self, a receding image of glorious and transcendent being, Fitzgerald expressed not only a personal disposition but a recurrent theme in American culture. In an exaggerated pure form, he struck what many regard as the unique chord in our national experience: a whole-hearted allegiance to an imagined future. This allegiance entails impatience with the present in all its imperfection and enjoins striving toward a yet unrealized state of grace. With maturity, the American dream commonly is scaled down to more modest proportions. The individual learns to tailor his goals, to limit the ideal, and to nourish his capacities for a more restricted achievement. Fitzgerald, however, was unusually tenacious, and his vision of the future was unusually full-blown. His desire encompassed the public life of the celebrity, the semi-private life of a star in a select social firmament, and the solitude of the literary craftsman. His refusal or inability to compromise these alternative and perhaps mutually exclusive selves may lie at

274

the root of his tragic unfulfillment. But that very disdain for discipline, that failure to conserve his personal resources, may also be germane to the marvelous zest that informs his best writing.

If Fitzgerald's ideal of self was marked by a catholicity so extreme as to thin out his talent in diffuse activities, it was at the same time distinguished by an intensity of literary aim. All that we know of his writing habits indicates a constant struggle to excel, to evoke precisely the right response from the reader by character and mood. His notebooks demonstrate how carefully, especially in his later period, he tried to create characters who would not make a psychologically false move. It seems likely, from the evidence of his last years in Hollywood and the incomplete fashioning of *The Last Tycoon,* that Fitzgerald might at length have muted the emphasis on himself as novelist extraordinary and devoted his life more thoroughly to art than had been the case. Nevertheless his foreshortened career stands dedicated to an ideal of self so intense and so demanding that it invites comparison with the Icarian myth.

In a recent essay, Henry A. Murray has described a psychological pattern which he terms the "Icarus complex." This pattern is an induction from a single intensive clinical history, although it is corroborated by a wealth of psychological and literary evidence. While Murray's elucidation of the complex is based on a variety of indices to his subject's personality, including projective tests, interviews, and observed behavior, Fitzgerald's life and work are so well documented that we are justified in seeking out a parallel configuration despite the lack of clinical knowledge in its strict sense. Fitzgerald, of course, does not conform to every facet of the Icarus complex; a scientifically isolated "type" never corresponds to any richly unique human being. Yet the psychologist is inevitably struck, in this instance, by an amazing correspondence between the themes exhibited in an exceedingly interesting male adolescent personality, studied clinically, and those exhibited in Fitzgerald's personality and the characters of his novels. These engaging parallels by no means "reduce" Fitzgerald to a clinical type; rather, they contribute to a coherent portrait of an extraordinarily talented writer.

The Icarus complex is distinguished by the following themes, most of which may be strikingly illustrated in the novelist: burning ambition and exhibitionism; desire to ascend to great heights; desire to be the center of all eyes; a precipitous fall; craving for immortality; depreciation and enthrallment of women. Obviously, the gifted and ambitious individuals of most societies exhibit some of these characteristics in some degree. The poet or philosopher may be peculiarly marked by them, according to Murray, and "for the fullest expression of the complex one must turn to ardent romantic poetry (Byron, Shelley), to mythic philosophy (Socrates in *Phaedrus,* or Nietzsche in *Thus Spake Zarathustra*), or to some form of up-yearning (erotic) mysticism." In significant literary and psychological respects, Fitzgerald may be viewed as a romantic poet.

Fitzgerald and his created figures abound in "burning" ambition and exhibitionism. As Arthur Mizener notes in *The Far Side of Paradise:* "As a small boy Fitzgerald lived, as he said later, 'with a great dream' and his object was always to realize that dream." His sights were set very high, and they continued to be on a transcendent scale long after the usual fantasies of adolescence. Two remarks he made in his early days are significant: "If I couldn't be perfect I wouldn't be anything," and, in undergraduate zeal to Edmund Wilson, "I want to be one of the greatest writers who ever lived, don't you?" The idealized self is perhaps a conspicuous feature of any artist's or any man's self-picture. What makes it unusual in Fitzgerald is the height of his aspiration, and his habit of comparing himself on a lifelong basis with the giants of literature. As Mizener observes, "But like Jay Gatsby's, his life was modeled on 'his Platonic conception of himself.' " And again, "He was thirty before experience succeeded in convincing him that 'life was [not] something you dominated if you were any good.' "

Exhibitionism and its complement, voyeurism, come through clearly. The endless parties of Scott and Zelda, their outrageous, funny, pathetic escapades, the final confession Fitzgerald wrote for *Esquire*—all contribute to the impression of a profound desire to exhibit, a desire not at all confined to the display of admirable qualities. It may well be that all writers are somewhat voyeuristic, that their stock in trade is a propensity to peer into other worlds, other styles of life. Fitzgerald, however, in his unalloyed curiosity about the milieu of the rich (the curiosity displayed in his story, "The Rich Boy," and embalmed in the famous exchange with Hemingway) showed extreme needs of this sort. Recall too the mood noted by Malcolm Cowley in Fitzgerald's Princeton days, the feeling that Eastern university life and the parties of the wealthy were to him like the candy store to the urchin, pressing his nose against the window to an exotic world.

All of Fitzgerald's heroes are ambitious, and all except Anthony Patch of *The Beautiful and Damned* are immoderately so. It should be remarked that their aspirations are not confined to a single path, for instance, to a vocation, but embrace many facets of work, love, and informal social intercourse. The heroes are self-consciously playing roles and striving for effects. Their eyes are on the future, on the creation of a dramatic personality and an orbit in which the personality may most graciously move. The two earliest heroes, Amory Blaine and Anthony Patch, aspire without fulfillment, although their dreams are not lessened by lack of success. Of Amory Blaine:

Always, after he was in bed, there were voices—indefinite, fading, enchanting—just outside his window, and before he fell asleep he would dream one of his favorite waking dreams, the one about becoming a great halfback or the one about the Japanese invasion, when he was rewarded by being made the youngest general in the world. It was always the becoming he dreamed of, never the being. This, too, was quite characteristic of Amory.

The later, more mature figures back up their ambition with genuine ability, but it is still overwhelming in magnitude. Jay Gatsby, Dick Diver, and Monroe Stahr each dream of brilliant success. Diver and Stahr are transcendent individuals in psychiatry and movie production, respectively, but strive even higher. The mysterious Gatsby is entirely transparent about his central concern, his dream of self:

The truth was that Jay Gatsby of West Egg, Long Island, sprang from his Platonic conception of himself. He was a Son of God, a phrase which, if it means anything, means just that—and he must be about his Father's business, the service of a vast, vulgar, and meretricious beauty. So he invented just the sort of Jay Gatsby that a seventeen-year-old boy would be likely to invent, and to this conception he was faithful to the end.

277

And as I sat there brooding on the old, unknown world, I thought of Gatsby's wonder when he first picked out the green light at the end of Daisy's dock. He had come a long way to this blue lawn, and his dream must have seemed so close that he could hardly fail to grasp it. He did not know that it was already behind him, somewhere back in that vast obscurity beyond the city, where the dark fields of the republic rolled on under the night.

Gatsby believed in the green light, the orgiastic future that year by year recedes before us. It eludes us then, but that's no matter—tomorrow we will run faster, stretch out our arms farther . . . And one fine morning——.

It is perhaps symptomatic that *The Great Gatsby* is generally acknowledged to be Fitzgerald's finest novel and one of the truly distinguished American works of the twentieth century. In addition to its marvelously taut form and precise language, *Gatsby* epitomizes the mystery and glamour of the future dream; without question, the struggle to fulfill a lofty unrealized conception of self is prominent in American values and central to Fitzgerald's psychic economy.

The desire to rise, leap, fly, and be tall among men is obviously akin to the zealous ambition which characterizes Fitzgerald and his characters. It is astonishing to find how often and how vividly images of flight occur in the novels. Indeed, *The Last Tycoon* is explicitly built around the transcontinental flights of its hero, Monroe Stahr, between Hollywood and New York, and Fitzgerald's notes show that flight was to have been an even more important theme in the unfinished portion. Fitzgerald appears as a literal Icarus in a curious description written by his wife Zelda in her avowedly autobiographical novel, *Save Me the Waltz:* "There seemed to be some heavenly support beneath his shoulder blades that lifted his feet from the ground, as if he secretly enjoyed the ability to fly but was walking as a compromise to convention." In his notes for *The Last Tycoon,* these images occur under the heading, "Airplane Trip":

My blue dream of being in a basket like a kite held by a rope against the wind.

It's fun to stretch and see the blue heavens spreading once more, spreading azure thighs for adventure.

The sexual symbolism of the latter is interestingly in keeping with the fantasies of the individual from whom the Icarus complex was originally derived; that young man dreamed of flying through the air on a maid's rump.

Probably the most coherent single expression of the ascension theme and Icarian imagery is found in the discussion of Monroe Stahr, the incredibly gifted Hollywood producer of *The Last Tycoon:*

"What I wanted to know," he told me ruefully, "is how he ever got to be Mr. Stahr."

I'm afraid Mr. Stahr could never have answered that one; for the embryo is not equipped with a memory. But I could answer a little. He had flown up very high to see, on strong wings, when he was young. And while he was up there, he had looked on all the kingdoms, with the kind of eyes that can stare straight into the sun. Beating his wings tenaciously— finally frantically—and keeping on beating them, he had stayed up there longer than most of us, and then, remembering all he had seen from his great height of how things were, he had settled gradually to earth.

Murray's next component is "a craving for unsolicited attention and admiration, a desire to attract and enchant all eyes, like a star in the firmament." Fitzgerald and his heroes display a keen appetite for this kind of adulation. The social worlds of the novels revolve around the heroes' persons, not simply because the story is told from their perspective but because they are in fact at the center of a universe.

From the start, Fitzgerald experienced the overwhelming admiration of others; for his mother, and later for teen-age companions, he was an admirable figure, glorying in the role of cynosure. Arthur Mizener speaks of "his mother's undiscriminating admiration." Fitzgerald himself later said, "I didn't know till 15 that there was anyone in the world except me." In the days of frantic partying, when in Zelda's familiar remark, "it was always tea-time or late at night," the Fitzgeralds stood in the center of a circle. One feels they never cared to stand anywhere else. It was as if they said, "Come, look, marvel at how we can be at once so witty and talented, so gay and handsome." The thirst for recognition, as writer and as person, may be related to the constant entertaining which helped insure a state of perpetual insolvency for an author whose novels and short stories were almost uniformly successful.

Brilliant and exciting gatherings of people, of the *best* people, invariably center on the magnetism of such protagonists as Gatsby, Dick Diver, and Monroe Stahr. The invited and uninvited guests of Gatsby's great house parties were perhaps as much in search of a legend as of free liquor; his very mystery and lack of identity served to focus a myth of distant, awe-inspiring personality. In one of the most intriguing passages of *Tender is the Night,* the girl Rosemary sees Dr. Richard Diver as symbol and center of a company so gay and rich and diverting that the world seems to balance at his dinner table. Any other setting, any other party, is cosmically irrelevant. But their *élan* is not a group achievement; it is created and controlled by Dick Diver and his wife, Nicole. An ephemeral thing, this grace and spiritual plenitude rests in Dick's hands, so that its continued existence depends upon his ability to maintain a somewhat euphoric mastery.

A variation of the theme is observed in *The Last Tycoon.* Here Stahr, while he is not the partying type, makes a dramatic entrance into a crowded club. At once all action stops, except the action of watching Stahr and whispering—as lesser figures do throughout the book—about his character and supposed motivations. Like all Fitzgerald heroes, Stahr asks a great deal of life; the notes for the novel make this clear, and the words underlined below might serve as a motif for the heroes as for their creator:

Back to the main theme: Stahr cannot bring himself to marry Thalia ("Kathleen," in the novel). It simply doesn't seem part of his life. He doesn't realize that she has become necessary to him. Previously his name has been associated with this or that well-known actress or society personality, and Thalia is poor, unfortunate, and tagged with a middle-class exterior that doesn't fit in with the grandeur Stahr demands of life.

Murray, finally, has recapitulated the blending of psychological elements which characterizes Icarus before his fall:

Already we begin to see a close, emotionally logical—indeed, an almost inevitable—connection, if not fusion, between ascensionism and cynosural narcism: the way to attract all eyes is to be very tall, to stand erect above the multitude, and best of all to rise in the air like a god.

Having attained a certain height, in most cases towering dominance, the hero falls like Icarus when the sun had melted his waxen wings. Of the five novels, only one concludes with the hero at or near the position he had held when the story opened. Amory Blaine, in *This Side of Paradise,* has lost romantic illusions but retains his youth and a life to come. Dick Diver (*Tender is the Night*) lives on, but is socially dead, corrupt, isolated from the mainstream of his profession (medicine) and his friends, and divorced from his beloved Nicole. Anthony Patch (*The Beautiful and Damned*) sails with his psychosis toward an unknown port. The remaining two, Gatsby and Stahr, meet violent death: Gatsby is shot, and Stahr, exemplifying Icarus, was to have died in an airplane crash at the end of *The Last Tycoon.* Fitzgerald seems to say that the gaudy dream—and the dreams are vital, for "the handle by which he took hold of his characters was their dreams"—is at length unrealizable, or, if realized, unsatisfying. It is, nevertheless, difficult to imagine any of these men as "settling down," as striking any kind of compromise with their aspirations or living an uneventful and undistinguished life. They are exciting to author and reader only while they are on top of the world and larger than life. Perhaps, then, Fitzgerald is also saying that the game is worth the candle and that one should have few regrets even if the descent from the heights is precipitous.

The life Fitzgerald lived, as well as the ones he wrote, hewed starkly to the Icarian theme. He went far up in popularity to become the poet of the Jazz Age and far up in critical esteem as the author of *The Great Gatsby.* His books brought wealth, fame, and a dramatic life style. He won the wife he sought, the Southern beauty who had once (before publication of *This Side of Paradise* and overnight success) seemed beyond his reach. Parties, travel, friendships with men and women of literary and social distinction—all these fell to him easily and quickly. Descent from such heights of self-realization could only be brought about by a cruel convergence of inner and outer circumstance.

The Fitzgeralds overspent to maintain the houses and clothes and parties which meant so much to both; saddled with debt and constant financial anxiety, the novelist was forced to write rapidly, to interrupt his plans for major works and produce saleable short stories. *Tender is the Night,* the effort of several years, failed to sell, although it is now recognized as one of his most exciting and sensitive novels; the popular explanation for this failure cites the fact that it deals with the personal problems of the wealthy and talented, a theme poorly calculated to interest Americans in the Depression year of 1933. Alcoholism began to interfere with his writing and living. Perhaps most telling of blows, the beautiful Zelda developed a psychosis which required hospitalization and destroyed family life. And so Fitzgerald fell to the depth in which he wrote that he now knew the dark night of the soul as described by St. John of the Cross, "where it is always three o'clock in the morning."

If Fitzgerald thus suffered the same fall from grandeur which he had charted for his heroes, it is most important to stress that his own story does not end at the nadir. Rather, he was able to come back part way toward artistic excellence if not toward the resumption of his total dramatic social role. The heart attack which foreshortened *The Last Tycoon* is believed by many critics to have interrupted his finest novel as well as to have ended a stubborn struggle for artistic rebirth and the revival of personal integrity.

The craving for immortality may be taken as intrinsic to the writer's role; in Herbert Read's phrase, he yearns for "a paper eternity." It is not strange, then, that Fitzgerald wanted his books to last. However, his heroes, none of them artists if one excepts the tentative longings of Amory Blaine and Anthony Patch, also strive for an immortality of a different variety, a type well-described by Murray.

> If resurrection (re-ascension) is not to be vouchsafed a man, there is the possibility of *replication,* which may be defined as the process whereby one or more persons are transformed in the image of the subject. It is the complement of identification, or emulation: the implanting of a memorable and impelling image of the self in the minds of others.

To imprint others with the seal of self, as a ring cuts an image in soft wax, is a prominent aim of Fitzgerald's chief characters. Thus the whole theme of *Gatsby* could be seen as Jay Gatsby's unforgettable impress of his self-conception on the mind and spirit of the narrator, Carraway. As Carraway says of this fascination:

> I wanted no more riotous excursions with privileged glimpses into the human heart. Only Gatsby, the man who gives his name to this book, was exempt from my reaction—Gatsby, who represented everything for which I have an unaffected scorn. If personality is an unbroken series of successful gestures, then there was something gorgeous about him, some heightened sensitivity to the promises of life, as if he were related to one of those intricate machines that register earthquakes ten thousand miles away.

So Dick Diver, too, lives on in the minds of those who surrounded him as an epitome of social grace. The last hero, Monroe Stahr, was to find his immortality by exerting a very powerful and specific influence following the plane crash that caused his death. Fitzgerald's notes tell us that Stahr's briefcase would be found in the wreckage by a small boy, and that its contents would then inspire the boy to follow an honorable, outstanding career.

Depreciation and enthrallment of women, a conception of them "as objects to be used for narcistic gains," is the one component of the Icarus complex for which the evidence in Fitzgerald is scant and often contradictory. It is true that the women his heroes marry or hope to marry are always, except in *The Last Tycoon,* creatures of unusual beauty and remoteness whose social status is high; thus marriage to them is a self-enhancing achievement which gratifies the hero's wish to be admired and envied. It is also true that in no case is a stable, lasting relationship achieved. An exceedingly narcistic view of women is given by Gatsby in his remark, on being told that the woman he desires really loves her husband, that, "in any case, it's only personal." That is, the personal concerns of another are inconsequential in the light of Gatsby's cosmic self. Finally, there is little doubt that Fitzgerald's own marriage to Zelda, the Southern patrician, represented both a triumphant achievement and a reward for his success with *This Side of Paradise.*

But depreciation is surely not a prominent feature of these relationships. Rather, the women in Fitzgerald are adored in a wholehearted way, in a rather quaint, old-fashioned mood of romantic chivalry. In some respects one feels his attitude toward them never advanced far beyond the worshipful gaze of the Ivy League undergraduate, circa 1920, toward the prettiest girl at the ball. This adoring stance also deepens and becomes enriched through the devotion lavished on the ill wife, on Nicole by Dick Diver and on Zelda by Fitzgerald. One is forced to conclude, then, that while women indeed fed the self-exaltation of the hero, they were also valued for themselves. As part of the dream and partners in reality, Fitzgerald's women secure a central place; they focus some of the most tender and moving passages in the novels.

The life and novels of Fitzgerald may thus be said to represent a sequence of themes characteristic of the clinical syndrome termed the "Icarus complex." This personality style overreaches, and founders on the insatiable quality of magnificent dreams, of idealized images. To analyze the progression of psychological elements is to see the writer more clearly, but decidedly not "to explain away" or undercut his creative achievement.

And one must of course beware of pushing an analogy too far; despite their similarities, the college student who modeled the Icarian career and Fitzgerald are quite different individuals. Fitzgerald was a successful writer and attained a very hard-won maturity, whereas the young man on whom the Icarus complex is based had not yet achieved his vocation or outgrown an adolescent attitude toward sex.

In striving for transcendent success, Fitzgerald accomplished much. A less noble conception of self might have produced less noble works of the imagination. Although he called himself "an indifferent caretaker of my talent," the astonishing fact is that, given the half-world of life with Zelda, life with alcohol, life with a party in the making or made, he sustained a recurrent creative thrust that affords us his small but fastidious artistic legacy.

II. Fitzgerald as Cultural Exemplar

A literary work, its creator's personality, and the cultural framework within which the work is written and read are always implicated in a network of relationships which forms the province of the sociology of literature. Although one may choose to emphasize a special aspect of this network, as in studies of creative personality or readership, the relationships are best seen as reciprocal and mutually enriching. A worthy social scientific approach to art should at once tell us something about the artistic object and something about human behavior, so that literary and behavioral analyses are both enhanced. Here I shall try to focus on Fitzgerald and his novels as exemplars of certain major patterns in American life, and to propose that while Fitzgerald is most often known as "the poet of the Jazz Age," he has a wider relevance than as a social historian of the 1920's.

If the novelist portrays social life, and moves us with his descriptive gift which evokes the essence of things seen and felt, it must be recognized that he also is an analyst. The perceptive novelist never merely describes at random, nor does he enunciate pure fantasy. Rather, he abstracts from the flow of experience and distinguishes significant elements of intrapsychic and interpersonal life. Like the scientist, a creative writer tries to make sense of the raw stuff of experience. But the writer employs different techniques, perhaps notably a rich—not parochial—and precise language, and he has a different end in view. The different end might be phrased as the artist's desire to convince others of his truths through immediate apprehension and assent to the felt rightness of what is said, in contrast to the scientist's wish for assent through logical demonstration or experimental replication. Despite all their precious and inerasable distinctions one from the other, there is an ultimate sense in which artist and scientist are alike in saying to the audience, "This is the way it is." The novelist is not an inexact sociologist. In most cases, and decidedly in Fitzgerald's, he is an intelligent man striving for entire precision in his report on the social universe.

Why should we, as students of American life, refer to Scott Fitzgerald, quite apart from whatever aesthetic sensibility we may feel toward his extraordinarily fluent style? Art may do at least three things for the social scientist: illumine, confirm, and stimulate. The novel illumines and illustrates what we think we know about our society, impressing known ideas upon us by its power of endowing them with dramatic life. It confirms our findings, in however singular a manner, by bringing us to realize that one very sensitive observer has remarked things we have also noted in our more pedestrian approaches. Finally, art stimulates by affording us fresh insights and ideas; we take these all the time from one another, from our own tradition and scholarly literature, since none of us can do first-hand research in more than a fragment of the social field. Why should we not then draw upon the record of a gifted researcher into the human situation, a novelist who thought long and experienced strenuously, who then reported what seemed to him the crucial features of American life?

Fitzgerald was very much part of the life of his times. His representativeness and immersion in the culture around him are shown both by his contemporary popularity (he was one of the few artists who gained both substantial literary esteem and a great deal of money from his work) and by his desire to live fully, often to his detriment as artist, in that decade and generation whose twin sobriquets of "roaring" and "lost" he so well earned. In addition to the glory and gray aftermath of a transient fame, he had staying power; his skill of craft, his aesthetic and humane talents, assured him of a good bit more than passing merit. If he is in the long run remembered as a minor novelist, and he will surely be remembered, the term "minor" will properly refer to his slender output rather than to flaws in the few novels he gave us. It may well be that some think Fitzgerald is dated just because he had such a fine ear for the speech and fine eye for the artifacts of the twenties. I should maintain on the contrary that American character and culture are plumbed in his art for a much longer run, that Gatsby's motor car and clothes and mansion may give way to the sports cars and split-levels of another day, but that Jay Gatsby the dreamer is as true to 1965 as to 1925.

The way in which Fitzgerald's novels, and to a lesser extent his life, will be employed here is cogently argued by Wolfenstein and Leites:

> The common day-dreams of a culture are in part the sources, in part the product of its popular myth, stories, plays, and films. Where these productions gain the sympathetic response of a wide audience, it is likely that their producers have tapped within themselves the reservoir of common day-dreams. Corresponding day-dreams, imperfectly formed and only partially conscious, are evoked in the audience and given more definite shape.[1]

As an ordering scheme for the relation of the literary vehicles to prominent American values, I shall hew fairly closely to the "value orientations" identified by Florence Kluckhohn.[2] No analytical system is able to apprehend fully the range and subtleties of cultural pluralism in an advanced industrial society, but these have the immense merit of combining general relevance to a host of philosophical essentials with specific linkage to behavior. The resonance of Fitzgerald's art for the American temper may be explained in part by the intimacy of his themes with certain dominant values. The degree of fidelity to core American dispositions raises problems in literature as in life, and Fitzgerald's excursions from the conventional pattern are often as interesting and revealing as his customary pursuit of the main goals down the main path. Let us see how the novels and the man adhere to the classic description of American belief and action.

FUTURE TIME

The tyranny of tomorrow is so frequently remarked as a feature of middle-class life that American orientation toward the future is quite taken for granted and seldom questioned or analyzed. It may be said to have two major aspects, which are unequally stressed by Fitzgerald. The more mundane element, and the less important in the novels, is the habit of rational planning toward ends whose accomplishment rests on deferred gratifications, training, saving, the husbanding of the self and its resources for an explicit later fulfillment. This is the world of thrift and Poor Richard, of correspondence courses and the down-payment on the cottage. It is a world too compulsive and tawdry for most of Fitzgerald's heroes, who want to run faster and more gracefully; his people are also more often of the upper-middle class, while the strict pattern of large renunciations and minor rewards seems more typically a lower-middle-class phenomenon. Nevertheless his gaudiest central figure was at length found to have rehearsed his sense of the future in just such a manner: after Gatsby's death his pitiful father arrives on the rich Long Island scene with a notebook which contains the adolescent Gatsby's schedule of self-improvement, a near-caricature of the vulgar Protes-

287

tant Ethic in its concern with habit training, hourly self-surveillance, and the last lovely admonition, "study needed inventions." It is significant that the more cautious and controlled facets of the future vision are so seldom seen in Fitzgerald's life or work. The missing pieces, the steps from dream to execution, are a clue to his and his heroes' failures, as they are also a clue to the grandeur of the dream itself.

Dreams are of course the second aspect of Americans' concern with the future. The deep desire to be and to experience that which is not yet informs our collective history of frontier and nationhood as it informs our personal histories of striving for the emergent self. Fitzgerald's men are imbued with a doctrine of personal manifest destiny. Here is perhaps the crux of his continued appeal and relevance, the great capacity to represent transcendent images of a future situation and a future self in believable and poignant terms. The novelist and his protagonists overreach, their visions founder on a fundamentally insatiable quality, but in the process they show us the tone and tragedy of our marriage to the future.

Gatsby's green light may serve as a symbol of the future dream, with the added overtone of the traffic metaphor which presses us to "go," to pursue the future with an exuberant energy. Margaret Mead has briefly and keenly evoked the theme of the unrealizable but demanding dream:

> By the very nature of the dream none can attain it, and each particular household falls short of the ideal. Each house lacks some detail that is included in the house which no one lives in. No mother can be all that an American mother should be, no romance have all the qualities that true love should show. And this, not because the ideal is so high, but because it is a dream of the future rather than an attempt to reproduce the past.[3]

The hero of *The Beautiful and Damned*, Anthony Patch, is made to live the entire novel in anxious anticipation of a heritage which would be enriching and enabling, only to fall before an insanity which debased his unearned wealth. Here Fitzgerald is highly realistic, implying that the dream alone is not enough if it is unmatched by talent and vigor. Fitzgerald himself, of course, was a willing hostage to his dream of a future as a great novelist; he

288

sought literary recognition, fame, wealth. But he had the equipment to make the dream effective, for if he harbored visions of a unique personal grandeur he also worked hard and perceptively at the novelist's craft.

Fitzgerald's chronology was not, however, exclusively attuned to the postponement of desire. Two of his most mature and fascinating heroes, the psychiatrist Dick Diver and the Hollywood producer Monroe Stahr, lived primarily in and for the present. And Fitzgerald too wished to live the dream right away, sacrificing his novels to the saleable short stories which afforded an instant cash return and the facilities for parties, travel, and a gaudy style of life. His lust for the present moment is related to the artist's need for sensory immediacy and to his intense drive for excellence and esteem in the form of quick reward. It should finally be remarked that Fitzgerald had the artist's respect for a tradition, that if he exemplified the American stance toward an imagined future he also lived with the insistent voice of a literary past, with the aesthetic conscience embodied in a Goethe or a Keats.

INDIVIDUALISM

Fitzgerald viewed the self as object and instrument; his goal was a particular image of selfhood, and his means were an exhaustive use of all that was in him. An individualistic version of human relationships is perhaps inseparable from the condition of being an artist at all in contemporary Western civilization. Fitzgerald not only lived his own life without much regard for collateral or lineal ties to others, but his novels really consist of heroic odysseys, of exfoliations of one person in the world that person shapes. It is a premise of the novels, as it is a premise of American culture, that unique individual destiny is the matter of first importance. Our attention is always centered on the hero's progress and personality; his lineage and his ties to others are significant only as they affect his rise in the world or as they reveal some aspect of his psychological make-up. Over the best of the novels there hangs an air of mystery, and this mystery is always focused on the hero: who he really is, where he comes from, what makes him run, where may he run to. Gatsby's acquaintances (he never had friends) search for the key to his motives and status; Dr. Richard Diver's secret is as much himself and his destiny as it is his wife's psychosis; Monroe Stahr in his mastery of film production requires explaining: "What I wanted to know—is how he ever got to be Mr. Stahr."

At heart, a very great deal of Fitzgerald's work is concerned with that most individualistic of problems, the struggle of a young man to make his way in a love affair, a profession, or a select social milieu. Success and money provided for Fitzgerald and his heroes a validation of self, but the validation required constant reinforcement in terms of social esteem. The concern is ever for the way the hero appears in his own and others' eyes. A heavy accent on the individual, when linked with the future dream and the belief in perfectibility, leads us to think of Fitzgerald as in one sense a very much more sophisticated and artistically worthy successor to Horatio Alger, Jr., as well as a genuine successor to the romantic novelist such as Stendhal or the young Goethe.

HUMAN PERFECTIBILITY

The American axiom that human nature is a thing to be cultivated, if not entirely redesigned, in a search for a more effective, coherent, and better-behaved personality is central in Fitzgerald's art. Each hero is intent on making himself fit to hold high position in the affairs of men and the affections of women. Part of the dream about the future is of course the picture of oneself as he will then hopefully be. Gatsby's self-improvement is the prototype of that conscious molding through which one may be, and perhaps more important may appear to be, in controlled mastery of the situation of action. Dick Diver is drawn as a man striving for physical perfection (hardening his body on "the flying rings at New Haven"), for intellectual discipline in his profession, for social distinction in his Riviera circle. Diver tries, moreover, to mold his ill wife Nicole and perfect her sanity. Monroe Stahr wants to become so alert and perceptive that he can direct a great artistic and business enterprise down to the tiniest detail.

It should be emphasized that Fitzgerald did not postulate a

benign or even a blandly neutral model of human nature. He embraced, rather, a strict code of self-control and gentlemanly inhibition which implied that the evil or mixed nature inherent in man must be disciplined if the characterological outcome were to be admirable. Some part of the fascination which the world of the rich and wellborn held for him was undoubtedly related to what he perceived as the aristocratic talent for self-control, for rounding the rough edges of passion and egotism. Fitzgerald had no illusion that men were any better than they should be; his stories repeatedly describe the outrageous behavior and moral decay of the man who lets himself go, who does not keep polishing his shield of honorable selfhood. Recall Tom and Daisy Buchanan of *The Great Gatsby*, who smashed things and then retreated behind their wall of money.

The novelist applied the doctrine of perfectibility to himself, and it was the belief in deliberate self-improvement that made his own dissipation and failures so hard to bear. Fitzgerald's dark night of the soul was the darker for being partly of his own devising. His notebooks and the letters to his daughter show how strenuously he tried to become a fine writer; self-exhortation is matched by the gently hortatory flavor of the letters to Scotty in which he poured forth heart, head, and artistic conscience. Despite the generous evidence in his novels and life that he conceived of personality as a flexible and improvable process, there always lies within the conviction of guilt and sin and root evil. His Irishness and his art alike led him to think of himself as a "spoiled priest," spoiled perhaps by pride and alcohol. Fitzgerald's concept of human perfectibility—and personal responsibility for the posture at length assumed—is nowhere better illustrated than in his remark that he had been "an indifferent caretaker of my talent."

MASTERY OF NATURE

Blending well with mastery of self is the theme of dominion over the natural world. Man's command of nature appears in Fitzgerald only by implication, since his is an urban, personality-centered universe, far from the pastoral dream. Nevertheless it is clear that to the novelist human desire is the great lever, that the individual's elaborate and energetic control of himself and other men is paralleled by his control of the dumb cosmos. Like a frontier American, Monroe Stahr drives for the gap in the mountain range, and this metaphor is used to stress his talent for decisive choice. A ready control of all kinds of resources is associated with the upper-class style of life which so obsessed Fitzgerald; one need instance only the extravagant fantasy of his short story, "The Diamond as Big as the Ritz," to demonstrate how surely the novelist captured the characteristic American drive to subject nature to human whim.

DOING AND BECOMING

The last of five key American values to be discussed here, that of active, persistent external effort to cope with problems of whatever variety, is probably least clear-cut in Fitzgerald. Certain of his protagonists are undeniably "doers," Monroe Stahr of *The Last Tycoon* serving as perhaps the best example. And Fitzgerald in his exacting work as artist was the doer incarnate, the laborer in language. Most of the heroes, however, and the author much of the time, devoted themselves rather to a quest for personal symmetry and interpersonal grace. They chose the alternate path termed "being-in-becoming," which emphasizes a rounded internal development and the pursuit of a thoroughly civilized style of life.

One might say that the author and his heroes are too much concerned with beauty, the beauty of objects as well as of a mannered and measured social intercourse, to follow precisely the American route of busyness and brusque efficacy. Again it is important to remark Fitzgerald's fondness for, and partial identification with, the upper class, for it is just in this class that one finds the national passion for activity shading off into a heightened concern with graceful living and humane breadth of personality.

Fitzgerald thus exemplifies certain primary themes in American culture, as much in his life as in his created social universe. Seldom has a writer been so exquisitely attuned to the main currents of his own place and time and yet so sensitive to the deeper patterns which endure through the history of a society. If Fitzgerald is representative of cultural themes, able to supply evidence and insight about characteristic American postures, this very representativeness may rest on his unusual capacity for simultaneously living in his culture and writing of it. In him we find the keenness of a detached observer wedded to the passion and spirited involvement of a participant. Of those novelists with whom he might most obviously be compared —the adventurous Hemingway, the reclusive Faulkner, the journalistic, crusading Sinclair Lewis—Fitzgerald came closest to being absorbed in his culture, bound to its governing aspirations, anchored in the kinds of concerns many of his nonliterary fellows shared.

SOCIAL CLASS

It is perhaps this thoroughgoing identification with the common dreams and anxieties of his milieu that makes Fitzgerald such an acute student of social differences. His acknowledged eye for telling details of language, dress, gesture, or decoration was related to an intense interest in the way Americans rank and evaluate one another. And the interest is, moreover, inseparable from Fitzgerald's own social position with its ambiguities of status and its perplexities about the process of rising or falling. Fitzgerald is exemplary in this aspect of his work because he chose not to stand apart from the excited strivings and the habits of invidious comparison which marked his—and our—era. The status envy which he exhibited at Princeton and seemingly ever after, the desire to ascend into a rich and exotic layer of life, made him in some ways a classically marginal man who responded swiftly to all the oscillations of a society on the move and on the make.

Lionel Trilling has observed that the traditional European novel has always pivoted on the facts of social differentiation:

If the English novel in its special concern with class does not . . . explore the deeper layers of personality, then the French novel in exploring these layers must start and end in class, and the Russian novel, exploring the ultimate possibilities of spirit, does the same—every situation in Dostoevski, no matter how spiritual, starts with a point of social pride and a certain number of rubles. The great novelists knew that manners indicate the largest intentions of men's souls as well as the smallest and they are perpetually concerned to catch the meaning of every dim implicit hint.

The American novel has shared this obsession, of course, although the rapidity of change in class structure and the absence of fixed hereditary categories has perhaps made our writers less adept and less confident in dealing with class alignments. Henry James, Edith Wharton, and Theodore Dreiser are all distinguished in their perceptions of social difference and distance; today, however, they are too specialized or too remote in time to afford substantial insight into contemporary patterns. Sinclair Lewis and John Marquand describe a society we recognize, although Lewis's view of class strikes us as rather naïve and clumsy. Marquand's aesthetic qualifications are probably inferior to Fitzgerald's, but between them we can gain a good deal of knowledge about a particular range of the class structure—roughly the upper middle class and the finer subdivisions of the upper class.

Fitzgerald nowhere tells us very much about status and its correlates in the social regions where most Americans live. He had no interest in the culture of poverty and slight interest in the workaday world of commerce and industry. What he does achieve is a remarkable perception of styles of life in the upper strata of the East and Midwest, and a fine sense of what these styles mean to the persons involved. The subjective impress, the psychological effect of holding a social position and striving to retain or enhance it, is delicately diagnosed. With his art, Fitzgerald enables us to enter the "little worlds" of class cultures and experience the social-psychological significance of status.

Ernest Hemingway is usually assumed to have come off the winner in his discussion of class with Fitzgerald. When Fitzgerald claimed that "the very rich are different from you and me," and Hemingway replied, "Yes, they have more money," we at once think of the tough-minded Hemingway puncturing a misty romantic notion. Yet Fitzgerald may have been in some senses the more realistic of the two, emphasizing deep-going differences in style and seeing money as an index to separate social universes which cannot readily be bridged in terms of cash alone. Fitzgerald had perceived a social fact which most analysts of social class would verify: that within broad limits the inhabitants of varied class levels live to themselves, immersed in a milieu of manner, value, and styled behavior which indeed makes the very rich "different from you and me."

There are many examples of this unusual sensitivity to social difference in his stories and in his life. Although Fitzgerald was early impressed with the peculiar glamour of the upper class, and seems as a Princeton undergraduate to have been naïvely susceptible to its alien charm, we find his maturing view to be in the true sense ambivalent: attracted, fascinated by a certain freedom, yet repelled by what he increasingly felt to be an enervating callousness. Thus the reckless cruelty of the Buchanans in contrast to Gatsby's innocent yearnings, and thus "The Rich Boy":

Let me tell you about the very rich. They are different from you and me. They possess and enjoy early, and it does something to them, makes them soft where we are hard, and cynical where we are trustful, in a way that, unless you were born rich, it is very difficult to understand. They think, deep in their hearts, that they are better than we are because we had to discover the compensations and refuges of life for ourselves. Even when they enter deep into our world or sink below us, they still think that they are better than we are. They are different.

Gatsby could never be at one with the Buchanans, could never penetrate their milieu, just as no one in "The Rich Boy" ever really shares Anson Hunter's ambience. When Fitzgerald dealt with the struggle for acceptance, the approach of a middle-class man to the environs of the rich, he sought and found the key detail. Dexter Green, the hero of "Winter Dreams," modulates his manner in shrewd recognition of the distinction between old and new money:

Next evening while he waited for her to come down-stairs, Dexter peopled the soft deep summer room and the sun-porch that opened from it with the men who had already loved Judy Jones. He knew the sort of men they were—the men who when he first went to college had entered from the great prep schools with graceful clothes and the deep tan of healthy summers. He had seen that, in one sense, he was better than these men. He was newer and stronger. Yet in acknowledging to himself that he wished his children to be like them he was admitting that he was but the rough, strong stuff from which they eternally sprang. .

When the time had come for him to wear good clothes, he had

known who were the best tailors in America, and the best tailors in America had made him the suit he wore this evening. He had acquired that particular reserve peculiar to his university, that set it off from other universities. He recognized the value to him of such a mannerism and he had adopted it; he knew that to be careless in dress and manner required more confidence than to be careful. But carelessness was for his children. His mother's name had been Krimelich. She was a Bohemian of the peasant class and she had talked broken English to the end of her days. Her son must keep to the set patterns.

So, too, Fitzgerald, in his own striving. Although he wrote his way to upper-middle-class respectability and won the judge's beautiful daughter as his bride, he could only describe—not master—the assured way of life which characterized his friends the Gerald Murphys and others of secure upper-class position.

Another facet of his exemplary role may be seen in his rehearsal of the ancient American dialectic between East Coast and Middle West, cosmopolitan and provincial, sophistication and angular virtue. One feels that Nick Carraway, the voice of *The Great Gatsby,* speaks for Fitzgerald in his disillusion with the falseness of East Egg, Long Island, and his determination to see the social world stand "at a kind of moral attention." The regional contrast is intimately bound up with the class contrast; the partly mythical egalitarianism of the continental fastness is poised against the partly actual hierarchy of the effete East. In Fitzgerald there is a constant struggle between St. Paul, Minnesota and the myriad settings of his adult career: Princeton, the Riviera, Long Island, Hollywood. In the classic vein, he remained the provincial young man even as he outwardly became a paragon of Manhattan worldliness. In a domestic version of Henry James's tension between wise Europe and young America, Fitzgerald was never quite certain of his regional and class identity; this very lack of sureness has of course been often remarked as typically American.

Fitzgerald tells us again and again that the attempt to breach class barriers is a perilous enterprise, requiring subtlety and courage. His heroes try, and they suffer. The gallant but untutored Gatsby, whose quest for status was presumably a mere adjunct to the winning of his dreamed Daisy, founders on the hard facts of social difference.

Dick Diver of *Tender is the Night* is much more than an upwardly mobile young professional; yet one of the things that shatters his promising psychiatric career is a noble desire to span two social worlds, the world of the very rich and the world of dedicated vocational striving.

The novelist's own life was coated with that "foul dust [which] floated in the wake" of Gatsby's dreams. It was Fitzgerald's goal to live in a style befitting the golden spokesman of a generation. He was by no means content to write a work of art; he had to live one, too, and his idea of the worthy literary career was inseparable from the rather gaudy style of one of his own protagonists. The remarkable merger of his identity with those of his heroes is baldly recounted:

> Books are like brothers. I am an only child. Gatsby my imaginary eldest brother, Amory my younger, Anthony my worry, Dick my comparatively good brother, but all of them far from home. When I have the courage to put the old white light on the home of my heart, then . . .

When Fitzgerald had the courage, which was often enough to give him genius, he turned a blinding light on his heart's home. One of the things he saw there was the heavy penalty exacted by the social ascent. He pitted the iron demands of artistic craftsmanship against the lust for the externals of life, the perquisites of social status. But the latter, except perhaps in his last years, never seemed to him only externals. As for so many men in the United States, they constituted for Fitzgerald a validation of self, a tangible symbol of personal worth. Thus his intermittent lapses from what he conceived to be his true literary vocation, his pursuit of the dollar through hasty magazine short stories, his grinding indebtedness, and the last bondage to Hollywood while he squared accounts. Looking back, he thought the concern with a heightened life style, the correlate of sustaining and enhancing social rank, was mistaken. And so he wrote to his daughter:

> I wish now I'd *never* relaxed or looked back—but said at the end of *The Great Gatsby*: "I've found my line—from now on this comes first. This is my immediate duty—without this I am nothing."

297

Perhaps Fitzgerald's inability to escape the system of social class, to blunt his vulnerability to invidious comparisons of external status, is ultimately revealing. If his personality structure was consonant with the Icarian theme, so much of his social behavior and his attitudes toward his society were consonant with major American values. If it would be an exaggeration to term the Icarus complex a characteristically American psychological type, we may at least affirm that there is something of Icarus—and something of Fitzgerald—at the very heart of our culture.

F. Scott Fitzgerald: Personality and Culture

[1] Martha Wolfenstein and N. Leites, *Movies: A Psychological Study* (New York: The Free Press of Glencoe, 1950), p. 13.

[2] Florence R. Kluckhohn, "Dominant and Substitute Profiles of Cultural Orientations: Their Significance for the Analysis of Social Stratification," *Social Forces*, XXVIII, No. 4 (May, 1950), 276-93.

[3] Margaret Mead, *Male and Female*. (New York: William Morrow & Co., Inc., 1949), p. 255.

Eleven

LITERATURE AND SOCIETY

Watt's elegant account of literature in social perspective might well serve as a paradigm for the sociological analysis of art. It is distinguished by an acute historical awareness, a catholicity of reference which dissuades us from an oversimplified version of the relations between literature and society. The sociologist, often too much inclined to take twentieth century industrial society as the measure of all things, can profit from this exposure to the rich variability of the artist's role, of literature's societal mirroring, of the functions of art.

Our understandable but dangerous enthusiasm for reading social history in literary works is properly bridled by Watt's analysis; he shows how seldom art may be construed as a direct, veridical rending of its creator's milieu, how often it must be seen as a partial, distorted, slanting image. As Kohn-Bramstedt wisely maintains:

. . . only a person who has a knowledge of a society from other sources than purely literary ones is able to find out if, and how far, certain social types and their behavior are

299

reproduced in the novel. . . . What is pure fancy, what realistic observation, and what only an expression of the desires of the author must be separated in each case in a subtle manner.

Yet Watt does not discourage the social scientist, or try to bar his profane excursions into what some purist critics regard as the sacred territory of art. Rather, he challenges the investigator to be more alert, more perceptive, more ingenious in his efforts to tease out meaningful connections between art and environment. Above all, he implies, a social analyst must be himself sensitive to literary values and receptive to the nuances of artistic tradition and formal patterning.

Again, we are disabused of the assumption that literature is either prepotent or utterly ineffective as an agent for modifying attitudes or promoting social change. We simply have a paucity of reliable knowledge about the consequences of literary experience for human behavior. This may well be an area to which social science research can make substantial future contributions, as the sociologist refines his investigatory skills and as the exposure of large numbers of people to the arts presumably increases in both scope and intensity. As Watt maintains, literature is a social as well as a private phenomenon; whether the artist's ideology inclines him to exalt or dismiss the supposed social relevance of his work, that relevance is inescapable as long as man remains the symbolic animal —as long, that is, as he remains human.

LITERATURE AND SOCIETY

Ian Watt

Conscious interest in the relation between literature and society is quite recent, mainly because it depends on a considerable

This essay is a slightly revised version of an article prepared for *Collier's Encyclopedia*. Used by permission of The Crowell-Collier Publishing Company.

degree of historical, sociological, and literary awareness. The problem was not really opened up until the late seventeenth century,
when the Ancients and Moderns controversy in England and France,
a debate about whether the achievement of modern European literature was comparable to that of classical Greece and Rome, naturally led to wide historical and social comparisons; to the idea, for
example, that epic poetry, which was then considered the supreme
literary genre, perhaps really belonged to a special kind of society,
and that this explained why, for all their efforts, the Renaissance
writers of national epics had obviously failed to rival Homer or
Virgil.

From then onward, and especially in Germany, literary scholarship gradually developed the concept of *Kulturgeschichte*—the
systematic study of human culture as a whole from a historical and
comparative perspective. At the end of the eighteenth century this
perspective was much widened by the growing Romantic interest
in folk tales and ballads, and by the work of such scholars as Bishop
Percy, Herder, and the Grimm brothers, work which drew attention
to the fact that there were long and important traditions of
popular as well as of classical literary expression. Meanwhile, in
France, De Bonald hit on the famous formula "literature is an expression of society" (1796), and in 1800 Madame de Staël published
her *De La Littérature considérée dans ses rapports avec les institutions sociales.* In the same year, but in England, Wordsworth's historic "Preface" to the *Lyrical Ballads* announced that one of the
aims of the new literary movement which we call Romanticism
was to create works whose matter and manner were adapted to a
much wider group than that for which their neoclassical predecessors had written, and to face the acute social and moral problems
set up by the Industrial Revolution's "increasing accumulation of
men in cities."

Since then a great deal has been written about the relations
between literature and society, but the main categories of enquiry
have remained fairly constant. To oversimplify, they may be reduced
to three: most obviously, there is the particular social position of
the writer, and the nature of his relation to his public; rather more
widely and elusively, there is the question of how far literature is
or ought to be a reflection of the society from which it springs;

Literature and Society

finally, and most generally, there are the ultimate problems of the social function of literature, and of how far literary values correspond to social ones.

The Social Context of the Writer

Taine's formula for the key forces which determine the author's literary product was *race, moment, milieu;* but the most directly determining factor is probably one specific aspect of the author's particular social *milieu*—his institutional context as a writer: how he makes his living; how far he and his fellows constitute a separate occupational group; the nature of his audience, and of his own individual relation to it. In all these matters there would seem to be an almost infinite range of possibilities; and yet historically there are actually certain fairly well-established institutional patterns of authorship, patterns which are closely related to the social structure of the time.

When the invention of writing first made possible the permanent recording of human thought and feeling, literacy was confined to a small social caste. Consequently in Babylon, Egypt, and Palestine, for instance, if we can judge by what remains, writing was used mainly to record the political and religious traditions of the past and the laws and practices of the present. One can hardly talk as yet of literature or of authors as such, since there was no clearly differentiated literary product or specialized professional role; those who could write merely utilized their laborious skill on stone or clay or papyrus for important public purposes. In China, where the nature of the particular writing system developed made literate prowess difficult and highly valued, literary ability, tested through examinations, became the basis for the selection of the ruling bureaucracy; and it was from this mandarin class that most of the creative writers were drawn. The long formal association in China of an esoteric literature with a powerful administrative elite is an extreme case of the generally close relationship of literature with social power, an association which seems to be almost universal under bureaucratic forms of government, and whose long tradition has Chaucer as its earliest illustrious representative in England.

302

In the West the invention of the alphabet prevented reading and writing from remaining the exclusive possession of a small elite. In any case the rudiments of the literary profession as such seem to have developed long before, in various small pastoral and tribal societies. The Greek rhapsodist, the Welsh bard, the Icelandic *sagamann,* and the Anglo-Saxon *scop* all made their livings by reciting or singing the heroic deeds and other memorable exploits of the tribal leaders, in the halls and courtyards of the local chieftains: out of these miscellaneous and partly improvised narratives epic poems were eventually composed and written down. Modern opinion, discarding the generous democratic enthusiasms of earlier theorists about collective or folk authorship, now tends to regard Homer and his mainly anonymous Northern analogues as highly skilled professional authors working on the basis of existing traditional, and usually oral, materials. Some of the bards, of course, were merely professional reciters who added little of their own; but others were both authors and reciters. This combination was repeated in medieval Europe: while some troubadours, jongleurs, minstrels, and minnesingers were mainly performers, others, like Arnaut Daniel and Wolfram von Eschenbach, also became famous as original authors. The directness and intimacy of the relationship of the Homeric bard or the medieval troubadour with his audience has since been much admired by later writers: Vachel Lindsay, for example, revived the art of the wandering minstrel early in this century; and so, in their fashion, have many later poets on the campus touring circuit.

The supreme example of harmonious reciprocity between author and audience, however, is probably that afforded by Periclean Athens. In theory, at least, every male citizen there was in some sense a literary performer, speaking on public affairs in the market place or taking part as author or actor in the great dramatic festivals which were a free and indeed obligatory part of community life; the great tragedians, Aeschylus, Sophocles and Euripides were not so much members of a separate professional class as citizens who had outshone their fellows in the common pursuit of one of the recognized forms of civic glory. This kind of integration of the author in the whole social group has also had some modern approximations: in the late Middle Ages, for example, the mystery and miracle plays were written and performed by members of the various trade guilds, and were an essential part of town life.

In modern times the historical successor to the bard as professional author, at least in the West, was the recipient of patronage. The system had developed in Greece after the decline of Athens, and achieved its most illustrious form in Rome under Augustus. There Maecenas made his name the symbol of discriminating patronage on behalf of the sovereign, dispensing munificent rewards to such inspired celebrators of the glories of the regime as Horace and Virgil. Something similar seems to have developed in the early days of many secure, wealthy, and leisured aristocracies: in Renaissance Italy, for example, or in the France of Richelieu and Louis XIV.

Royal patronage was often succeeded by a more casual kind of patronage by the rich; in the Rome of Martial and Juvenal, for example, or in the England of Alexander Pope, we hear much of abuses of the system, with needy authors vying with each other to flatter whoever might be expected to repay them with rich food or gold coin. This kind of private patronage, however, was eventually superseded by that of the reading public in general. In the later days of Imperial Rome the presence of a huge leisured and literate class had combined with an abundance of cheap slave labor to produce something like the modern book trade: publishing houses with large staffs of well-trained slave copyists could turn out editions of several hundred by hand in a few days. But it was only with the invention of movable-type printing late in the fifteenth century, and the subsequent increase of popular literacy, that a reading public arose large enough to enable authors to rely entirely and directly on the sales of their works.

It took some time for this, our modern system, to replace other methods. At first, for example, the press was used primarily for making more widely available educational and religious texts: the spread of printing owes much to the Protestant stress on reading the Bible, especially in vernacular translations such as Martin Luther's. For several centuries, however, writers of secular literature found their support elsewhere. Thus Shakespeare depended on private and court patronage as well as on the boxoffice receipts of the theatrical company in which he was a shareholder, whereas most of his contemporaries sought noble patrons or combined literature with clerical careers; only a few unfortunate hacks relied entirely on writing for the market, producing popular, ephemeral, and ill-paid works for the booksellers. It was not until after the Copyright Act of 1709 that the author's ownership of his own literary works was legally assured; and then there slowly arose the modern system of royalties, where the author does not, as previously, sell his work outright to the bookseller, but receives an agreed percentage of sales.

The development of the royalty system in turn depended on a considerable scale of purchases by the public. This was made possible by the great expansion of middle-class leisure and literacy brought about by industrialism and urbanization toward the end of the eighteenth century. Later, the power press and other technological advances early in the nineteenth century made it possible to produce huge numbers of newspapers and magazines that were cheap enough for some working-class pockets, and thus led to the mass reading publics of today.

The complement of the mass public is the professional author. Evidence of the existence of a considerable group of professional writers, dependent wholly or mainly upon publishers for their living, is first reflected in the late seventeenth century by the frequent attacks of satirists on the starved hacks of Grub Street. By the middle of the eighteenth century the author by profession had finally secured somewhat more respectful recognition, and a good many writers, such as Dr. Johnson, were able to live very comfortably without recourse to patronage.

The economic dependence of authors on large sales, combined with social, and consequently educational, stratification, has had profound literary consequences. As early as the time of the Ptolemies, for instance, there existed quite separate classical and popular bodies of writing for the vast urban society of Alexandria; but as, with printing and modern industrialization, the reading public gradually expanded from the thousands of the eighteenth century to the millions of today, the ensuing literary stratifications became much more marked, and were more and more systematically exploited by the publishing industry. Some of the early nineteenth century writers in France and England were very much aware of the tendency: in 1859 Saint Beuve coined the phrase "industrial literature"—potboiling wordage produced to the specific requirements of mass journalism; and in 1881 John Ruskin attacked the "excitement of the lower passions" which characterized the works of the "railroad-station novelist." Today we have *Time* magazine, whose style and content are no longer those of the individual writer but are the hallmarks of a vast collective enterprise; whereas at the other extreme are the little magazines, produced by and for the "highbrows"—the word apparently dates only from 1908.[1] Characteristically, it is in the unremunerative pages of the highbrow quarterlies that many of the great masterpieces of our time have appeared, from Joyce's *Ulysses* to T. S. Eliot's *The Waste Land.*

The present social and economic context of authorship thus reflects certain features of modern society in general. There exists, for a few authors, the possibility of an unprecedentedly complete freedom of individual expression, but only for a minute, fragmented, and very special kind of audience; while there is an equally unprecedented and usually decisive pressure on the majority of professional writers to conform to the demands of the giant publishing organizations which offer glittering rewards for alertly docile service in entertaining the masses.

Literature as a Reflection of Society

There is a rather misleading simplicity about the word "reflects." In some senses all writing cannot but be a "reflection" of society, since it contains many elements which are socially derived. Language, to begin with, is a social product; and most writing—certainly most literature—is related to some established tradition or model of expression. More specifically, literary works usually reflect various surface features of the life of a society. Yet although the clothes and meals and customs described are rarely invented, they may not be those current at the time of writing; and since this is often true of more important matters, literature cannot be assumed to be necessarily a reliable reflection of the society of any specific period. Spenser, for example, "writ in no language" according to Ben Jonson, meaning that his language was an invented conglomerate of archaic and contemporary forms; so indeed was the society which the *Faerie Queene* described. Nor is Spenser an exceptional case: there is a very general tendency for well-established literary traditions to foster a conscious or unconscious archaism of matter or manner.

There are many other reasons why it is dangerous for the social historian to assume that any particular literary work is an accurate reflection of the author's society, although, of course, it may offer invaluable illumination or confirmation of matters known or surmised from other sources. Every individual's social experience is idiosyncratic in many ways, and if he is a writer this colors the selection and presentation of every social detail in his works. Thus Chaucer, in the "Prologue" to *The Canterbury Tales,* undoubtedly gives us our most vivid description of the society of his day; but it is in some ways a very incomplete and prejudiced description: seemingly he didn't care for merchants or tradesmen or ecclesiastical dignitaries, and wasn't much interested in the urban or rural proletariat. Yet actually the selections and exclusions may be not a matter of Chaucer's personal outlook on society at all, but merely the more or less accidental result of Chaucer's particular literary subject: the lowest orders of society could not afford to go on pilgrimages, and that happened to be what Chaucer was writing about. Certainly we can't assume from the character of the Wife of Bath that fourteenth century England contained no faithful married women; but at most that—as we should perhaps expect—their activities had less literary appeal.

Literary genres often reflect the social attitudes of the particular group which produced them, rather than that of the society which their content overtly portrays. Pastoral poetry, for example, does not tell us much about the economy or institutions of the Sicilian shepherds whose lives it pretends to describe, but it does reveal the taste for a fashionable kind of escape which arose in the later days of Greece and Rome among certain urban and leisured audiences. The influences of the author's particular social orientation in distorting his picture of social reality may not be conscious, but it is always present to some degree. Most of the court literature of the past made the nobles much more noble and the rustics much more rustic than they were in reality; while in the last hundred years the various radical, socialist, and communist movements have produced proletarian fiction in which the picture of the worker is a good deal more heroic or tragic than would probably be substantiated by objective sociological investigation.

Even the kinds of writing which aim at the most literal and detailed description of their society are far from being sociologically reliable mirror images of reality; for, quite apart from the influences of the social group, the author's own individual temperament and his personal ideology play a compelling, though usually unconscious, role. In Zola's novels, for example, the novelist's individual personality is continuously present, despite his resolute attempt at objective reporting; and in general the quasi-scientific Naturalist ideology, with its doctrine of the crushing influence of the environment, usually tended to produce fictional characters who were a good deal less crush-proof than the human average, and to place them in circumstances that were exceptionally crushing.

On the other hand the opposite position is also true: literature which makes no pretence whatever at reflecting social reality always does so in some form, however individual, abstract, or unrealistic that reflection may at first sight appear. *Alice in Wonderland,* for instance, or Kafka's *The Castle* are full of brilliant insights into the essence of the social world of their authors, but these insights only become manifest after a patient and imaginative interpretation of the fantasy or symbolism through which they are expressed.

Literature, then, reflects society, but it usually does so with various degrees of indirectness and selectivity. The particular "society" which it reflects is often equally difficult to determine; we hardly know, for instance, how far Homer describes the period of the Trojan War, and how far his own. Then again, as societies become larger and less homogeneous, they become more difficult to portray, merely because of their scale and complexity. Whatever the historical period may actually be, Homer at least gives us a sense of knowing and understanding a whole society; but no one could possibly attempt anything along the same lines for modern America, for example, if only because no single individual can have personal knowledge of more than a minute fraction of it.

Nor is the difficulty only a question of the scale and complexity of modern society as a literary subject matter; for this increased scale and complexity also modify the author's personal situation in society: he becomes more a member of a specialized social group and less a representative of the community in general.

In early eighteenth century England, for example, the interests and values of the middle class dominated the subject matter, the literary treatment, and the moral orientation of such novelists as Defoe and Richardson. But by the middle of the eighteenth century in France, and soon after in England, the professional writer tended to belong to a particular group of specialists, the intelligentsia, which regarded itself, and with some measure of justice, as some-how outside or above the class system as a whole. This feeling of separateness increased during the nineteenth century. In France, for example, the growing divorce of intellectuals and artists from established social institutions produced Bohemianism—a limbo as unrooted in any defined temporal or social environment as Shake-speare's Bohemia; whereas, in the United States, the even greater isolation of intellectuals produced, in the novels of Hawthorne and Melville, for instance, a more agonized anticipation of the social alienation of most great twentieth century writers.

The modern author, then, is in a problematic situation as re-gards his portrayal of society at large; and this, not only because of social fragmentation in general, or because of his personal ideologi-cal commitments, but also because of the drastic changes in the im-mediate social and economic context of authorship which have been referred to previously. Socially, the author belongs to a small pro-fessional group; economically, he depends directly on the modern publishing industry and their mass media. The author thus operates in a literary climate where the crucial decisions about the kind of social reflection he will create are based on an even lower estimate of what the public wants in the way of sexual and social fantasy than is probably the case.

Many successful writers, with more or less cynicism, provide the appropriate literary stimuli, stimuli which bear little recogniza-ble relation to the shape of social reality. The great best-sellers of today, for example, are Mickey Spillane and Erskine Caldwell (whose *God's Little Acre* was the first novel to sell over ten million copies); what they most obviously have in common is a frantic primitivist revolt against social controls, especially those on sexual and aggressive impulses. This kind of revolt, and the amazing popularity of works which embody it, may well be tokens of some deep psycho-social breakdown; but we must not forget that there may be quite different explanations for the nature of such fiction, explanations which are based on the assumption that the success of this kind of fiction depends precisely on its not being a reflection of contemporary reality. For such works must, to begin with, be regarded as the particular modern embodiments of the age-old and almost universal tendency to enjoy imaginative gratifications of impulses which are largely denied in social life. Nor is the brutalized vulgarity with which these impulses are gratified in much contemporary writing necessarily a reflection of the prevalence of such impulses in contemporary society: it may only be the result of intensified commercial exploitation of an ever-increasing reading public.

This would be one example of how literature may be a reflection of its society only in a very special and indirect sense; and there are many other such examples. One can at least assert, however, that the writer always reflects his society in some way. However little, for example, he may intend to portray the reality of his time, he is inevitably responsive, directly or indirectly, to changing patterns, not only of mass fantasies, but of basic social values and goals. Thus, as Leo Lowenthal has demonstrated,[2] in the last decades the great majority of biographies in popular magazines have no longer dealt with "heroes" drawn from business, politics, or the professions, but with men and women in the world of popular entertainment.

The responsiveness of the author to the social patterns of his time cannot usually be so conveniently demonstrated: it is rarely susceptible of statistical analysis. But a reflection of social reality is always there, if we can find it; and not only in those writers, usually of the middle rank, who, like Trollope or Marquand, consciously set themselves the task of chronicling the average life of their time, but in every kind of writer, once we know how to interpret him. Mickey Spillane is not the Tolstoy of our era; but he belongs to it, and tells us something about it.

Social Function of Literature

Almost every society has its venerated classics—wisdom books, national epics, devotional hymns—which are taught to the young and which make available to the whole community a common background of knowledge, belief, and aspiration. It is always difficult, however, to assess the functional efficacy of such a literature, because there is obviously a particularly wide gap in the case of national and religious classics between public attitudes and private behavior. This gap has probably widened somewhat in modern times. Many recent studies of the social role of reading and of exposure to mass communications suggest mainly negative conclusions. Yet these are hardly final. That few people read the Bible does not disprove its importance as the source of much of our speech and our approved social and moral attitudes; then again, it is always difficult to decide whether the social values derive from the literary work, or vice versa; and in any case we should remember that the best literature by its very nature deals with matters of such delicate complexity that they can hardly be discussed except in their own terms, terms which render them virtually inaccessible to empirical study.

It is much easier, fortunately, to deal with the different ideas that have been held about what the social function of literature ought to be.

One extreme position is that associated with the Romantic poets, who tended to regard themselves as the lineal successors of the priests and the prophets: in their different ways Blake and Wordsworth and Shelley, for example, conceived of themselves as endowed by their private imaginative inspiration with the duty of leading humanity to a new and better world. Somewhat similar ideas about the function of literature as an innovating and reforming force are occasionally found earlier in such religious radicals as Milton, and also in such later political enemies of the institutions of their time as Voltaire, Rousseau, and the whole group of Encyclopaedists, writers whose often clandestine publications were an important factor in bringing about the French Revolution. Today, this conception of the reforming role of the writer survives in various forms; from the notion of the writer as a man of highly original moral, social, or literary beliefs, to the "fearless crusaders" of the newspapers.

At the other extreme is the idea that literature ought to limit its function to giving pleasure, whether through humor, wish-fulfillment, excitement, or intrinsic aesthetic perfection: in this idea, the doctrine of art for art's sake joins hands with the practice of the box office, and disregards not only the values inherent in any truthful report on social reality, but also the fact that an antisocial literature is itself a social reality with many important (and often deplorable) consequences.

The classical and perhaps the most defensible position on this issue is essentially a compromise: literature should instruct by pleasing—*delectando pariterque monendo*. "Pleasing" goes without saying, as long as we remember that there are many kinds and degrees of pleasure, some of them the reward of considerable effort. As for "instructing," the problem is more complicated. For one thing, a conscious didactic purpose may never have been a very useful thing for a writer: most primarily didactic or propagandist writing has little social effect, and, incidentally, succeeds even more rarely in being valuable as literature. It is also apparent that a didactic purpose is only possible to the writer if he accepts the major social, moral, and religious values of his society; and this acceptance has become less and less common of late. Here the effects of the individualist ideology of the last few centuries have been reinforced by the very widespread opposition of the modern intellectual elite to the predominantly Philistine and materialist values of its society in general. As a result, very few twentieth century writers have been able to follow the example of the many great writers of the past who endorsed the main social and moral orthodoxies of their time.

This discrepancy between past and present writers, however, is only partial, for, whatever they may themselves have intended, the works of Sophocles and Shakespeare, Goethe and Tolstoy, are essentially didactic only in the sense that our social and moral awareness is increased by imaginative participation in the works of those who have been supremely responsive to the realities of human experience: realities, of course, which always have a very important social component.

From this perspective the literary opposition between the Realist and Naturalist insistence on the liberal description of the actual social worlds, and the Parnassian and Symbolist reassertion of the artistic autonomy of imaginative creation, is seen to be a good deal less than absolute. For, although there is an age-old divergence between those who see man as essentially a social being, and those who insist on his individual uniqueness, the force of the contradiction begins to disappear the moment a writer puts pen to paper: as W. B. Yeats put it, "art is the social act of a solitary man."

It is a social act, however, of a very special kind, and one which reminds us that "literature and society" can be a misleading phrase in yet another way, because it suggests a more absolute distinction between the two terms than is actually the case. If only because, in one perfectly valid sense, literature *is* its own society: it is the subtlest and the most enduring means which man has devised for communicating with his fellows; and not the least of its functions is to give those who have learned its language something that no other society has ever afforded.

Bibliography

The subject is too vast and dispersed for reasonable documentation to be possible; and the following brief bibliography hardly scratches the surface. Still, the following are recommended on their particular topics.

Denney, Reuel, *The Astonished Muse* (Chicago: University of Chicago Press, 1957).

Duncan, Hugh D., *Language and Literature in Society* (Chicago: University of Chicago Press, 1953).

Edwin H. Miller, *The Professional Writer in Elizabethan England* (Cambridge: Harvard University Press, 1959).

Escarpit, Robert, *Sociologie de la littérature* (Paris: Presses Universitaires de France, 1958).

Hart, James D., *The Popular Book* (New York: Oxford University Press, 1950).

Hauser, Arnold, *The Social History of Art,* I and II (New York: Alfred A. Knopf, Inc., 1951).

Leavis, Queenie D., *Fiction and the Reading Public* (London: Chatto & Windus, Ltd., 1932).

Levin L. Schucking, *The Sociology of Literary Taste,* 1931, trans. E. W. Dickes (London: Kegan Paul, 1944).

Lowenthal, Leo, *Literature and the Image of Man . . . 1600-1900* (Boston: Beacon Press, 1957).

———, *Literature, Popular Culture and Society* (Englewood Cliffs, N.J.: Prentice-Hall, Inc., 1961).

Raymond Williams, *Culture and Society, 1780-1950* (London: Chatto & Windus, Ltd., 1958).

Thomas F. Marshall, with George K. Smart and Louis J. Budd, *Literature and Society, 1950-1955: Selective Bibliography* (Coral Gables, Fla.: University of Miami Press, 1956).

Literature and Society

[1] Mitford M. Mathews, *Dictionary of Americanisms;* "highbrow" and "lowbrow" were given wide currency, in a somewhat special sense, by Van Wyck Brooks in his essay *America's Coming of Age,* published in 1915.

[2] In "Biographies in Popular Magazines," *Radio Research 1942-1943,* Paul F. Lazarsfeld and Frank Stanton, eds. (New York: 1944); reprinted in *American Social Patterns,* William Petersen, ed. (Doubleday Anchor, New York: 1956), pp. 63-118.

Twelve

THE HIGH CULTURE OF THE AGE

Running through most social analyses of the arts, and prominent in the descriptions of artistic roles in the early chapters of this book, is a tension between what Shils terms "high" culture and what he terms "mediocre" or "brutal" culture. Although this symposium is exclusively concerned with the products and producers of high culture, it seems impossible to avoid seeing these in a framework of competition with lesser expressions of man's "need to symbolize." The modern artist's vulnerability to the rigors of the marketplace, where inferior works presumably drive out superior creations in a kind of aesthetic Gresham's Law, is a common theme in most critiques of the artist's position. Further, many contemporary writers—both literary men and social scientists—fear that art of the highest quality may be submerged by the rising tide of "mass culture" or popular entertainment. The age, then, is conventionally judged inimical to both high culture and those artists and intellectuals who create it.

Although Shils is a defender, not to say an apostle, of high culture, he seriously questions the merit of these prevalent conceptions. The easy assumption that ours is the worst of times for art and artist, for devoted followers of imagination and intellect, is the target of a searching comparative examination. Without glossing over the very real problems generated for the artist by an era of specialization, organization, and rampant trivial amusement, Shils effectively disabuses us of the notion that high culture has drastically fallen in quality and of the related thesis that artist and intellectual are uniquely harassed in contemporary society. He shows how selective is our superficial evaluation of the cultural products of other centuries, how limited in range to a very unusual sample of the best and the enduring. He contends, too, that the trials of the artist today may be different in kind but are surely not heightened in severity when set against those of other times and places.

Most importantly, Shils goes on to assess the contemporary scene in precise, sober terms, illuminating both the advantages and the disabilities which characterize artistic and intellectual activity. He properly places high culture in a dense social framework, elucidating its relation to particular aspects of the social structure. For instance, the immense expansion in higher education—presumably inseparable from mass literacy in an elaborately technological society—is weighed not only for its potentially negative implications, such as a dilution of the quality with which high culture is transmitted, but also for its potentially positive stimulus to high culture through university artistic patronage and the wider cultivation of taste. Again, the decline of private patronage for the cultural innovator is viewed in the context of the public, and probably more even handed, support afforded by government and the foundations. Shils remarks the peculiar hazards of American society, the Philistinism of the specialist outside his "field," the weak and tattered fabric of the intellectual community, the inevitable seductiveness of blandly mediocre cultural activity. But he notes two vital things: that a healthy pluralistic society cannot and should not be limited to an exclusive focus on refined culture ("There are real needs for the brutal, the trivial, and the frivolous . . ."); and that artists and

316

intellectuals have defined tasks, have a vocation which should be their primary and energetic concern.

Abjuring a naïve sociological determinism, he sees in the intellectual a potent initiating force. He commends those involved in high culture to enact their appointed roles: to create, conserve, and disseminate the best in art and thought. He would revive in us the nerve to face the poet's high calling, the steady increase of consciousness.

THE HIGH CULTURE OF THE AGE

Edward Shils

I

For centuries, in the great but, by present standards, not very populous societies of the past, the life of the intellect was carried on by very small numbers of persons. What could have been the number, in fourth century Rome, of the producers of intellectual objects —poets, historians, moral and natural philosophers, grammarians, mathematicians, epigrammatists, dramatists, speculators on the affairs of the commonwealth, teachers of law and rhetoric, and all the other subjects a highly educated Roman was supposed to know? How many consumers of their works and ministrations were there —studious and reflective civil servants, lawyers and politicians, well-read landowners, great figures of the state who cultivated and patronized literary men—all these together in Rome itself must have been a rather small circle of men. Five thousand persons at any one time might not be too outrageous a guess. It could not have been very great—the number of copies of each book was small, so that very few persons could have led a very intense and diversified intellectual life. There was not enough in quantity or diversity on which many could feed.

Let us take the whole of England in 1688. The inheritance was much richer and activities more diversified. The numbers of those who devoted themselves to intellectual pursuits were surely greater than in Rome, although the total population which could be drawn on was smaller. There were two universities, numerous grammar schools with educated teachers, a thriving theater, a book-publishing trade far larger in its output than the Roman book-copying systems. There was a national church with an administrative staff in which educated men could find a place. There were dissenting sects which took theological study with great seriousness. There were 10,000 clergymen, men of education and intellectual concern. The civil service might have been more dilapidated than the Roman bureaucracy of the third century, but the mode of recruitment meant that there were always likely to be some men of intellectual training and interests among them. There were 10,000 of these. There was a considerable gentry, of whom there must have been a considerable minority interested in intellectual things. There was a legal profession of almost 10,000. There was a medical profession. There were playwrights and actors, writers trying to live from their writing of potboilers or from the patronage of the great. There were artists and musicians, composers and performers. Intellectually, England in this time was at one of the peaks of world history. Its plays and poetry are among the greatest achievements of the human race; it was the home of a group of the very greatest scientists in the whole history of science; philosophy and political thought saw some of their greatest achievements brought forth at this time. Modern historical scholarship was taking form. But the numbers of creative spirits were small. They, their audience, and the ranks of the less creative who helped to supply this audience with instruction and entertainment—although larger by many fold than the genuinely creative—were, taken all together, probably fewer than 70,000.

In any one of the great contemporary societies of the West, the United States or Great Britain or France or Western Germany, the situation is markedly different. The intellectual institutions, universities, technological colleges, research institutes, public university libraries, bibliographic services, publishing houses, the better newspapers, reviews and periodicals, sound broadcasting and television, learned societies and academies, all engage great numbers of highly educated persons, many of whom are very productive, some of whom are creative at the level of genius. They provide intellectual services for a vast audience of students, readers, viewers and listeners, as well as for the narrower, but nonetheless very large, circle of the productive whose works must be assessed, selected, and graded to enable other producers and the vast audience of consumers to have an approximate map of the intellectual continent. College and university teachers, scientists, authors, journalists, artists must come to more than a half million in the United States alone. The audience is very much larger, since the professions and occupations from which the audience of intellectual work is generally constituted were more than four million in 1950 in the United States. The magnitudes are not too different in Great Britain, Western Germany, and France.

The sheer volume and diversity of production in the intellectual (including expressive) domain are incomparably greater than in any other epoch. As compared with the middle of the nineteenth century or the beginning of the twentieth century, the stock of intellectual "goods" is enormous, and it goes on expanding in the second half of this century. The inheritance from the past is preserved, and the increment enriches the stock and adds to the intellectual wealth and burden of the oncoming generation of each successive decade.

But what of the quality of this oceanic outpouring? Does the quantitative increase automatically entail an improvement in quality? Is the truth of science in any subject simply a function of the amount of work done? Does history become truer and does it penetrate to the essentials better simply by virtue of the number of historians and the amount of work they perform? Is the quality of poetry improved as a result of an increase in the amount of poetry written and published? Although a proper answer requires some qualifications, a first approximation to an adequate answer may be made by saying "Of course not."

Still, the overwhelming multiplication of the personnel, provision, and output of the intellectual activities of our society is not without some influence. Some persons would say, as Mr. Kingsley

319

Amis has said of the expansion of the numbers of university students in the United Kingdom, "More is worse." There are others who, interpreting "more" as derivative of "modern," would go further and say that "modern is worse."

It almost seems that no sooner had "The Battle of the Books," *"la Querelle des anciens et modernes,"* been won by modernity than some of the beneficiaries of the victory turned around and proclaimed its nullity. This diminution-in-growth had been traced by certain contemporaries to the very nature of modern society in its latest phase, to the nature of mass society. This concern is not a new one. Scarcely had modernity accredited itself when its derogation began in a new form. From the *Discours sur les Sciences et les Arts* onward, a clamorous flood has risen. The Parisian mob, comprised mainly of those often alleged buttresses of order, the *artisanat*, set loose a specter which sensitive and ungenerous imaginations transformed into a pandemonium of culture-destroying devils. The years 1830, 1848, and 1871 horrified many of the European high intelligentsia and made them fear the new age.

Today the detractors of mass society look upon that great and stuffy bourgeois age, which preceded the formation of "mass society," as a wonderful, irretrievably lost age of intellectual and artistic creativity, of an earnest moral quality of a genuine individuality and dignity of the mind. Some of the best spirits of the time, ancestors of the present anxiety, claimed even then to see the first erosion which the democratic flood was to cause to the culture of the educated classes. Their criticisms were not specific. They confused the Philistine vulgarity of the bourgeoisie with the barbarity of the populace. They rendered up no just comparison of their own age and some better past, and in some respects they did no more than repeat the ancient denunciations of the present as a sorry falling away from a better, more virtuous past. The recently prevailing conception of "mass society" in most intellectual circles is only the latest form of this unexamined devil whose mere existence degrades the culture of his betters.

Of course it is conceivable that our present high culture, viewed from a sure and detached standpoint, is poorer than the high culture of any comparable span of years in the past. There might be any number of reasons or causes for that deterioration. The distribution and efflorescence of genius are mysterious matters.

There may be waves of cultural movement which we cannot discern. It is conceivable, although not very likely, that our neural equipment is poorer than that of our ancestors. And even if it is as good, it might be argued that our cultural traditions have passed their point of culmination. It may be that our cultural traditions have reached exhaustion; that they contain no possibilities of further development, that they offer no point of departure even for creative minds. These are possibilities which must be considered if we conclude that our contemporary culture has sunk or is sinking below the level of those ages which have preceded us. But has high culture really declined in quality?

Has the culture of the past forty years—which is the approximate age of "mass society"—deteriorated, as its detractors claim?

In our own time, we are surrounded by the easily visible debris of recent, unsuccessful aspirations to high achievement and by the newly formed rubbish of that mediocre culture which seeks no attainment higher than mediocrity. It takes many decades, perhaps a century, for this poor stuff to be washed away into the silt with which only research students, curio-hunting dilettantes, and scholarly investigators will concern themselves in the future. This process has already occurred for the output of the preceding centuries of the modern epoch, and those who regard themselves as the vessels of refined culture generally think only of the great classics when they think of something with which to contrast randomly selected instances of vulgar mediocrity. When, out of perversity or curiosity or for reasons of scholarship, they exhume the otherwise neglected trivia of the past, they know what they are doing. They know that they are dealing with what is inferior. They do not think that its mediocrity diminishes what is great in the age which they study. In contrast with this, films of the poorest quality, television silliness, journalistic beastliness are unqualifiedly presented as characteristic of the style of the present age and as significant of the whole.

Our present cultural cosmos, like any other, is far from homogeneous and its coordinates and strata, cutting across us and surrounding us, do not form a determinate map in our minds. Regardless of whether the quality of our contemporary refined culture were superior to that of the past, the task of its location and assessment would be very hard.

The evidence of our decline is not, however, very impressive. It is likely that no one in our age can leap beyond the inherited stock in the way in which Galileo or Copernicus or Newton did in physics, or Harvey in physiology, or Boyle in chemistry, or Hobbes in political philosophy. Individual genius might be as great, but the vast and concerted effort and the density of achievement—which is surely on a higher level than it was in the greatest decades of the seventeenth century—make an equally striking advance more difficult to encompass. In all these domains of intellectual work in which there is in general a unilinear course of development, the state of knowledge is more advanced than it was two and a half centuries ago. It is more advanced than it was a century or a half century ago. The advance is not just an advance in the quantity of verified details, although this is not irrelevant. The understanding of the laws of the universe is more comprehensive, deeper, and more differentiated—we understand important things now that we did not understand then. The same obtains in fields other than physics or physiology or genetics. It is proportionately as true of the lesser disciplines like the study of politics or sociology and linguistics. There is no Locke or Hobbes who has apprehended such a fundamental theme with such clarity and precision, or who has penetrated so deeply into one root of man's existence and then traced its ramifications. Yet, in a way we have advanced beyond them, and so the level of performance attained by the best of our age is in advance of that attained by seventeenth century political philosophy, even if the magnitude of the accomplishment of any single individual thinker falls beneath that of the geniuses of the earlier century and even if some of the insights of seventeenth-century writers are not widely possessed among us.

Let us look at the United States, which is the cultural nightmare of those dreamers, European and American, who in their sleep produce the clichés which come from the surface of thought and from the depths of fear and animosity. Is American science on a lower level now than it was fifty years ago? Are the best of American literary critics less perceptive, less elegant in their interpretation, more superficial in their grasp of motives than their predecessors of the period before World War I? Is American painting now inferior to what it was then? Are our playwrights and novelists poorer than their like of fifty years ago?

It might be answered that things are culturally as good as they are in America today because we still draw so much from Europe—from distant models and from recent refugees and immigrants—and that America has gone forward by adding to itself what was extruded from Europe in its decades of self-destruction. Certainly American culture, which was first the creation of European culture, has continued to benefit immeasurably from the works of the most superior quality which still appear in Europe, even after the silence and desolation of two hideous wars. No American, even if he has completely emancipated himself from provincial fascination with the old metropolis, can afford to be ignorant of what is being accomplished by his colleagues in Europe, whether his field be physics, chemistry, sociology, anthropology, journalism, or literary criticism. It is right that such should be the situation. Participation as an equal contributor and beneficiary in the Western intellectual community implies no deficiency in creativity.

There are certain other features of intellectual life in the present period which call for attention when the quality of the age is placed in question. The present century has experienced an extension of its horizon and a fertilization of its sympathies of the sort which has never been seen in the Western world or in any great civilization—and certainly not least in the United States. Indeed, it is in America that this new sensibility, disciplined by active research, has developed most uniquely. Of course oriental studies began in the eighteenth century and flourished in the nineteenth century; the great work of exploration and their chronicles began much earlier and continued as long as there were unexplored territories. Nonetheless, it must be acknowledged that the range of curiosity and the openness of sentiment have never been as great as they are now nor, for that matter, more generously and discriminatingly intelligent than they are now. The artistic, political, social, and religious life of civilizations outside our own has never been studied so much nor so soberly and humanely appreciated as it is in the past several decades. And all this is under conditions of very great difficulty, when the quantity of what there is to travel to, to see, to listen to, to read has never been greater—and when we are having to concede that our own civilization is not as ascendant in every regard as one's immediate ancestors thought it was. In this new renascence of oriental studies, America has had a great share and that largely in the years since World War II. It is no diminution of the reality of this accomplishment to acknowledge that the occasion has been the political transformations of the postwar world or that the wherewithal has come from a government involved in a "cold war" or from the munificence of a prosperous capitalistic economy.

Nor do I think that the standards of moral and civic integrity of the American intellectual classes have sunk particularly. It must be agreed that the thirty years after World War I saw degrees of insult and submission of intellectuals in very many countries, including the United States, which were appalling to those who witnessed from afar and even more appalling to those who had to submit.

There were, it is true, a few intellectuals who affirmed the will of their silly and not very effectual tormentors in America. A much larger number, coming out of an apolitical cocoon, became protagonists of doctrines which were injurious to intellectual life abroad and which bespoke a frivolous ignorance on their own part. Even the featherbrained leftism of the thirties was in a sense an advancement in moral sympathy and in the concern for justice. It was, moreover, accompanied by a growth in intellectual civility such as had been absent from the public life of the country for many decades.

Simultaneously the influence and status of the intellectual classes have increased markedly. In the prosperity of their institutions and in the opportunities for research and publication the situation has never been more indulgent to the intellectual life of the country.

Nonetheless these latter considerations are peripheral to the immediate issue of the equality of contemporary intellectual life; their greater relevance will be made apparent later on.

II

Let us return to the consideration of the charge that our culture is in decline. It is a broad charge, very vague in its objects, and any rebuttal is bound to suffer from the grossness of the terms in which the problem is set. It is a criticism that intermingles without discrimination individual creative genius and the average level of production, the creators and their audiences, works and institutions, the general level of culture in the society and the cultural condition of the intellectual classes. It is a criticism characterized by the arbitrariness of its comparison of the bases of our own age with the heights of achievement in much longer periods of the past. Nor does the criticism bear in mind that in assessing contemporary culture it is comparing individuals who have not completed their careers with great figures of the past whose greatness is assessed on the basis of a completed career of great works. The argument for a decline is a poor argument and is more poorly put than it need be.

That there is a *consciousness* of decline is undeniable. Many intellectuals in Western Europe and the United States are beset by a malaise, by the malaise of a sense of isolation, of disregard, or lack of sympathy, of a feeling of loss of an appreciative contact with that most important of all audiences, the audience formed by those who exercise power in society.

But there is nothing new in this complaint. Romanticism antedates mass society and in a multitude of shapes it is still far from dead. It still lives among us with full vitality and in many transformations. It was a cardinal tenet of Romanticism that the creative person was cut off from his own society and that he was despised by its rulers. The contemporary romantic intellectual has, in addition, as a precipitate of revolutionary and populistic traditions, an acute sense of the cleavage between himself and the people. Unlike his antecedents—even up to the 1940's—he does not seek to immerse himself in them (or at least, in his idea of them). He does not regard them as models or as repositories of the highest values, as many Asian and African intellectuals, and as populist intellectuals, do. He is, instead, repelled by them. In the imagination of the present-day intellectual who has given up the substance of the revolutionary tradition while retaining its categories, the mass of the population is utterly alien to culturally significant things. It manifests the deficient sympathy with refined cultural things, the crudity of mind, the preoccupation with worthless matters, which he previously found in his rulers, particularly the new rulers of his country's economic life. In a way, the mass has acquired the character it had before Romanticism and revolution took dominion over intellectual life, but unlike the writers of the seventeenth century, who attended to the populace only occasionally when it became turbulent, the contemporary critics of mass society cannot remove their minds from it as a continuous threat.

The too noisy, too visible, too tangible presence of mediocre and brutal culture, from which the mind can no longer be averted, has heightened his anguish. Whereas intellectuals of the earlier ages of modern society could remain indifferent to and ignorant of the impoverished cultural consumption of most of the members of their own society, this privilege is no longer given to contemporary intellectuals. Modern society is democratic and the masses are on the minds of the intellectuals, particularly those who were once socialists who thought the working class was ready to become the heir of classical philosophy. Then, too, by virtue of their own role in the production and reproduction of these works of mediocre and brutal culture, and the evident and visible enjoyment of many of them by their consumers—including many intellectuals—intellectuals are as familiar with the manufacture of popular entertainment in daily and periodical press, the films, and the television as their intellectual ancestors were with the heartless stinginess of patrons and the arbitrariness and frivolity of authority.

These interpretations of the motives and traditions of those who see the cultural inheritance and contemporary creativity menaced by the masses are not an adequate reply to their arguments, even though they rightly serve to set us on guard against them. The arguments themselves must be considered. Is the high culture of the age really endangered by mass society? To what extent do such dangers as do exist differ from earlier dangers? To what extent do these dangers derive from mass society; to what extent from other sources?

High culture is not today, and never has been, the culture of an entire society. Even if it were to become the culture of the whole society to a much greater extent than it has ever been before, high culture must necessarily be in a state of tension *vis-à-vis* the rest of its society. If the producers and the consumers of refined culture see further and more deeply than their contemporaries, if they have more subtle and more lively sensibilities, if they do not accept the received traditions and the acknowledged deities as much as their less creative and less sensitive contemporaries, whatever they say or believe or discover is bound to arouse a certain measure of hostility in some of their fellow countrymen.

Are intellectuals more endangered in mass society by the jealousy and distrust of the powerful than in other social orders? Censorship, arrest, and exile are nothing new. Can the occasional flurries of the interfering anti-intellectualism of American politicians and businessmen be placed on the same plane with the restraints imposed in Communist Russia and China, Fascist Italy, and Spain, or National Socialist Germany, none of which are or were mass societies in the sense that the contemporary United States is or as the United Kingdom, Western Germany, and France are becoming? Do the inane and exasperating intrusions of advertisers on the television screen represent a greater intrusion into the creative sphere than the prosecutions of Flaubert and Baudelaire in nineteenth-century France, and the moral censorship which Mrs. Grundy has exercised so coarsely in Victorian Britain and America, or the political and religious censorship practiced in eighteenth-century France? Athenian society was no mass society, and there were no advertisers there, yet Socrates was executed. I do not wish to belittle recent interferences with intellectual or artistic liberty in the United States and Western Europe, but I do wish to stress that they are not unique to mass society, that they are not more severe in mass society than in other societies, and that they do not even derive in most cases from the "mass" character of mass society.

There is one particular feature of mass society which does generate tension when confronted with refined culture. This is populism, which has been a recurrent element in the hostility of some American politicians against intellectuals. There is no doubt that this is a distraction to intellectual life, both within the intellectual classes and outside their boundaries. But politicians, even the least populist and those who share authority with them, have never lacked legitimations for action against those whom they have regarded as guilty of *lèse-majesté* or sacrilege. At bottom, these are the risks which intellectuals must run if they are to continue to be intellectuals. Thus if they are intellectuals, the livelier among them must engage in the reinterpretation and transformation of the traditions which they receive from earlier generations and which they inevitably share in some measure with their fellow countrymen. Their fellow sharers do not enjoy having the tails of their sacred cows twisted by intellectuals, and that is so whether the society is a mass society or an oligarchical one. A mass society has its own special dangers, persecutory and corrupting, but I doubt whether the magnitude of the dangers places mass society in a uniquely destructive position.

It is sometimes asserted that the culture of mass society produces its insidious effects in roundabout ways that constitute a greater danger than the crude external pressures employed by the rulers of earlier societies. It seduces, it is said, rather than constrains. It offers opportunities for large incomes to those who will agree to the terms of employment offered by the institutions which are organized for the production of works of inferior value. Television, the films, the popular press, the advertising industry do attract to themselves considerable numbers of persons of some moderate intellectual quality. But does this opportunity, and even its acceptance, necessarily damage the high culture? There are two questions to be raised here. First of all, is the person with outstanding gifts destructible in any way other than physically? If his talents are accompanied by the strength of motion and by the self-confidence which is so often associated with the successful exercise of talent, he is not likely to be drawn out of the category of activity in which his talents have found an adequate field of exercise. Then even if tempted by money and fame, he is drawn into another field, for example, from literature into films or from scholarship into journalism, his talents are very likely to show themselves there.

The argument against which I am contending implies that certain genres are incapable of offering an occasion for important achievement; entry into them is the equivalent of self-condemnation to ruin. The very fact that, here and there in the mass media, on

328

television and in the films, work of superior quality comes forth seems to be evidence that genuine talent is not inevitably squandered once it leaves the traditional media of refined culture to work in the mass media, which tend on the whole to present mediocre and brutal culture.

It is, of course, possible for men to waste their talents: to corrupt themselves for the pleasures of office, for the favor of authority, for popularity, for income, or for the simple pleasure of self-destruction. Qualitatively, the financial temptations of work in the media of mass communications are of the same order as the other temptations which intellectuals encounter. Quantitatively, they extend to more persons and offer more imposing rewards in extreme instances. There are many more opportunities now for intellectuals to earn large sums of money in the production of intentionally inferior cultural objects than there were before the development of the mass media. Literature is the field most likely to be affected by the temptations. There must be some unknown talents which were really distracted and ruined by the style of life and the commercial concerns of the film world. James Agee, Nathaniel West, and F. Scott Fitzgerald are the frequently cited instances; but it is excessively simplistic to attribute the miseries of these talented men to the frustrations of Hollywood alone, just as it is undeniable that, despite their miseries, they left behind works of genuine value. Poets and artists and other men have gone to the dogs before the temptations of Hollywood were invented, and there are many paths to the dogs which are followed now and which have little to do with Hollywood. Not all literary men, poets, scholars, painters, scientists, teachers have been tempted or have yielded to the temptation—even if we concede, which we do not, that their experience in the mass media prevents them from finding creative expression either in the mass media or outside them.

Popularization is something cited by the critics of mass society as one of the ways in which superior culture is being eroded. Popularization is, of course, not just a product of mass society. It is a product of a state of complexity in the development of a subject where it ceases to be directly or immediately intelligible to the layman. It is not just the ignorant brute or the passive one fixed before the television screen who is in need of popularization today. In so many fields of research in science and scholarship, the output is so large that it is difficult for an outsider—even a scientist or scholar —to penetrate into it even if he can get through the terminology. Without popularization, the ravages of specialization would be even worse than they are. Still, there is popularization and popularization, and perhaps the critics of mass culture have in mind popularization beneath the level of the *New Scientist* or *The Scientific American*. They have in mind presumably *Life* or *Reader's Digest* as organs of popularization. These are assuredly not parts of our high culture, but it is extremely difficult to see what harm they do. No person with a serious concern about intellectual matters draws on these magazines to sustain his mind, and those who do read them do not enter in the circle of the high intellectual activities of our society. Hence, if they are harmful, they are harmful only to the writers and editors of these journals, and since some of these have serious intellectual pretensions and mingle with intellectuals, they might do harm in this way.

First let us consider whether writing occasionally for a popular journal or newspaper or broadcasting in a popular program is injurious to the intellectual or expressive capacities of a man or woman. To begin at the top, the late R. H. Tawney's scholarship and literary style certainly did not deteriorate because, at an early stage of his career, he was a tutor of the Workers' Educational Association. Professor Raymond Aron's thought has not become less subtle or less forceful because he writes occasionally in *The New York Times Magazine* and much more frequently in *Figaro;* Bertrand Russell suffers no intellectual injury from articles in *Look;* Professor A. J. Ayer is not a poorer philosopher nor Professor Fred Hoyle a poorer astronomer because they are such excellent broadcasters. There is no reason why an intellectual of pre-eminent gifts should become soft in the brain from writing articles, from time to time, for an audience unable to comprehend his usual level of analysis and exposition. An intellectual who devotes all his efforts to popularization would naturally, in the course of time, cease to have anything of his own to popularize and would have to become a popularizer of the works of other persons. But there is no evidence whatsoever that persons who are capable of serious creative work, who are strongly impelled to it, and who do in fact devote a good deal of their energy to serious creative effort, are being unwittingly debilitated by occasional activities of popularization. The contact between a scientist and a popularizer with some scientific qualification does no harm to the scientific work of the former. American, British, and French science in the past forty years has certainly not been harmed by the development of the new branch of journalism called "scientific popularization." How many of our few outstanding political philosophers have been lost to their calling through becoming political analysts? [1] There is probably a process of selection which separates those who can create and who are strongly impelled to do so from those who, having been trained in a discipline, devote themselves to making its results intelligible to the inexpert instead of adding to its results.

But what about the popularizers themselves? What harm do they do? As far as I can see, they do no harm at all to those who read their work or to those whose work they popularize. They might do themselves a little harm; they might feel guilty of vulgarity because they share certain common prejudices of intellectuals. They might feel inferior and unhappy because, quite reasonably, they regard their own category of activity as of a lower intellectual dignity than those whose works they popularize. They might make a few poor characters in the intellectual world jealous because they have not chosen the works of these persons to popularize. Neither they themselves nor their popularizing writings really afflict the main currents of the decisive forces of the subjects they touch. Has American sociology been made better or worse because Professor David Riesman appeared on the cover of *Time,* or because Professor Robert Merton was the object of a *New Yorker* profile?

The production of works of inferior culture need not, however, the argument goes, destroy superior culture by striking directly at its producers, either constrainingly or seductively. It can deprive them of their market, and especially of the discriminating audience which they need to keep their skills at the highest pitch. The deformation of the taste of those consumers whose natural discriminatory powers are not so great that they can dispense with the support which a clearly ascendant and superior cultural environment provides is certainly a possibility. There must be many people in all Western countries and certainly in the United States, who would have a better content to their cultural existence if they had no choice of a poorer one. They might indeed have better lives if they were not allowed to sink to the level which at present, all things given, they enjoy more than the refined culture of their intellectual contemporaries. In other words, things could be, in one sense or another, much better than they are—or they would at least look better, like military piety under conditions of compulsory church parade—if the mass of the population were not allowed to expose themselves to the mass media.

The culture of the mass media might impede the improvement of public taste. The fact remains, however, that in the United States and Great Britain today, discrimination in a small minority —probably larger in numbers than it was at the end of the nineteenth century or than it is in England today—is as acutely perceptive as it ever was. The quality of literary criticism in the best American and British reviews is as informed, as penetrating, and as reflective as it was fifty years ago in these two countries. The public for the works which are criticized in these reviews is probably larger than it once was. If it were much larger, the external cultural tone of these societies would be more seemly and these reviews would be a more secure assurance to creative intellectuals that the resonance which they need is present. But there is at least a minimal resonance, enough to help to maintain a quite respectable standard of performance in the various fields of refined cultural production. There are certainly no grounds for predicting that it is bound to shrink in the future.

If no inferior cultural products were available, some of the thus liberated purchasing power might be spent on superior products. This would be to the economic advantage of those intellectuals who live from the market, and it might also raise somewhat more the general level of culture. This was the situation in Britain during World War II, and it is probably the situation in the Soviet Union today. In Britain, after the war, once inferior cultural objects became available in larger supply, the prosperity of serious booksellers declined pronouncedly. The same would probably occur in the Soviet Union if a larger range of consumers goods, cultural and other, were to enter the market.

When, therefore, public demand is free to obtain the objects it desires, the market for refined cultural objects, given the present distribution of tastes, is restricted, and enterprisers with capital to invest will not rush in to use their resources in areas of the market where the return is relatively poor. Yet are there many manuscripts of books of outstanding merit lying unpublished today? It is true that if there is more money to be made in publishing or broadcasting works of poor quality, investors will not put their money into the production of better works for less remunerative markets. This is the principle, but for various reasons the principle does not quite work out in reality. There are investors whom irrationality or devotion to more valuable cultural activities commits to the acceptance of smaller returns on their capital. Many publishers pay for the publication of superior works with a smaller market from the proceeds of publishing less valuable works with a larger market. They do so because it has been the tradition of their trade to do so and because they are, although in business for profit, also concerned to adhere to the traditions of superior culture.

The relative unprofitability of the market for high cultural objects is compensated therefore by the existence of these enterprisers who are motivated by considerations other than of the largest possible return on their investments. It is possible that the newly developed interest of larger-scale investors who have not shared in the tradition of the book-publishing trade might change this for the worse. It remains to be seen; but meanwhile there is no certainty that it will in all cases. Some of them will want the prestige, which is, in part, associated with the renunciation of profit, and they too will become assimilated into the traditional responsibilities which have never been absent from this branch of business enterprise.

The argument that the operation of the laws of the market results in the constriction of the superior cultural sphere is wrong in fact and problematic in its ethical postulate. It is problematic ethically because it implies that persons with inadequate cultural discrimination should not be allowed to gratify their desires; it is also problematic because it implies that a coercively imposed superior culture would be the genuine thing. It is wrong in fact because the market is not so completely uncongenial to superior cultural goods and because superior culture does not depend, never has depended, and never should depend entirely on the market.

We often hear the old system of patronage praised by those who bemoan its passing and contrast it with the vulgar insensitivity of the rich of the present century. It is well to remember, however, what misery and humiliation the older individual patronage often imposed on its beneficiaries, how capricious and irregular it was, and how few were affected by it during the period of its greatest prevalence.

The direct private patronage of individual intellectuals by individual patrons still exists, but it plays a scant role. The place of the older form of patronage and subsidy has been taken by the universities, the state, and the private foundations, and with all their deficiencies they appear to be more liberal, more generous, and more just than their counterparts in earlier centuries.

It is only in modern times, with the growth of a literate reading public, that it has become possible for even a small number of authors to maintain themselves from the sale of their literary works, and for a larger number to supplement their not quite adequate literary or artistic earnings by teaching or by occasional journalism. Television and films have extended these supplementary opportunities. Just as good books with small circulations need the financial support of other and often poorer books with larger circulations, painters need the support of art schools, foundations, museums, churches, and private collectors. Scientists and scholars could never conduct their research for the returns they can get from the sale of their output. Only recently have scientists in certain countries begun to sell their services collectively to governmental bodies on a contractual basis, but the purchasers of their sources (or their output) are not business enterprisers who sell the resultant scientific discoveries or inventions in a market.

So it does not seem to me that there is much to the critics' arguments about the corrupting effects of mass and commercial culture on the creators of high cultural works of the genres of higher culture, and the pre-emption of the market for such works. The situation of high culture is, however, far from perfect. There are many flaws and dangers, and it is to some of these that I shall now address myself.

III

The transformation of the role of the intellectual from the amateur pursuit of a rentier or landlord, or of a civil servant or courtier, to a profession has been accompanied by an increased complication in the organization of intellectual institutions. Reproduction and distribution—even if only for copying a manuscript by hand—have always required some organization, and the production of plays could not have come about without organization. But the practice of philosophizing, of writing poetry or history, and of conducting scientific research were individual efforts, bound into a social framework through the assimilation of a tradition, by study under a master and by informal communication by oral discussion and correspondence. The writing of poetry is still that way; so is the writing of novels. But history is no longer that, and science is that way even less than history. Historical research nowadays entails an intricate system of training in historiography, elaborately organized archives, bodies which grant funds to scholars to enable them to travel to "their" documents; it requires a network of publishers, editors, and reviewers. Sometimes historical writing is even collaborative. Scientific research nowadays demands a tremendously elaborate and costly institutional system—science teaching at the secondary school level, university teaching, research training, the manufacture and procurement of very costly apparatus, a complex of journals with their editorial boards and referees, and the research itself is now often collaborative within a given laboratory and co-operatively competitive among laboratories over a far-flung territory. Painting and sculpture are still organizationally what they were in the Middle Ages and early modern times; commissioning is probably no more organized than it was, but the sale and distribution of paintings and sculptures are immeasurably more differentiated and dense than they were. The development of the devices of mechanical reproduction in the film, radio, and television have bred a mighty bureaucracy into which the creator of the work being filmed, broadcast, or televised fits himself with various degrees of comfort or discomfort.

The greatest organizational changes have occurred in connection with the financial support and the administration of intellectual institutions. The diminution almost to extinction of the amateur scientist and scholar, the great growth in the numbers of universities, and the increased proportion of all cultural life that they embrace, have meant that contemporary intellectual life is set in a far denser institutional matrix than it ever has been in the past. Applications, authorization, planned division of labor, scheduling, periodic reporting, all play a greater part now in culture than they did at an earlier age when deliberately coordinated action was unthought of or dispensable. Change in the nature of the tasks of intellectual work and the devices it uses, the increase in the quantity of intellectual activity, its greater dependence for external financial support, as well as a change in the pattern of private patronage, have all helped to make the organization of financial provision more intricate than it ever was before. Culture has become more costly, and the intellectual worker is less capable of bearing its cost. It is carried on less frequently by rentier-amateurs or businessmen with intellectual interests. As a result, the producer must now be supported by the sale of his services as a teacher or as a research worker. But his salary as a teacher or research worker cannot pay for the material and equipment he needs to do his creative work, nor can it pay the other expenses, such as the travel, secretarial, and technical assistance, which is needed or which it is thought is needed. Equipment is much more complicated now than it once was, and far more expensive. Even in the social sciences, which up to thirty or forty years ago were like philosophy in their financial requirements, certain techniques of research, such as the sample survey and the use of statistical methods, have greatly increased the cost of a single piece of research. In the humanistic subjects, too, microfilming, the use of computers, and radioactive dating have introduced new financial necessities. All of these have called for an institutional machinery for receiving applications for funds from research workers, for assessing the applications and allocating funds. They have also required further organization to administer the funds in the institution to which they are granted. Committees are in frequent session to make decisions or advise on making them.

Since so much of this money comes from government and from

a relatively small number of philanthropic foundations, it would appear that the direction and range of intellectual development is now subject to control from a small number of centers outside the intellectual community proper. In principle, this possibility certainly exists. In fact, it had hardly done so, even though it had changed the structure of decision making. Neither in Great Britain nor in the United States is the expenditure of the funds allocated by governments or private patrons for research and cultural activities in general independently of the control of members of the intellectual community. Through incumbency in the decision making posts or through advisory functions, members of the intellectual community exercise a very far-reaching control over the direction which research and teaching will take. The diversity of governmental and philanthropic sources assures also that, even if one group had a clear and firm idea of the direction into which it would like to steer a branch of cultural life, it could hardly do so because of the existence of alternative sources of funds. The volume of funds, too, and the desire to please also give assurance that only the most eccentric proposals will not find support—and even then the eccentricity which does find support is often amazing in its extremity. A new stratum of intellectual-political-bureaucratic roles has grown up as part of this situation. Persons of intellectual qualifications and achievements are drawn into administrative and policy-making roles in the intellectual community on a grander scale than ever before. In some cases the drawing off of these persons is a loss to intellectual creativity, but in others, it represents a new stage in a career, which was once creative, and which has ceased to be creative. Since, on the whole, these persons maintain very intimate relationships with the intellectual community and depend for their sustenance and esteem on the opinion of the intellectual community, their ideas and standards—for better or for worse—are pretty much the ideas of their fellow members of this community.

Of course, in the increasingly important part of science which depends on governmental financial support, the preoccupation with national defense affects the direction of expenditure. Even within the limits of the direction, however, the free choice of the academic-scientific community plays a very important part through influential advisory functions and through a certain respect for basic research.

Scholarly and scientific creativity has, at least thus far, suffered no harm from the administrative encrustation brought about by its greater scale, cost, and division of labor. This observation applies to the universities which have been especially favored. But very much research is at present conducted by industrial and commercial enterprises as well as by governmental bodies. These are in the main concentrated on technological problems, and although the level of scientific skill is high, the problems on which the scientists work belong more to the realms of technology than of basic science proper. In this field, on the whole, the autonomy of intellectual work is foregone, but even here, not entirely. Certain institutions doing the most original work grant a great deal of autonomy to their scientists to choose their problems within the general field of common interest. Since recruitment is voluntary, the field of work chosen often corresponds to the dominant intellectual interest of the individual scientists. All this notwithstanding, this sector of the intellectual community is definitely one on which the considerations of national power, private profitability, and public welfare have taken a place alongside and even superior to scientific curiosity and in internal directions of science itself.

The numbers of scientists employed in these types of institutions are likely to grow in the coming decades. What will be the impact of this growth of applied science on the quality of creative intellectual life? Applied science at present is largely derivative from the university science; the university's standard of work remains uppermost, particularly in those laboratories with the highest aspirations and the highest prestige. The relationships of these latter laboratories to the centers of intellectual creativity will remain close, with the major universities continuing to have the upper hand. They will supply the leading members of the staffs, and their teaching and publications will provide the general theoretical orientations guiding the technological research. Their pattern of organization—one in which the freedom to follow one's bent is predominant—will embody the standard by which the organization of governmental and industrial laboratories will be judged, by scientists inside and outside them and by responsible administrators of science. There appears, therefore, to be little likelihood that the scientific culture of the universities will be swamped by the outlook of more bureaucratically conducted institutions; the chances are better for an increased approximation to the university standard of organization on the part of the governmental and industrial scientific institutions.

This, however, is not the whole story. As the numbers of scientists in industrial and governmental laboratories increase, the universities will have the task of training their prospective staff members. This has for a long time been the case in chemistry; it has begun to be so in physics, in statistics, mathematics, etc., as well as in much less developed subjects like sociology and psychology.

Will the greatly increased numbers of university students— which are a result of mass society in the sense that they are the product of a widely diffused expansion of the desire for enhanced dignity—damage the high culture of our society? There is indeed a general apprehension that they will do so. They need not do so if the newly recruited students are of an intellectual caliber equal to the students of earlier generations. There must certainly, in most countries, including the United States, be many young people of university standard of intelligence who are not in the universities. Many lack the motivation and the culture to use their intelligence most effectively; they come from families which inhibit their social self-confidence and they are fearful of letting themselves go intellectually. Furthermore, in the United States especially, the quality of elementary and secondary instruction is such that capacities are not aroused, or are permitted to atrophy. There are, in any case, even with the system of state scholarships and similar aids to the offspring of the economically poorer sections of the population, many who do not get into effective contact with the machinery of the higher culture of our society. There seem, therefore, to be veins of undeveloped talent which could enable the considerable quantitative expansion which is probable in the next decades to permit the maintenance of the present level of attainment.

Increased numbers could pull the cultural level of the peak downward if they afflicted all universities and every post within every university equally. But they will not do so. The greatest universities and even the fairly good ones are not going to let their best men be swamped by routine teaching and administration—and the best men would find a way around the efforts of students and administrators to engulf them.

The past fifty years offer further evidence that increased numbers do not inevitably cause deterioration. Those who claim that the high culture of this age has deteriorated never allow their minds to turn to the universities and to compare the American university now with what it was before World War I. The standard was not forced lower by the proven incompetence of all the children to learn more and better than they did.

Of course, the expansion of the numbers in universities would result in a lower average if the hitherto existing mechanisms of selection had worked so perfectly that there were no young people above a certain level of capacity and character who had been excluded in the past, and if all the previously admitted college and university students had been above that level of capacity and character. This was obviously not the case. The indolent, fun-loving undergraduates at Princeton or Harvard or Chicago or Berkeley fifty years ago were no different from the mass of the young men at the great state universities like Michigan, Minnesota, Illinois, or California today. They are probably even a little better by virtue of having more sophisticated intellectual formation than their predecessors of a half-century ago. The American universities today are better institutions intellectually than they were fifty years ago, when their student bodies and staffs were much smaller. There are more American universities at which important scientific and scholarly research and teaching are done now than then, and the number of persons who are creative and not just productive is very much greater now than then. Numbers as such will not corrupt standards as long as the standard appropriate to the less gifted does not become the standard regarded as appropriate to the more gifted. It certainly need not become so. A self-respecting community of science and scholarship will be able to resist the pressure of the opinion of the indolent among the students and of the demagogic among the politicians to replace a more demanding standard by a slacker one.

IV

The state and position of intellectual life in society are not merely functions of the quality of the works created. Intellectual life needs an audience to form the community within which creation can go on and in which those who are to transmit what is created to the wider society can receive the sustenance they need. Intellectual life depends, therefore, on institutions of communication through which the works can be assessed, selected, and disseminated. In the spheres of scientific and scholarly work, the contemporary situation is almost too prosperous. So many books are published and journals go on multiplying past the capacity of any one human mind, even a moderately specialized mind, to survey and pass on their contents. The scientific and scholarly worlds have, however, met this situation by a mechanism of selection which protects the individual scientist and scholar from being inundated. An informal, vague, and loosely conceived hierarchy of journals, publishing houses and research centers has become established in the opinion of the various scientific and scholarly subcommunities, and works which originate in or pass through these institutions are given more attention than others which do not. This is supplemented by the network of individual acquaintanceship and the distribution of publications along the paths of this network. Finally, more massively, as a final protection against the flood, there are the huge apparatuses of bibliographical indexing, abstracting, and information-retrieval services. By these means an international scientific community is maintained. But the audiences of especially scholarly and scientific work, except for marginal exceptions, are the scholarly and scientific communities. There is practically no laity for scientific work[2] in the sense that there are religious, artistic, and literary laities. The laity of scholarship within the United States, although probably not becoming smaller than it was, is not growing. The audience of scholarly works is increasingly becoming as sharply defined and as identical with the community of creators and reproducers as it is in the scientific sphere. The laity of art and literature and social and political analysis is what used to be called

341

the educated public. The situation here is not what one would like to see.

Where, as in the United States today, there is a danger of centrifugality within the intellectual classes arising from their numbers, their spatial dispersion, and their professional specialization, there is too little to give a sense of intellectual community to our large intellectual classes. Without this sense of community, with the broadening of responsiveness which it carries with it, the educated classes will slacken their standards in those matters in which they are receptive rather than creative, and they will not exercise the collective influence which they should in the country at large or in their localities.

The organs of communication of arts, literature, and social and political analysis are the serious daily press and the reviews. In this category of intellectual institutions, the United States, which has done so much in the technology and organization of mass communication, seems to suffer particularly from the deficiencies of its system of intellectual communication. Other Western countries, with many imperfections, have a small, serious press which is not only serious and responsible politically, but also culturally. The same cannot be said for the United States, where serious and responsible press, which does exist, is—unless *The New York Times* becomes a national newspaper—restricted in circulation to locality and region. The handful of good newspapers in the United States—such as *The Washington Post* and *The St. Louis Post-Dispatch,* are much more confined to their area of origin than *The New York Times.* All these papers, moreover, are extremely feeble culturally. It is true that *The New York Times* makes some effort in this direction, but, especially in its literary assessments, it deliberately "writes down" to a presumptively unqualified audience. The other dailies are almost unmentionable culturally. Their book reviews are negligible in quality and in quantity and the level of the political and social analysis in their leaders and features, except for a very small number of syndicated features, is distressing. Chicago, San Francisco, Los Angeles, Philadelphia, New Orleans, Detroit all suffer from the intellectual nullity of their local press. There is, moreover, no regular making up of the deficiency by the radio or television or by the weekly reviews. *The Nation* and *The New Republic,* which some

342

decades ago provided something quite comparable in journalistic and intellectual merit to *The New Statesman* and *The Spectator,* have been for many years in a condition of pathetic paltriness. Part of their misfortunes has arisen from their own poor editorial direction, their fellow-traveling, which persisted longer than that of their audiences, and the ineptitude of their efforts to make themselves competitively "popular." [3] Even had they been better, they might not have been able to withstand the drawing power of *Time,* which, with all its vices of prejudice, arrogance and cleverness, has, in recent years, performed the function of supplying information about the larger world of politics and culture more satisfactorily than either of our two intellectual weeklies. However well *Time* were to perform its self-appointed task, its accomplishment would still be different from what a journal, which aspires to sell only 100,000 copies and to reach one-third of a million readers, should be. *Time*'s conception of its audience, leaving out the distortions of snobbery, is inevitably different from a weekly with a more stringent standard. A proper weekly, in the tradition of the best weeklies of the century, must assume its audience to be highly intelligent, highly and broadly educated, well informed and curious to know and pass a complex judgment about a wide variety of things.

The absence of a passable intellectual weekly[4] does damage to American intellectual life. The country is so large, the intellectuals are so scattered, and their superior training and practice are so specialized that a continuous and discriminating focus on a wide variety of cultural, social, and political matters, beyond their immediate speciality, would do much to raise the level of discourse and offset the Philistinizing consequences of specialization. There is at present no shortage of monthly and bi-monthly and quarterly reviews of the highest quality in the natural sciences. Even in the social sciences and in the humanistic disciplines the situation is tolerable. For those, however, who would concern themselves with matters outside their professional specialities, the situation is very unsatisfactory. The highbrow reviews, insofar as they are not self-consciously "little magazines," are excessively academic (written by professors for professors and their research students)[5] and below them there is a nothingness until we reach *Saturday Review,* which is an organ for secondary school teachers, and *The New Leader.*[6]

343

Harper's Magazine, the *Atlantic* and *The Reporter* are good enough in their way for the same audience as enjoys the *Saturday Review,* but their weakness becomes all too evident when they are compared with *Encounter.*

This situation is perhaps partly a result of the draining off of the best talents for intellectual journalism to the mass media on the one side and the university social sciences on the other. It is also a result of the high cost of production of intellectual goods in the United States and the greater capital resources of the mass media and the universities. In part, too, it is a result of the antecedent weakness of the wider cultural attachments of the educated classes in the United States. This is, in turn, a product of an unthinking rush into specialization, as a way of correcting, at a later stage, the deteriorated state of elementary and secondary education and the slovenly inefficiency of so much undergraduate education.[7]

The unenthusiastic acceptance, which remains nonetheless an acceptance, of the local daily press and of the national periodical press in their present condition is the fundamental obstacle to the improvement of the extra-university intellectual institutions in the United States. Just as they have learned to exist without bookshops, so American intellectuals have learned to exist without a decent intellectual press. They suffer its ill-effects, but they do not feel them. Their consciously perceived needs are met by their professional organs, by their university libraries and laboratories. As a result, alongside a very high level of proficiency and the occasional peaks of genius in intellectual production, the educated classes of the United States are, outside their specialized professions, Philistines in their intellectual consumption.

V

The boorish and complacent ignorance of university graduates and the distrust or superciliousness toward high culture exhibited by university professors in the humanities and social sciences, in the medical and law schools of this country, outside their special subjects, and by journalists and broadcasters to say nothing of lawyers, engineers and physicians, cannot be denied except by those who share these qualities. The near illiteracy of so much of the American press, the crudity of judgment of our news commentators, the unletteredness of our civil servants, the uncritical ingenuity of our lawyers, the yawping vulgarity of our publishers, or at least those who write their jacket blurbs and their advertising copy, can give little comfort.

The political, economic, military, and technological elites are no better, but they at least do not allege that they are the custodians and practitioners of high culture, even though some of them are.

It is true that these are phenomena of the periphery of our cultural creativity. The center is very much alive. Its vitality, its curiosity, its openness are its virtues. They are the virtues of un-inhibitedness, of letting oneself go, of being whatever one "is." This results in much trash and nonsense in the effort to be creative, as well as some brilliant originality. It also results in the culturally inert complacency of the consuming and reproducing intellectuals in the United States. This emptiness of the cultural cupboard of the educated classes outside the creative minority in the sciences, scholarship, and the arts is not simply disagreeable to contemplate; it is full of consequence. It is probably the main reason for the unseemly quality of much of the mass communications in America; quite the opposite of what is believed by those who see mass culture, that is, the culture of the mass media, as an infection doing harm to the culture of the educated class, it is the poor culture of the educated classes which is doing harm to mass culture. It is the ab-dication of the educated classes that opens the way to the infiltra-tion of so much mediocre and brutal stuff in our popular culture. It is not that a proper intellectual carriage within the educated classes would be accepted as a model by the less educated portions of American society. The latter would not necessarily accept what might be offered to them by a more solidary intellectual front domi-nating all the main positions from which cultural objects are dis-tributed. Even in a situation without alternatives, they might be obdurate. Nonetheless, all these considerations are entirely imagi-nary in the present situation. At present, there is no such unity of standards or such a cultural consensus between the creative center and the consuming and reproductive periphery. Why does this dissensus within the educated classes exist, and to what extent is it a consequence of mass culture?

It is to some extent a product of the sheer size of the educated classes and the multiplicity of intellectual institutions. A large intellectual class is inherently bound to be more dissensual in its standards and in its cultural substance than a small one. That much is to be attributed to mass society. Other determinants antedate mass society in their origins.

The dour-spirited Puritanism which looked on aesthetic expression as self-indulgence appeared in America and Britain long before mass society. The complacent and often rude provincialism of the American middle classes, which originally distrusted the artistic and literary elements of high culture because it believed them to be Eastern, urban and connected with an Anglophile patrician upper class, does not come from the culture of a mass society. It was found in all classes, in the plutocracy, in the mercantile middle class, in the small town Philistine physician, lawyer, banker, and merchant. If the term "mass" is not just a "cuss word" and refers primarily to the urban proletariat, as its originators intended, and to the "new middle class" of clerks, which later critics added to the earlier meaning, then the bearers of that unpleasant provincialism were not of the masses at all. America was not a mass society in the nineteenth century—it was a differentiated society in which pronounced equalitarian sentiments often took on a populistic form. Mass society is its offspring, not the other way around. Much of its culture, although mediocre, sentimental, and brutal, was produced neither in the institutions nor by the professional personnel now producing the culture of mass society. The greatest achievements of this anticultural high culture from Mark Twain to Theodore Dreiser were certainly not a product of mass culture any more than its inferior and much more common manifestations.

The dominant high culture of nineteenth-century America was stained with the faded colors of the gentility of the cultivated classes of New England and the Middle Atlantic States. It did not enjoy a hospitable reception in the Middle West—in the common pattern of provincial hostility toward the metropolis. American provincial culture in the nineteenth century was a variant of the British provincial dissenting culture that Matthew Arnold disparaged in *Culture and Anarchy*. Whereas this mediocre provincial culture collapsed in England after the First World War, in America it survived in powerful form until very recently, and its traces are still with us.

In practically every differentiated society high culture arouses some distrust, and the nature of the provincial Victorianism of nineteenth-century America and the sensitive zones in which revolt against it took place accentuated this distrust. Furthermore, American Victorian respectability was an integral part of a larger landscape in which rough manliness, rude patriotism, and touchy equalitarianism were no less important. The political and economic elites of American society were figures in this landscape, and very few of them indeed, until very recently, have felt any obligation to cover themselves with a thin covering of high literary and artistic culture, such as their opposite numbers do in Great Britain and France.

Against this background of Puritan, populist, and provincial tradition and sentiment, the educational system of the United States in the past decades has created a scientific technical and scholarly intelligentsia of an increasingly outstanding merit, which neither forms nor enters into a self-consciously coherent intellectual community. Whereas secondary education became less intellectual in its content, and undergraduate university and collegiate education, for the most part, was dissipated in courses of study of very low intensity and little discipline, very superior and vigorous systems of postgraduate education and professional training developed. In trying to make up for lost ground and seeking to make as deep and thorough a penetration into a rapidly growing body of knowledge, postgraduate training in each discipline has had to become highly specialized.

This impetus toward specialization has been heightened by the internal diversification of scientific knowledge and by the growth of the population pursuing postgraduate studies and conducting research as a profession. The natural development of science has greatly increased the volume of literature and the intricacy of detail which a student must cover in each discipline. The increasing number of students and the necessity for each of them to do a piece of research which no one has ever done before has tended to narrow further the concentration within the discipline imposed by the internal evolution of the subject.[8]

The product of these educational and scientific developments has been a specialist, who shares little of the inherited culture and whose views and tastes outside his own speciality are too often like those of a much less educated person with a lower income and a smaller responsibility for the guidance of his country and the care of its cultural and moral inheritance. Except for those strong and expansive personalities whose curiosity and sensitivity lead them to the discovery and experience of what their education has failed to give them, the well-trained and competent American scientist, scholar, or technologist possesses a very meager and miscellaneous knowledge outside his special subject. More important, perhaps, than the meagerness and fragmentariness of his knowledge is the indifference, callowness and indiscriminateness of his judgment about the very things for which the highly educated in any society have a special responsibility.

One might interject at this point the question whether it really makes any difference if there is so much specialization. Might not the problem be the product of a humanistic snobbery affronted by the growth of science and technology outside the influence of conventional cultural concerns? Is there any value in a community of culture within the educated classes, apart from the value for the individual, and for the entire aggregate of individuals, of understanding and experiencing the world at the levels made possible by the greatest geniuses in the wide variety? Is there any value in a coherent educated class? Might not the very setting of the problem be a prejudice derived from a false image and a nostalgic attachment to some past age, no more truthful than the image of early capitalistic society put forward by the critics of mass society?

My conception of the unity of the intellectual class is in part derived from eighteenth-century France and especially nineteenth- and early twentieth-century Britain when, especially in the latter, there was some approximation to the reality of a coherent educated class, not by any means unitary in its political or ethical outlook but unified by sharing a common culture, and having some sense of affinity despite all opposition and antagonism. The unity of the educated class is desirable because it is important for the maintenance and diffusion of our cultural inheritance. It is important for improving the quality of judgment concerning ethical, political, cultural, religious, and social policies; it is important for establishing and upholding the authority of the educated classes in their particular vocation, which is the formation of opinion throughout society.

If it be answered, especially to the last point, that it is undemocratic to think that the educated classes should enjoy a particular authority—entirely uncoercive and voluntarily assented to—then the answer is that it is not the sole function of education to produce experts and technicians. It is also their task to enlighten their own judgment, to make it more informed, detached, and disciplined and to make that judgment heard and seriously considered throughout their respective societies. Their authority would be enhanced if they possessed more of a common universe of discourse, a more mutually intelligible idiom, which, despite inevitable and desirable diversity, would improve the quality of argument and enhance its persuasiveness.

A full solidarity of the educated classes and their closure *vis-à-vis* the rest of the society is unrealizable, and it is also not desirable that it should be fully attained. The unbroken unity of the highly educated in the face of the rest of the society would produce a hierarchy and a disjunction which would be very undesirable. There is, however, no danger of this at present in any country and least of all in America. The dangers of segregation consequent on specialization seem much more imminent.

In the present century we have experienced the dissolution of "the educated public," that coherent, although unorganized, public for the objects of high culture; the public which appreciates cultural objects which are not of immediate professional significance. The incorporation of so much of our higher cultural production and creativity into the universities represents a great improvement in the activity of our universities. It is a process which is more advanced in America, but it is already visible in Great Britain. It is part of the process of dissolution of a transprofessional public

349

for higher culture; it contributes to it, too, since the universities are among the most important agents of intellectual specialization and the professionalization which is akin to it.

The ascent of the universities to preponderance in the life of high culture in the United States, and increasingly, though not yet to the same extent, in Europe, is a further instance of the segregation which follows on specialization. Too much of the public for intellectual products in the United States is increasingly in the universities, among teachers, research workers, and postgraduate students. It is the same among the producers. Intellectual institutions are beginning to supply their own and each other's audiences, while the larger public which is not concentrating on intellectual things becomes the audience for intentionally mediocre culture and for inferior culture produced primarily for light entertainment, diversion, and commercial advantage. Thus the university public is large and its quality is good, but it is in danger of being too isolated for the cultural and social good of its own society.

The production of refined culture may be vocational without damage to creativity, and, in fact, certain types of such production, such as science and some branches of scholarship, must be vocational if they are to be carried on at all. It is injurious, however, to the fruitful impact of the universities on their society if they concentrate too much of the intellectual life of the country within themselves. It means that they reach the public too much within a limited age range and largely when they are in the status of students. For the rest, their influence is exercised in advisory capacities to government and through popularization to a much less well qualified public. The larger public dries up.

It would, of course, be a disregard for the truth to overlook the extraordinary vitality of the contemporary American university, even fairly far down the scale. Vitality by its nature is diffuse and inflammatory. It is possible, therefore, that, despite the densely specialized clutter of the postgraduate system and the prevailing pattern of research which is partly a cause and partly a result of that system, this vitality will do more than withstand the pressures of the intellectual life in the universities arising from segregation. It is possible that the vitality will spread and ignite interest and curiosity and stringent standards along a broader front within the intellectual classes than the specialized training would indicate.

Specialization has lessened the coherence of the intellectual community. It has dispersed its focus of attention and thus left ungratified cultural needs, which the mediocre and brutal culture of the mass media have been called in to satisfy amidst the dimness of private life. The consumption of inferior and mediocre culture is the consequence, not the cause, of the desert which covers much of our educated classes.

This, however, is only one side of the picture. It is possible that the wastes of secondary and undergraduate education will be brought under lively cultivation through the vitality of the new generation of college teachers who are at present, together with the postgraduate students, among the chief consumers and reproducers of refined culture. It is quite possible that a lively and discriminatingly critical public will be generated by the liberation of powers which an affluent and equalitarian mass society make possible. Without being formed by or through the universities, the mass of our society will be inchoate, and its share in intellectual traditions will be extremely fragmentary. Its contributions to public life will be deprived of the mollifying and rational influence of these traditions. This new public, impelled by its own newly released curiosity and creativity, a product of economic affluence and moral equality, might reach out toward the great cultural tradition, much like the extraordinary movement of self-education which flourished in the elite of the working classes in the nineteenth century and early twentieth century, prior to the spread of public education and the hegemony of party-Marxism.

There is much talent hidden in the classes which do not participate seriously in the higher intellectual life. They are human beings, and the categories of their existence contain the possibility of intellectual, moral, and expressive development. More of their powers could well be exerted in the sphere of higher culture without a loss of genuineness. Not that their lives should become either professionally intellectual or exclusively preoccupied with matters of higher culture. There are many merits in the genres of culture which are at present alien to high culture. There are real needs for the brutal, the trivial, and the frivolous in all strata of society, and their extirpation is neither desirable nor feasible. But within these limits a great improvement is possible.

VI

The responsibility of the custodians and practitioners of the various genres of high culture—science, literature, art, scholarship, philosophy—is to do their work as well as they can. The job is a threefold one. The first is to discover or create something true, genuine, and important to perceive, experience, and express in a way which adds to the value of the stock of culture of the human race. The second task is the conservation and reinterpretation of the inheritance. The third is the maintenance and extension of the influence of high culture in the other sectors of the society.

The responsibility is the same in all differentiated societies. It is not just a responsibility which is attributed by an outsider to the practitioners of high culture, but one which is inherent in the intellectual's role and which is sensed in varying degrees wherever intellectual life is practiced. It is particularly felt by the more creative intellectuals. Not all three responsibilities are accepted with equal fullness.

The effective performance of its first task is not entirely independent of the second, although the balance might vary. In our own society, for example, the emphasis lies more heavily on creativity than on conservation. Nonetheless, any sector of high culture, if it is to be creative, must look to the protection of its own *tradition* and its own *internal coherence*. The progress of high culture—and its continued self-renewal and expansion—require that there should be a continuous contact with tradition, not simply to reproduce it but to take it as its own point of departure. It is not that creativity would be entirely impossible without the platform of tradition on which to stand. It would, however, be so much less rich in its achievement if it were not enabled to avoid the false paths rejected by past experience and to take advantage of the openings indicated by what has gone before. Contact with tradition discloses new possibilities even to the most creative mind.

The reception of tradition in a manner which allows freedom

to move about easily within it and away from it goes hand in hand with the internal coherence of the intellectual community or the subcommunities within it. This in turn is intimately connected with self-esteem. The custodians, the reproducers, the teachers of the sciences and arts, must feel themselves to be performing a vital task, as indispensable to the well-being of the race as are the labors of manual workers or the exertions of administrators and technologists—and even more constitutive of its greatness.

It has not been easy to maintain such an attitude in the United States. The equalitarian moral tone of American society is not conducive to such an attitude, nor is the predominant tone of unfriendliness toward high culture which appears to emanate from the economic, political, and technological elites, however brilliant and important the exceptions.

The mood begins at the earliest stages of education. Children who come, as most necessarily do, from families in which there is little experience of high culture, acquire their first orientation from their teachers. Overworked, underpaid teachers, not well educated themselves, are scarcely capable of representing with persuasive conviction the high culture of their civilization. Even at the level of secondary education, the situation is not especially favorable.

The older traditions have often been dealt with and in more recent years are widely ramified; the state of municipal finance, the armaments program of the Federal Government, the traditional conception of the separation of Church and State, the diversion of so much talent into the mass-communications industry, the outlook of educational progressivism, are only a few of the factors which hamper the effective reception of the inheritance of high culture in American schools. The position becomes more favorable at the level of undergraduate education, but it is still extremely uneven, and the inimical traditions are difficult to weather. The result is a public opinion which is much too indifferent to the values of its inheritance of high culture, far too unconnected with it.

The prospect is uncertain. Sporadically, here and there, in television and in the widespread sale of paperbound books, and in the alarm of an occasionally humiliated national pride, and above all in the great expansion of postgraduate education, which might soon manifest itself in an improved undergraduate intellectual life, there are signs that the situation is unstable and that it might indeed change for the better. Unless it does, one of the most vital supports of the system of high culture and of the formation of an intellectual community which cuts across the boundaries of professional specialization will be lacking in the United States. Not only will the public life of the country be poorer, but the quality of life as a whole in the society will be poorer. Opinion on political, economic, and social matters will have a poorer guidance, and the style of life of the mass of the population will be more frivolous and petty than it need be.

Yet, even failure in this sphere might still leave fairly unimpaired the capacity to meet the first obligation of an intellectual class which is to do intellectual work creatively. The experience of the country since World War I would support the contention. The country is, moreover, committed to science and to higher education in a way which appears oddly incommensurate with its other dispositions. Thus at this superior level, despite the pressures and distractions of a populistic mass society, the prospects of the maintenance of creativity are good. There is always the chance in the United States that a spotty resurgence of demagogic populism will harass intellectuals in the way it has done occasionally in the past. Yet if experience is to guide our judgment, it should be remembered that the unpleasantness of the time of McCarthy did not derail the serious intellectual life of the country. It is true that the attractions often described by the critics of mass culture will exist, and they will lure away and spoil some talented persons. But they will not ruin all whom they attract, and some of them will surely continue and might even expand the present small amount of outstanding work done in those fields.

Serious intellectuals have never been free of pressure from other sectors of their society. The intellectual sectors, like any other sectors performing specialized roles, are always somewhat removed from other sectors of their society, and this is so, regardless of the role of the intellectuals in economic and political life. The external world is always jealous of the devotion of the intellectuals to their gods and of the implicit criticism that such devotion directs against the ruling values of the other sectors of society. Intellectuals have always had before them the task of continuing their own tradition, developing it, differentiating it, improving it as best they could. They have always had to contend with church, state, and party, with merchants and soldiers who have sought to enlist them in their service and to restrict and damage them in word and deed if they did not yield to the blandishments and threats. The present situation has much in common with the past. The responsibilities of intellectuals also remain the same—to serve the standards which they discern and develop and to find a way of rendering unto Caesar what is Caesar's without renouncing what belongs to their own proper realm.

It has not been easy for intellectuals to find the right relation to their society, whether it be a civil mass society, an aristocratic oligarchy, or a tyranny with populistic pretensions. In some respects the situation is more favorable than it has ever been in America. Public opinion and political opinion especially are firmly convinced of their need for the intellectual institutions which train specialized professionals and which do research. Intellectuals have, over the past three decades, come into positions of influence in the economy and polity, which the country had not known for about a century. They occupy powerful positions in the mass-communications system. For all this to bear the desired fruit in an adequate performance of the third function which lies in the guidance of society, some greater degree of closure of the intellectual community as a whole is required. It must be a closure which transcends specialization. If this is attained, then the many channels of intellectual, social, political, and economic influence which intellectuals now occupy will make possible a very great improvement in the intellectual style of the wider reaches of our society.

*   *   *   *   *

Digression on the *avant garde*

The question has recently been raised as to whether the maintenance of high culture necessitates an *avant garde*. An *avant garde*, in the most general sense, is as necessary as it is inevitable, if the field of work continues to attract living human beings with creative capacities. It is given in the nature of creativity. Creativity involves a partial incorporation of tradition, but it also involves a partial rejection of tradition. The *avant garde,* which tends to emphasize the element of rejection, quite understandably, very often fails to appreciate how much of the rejected tradition it is incorporating. The *avant garde* may wear workman's caps or any other garb; it may conduct its personal relations in a bohemian fashion or in the most respectable manner. These types of behavior are quite irrelevant to the way in which the *avant garde* performs its innovative, reinterpretative role with regard to inherited traditions. The *avant garde* is as much a phenomenon of science and scholarship as it is of art and literature.

In all fields of culture, the reception and transformation of traditions are the essential things. Transformative powers are not equally distributed through the whole intellectual community. Many of its members are solely reproductive, many others seek to transform and reinterpret but fail, and only a few succeed in their efforts.

There is probably, however, some difference between the organization of innovation in the more institutionalized fields of science and scholarship on the one hand, and the less organized fields of art and literature on the other. In the latter fields, the young, especially, who conceive of themselves as an *avant garde*—including both the successes and the failures—have tended since the eighteenth century to segregate themselves from the rest of the intellectual community, on the basis, not of their achievements, but of their aspirations. They have developed their own traditions, not all of which are essential to intellectual creativity and some of which even serve as a substitute in those who lack it.

One of the more remarkable developments of recent years in the West is the assimilation of the culture of the *avant garde* in the more routine and even Philistine cultural circles. The enfeeblement of the institutions for the inculcation of the traditional or conventional high culture—and a rebellion against its diminished authority—opens the way as much to the penetration of often trivial *avant garde* culture as it does to the penetration of an even more trivial mediocre and brutal culture.

The drawing-in of left-wing horns in the United States in the

1950's has led to the question as to whether intellectual creativity—or as it is called in artistic and literary circles, an *avant garde*—is necessarily linked with revolutionary attitudes in political and economic matters. From the standpoint of logical necessity or of reasonable common sense, there is obviously no such obligatory link. Why should an original feeling for color or form or a new conception of light require the belief that the existing social order should be transformed, that property should be brought under public ownership, women rendered equal to men, aristocracy abolished, and kinship connections diminished in their importance? Nevertheless, there has grown up an affinity between the *avant garde* variant of high culture and revolutionary dispositions, and this has not been entirely an accident. There is some psychological linkage between the rejection of tradition in the cultural sphere and the rejection of tradition in the social and political spheres. It is an affinity which is unnecessary to cultural creation—it is probably its consequence. This affinity has had many merits and many lasting achievements to its credit. It has given color to the cultural life of an entire century and a half. It has sharpened our moral conscience and heightened and distorted our sensibilities to the nature of the society in which we have been living. It has also added to the disorder of political life and has aggravated the inevitably never perfect harmonious relations between high culture and civil society. The atrophy of this aspect of *avant garde* culture would not be a loss, but it is not very likely, and its persistence will just have to be borne.

* * * * *

The need to maintain continuity with the past is not more important than the need to maintain community among those now living in the present. In some respects the position in the United States is advantageous. In the new generation of literary men, there are many who have had a wide range of experience in their late teens and early twenties. They come, moreover, from beyond the limits of the educated classes and so they have a more extensive range of sympathy than their counterparts in Great Britain. Once, however, they are under way in their careers, they tend to lose this wider contact and to confine themselves inordinately to literary circles or to universities or to literary circles within universities.

In the more formally disciplined intellectual activities of science and scholarship, the range of external connections varies. Scientists have come increasingly to concern themselves with the world outside the laboratory. Not only are many employed in industry and government, but even those who remain within the university have developed a greater interest and a wider range of sympathy in politics. They serve the government in many important capacities. Professional social scientists are not confined to their cloisters but are out in society as investigators, which gives them a unilateral and unprecedented intimacy of a special kind with many parts of society. They, too, have become more civil than ever before in their history. In most respects, the civility of American intellectuals has gone further than at any time since the Jacksonian revolution.

All these improvements notwithstanding, there is no doubt that the main "political" tradition by which most of our literary, artistic, and social science intellectuals have lived in America is unsatisfactory. The fault does not lie exclusively with the intellectuals. The Philistine, puritanical provincialism of our elites has contributed its share to the troubles. Crude and passionate irrelevance, and disregard for the public interest have added to them, and nowadays, the mere existence of nuclear weapons fastens onto the political elite a burden which is monstrously difficult to carry and of which they cannot divest themselves. All these things have been repellent to intellectuals, for good reasons and bad ones. There have been bad reasons for being antipolitical or anticivil, and the American intellectuals have had their fair share in them. Until recently the intellectuals had not been forthcoming in their efforts to ameliorate the situation. Even now, when things are improving in the relations of politicians and intellectuals, the almost immovable international situation has become a point at which so many of the older antipolitical prejudices are expressed in a contemporary idiom, as if they arise simply from a confrontation of the actual situation.

One of the responsibilities implied by the obligation to maintain good relations with the nonintellectual elite is the "civilization" of political life, that is, the infusion of the standards and concerns of a serious, intellectually disciplined contemplation of the deeper issues of political life into everyday politics. Our intellectuals have, in the main, lectured politicians from the outside, upbraided them, looked down their noses at them, opposed them, and suspected those of their fellow intellectuals who have become politicians of moral corruption and intellectual betrayal. The intellectuals who, in any country, have taken on themselves the care and cultivation of high culture, are, by prominence, influence, and self-consciousness, part of the differentiated elite of their society. But in the United States they have not usually felt themselves to be bound, by an invisible filiation, to the political, economic, ecclesiastical, military, and technological elites.[9] They tended to feel isolated and seldom brought their influence to bear in a way that would have continued the practice of the Founding Fathers, the practice in which philosophy and men of affairs collaborated in the formation of an enduring constitution. The civilization of politics, the infusion of the best that intellectual activity has into the practice of politics and government, is one great possibility of modern society. Naturally, it can never wholly succeed. Politics are too strenuous, the machinery of power warps the sensibilities too much for the wisdom of detachment ever to dominate them completely. Deciding is different from contemplating the differentiation of reality, and the tensions of alternatives are always greater than they look from a distance. Still some interpenetration is possible—certainly more than we have had in the United States. Such improvement is the condition of a better polity and of the better understanding which the intellectual community needs from the rest of society.

The "civilization" of political life is only one aspect of the "process of civilization," which is the expansion of the culture of the center into the peripheries of society. In this particular context, the "process of civilization" is the diffusion of some elements of high culture into the areas of society normally consuming mediocre and brutal culture.

Within the limits mentioned earlier in this essay, the prospects here seem to be moderately good. The mutual interpenetration, at certain points, of the producers of high culture and the producers of mediocre culture, has resulted in an expansion of the elements of high culture toward persons whose usual inclinations do not lead them to seek it out just as it has increased the consumption of mediocre and brutal culture among persons whose equals in occupation, education, and income might in the past have been resistant. Popularization which brings a better content, although eradicating refinements, helps in this. Not all of the expansion is popularization; much of it is the presentation (and consumption) of works of genuinely high culture. An improvement of our educational system at the elementary and secondary levels, which is entirely practicable, would also further this process of a broadening civilization. The better education of the passions which a richer, less scarcity-harassed society can afford, the opening and enrichment of sensibility which leisure and a diversified environment can make possible, a more fruitful use of available intelligence, can also push forward the "process of civilization."

Of course, men will remain men into the foreseeable future; their capacities to understand, create, and experience will vary, and very many are probably destined to find their pleasure and their salvation at other and lower cultural levels. For the others, the prospect of a more dignified and richer cultural life does not seem to be out of the question.

The urgent desirability of this accomplishment certainly does not mean that all must be engaged in it. Such rearrangement of the division of labor would be like a floral industry which never grew new flowers but dealt only in cut flowers. In a short time, the high culture which would be transmitted through the "process of civilization" would desiccate and fade. There would be no new creations to replace and give freshness to the inherited cultural stock.

Popularized high culture and original high culture transmitted to a new audience must have the same contemporaneity, the same feeling of being in contact with what is most vital in life as it is being lived in the present, as the high culture produced and consumed by the intellectuals. (We might reformulate here the Crocean notion in the following terms: "all culture is present culture.") The greatest monuments of our inherited high heritage are made vital by our contact with them through our own present cultural experience, and the enlivenment of our minds by contemporary creativity.

Thus, if the periphery is not to be polished while the center withers and becomes dusty, the first obligation of the intellectuals is to look after intellectual things, to concentrate their powers on production and consumption of particular works of philosophy, art, science, literature, or scholarship, to receive the traditions in which these works stand with a discriminating readiness to accept, elaborate, or reject. If that is done, there will be nothing to fear for the movement of culture in a rich, large-scale, mass society.

The High Culture of the Age

[1] Mr. Walter Lippmann's name comes to mind at this point: is *The Public Philosophy* a markedly poorer book than *Public Opinion* or *The Drift Diplomacy?* Are Professor Denis Brogan's later books *The French Republic* or *The Price of Revolution* markedly poorer than the books he wrote before he became a broadcaster and journalist? Bertrand de Jouvenel is one of the most eminent of contemporary political thinkers; he earns his livelihood by an intense journalistic activity.

[2] The lay audience of science consists of the scientists who are not the specialists in a particular topic but who had a general intellectual and technical interest and who can follow technical exposition with some understanding. Beyond that is a more genuine laity, which must have popularized science: industrialists, government officials, military men, who depend on scientific advisers who tell them what and how the results, once attained, are utilizable for their various ends.

[3] *The New Republic* is now showing signs of recovery, but it has much ground to regain. It is here that the critics of the cultural consequences of a mass society do score a point. The intellectual weeklies have been forced into an inferior position in the competition for editorial talent and for readership by the weeklies of mass circulation.

[4] *Commonweal* exists on a higher intellectual plane than our two secular weeklies, but its Roman Catholic preoccupations restrict the generality of its appeal.

[5] These generally excellent reviews are not a substitute. They are not only too academic; they are also too infrequent, and they are too apolitical. Even where they are not, as in the case of the *Partisan Review* or *Commentary,* they cannot maintain a continuous flow of comment and coverage.

[6] Oddly enough, the direct heir of what Trotsky called "socialism for dentists," *The New Leader* was, as a weekly, the best of them, but it was too often written for persons who were assumed by its authors to know nothing of the subject before reading their particular articles. It presupposed an anti-Communist attitude.

⁷ The poor quality of the earlier levels of American educational system was a result of the rapid expansion of educational provision and has been supported by the populistic and antitraditional prejudices of educationists. The poor quality is not the result of the demands of the mass for a poorer education or of their insistence on a lower cultural level. They probably would not have resisted had they been offered something better.

⁸ The romantic idea of originality, which claimed that genius must go its own *unique* way, has been transposed into an idea of originality that demands that the subject matter should be *unique* to the investigator. This led to much specialized triviality in humanistic and social science research, even before the present stampede of research workers treading down topic after topic. The increased number of university presses and their hunger for manuscripts have shown what is afoot. Authors otherwise incapable of life are revived and then re-embalmed in public form. In the past, the dissertation very seldom became a book, and when it did it was usually as one of a series as much intended for the learned world as the most specialized periodical. The patriotism which led to the busy work of American studies is responsible for much of the digging up of once sealed and forgotten intellectual cemeteries. But the alternative of studying the monuments is equally problematic. How many more books can Herman Melville or Mark Twain or Henry James stand?

⁹ This is not a condition unique to the United States. Only Great Britain has managed to avoid it for most of the period since the French Revolution. (The past few years show that such good fortune does not always endure. In some respects at least, the relations of politicians and intellectuals in Great Britain is now worse than it has been for some time in the United States.)

Thirteen

CONTENT AND METHOD IN THE
STUDY OF THE HIGHER ARTS

Throughout this volume we have been concerned, usually implicitly, with the kinds of issues Dornbusch
enunciates in his discussion of methodology. Most
essays in the sociology and psychology of the arts have
represented the unique excursions of sensitive individuals rather than sustained scientific efforts to test the
truth of propositions. Part of this situation probably
resides in the fact that it is extremely difficult, in the
world of art, to devise propositions which are at once
meaningful and susceptible of proof or disproof. And
Dornbusch would reply: "Extremely difficult, yes, but
not impossible." Part, too, of the singular, impressionistic nature of work in this field may be traced to the
dispositions of scholars who profess such interests; they
are usually persons of humanistic bent who are little
inclined toward experimental science in any of their
professional endeavors.

One can only agree with Dornbusch that the
sociology of art deserves much better from its practitioners in the way of rigorous statement and inventive

research strategies. As he suggests, there are many possible avenues for discovering what really happens as art is made, perceived, and evaluated. As yet, we have seen in the arts very few of the ingenious studies which characterize other subjects like, say, opinion research or the analysis of small-group interaction. Studies of the creative process and of the induction and socialization of neophytes in the arts have made some progress in recent years; indeed, the early papers in this volume represent modest contributions to these topics. The case studies and the broader historical analyses of later essays treat more vexed problems of aesthetic content and societal response. In general, these papers are open to Dornbusch's criticisms about reliability and definition of terms. In the present collection, the Whites' treatment of French painting and social structure is closest in spirit to methodological rigor, resting as it does on a very sophisticated scheme of computation and extrapolation. Nash's and Griff's papers, on composers and painters, respectively, show evidence of concern for sampling, whereas Lowenthal's examination of Dostoevski's critics is exhaustive.

Although Dornbusch's strictures may be seen as a healthy corrective to the rather free-wheeling studies presented here, they do not and cannot mean that such efforts are without value. Many would disagree with his assertion that history is not a "behavioral science" (unless this term is very narrowly conceived), and some of the best work in the sociology of art relies precisely on the historian's favored techniques of close reading, the sifting of evidence, and subjective integration of findings into a coherent description. Impressionistic, intuitive, perhaps in some respects "prescientific," the papers gathered here rest primarily on the capacities of their individual authors. They are in themselves worthy, and they may well set the stage for certain more detailed studies such as Dornbusch recommends. Students of the arts might well heed one of his closing remarks: "When we undertake the impossible, for we believe our attempt to be better than nothing, the obligation to be self-critical remains."

CONTENT AND METHOD IN THE STUDY OF THE HIGHER ARTS

Sanford M. Dornbusch

This essay is primarily concerned with methodology, but it necessarily has invaded the area of content. It is not just that methodology without content tends to be a sterile exercise, but that consideration of methodology in this burgeoning area has led to consideration of some new lines of inquiry.

Methodological rigor is an inappropriate area for much current research in the higher arts. Ideally, the scientific method requires theories from which deductions can be made, and these deductions must be translatable into testable hypotheses. For my own field, sociology, the application of this ideal would cause any unbiased investigator to throw out almost all of what passes for knowledge. But there must be a baby somewhere in that bath water, and we hesitate to scrap any set of cumulative findings. In an area of genuine intellectual interest like the study of the higher arts, if rigorous knowledge is not present, there is at least some justification for compromise, half steps, and approaches to the scientific model. The arts are too important an area of human experience to await developments in other fields before the scientific method is even imperfectly applied to the understanding of their development and place in society.

Realistically, then, what can be done for the next few intellectual generations? I believe that the behavioral science contribution will be twofold: (1) at a minimum, to emphasize that no science can use unreliable data, and that intersubjective reliability is a necessity and not an aspiration; (2) to redefine certain problems so that research in the higher arts can be related to and draw upon the main body of ongoing research in the behavioral sciences.

The remainder of this paper will discuss these two approaches again and again. The organization of the essay will necessarily interweave them, and this is a healthy condition. The burden of the argument is to stress ways in which existing methods make possible research in the arts which has not yet been attempted.

I believe in coexistence. There is no need to limit the free operation of the intellectual market place. There is no need for hair-pulling evaluations of the body of current research. This essay merely represents an attempt to portray alternative strategies to those suggested by most of the chapters in this volume. In addition, the search for methodological sophistication should not be seen as endangering the study of aesthetics as a branch of philosophy or the appreciation of the creative impulse.

A study in one of my courses at Harvard showed that hostility to behavioral science was greater for students in the humanities than for majors in the physical sciences. The explanation appears to be a defense of home territory against the pretentious interlopers. Even a cursory glance at the preceding essays, and, hopefully, the reading of this chapter, will make clear the friendly intentions of the behavioral science visitors. The artistic act is *sui generis,* but that does not preclude the meaningful search for its context. Understanding about light rays and prisms does not make the sunrise less beautiful.

History is not a behavioral science. As a historian happily wallows in complexity, the scientist seeks simplicity in the form of abstract generalizations. Art, which has always been produced within the context of an historical epoch, demands the services of both groups. Most behavioral scientists, discussing the relation of art to social circumstances, tend to be far from circumspect in their treatment of the complexity of an historical period. Particular periods are labeled and, once named, the era has a monolithic quality which it did not have prior to being tagged. It is a little maddening to observe the blithe superficiality with which behavioral scientists have summarily treated whole societies.

The temptation is understandable. If the behavioral scientist is to produce general propositions, the presence of so many uncontrolled variables develops a cultivated blindness. But to develop simplicity by ignoring complexities is ruinous. Instead, the scientist should face up to his problems, and, through such methods as experimentation and the comparative approach, he may be able to move toward abstraction. By some means, the researcher must attempt to escape from the too-abundant variables and provide a basis for replication of his findings.

Not only artists may be surprised by the suggestion that experimentation can be introduced in the artistic arena. Many behavioral scientists are quick to point out the difficulty in moving from experimental treatments to the understanding of a problem in the field. Nevertheless, for certain limited objectives, experimentation may be the best vehicle. For example, current research in communication and persuasion provides excellent models for studying the communication process from artists to work to audience. Variations in art objects and level of audience under controlled conditions can go beyond the usual verbiage about the complex interaction among artists and publics.

One cannot randomly assign a person to be an artist, but random assignment of members of the audience is commonplace. Many variations on this design are feasible. The variable of interest may be artistic style. Representative works may be shown to randomly selected groups, and it is only the lack of imagination of the researcher which limits his study of what gets communicated. Perhaps we are interested in the effect of training upon audience appreciation. Because, in the current social structure, training in art appreciation is associated with a host of variables, from social class to length of hair, experimentation is the best means for unscrambling the interactions and assessing the impact of training alone. Random assignment to a training group or control group is simple. The experimenter may then introduce additional variations in types of training, types of art experience to be communicated, and types of populations from which he draws his samples.

Communications research may also be used to relate artistic intention to audience response. As every artist can testify, the reaction to his work is often surprising, and often lamentable. A simple design would have artists recording their intent, empathically judging audience reaction, and then having some evidence of audience reaction fed back to the artist for his evaluation and guidance. Such

367

research may aid in understanding the complex process of inter-action and evaluation among members of the total artistic com-munity.

The experimental approach may also contribute to the assess-ment of the reliability of the standards of evaluation and analysis among elite evaluators. In the world of music and art, juries of trained experts are typically used to allocate rewards, such as prizes or space in an exhibition. It would be simple to develop tests of the impact of communication among jury members, for juries often for-bid communication in the early stages of judging. Our concern with reliability goes beyond the degree of agreement as to whether a work of art is worthy. We can move to the reliability of the assign-ment of works with respect to particular sets of standards. For exam-ple, one may use the terms employed by art critics in their printed reviews in order to develop a set of categories which appear relevant to them. Then, a set of critics may be asked to independently judge the same works of art in order to assess the reliability of their categorizations.

In the study of psychotherapy, a common design is to have psychiatrists and psychologists of differing persuasions evaluate the same cases. This provides a basis for determining the relative relia-bility of different dimensions of personality and, also, for assigning the evaluators into types. Sometimes these types of psychotherapists show the impact of their training and identification, and sometimes common life experiences have a greater impact than earlier affilia-tion. In the world of art, there is much distrust of the qualifications and standards of the judges of artistic performance. Ignorant laymen are not much more suspicious than unsuccessful practitioners. By applying the methods of clinical researchers to a sample of critics and common art objects, one could move beyond reliability to the clarification of particular dimensions of judgment and typologies of judges. The design could easily be expanded to compare the pro-cedures of laymen and practitioners with those of critics. In addi-tion, such research may, in turn, assist students of content analysis in relating reliability to the competence of judges. Too often, the college sophomore is not only the subject of the research but also the analyst.

The socialization of the artist and his audience may also be

Content and Method in the Study of the Higher Arts

studied by the application of methods developed elsewhere in the behavioral sciences. The typical model for socialization is the child's internalization of society's standards of morality and behavior. But life does not end at six years of age, and society's pressure even influences the funeral director. As human beings enter new groups, they are assimilated; that is, they learn to internalize a new set of standards. There is no reason why socialization and assimilation should not be studied with respect to the standards of artistic judgment. Agreement is agreement, whether the consensus is on the number system, marriage system, form of a novel, or balance of a painting.

The standards of judgment may be immutable, or they may be variable social products. In either case, those standards must be taught and learned. Despite the methodological pitfalls, panel studies with experimental groups and control groups may be the best device to understand how this type of socialization takes place, and the interrelationship of artistic standards with other standards of behavior. Art is part of the moral order, and social scientists must learn how order is created.

If we ask why such topics have long been ignored, a possible answer is the bias of the social scientist. Every generation laughs at the products of its predecessors, but it takes some objectivity, more than most social scientists have, to objectively view those central values which give life meaning, such as religion and art. But the history of artistic reputations often resembles a roller-coaster ride. Certainly, the evidence of variability in judgment should be sufficient basis for concern about the rise and fall of the standards themselves.

Unfortunately, on a broad historical scale, behavioral scientists are forced to emulate art historians, critics, and philosophers. The field of collective behavior, which should give social scientists a general theoretical orientation, has developed cumulative knowledge predominantly in the areas of crowd behavior and mass communication. The study of collective dispositions, to paraphrase Herbert Blumer, is the analysis of those subtle shifts in societal orientation which unify the elements of social behavior that are continually changing. Science influences art; art influences fashion, and there are fashions in science. What do we know about collective dispositions? Nothing. The social scientist must not be too harsh in judging those who leap into the void. Those who cannot do better had best be silent.

Further, the study of social movements is not very advanced, but at least the study of artistic groups as social movements can provide cases for the development of general propositions. Art movements are not less real than political movements. The generalizations that are beginning to develop in the political area may accordingly be appropriately tested in the study of Les Fauves or the Ash Can School.

Shifting perspective only slightly, it is possible to take advantage of the often noted similarity between artistic and scientific creativity. Innovation and diffusion processes are present in the art world as in the world of science. Probably, diffusion is simpler to analyze with existing techniques than is innovation, but studies in the history of science provide a good model for both. There is, perhaps, an understandable tendency to focus on leaders in art, but we can only understand the societal basis for their achievements if we study their unsuccessful precursors and their less famous followers. History might be written as a succession of biographies of great men, but behavioral scientists believe there are additional chapters to the story.

Art is an institution. Therefore, we may employ techniques of study developed in the analysis of other institutions. A major approach is the comparative method. On the grand scale, this method demands sophisticated selection of major historical periods and cultural areas, so as to test an abstract proposition. In the fashion of Weber, this method requires broad historical knowledge of art and society, and the ability to spot the important dimensions of difference. On a less grandiose note, many propositions can be tested by taking advantage of the complexity of contemporary societies and the variability of the many subcultures they contain.

Many statements about the relation of a work of art to the society which produced it can be translated into testable hypotheses by noting the existence of groups in the society which differ on relevant characteristics. As in William James' *Varieties of Religious Experience,* contemporary life provides many persons and groups which are similar to the modal groups in earlier periods. The investigator must be careful, however, to measure the differing groups on his explanatory characteristic when measuring their diverse productions of art or reactions to it. He cannot trust his intuition, but requires reliable confirmation.

Most artists search out peers who will give them social support. We are not surprised that New York is a cultural center, but we vainly seek to explain the eminence of Concord, Massachusetts. Large cities provide a sufficient base where even the most bizarre sentiments may be standard for some group. But if nonconformity on a societal level may still imply conformity within a small group, there are general questions of human behavior which can be studied in the world of the artist. The relationship between such conformity and creativity is one aspect, while individual differences in the need for support from peers may be another. It is important to note that coincidence of opinion between a particular artist and his peers does not in itself indicate that they are a reference group for him. The reference group for an individual is not a group which thinks or acts as he does. It is a group which molds his opinion, whose opinion of him is of sufficient importance so that he changes to gain its approval.

The artists are the key personnel in the art institution. Obviously, social-psychological studies of their self-conception and their perception of others are needed. In a world which tends to be hostile toward their aspirations, they provide a basis for understanding internalization of standards with relatively little societal support. Yet, such research must not merely study persons currently involved in the art world. The drop-out rate is high, and the sample of current artists is a biased one. Perhaps it will be necessary simultaneously to study social-psychological processes among artists, former artists, and laymen.

In conclusion, I would like to stress both my conviction that behavioral scientists who study art and are unconcerned about reliability should at least feel guilty, and my respect for the enterprise to which they are dedicated. Much that can be done has not yet been done, even after granting that the behavioral sciences are in their infancy. Much that should be done cannot be done at this time. When we undertake the impossible, for we believe our attempt to be better than nothing, the obligation to be self-critical remains. Too often in the past, I believe, the study of the higher arts has been so defensive in its orientation that self-criticism has been viewed as improperly defeatist. With the appearance of this volume, it is to be hoped that the growing respectability of the field will enable its researchers to view themselves as behavioral scientists who happen to be studying the social context of artistic creation.